MULTIDISCIPLINARY PERSPECTIVES ON INSTITUTIONAL DISCRIMINATION

Multidisciplinary Perspectives on Institutional Discrimination: Global Injustice, Local Responses examines how institutions shape contemporary forms of displacement and victimisation across settings such as colonial governance, justice systems, climate-related harm, and algorithmic discrimination. Its central claim is that institutions, through routine procedures, classifications, legal interpretations, and administrative practices, can produce, intensify, and normalise victimisation.

The book asks how these dynamics may be interrupted or mitigated, foregrounding community empowerment, legal mobilisation, and institutional transformation. Each chapter combines rigorous academic analysis with real-world applications, offering theoretical frameworks while pointing towards practical pathways for justice, resilience, and reconciliation. Overall, the volume reveals how power erodes identity, security, rights, and attachments to place and argues that recovering collective agency is crucial to repairing and advancing justice.

This volume serves academics, postgraduate students, and practitioners working across sociology, law, criminology, political science, and environmental studies and will also provide valuable insights for policymakers, human rights advocates, and community organisers seeking to understand and address systemic injustices through bottom-up approaches.

Rosanna Amato is Researcher at the Institute of Legal Informatics and Judicial Systems (IGSG), National Research Council of Italy (CNR), Italy.

Patrícia Branco is Researcher at the Centre for Social Studies (CES) at the University of Coimbra, Portugal.

Francesco Contini is Research Director of the Institute of Legal Informatics and Judicial Systems (IGSG), National Research Council of Italy (CNR), Italy.

MULTIDISCIPLINARY PERSPECTIVES ON INSTITUTIONAL DISCRIMINATION

Global Injustice, Local Responses

Edited by Rosanna Amato, Patrícia Branco and Francesco Contini

Routledge
Taylor & Francis Group
LONDON AND NEW YORK

Designed cover image: Getty Images

First published 2027
by Routledge
4 Park Square, Milton Park, Abingdon, Oxon OX14 4RN

and by Routledge
605 Third Avenue, New York, NY 10158

Routledge is an imprint of the Taylor & Francis Group, an informa business

British Library Cataloguing-in-Publication Data
A catalogue record for this book is available from the British Library

ISBN: 978-1-041-27156-7 (hbk)
ISBN: 978-1-041-27144-4 (pbk)
ISBN: 978-1-003-75297-4 (ebk)

DOI: 10.4324/9781003752974

Typeset in Times New Roman
by Apex CoVantage, LLC

CONTENTS

CONTRIBUTORS

Rosanna Amato has a PhD in European law and works as a researcher at the Institute of Legal Informatics and Judicial Systems of the National Research Council of Italy (IGSG-CNR). Her work focuses on the administration of justice, particularly organisational and operational dynamics and inter-institutional coordination. She examines how organisation and institutional practices shape the effective exercise of rights, with a specific focus on the protection of crime victims and gender-based violence. Her research also covers international judicial cooperation, digitalisation, and access to justice and the interface between justice and health institutions. She provides technical assistance to national and international institutions and is a member of the Council of Europe's Gender Equality expert pool and the co-managing editor of the *International Journal for Court Administration.*

Thalia Anthony is Professor of Law at the University of Technology Sydney. whose research examines the adverse impacts of criminal laws and practices on First Nations peoples. She works collaboratively with Aboriginal people in prisons and communities to build self-determination outside of carceral system. She has a partnership with the Victorian Aboriginal Legal Service to provide community justice reports in Aboriginal peoples' sentencing matters. This partnership was recognised in international criminology and engagement awards in 2024. Her research is published in *Indigenous People, Crime and Punishment* (Routledge, 2013), *Decolonising Criminology* (with Blagg, Palgrave 2019), and *The Palgrave Handbook of Racial Injustice and Resistance* (2026). Professor Anthony's research is cited in UN documents, Supreme Court decisions, and parliamentary debates. She has been listed three times by *The Conversation* as Australia's Top 50 Public Intellectuals.

Patrícia Branco is Researcher at the Centre for Social Studies of the University of Coimbra (CES/UC), working under Thematic Line 2—Democracy, Justice and Human Rights. Within the Scientific Employment Stimulus Programme (CEEC-IND/00126/2017), she coordinated the project "FORK. Food, Regulation, Kinship: considerations on contemporary law, families and parenthood through the lenses of food" (2019–2025). Her research interests and publications focus on judicial architecture and spaces of justice; the transformations in family, children and youth law and its intersections with gender, juvenile delinquency and crime; the relationship between law and the humanities; and the interplay between food and law.

Davide Carnevali is Senior Researcher at the Institute of Legal Informatics and Judicial Systems of the National Research Council of Italy—IGSG-CNR. His interdisciplinary background lies at the intersection of law, political science, and organisational and socio-technical studies. His areas of comparative scientific interest include the judicial systems' institutional setting and reforms, justice administration and management, techno-organisational innovations in the justice sector, access to justice, and evaluation and improvement of the quality of justice.

Paula Casaleiro is Researcher at the Centre for Social Studies of the University of Coimbra (CES/UC) and Member of the Permanent Observatory of Justice (OPJ/CES), where she coordinates and integrates multiple national and international research projects. She has a PhD in sociology of law and an MA in sociology at the School of Economics of the University of Coimbra. Her research interests and publications focus on the issue of family and children law and justice, law and science, and working conditions on judicial systems.

Fabrício Castagna Lunardi holds a post-doctorate in law from the Center for Human Rights at the Faculty of Law of the University of Coimbra; a doctorate and master's degree in law, state, and constitution from the University of Brasília (UnB); and a bachelor's degree in law from the Federal University of Santa Maria (UFSM). Coordinator and professor of the master's program in law and judiciary at the National School for the Training and Improvement of Magistrates (ENFAM). Chairholder of the UNESCO Chair on Digital Justice, Access to Rights and Freedom of Expression. Judge of the Court of Justice of the Federal District, Brazil. He has authored over 40 books and 80 scientific articles on topics related to the justice system. His areas of interest include digital justice, judicial governance, judicial process, access to justice, and minority rights.

Francesco Contini is Research Director at the Institute of Legal Informatics and Judicial Systems of the National Research Council of Italy. His work examines the evolution of judicial systems, focusing on digital transformation, managerial innovation, and the quality of justice. Since 2017, he has been studying the impact and implications of artificial intelligence on judicial systems, particularly its effects on the fundamental judicial values enshrined in Article 6(1) of the European Convention of Human Rights (ECHR) and its intersections with judicial governance. He collaborates with international organisations to promote judicial reforms across Europe, Africa, and Asia.

Madalena Duarte is a sociologist. She is Associate Professor at the Faculty of Economics, University of Coimbra, and Research Fellow at the Centre for Social Studies (CES/UC). She has coordinated several research projects on the sociology of law, criminology, and gender-based violence. She has published extensively in these fields, including the book *O papel do Direito e dos Tribunais na violência contra as mulheres* (*The Role of the Law and the Courts in Violence against Women*) (2023).

Luis Gómez Romero migrated from Mexico to Australia in June 2013 to join the School of Law at the University of Wollongong, where he is currently a senior lecturer and a member of the Legal Intersections Research Centre. As a scholar of law and humanities, he has published extensively on migration, human rights, and violence in Latin American law and politics. His latest major work, co-authored with Desmond Manderson, is *Twenty Minutes with the Devil* (2022), a playscript inspired by the capture of Joaquín 'El Chapo' Guzmán.

Richard Mohr is an urban and legal sociologist who has worked in community health, planning and evaluation, teaching, and research. He has taught in schools of architecture, history and philosophy of science, sociology and law at Sydney University, UNSW, Macquarie University, McGill University, and the University of Wollongong. Over the past 30 years, his research has been supported by the University of Wollongong, IISL Oñati and IGSG-CNR Bologna. He incorporated the consulting company Social Research Policy and Planning PL in 1991 and continues as a director, with Dr Margot Rawsthorne as principal. His work is available at http://independentresearcher.academia.edu/RichardMohr.

Ana Oliveira is a sociologist and researcher at the Interdisciplinary Centre of Social Sciences (CICS.NOVA), Faculty of Social Sciences and Humanities, NOVA University Lisbon (NOVA FCSH). Oliveira's research explores the social and cultural studies of law, with particular attention to the legal status of sex and sexuality.

Elena Alina Onțanu is Assistant Professor of Global and Comparative Private Law at Tilburg University (The Netherlands) and a lawyer with the Bucharest Bar Association (Romania). She is the co-manager and editor of the *International Journal for Court Administration* and an editor of the European Association of Private Law Blog (EAPIL Blog). Alina received a starter grant from the Dutch Ministry of

Education, Culture, and Science to conduct research on court and out-of-court procedures titled "Reimagining Access and Procedural Justice in an e-Justice Geography". Her research interests focus on cross-border litigation and dispute resolution, e-justice, techno-legal platforms, AI, and quality of justice.

Jocelynne A. Scutt is a barrister and human rights lawyer of the Bar of England and Wales, and the Victorian Bar (Australia). A writer and filmmaker, her latest books are *Women, Power and Autonomy—Rights, Respect and Representation in Law and Society* (edited collection, 2025), *Rage Wage for Equal Pay—Australia's Long, Long Struggle* (2024), *Beauty, Women's Bodies and the Law—Performances in Plastic* (2020), *Women, Law and Culture—Conformity, Contradiction and Conflict* (edited collection, 2016), and *Women and Magna Carta—A Treaty for Rights or Wrongs* (2016) (all published by Palgrave Macmillan), and her films include *Filming Shelley's Frankenstein in Italy* (in progress).

Luciana Sotero is Assistant Professor at the Faculty of Psychology and Educational Sciences, University of Coimbra, and researcher at the Centre for Social Studies (CES/UC). She holds a PhD in clinical psychology, specialising in family psychology and family intervention. Her academic work is situated at the intersection of research, teaching, and clinical practice, with a particular focus on systemic psychology and family therapy. Her research agenda seeks to understand how families navigate crises, engage in therapeutic change processes, and adapt to contemporary social transformations.

Gabrielle Tatith Pereira is Attorney General of the Federal Senate. She is a PhD student at the Complutense University of Madrid. Master's degree in Constitution and Society from the Brazilian Institute of Education, Development and Research (IDP). Bachelor's degree in laws from the Federal University of Santa Maria (UFSM). Member of the Permanent Committee for Gender and Race Equity of the Federal Senate. Her areas of interest are related to gender equality, parliamentary law, and gender-based political violence.

Bryan Vargas Reyes is a PhD student in postcolonialisms and global citizenship at the University of Coimbra, where he studies the rights of nature and the climate change. He has a bachelor's degree in law and has completed a master's degree in political studies, both at the National University of Colombia (Bogotá), where he has developed various research projects on indigenous peoples as Research Assistant. He has experience of empirical work in rural contexts with indigenous peoples in Colombia. His scientific work involves sociology of law, legal pluralism, the rights of indigenous peoples, and critical theory. His publications have focused on the indigenous peoples of Cauca (Colombia) and the strategic use of law in processes of social resistance.

Marco Velicogna is Researcher at the Research Institute on Legal Informatics and Justice Systems of the National Research Council of Italy (IGSG-CNR), where he studies the justice systems' transformations. His work focuses on e-Justice, court administration, judicial reform, and the practical impact of technology on legal institutions. Over the years, he has contributed to major European projects such as e-CODEX and collaborated with national and international institutions, including the Council of Europe, UNODC, and several Ministries of Justice. His publications explore cross-border justice, e-Justice, and, more recently, AI and accountability in judicial proceedings.

Anne Wallace is Adjunct Professor at La Trobe University and holds the following qualifications: LLB (UTas) 1981, LLM (U Melb) 2002, and PhD (Syd U) 2012. Over her 35-year career, including roles as a practising lawyer, Deputy Executive Director of the Australasian Institute of Judicial Administration, and law academic, she has been involved in a wide range of training, research, and evaluation projects in courts and tribunals. Anne's research has specialised in the application and implications of technology in courts (access, privacy, videoconferencing and social media), as well as projects on judicial workload allocation, court safety and security, court workforce development, and judicial education.

INTRODUCTION

Rosanna Amato, Patrícia Branco, Francesco Contini, and Richard Mohr

Multidisciplinary Perspectives on Institutional Discrimination: Global Injustice, Local Responses examines how institutions shape contemporary forms of displacement and victimisation across diverse settings, from colonial governance and justice systems to climate-related harm and algorithmic decision-making. Its central claim is that institutions do not merely fail to prevent injustice: through routine procedures, classifications, legal interpretations, and administrative practices, they can actively produce, intensify, and normalise victimisation. At the same time, the book asks how these dynamics may be interrupted or mitigated, foregrounding community empowerment, legal mobilisation, and institutional transformation as pathways forwards.

This volume engages with a large body of works that have explored specific forms of injustice, including racism and colonial dispossession, intimate partner violence, climate-related displacement, and algorithmic discrimination. Works such as Butler and Athanasiou (2013) have provided an important theoretical language for thinking about the loss of land, agency, and recognition, while more recent studies have examined the institutional lives of racism across migration, health, science, and colonial governance (Anthony et al., 2023; Bhagat, 2024; Liverpool, 2024; Saini, 2019).

Evaluation and impact assessments on intimate partner violence and justice-system regulative reform have shown how legal recognition does not automatically translate into protection (European Commission, 2022; GREVIO, 2022). The works on intimate partner violence, risk, and security have shown how law, policy, and advocacy respond to gendered violence in different contexts while also exposing the limits of formal protection (Stith & Spencer, 2021; Sudderth, 2024).

Likewise, studies on climate migration, loss and damage, and algorithmic systems have exposed the new forms of vulnerability produced by environmental

DOI: 10.4324/9781003752974-1

crises and digital infrastructures. For instance, several works have explored the dynamics and social impacts of climate migration (Mechler et al., 2019; Nicholson & Mayer, 2023), while other contributions have also made clear how algorithms create inequality, increase control over people, and spread victimisation (Eubanks, 2018; Pasquale, 2015).

This book builds on these contributions but with a different approach. Instead of treating injustices as separate and disconnected fields, it brings them into a shared analytical frame, showing how victimisation and displacement are produced through recurring institutional dynamics: classificatory practices, administrative closure, unequal access to redress, and the shifting of responsibility onto those most affected. Across three parts, the volume highlights community empowerment, legal mobilisation, and transformation as routes to redress. Thus, the book offers an original contribution to the debates, proposing a genuine interdisciplinary approach. It shows that different types of harm are connected, as they all stem from the ways institutions create and manage vulnerability, exclusion, and resistance.

The volume's interdisciplinary approach emerged from a 2024 call for papers that invited legal, socio-legal, political, and organisational perspectives on displacement, victimisation, and institutional discrimination. Workshop discussions among all the participants sharpened a common analytical focus: instead of treating harm solely as an outcome, the contributions examine how institutions generate and normalise exclusion through administrative routines, classificatory systems, legal interpretation, and policy implementation. To investigate these processes, the book relies on qualitative approaches—especially in-depth interviews and longitudinal case studies—to connect lived experience with institutional dynamics. Building on this analysis, the book then addresses normative questions, asking how rights, voice, and agency may be restored, and under what conditions communities, intermediary actors, and institutions can open pathways to resistance, repair, and transformation.

Each chapter analyses a case, identifies the dynamics of displacement, and explores responses. Overall, the volume aims to reveal how power erodes identity, security, rights and attachments to place to consider ways to disrupt these patterns. Ultimately, it argues that recovering collective agency is crucial to repairing and advancing justice.

Part I brings together analyses of how colonialism continues to shape contemporary societies through enduring forms of violence, discrimination, and exclusion. The chapters show that colonisation is not confined to the past but persists through dispossession, conquest, and the institutional management of harm, visible in prisons, policing, judicial practices, and enforced disappearances. The chapters also examine the symbolic frameworks that sustain these realities as the intertwining role of law and myth as instruments of colonial power. Law structures domination through rules, institutions, and official authority. Myth legitimises it through narratives of civilisation, protection, and legal superiority. Together, they obscure and normalise the violence of colonial rule, while subordinating Indigenous norms, histories, and experiences. At the same time, the chapters foreground resistance and survival. Indigenous law, memory, mourning, storytelling, and cultural practice endure despite repression.

In the first chapter, *Richard Mohr's* study of displacement begins by noting the long history of exile as punishment, seeing its roots in republican citizenship and the Christian tradition of expulsion from Eden. He sees subsequent justifications of expulsion, on the grounds of property and rights, sitting uneasily in colonising missions since the rise of liberalism. The original inhabitants could only be displaced by denying their existence or their capacity to claim human rights. Subsequent histories, Mohr argues, show the consequences of these denials, with the continuing existence of the colonised peoples haunting settler narratives, with terrible consequences.

Luis Gómez Romero studies the haunting of modern Mexico by *la Llorona*, the woman who weeps for her lost children in persistent myths and legends (Chapter 2). Arising in the early days of colonisation, she commemorates what the colonised peoples lost: in lives and in culture. The colonial conquest lives on in these haunted memories. Gómez then relates those losses to the lives sacrificed to the recent violence in Mexico, since the 1990s. He sees *la Llorona* as exemplary of the need to hold on to the memory of the past and the inspiration of the ever-present dead as a perpetual demand for justice.

Thalia Anthony's study of First Nations women in Australian prisons understands their displacement as a loss—of freedom, of family, of Country—equivalent to a social death (Chapter 3). And yet those women are able to hold onto their identities through the persistence of community and culture in their relationships and bonds with each other. Coming from different Nations across the colonial state, they nonetheless understand their lives and communities through the histories and injustices they have shared. Like *la Llorona*, they have lost children: their own and those of the Stolen Generations. Yet they endure through communal bonds and active memory.

Colombia's recognition of First Nations law is the subject of *Bryan Vargas Reyes'* Chapter 4. Describing how this development was achieved, he then analyses the pitfalls of application through Colombia's (post)colonial courts. Despite the formal recognition of the indigenous laws, the courts fail to properly account for them *as law*. Instead, their force is diluted to a status more like culture, relegated to history. Vargas observes that Western state law, insisting on its own all-powerful rationality, dismisses other laws as myth.

Part II focuses on the persistence of victim vulnerability within justice systems despite the relevant legal improvements that have occurred in many regions. While criminal, family, and policy frameworks have recognised and strengthened victims' rights, effective protection is still lagging. Hence, the chapters offer a counter probe to the works presented in Parts I and III: an investigation into why reforms aimed at reducing discrimination and protecting vulnerable individuals and best legal standards struggle to achieve their intended goals.

The chapters show how organisational arrangements, interpretative practices, administrative classification, institutional logics and temporal dynamics mediate and limit the intended protective function of the legal system. Indifference to victims and vulnerability persists within procedures that are formally compliant, normatively coherent, and institutionally legitimate as a consequence of deeply rooted cognitive, administrative and judicial practices. Building on this premise, the contributions approach the relationship between formal guarantees and effective protection from different analytical angles and at different levels of detail.

Gabrielle Tatith Pereira and *Fabrício Castagna Lunardi* (Chapter 5) situate the discussion within a concrete national context. Their examination of Brazil's domestic violence framework maps a comprehensive array of norms and policies, highlighting the multidimensional nature of state intervention and its attention to intersectional vulnerabilities. Without assessing outcomes, the chapter makes visible the scope and internal complexity of the existing institutional architecture.

In Chapter 6, *Davide Carnevali* moves from the acknowledgement that normative frameworks are now consolidated across OECD countries to advance a policy-oriented critique of the gap between the formal recognition of victims' rights and their practical implementation. Analysing national experiences through the lenses of multi-agency approaches and people-centred justice, the chapter identifies factors such as the self-referentiality and closure of justice institutions as critical to the effective implementation of the new regulatory frameworks. It then argues that applying such an approach is desirable, fostering inter-institutional coordination and the treatment and protection of vulnerable justice seekers.

Paula Casaleiro, Patrícia Branco, and *Luciana Sotero's* Chapter 7 narrows and deepens the analysis, focusing on family law and the application of the "best interests of the child" criterion. The work highlights the tension between normative flexibility and operational routinisation. Although formally open-ended, this principle results in structured procedural habits, statutory presumptions—including shared parental responsibility—and institutional constraints such as time pressures and caseload management. Drawing on qualitative interviews, Casaleiro and colleagues shows how hearings may compress complex relational histories and how discretion, while formally present, operates within organisational boundaries. This makes Carnevali's rationale visible in concrete, detailed terms.

This is further complemented by the analysis of *Madalena Duarte* and *Ana Oliveira* on the trajectory that precedes homicide in domestic violence cases in Chapter 8. By tracing patterns between prior domestic violence complaints and subsequent lethal outcomes, they foreground the role of judicial interpretation, evidentiary assessment, and sentencing practices within a broader continuum of violence. Intimate partner homicide thus appears not as an isolated rupture but as a phenomenon embedded in earlier institutional responses. It shows how the assessments of credibility, cooperation, and relational dynamics shape judicial reasoning and how institutional timing becomes decisive: what happens upstream (or fails to happen) may condition later escalation.

These findings intersect with those of Casaleiro, Branco and Sotero and with *Rosanna Amato's* analysis of post-separation vulnerability, stressing how interpretative practices shape the scope and limits of protection (Chapter 9). Amato, indeed, relocates the problem of protection from formal entitlement to organisational practice. The dilemma of "protect by displacing" exposes the conditions under which safety becomes operationalised, particularly when protection is linked to victim relocation. Protection orders emerge as non-self-executing instruments whose effectiveness depends on continuity, monitoring, and specialised case management. The analysis of an innovative practice illustrates how organisational design can influence the trajectory of an intervention at an early stage, resonating with Duarte and Oliveira's emphasis on the significance of upstream institutional response.

Part III examines how environmental, digital, and administrative systems generate victimisation while obscuring responsibility. The four chapters show that injustice, today, is often derived or mediated by infrastructures that appear technical, neutral, or inevitable but are not. They have the capacity to cause widespread harm to users or vulnerable groups while rejecting any responsibility for that harm.

The section opens with *Jocelynne A. Scutt's* Chapter 10, which places climate change at the centre of contemporary patterns of displacement and exploitation. Its argument is that global warming and environmental degradation generate the conditions in which trafficking, displacement, and new forms of vulnerability emerge. Climate injustice is thus shown to be directly connected to victimisation, especially for women, children, and disadvantaged communities. The chapter also highlights attempts to respond through law and litigation, asking whether legal frameworks can move beyond reactive remedies and address the systemic roots of displacement and exploitation.

Elena Alina Onțanu's Chapter 11 shifts the focus from environmental systems to digital platforms, but it retains Scutt's concern with asymmetrical power and institutional dependency. It argues that online platform dispute resolution offers accessible and rapid forms of settlement yet does so outside the procedural guarantees usually associated with justice. Because platforms define the rules, control access, adjudicate disputes, and enforce outcomes, they exercise a form of concentrated private power that resembles a neo-feudal system. The risk is that decisions based on fair trial standards will be replaced by commercially driven decision-making. The legal analysis rooted in the EU Digital Services Act framework shows how platform governance can produce new forms of exclusion while blurring the line between market regulation and adjudication.

Marco Velicogna develops this analysis further. Chapter 12 investigates the Horizon scandal in the UK, showing that the injustice—in terms of thousands of postmasters unjustly accused of fraud—did not stem from software error alone but from a broader sociotechnical arrangement in which digital records acquired evidentiary authority while accountability for their failures was displaced from system owners and managers onto system users. Hence, the chapter reveals how institutions can transform contestable technological outputs into almost unchallengeable legal reality, with devastating consequences for those caught within the system.

Francesco Contini and *Anne Wallace's* chapter closes the series by extending the inquiry into the field of welfare administration through a comparison of Australia's Robodebt and the Dutch childcare benefits scandal. Their chapter shows how automated decision-making in public administration can entrench discrimination, shift the burden of proof, and inflict severe harms on already vulnerable groups. At the same time, it underscores the limits of judicial redress when harms are systemic, opaque, and widely distributed. Courts remain crucial, but legal remedies often arrive late and incompletely. For this reason, the chapter highlights the roles of civil society, unions, NGOs, and other intermediary actors in transforming scattered grievances into collective claims and enabling accountability.

In the concluding chapter, *Rosanna Amato, Patrícia Branco, Francesco Contini, and Richard Mohr* bring together the book's central claim that colonial violence, failures of justice systems, algorithmic discrimination, and climate-related harm are not isolated phenomena but different expressions of how institutions produce, stabilise, and normalise injustice. It shows how harm is processed through legal categories, administrative routines, and technological systems that make violence appear ordinary, neutral, or unavoidable. It explores the connections seen throughout the book between victimisation and displacement. Displacement is not only spatial but also often involves the loss of rights, recognition, credibility, and the capacity to contest institutional decisions. The chapter also highlights recurring patterns of opacity, institutional closure, and the transfer of responsibility from the perpetrators onto victims. At the same time, it argues that communities do not simply endure harm: through memory, mourning, collective action, storytelling, and local forms of organisation, they create pathways of resistance and repair. Ultimately, the chapter restates the book's call for more open, contestable, and responsive institutions grounded in accountability and community empowerment.

References

Anthony, T., Sherwood, J., Blagg, H., & Tranter, K. (Eds.). (2023). *Unsettling Colonial Automobilities: Criminalisation and Contested Sovereignties*: Emerald Publishing Limited.

Bhagat, A. (2024). *Governing the Displaced: Race and Ambivalence in Global Capitalism*: Cornell University Press.

Butler, J., & Athanasiou, A. (2013). *Dispossession: The Performative in the Political*: Polity Press.

Eubanks, V. (2018). *Automating Inequality: How High-Tech Tools Profile, Police, and Punish the Poor*: St. Martin's Press.

European Commission. (2022). *Commission Staff Working Document Impact Assessment Report Accompanying the Document Proposal for a Directive of the European Parliament and of the Council on Combating Violence against Women and Domestic Violence (ST 7042 2022 ADD 4)*. Retrieved from Brussels: https://eur-lex.europa.eu/legal-content/EN/TXT/PDF/?uri=CONSIL:ST_7042_2022_ADD_4

GREVIO. (2022). *Mid-Term Horizontal Review of GREVIO Baseline Evaluation Reports (2022)*. Retrieved from Strasbourg: https://edoc.coe.int/en/violence-against-women/11030-mid-term-horizontal-review-of-grevio-baseline-evaluation-reports.html

Liverpool, L. (2024). *Systemic: How Racism Is Making Us Ill*: Bloomsbury Publishing.

Mechler, R., Bouwer, L. M., Schinko, T., Surminski, S., & Linnerooth-Bayer, J. (Eds.). (2019). *Loss and Damage from Climate Change: Concepts, Methods and Policy Options*: Springer.

Nicholson, C., & Mayer, B. (Eds.). (2023). *Climate Migration: Critical Perspectives for Law, Policy, and Research*: Hart Publishing.

Pasquale, F. (2015). *The Black Box Society: The Secret Algorithms That Control Money and Information*. Cambridge, MA: Harvard University Press.

Saini, A. (2019). *Superior: The Return of Race Science*: 4th Estate.

Stith, S. M., & Spencer, C. M. (Eds.). (2021). *International Perspectives on Intimate Partner Violence: Challenges and Opportunities*: Springer.

Sudderth, L. K. (2024). *Changing Communities in Challenging Contexts to Address Intimate Partner Violence: Doing the Impossible*: Palgrave Macmillan.

PART I

Changing displacement storytelling

1

DISPLACEMENT AS PUNISHMENT

Exiles, victims, and the imperialism of suffering

Richard Mohr

Introduction

Rights or punishment

This chapter begins with a history of displacement that predates the contemporary liberal paradigm of rights. After critiquing the move to a liberal paradigm for attachments to place, it studies two cases of displacement arising from colonisation.

In today's dominant liberal regimes, we live or stay in a place through a right to property or a contractual right to occupation. Attachments to place, and the legal and moral means of expulsion from places, have a far deeper history than liberalism's. To argue for a "right to place", adopting the liberal rights paradigm, cannot succeed against the overwhelming force of property rights in that tradition. In the interests of finding a more robust intellectual footing for arguments against displacement, I trace the history of displacement as punishment from the Garden of Eden, through Roman republicanism, to contemporary neo-imperialism in Australia and Palestine.

In opening this collection of studies, I ask one of the most basic questions about a theme that unites them: displacement and victimisation. Why or how do we consider displaced people victims? Are people "victimised" by being forced to move away from a particular place or a virtual environment? In the examples shared by this and other chapters, that place might be a particular jurisdiction, such as a city state, or an area that sustains and nurtures a community of people through mutual connections to the land. Cases of displacement in the following chapters include expulsion from a domestic residence, commonly the result of the violence of an

DOI: 10.4324/9781003752974-3

intimate partner. In these instances, people can be displaced by fleeing violence, by violent removal, or by the destruction of their economic or ecological links to place or land. Later chapters also recognise that people can be displaced by on-line platforms used for government, trade, or communication. They may, in the first instance, be displaced from the electronic platform itself, but this can lead to further, physical, displacement when they suffer extreme hardship as a result. The instances of displacement selected in my present study are local in the sense that they are place-specific. Yet they each have a national dimension, and their global relevance will be clearly shown in the history of imperialism.

Outline of the chapter

My argument relates specific local histories to broad traditions of thought and geopolitics—in short, ideologies. In the next section I outline three baseline ideologies underlying displacement:

- Morally justified exile, as from the Garden of Eden.
- Physical and political expulsion, by which one is deprived of all civic status and is expelled from humanity itself.
- The liberal calculus of rights, whereby property rights generally trump all others, with major political consequences for rich and poor.

Following these relatively straightforward justifications, my case studies reveal some of the tortuous justifications for imperialist displacement. The case studies in colonial dispossession and punishment explored in the third section are as follows:

- Australia, founded as a penal colony for the expulsion of convicts from Britain, which has to this day used a variety of justifications for displacing, killing, and punishing the First Nations of the continent it expropriated.
- Palestine, where Regulation 119 of the British Mandate, providing for the "unusual punitive action"[1] of destroying any "house, structure or anything growing on the land",[2] has cast a long shadow of expropriation, death, and destruction.

In a concluding section, I compare the various narratives of imperialism and exile to the three paradigmatic justifications outlined in the Section "Historical Justifications for Displacement". Taken together with other neo- and post-imperialist narratives, these apologias reveal an extraordinary interplay between claims to heroism and pathos, victimhood and survival. Far from the coherence of the basic ideologies—Christian, Republican, and Liberal—a hermeneutic analysis (as outlined by Ricoeur 1973) reveals imperialist justifications to be a tangle of contradictions, misrecognition, and bad faith. In conclusion, I reveal neo-colonial delusions that have painted the oppressors as the victims, terrorised by the very presence of the displaced and particularly their children, who must be punished for their existence—for still existing here—by incarceration and death.

Historical justifications for displacement

I identify three "ideal types" in the history of exile, expulsion, and displacement. Each one has a long history and some coherence in its moral and political stance.

Republican

The democratic and republican ideals of Ancient Greece and Rome linked residence in the city state or imperial capital to the status of citizenship. The life of the political man (always masculine) was defined by this status. It was a privilege that could be granted (in Rome) or taken away. Punishments in Athens ranged from fines and imprisonment to death and included "exile from the city (which could be amplified with the confiscation of property and/or the razing of the convict's house)" (Allen 2003, p. 16). Roman punishments included *interdictio, relegatio,* and *deportatio*. Of these, *interdictio* and *deportatio* involved permanent loss of citizenship rights: in the former, one chose where to go, while *deportatio* was *to* a specific place. Given these different sentences, some took it more harshly than others. Ovid's bitter exile to the shores of the Black Sea, described in his own poetry, forms the basis for Australian author David Malouf's touching novel *An Imaginary Life*.[3] In contrast, Agrippinus reportedly responded to his sentence of *relegatio* (which could be temporary and did not involve a complete loss of property or withdrawal of citizenship) saying, "Well then, let us go to Aricia and take our lunch there" (Gibney 2020, p. 7).

Christian

In Medieval Europe banishment was adopted from Roman law, as an intermediate punishment between flogging and death. Now it had Christian justifications, since exile from the Garden of Eden had been God's first punishment of humanity. "Public shaming and dramatic exclusion from the community" were considered more punitive than direct physical pain, though often the sentence included both (Gibney 2020, p. 9, quoting Tarlow and Lowman 2018). While not as severe as physical death, banishment was nonetheless conceived as a social death, or *morte civile*, entailing the loss of status and property, as in republican regimes.

In the seventeenth and eighteenth centuries banishment was criticised by Voltaire, among others, for simply shifting the problem—that is, the offender—into someone else's jurisdiction. By the early nineteenth century Benjamin Constant objected that the practice was cruel and contrary to individual rights. Yet even this professed liberal accepted that exile could be imposed by a properly constituted tribunal applying a formal law specifying such punishment (Gibney 2020, pp. 19–20).

Liberal

Liberalism arose out of Enlightenment challenges to divine right and other Christian sources of state authority. After the French Revolution and various accommodations in other states, a new secular compact was required, supporting state law on liberal principles. This typically required the state to respect property rights and other interests of the bourgeoisie.

Over time the liberal emphasis on individual rights trumped the state's prerogative to displace. Yet those rights did not preclude displacement. Rather, they determined *who could be displaced*: generally, the poor, the colonised, and the outsider. Imperialism, forged in liberalism's formative era, sharply circumscribed who had rights, as will be discussed in the next section. Even back in the metropole (particularly in Britain), the increasing dominance of property rights and the enclosure of the commons justified a new wave of displacement. To the present day, only property ownership guarantees a secure attachment to place. Particularly in Australia, where tenants' rights have been practically non-existent, displacement from home is an ever-present threat unless you own it. Whole communities can be displaced by the ineluctable economics of property, as when the poor are displaced by the rich. Gentrification is one consequence of this logic of property as the only guarantee of security in place.

Arguments based on rights, such as a right to the city (Lefebvre 2009 [1967]; Mitchell 2003), right to community (Hubbard and Lees 2018), right to stay put (Newman and Wyly 2006), or a right to place (Samara 2014), have gained little purchase against liberalism's holy grail of property rights. Attachments to place have no part in the liberal regime. As the rich have enclosed the commons and bid up the price of real estate, the poor just have to move on. With the apparent certainty of a law of nature, the laws of the liberal state dictate where we live and how we access the economic resources that sustain us, whether food-bearing land or jobs. Following my own attempts to argue for rights to place and the city (Mohr 2020), this inquiry gives up on rights and instead argues that *punishment* is the more salient concept.

Two case studies

3.1 Displacement: Australia and Palestine

The following case studies of the colonial practices of displacement in Australia and Palestine consider some of the legal and ideological claims that underlie them. In both cases people were displaced, with varying degrees of free will or compulsion, from their homelands to the lands of other people. Australia was first colonised as a penal settlement when exile was still explicitly a form of punishment, derived from both Republican and Christian traditions. This was no longer an acceptable foundation by the twentieth century, when Australia and Israel both became independent states. Each state was to be faced with the dilemma arising from liberal claims to human rights. This led to the contortions and delusions that will be analysed in the conclusion to this chapter.

Imperialism initially offered an alternative solution to the objection that punitive displacement simply shifted the problem onto another's jurisdiction. Australia's colonisation relied on the convicts who were transported from the metropole to a place claimed by the Crown as *terra nullius* colonised Australia. The displacement of European Jews, from the Spanish expulsion of 1492 to centuries of state- and mob-led pogroms and Nazi barbarity, is another example of mass displacement and victimisation. Before Jewish Zionism, nineteenth- century Christians who advocated for Jews to be resettled promoted the notion that the Jews, as " 'a people without a country",' should take a "country without a people", i.e. —that is, Palestine.[4] There are parallels between the European justification for granting Palestine to an Israeli state, and the colonisation of Australia. Expropriating other people's land for settlement by a new population underlies these case studies in displacement. To justify colonisation without treaty, agreement, or formal conquest, Australia had to be classed as *terra nullius*. Similar considerations apply to Palestine, regardless of whether the claims denying the existence of "a people" were made by Christians, Jews, or European politicians. Either country could only be annexed by negating the existence of the people who had really lived on it for millennia. All the colonial denials—of nationhood, identity, or cultivation of the land—come up against the same awkward truth: that certain actually existing people must be regarded as either not truly human, or they have no attachment to their lands. Either way they are classed as *displaceable*. The moral flaws and counterfactuals in these justifications inevitably eat them away from within. Over time new and, as will be shown, increasingly bizarre justifications continue to be invented.

Practices of displacement 1: Missions, stations, and reserves

Beyond the legal fiction of *terra nullius*, the actual process of colonising Australia generally moved through stages of negotiation, accommodation, massacres, and removal to places where First Nations people could be corralled and controlled. Negotiation and accommodation were characteristic of first contacts. As settlers went beyond any reasonable accommodation—stealing resources, abusing women, and other acts of violence—resistance led to frontier wars. Resulting massacres overwhelmingly (though not exclusively) involved the murder of the First Peoples,[5] due to the imbalance of access to implements of war, from guns and poison to horses. Once the roads, fences, and police forces of colonisation were established, whole populations (who had not been shot, hacked to death, poisoned, or died of introduced diseases) would be moved off the lands they had cared for, revered, and lived off for millennia.

Removal was achieved by allocating spaces for Aboriginal people to live. These spaces were classed as missions, boys' and girls' homes (for children who had been taken from their families), reserves and stations (i.e. White-owned farms or ranches). These involved varying degrees of internal control and oppression, but common characteristics included suppression of languages and culture, randomly mixing people from different lands and nations, exploitation of labour (homes and stations), and controlling everyday life, including marriage and movement.[6] These practices continued into the second half of the twentieth century.

Designed to concentrate diverse people away from their ancestral lands, the boundaries of these spaces were not as tangible as the barbed wire fences of concentration camps. The bounds of these reserves, missions, and so on were policed by provisions of the various acts[7] governing the actions and movements of Aboriginal people throughout the colonies (and, after independence, the state or nation). In addition, the state police have used arrest and "move on" provisions of a variety of other acts (HREOC 1991, p. 90; Anthony et al. 2024, pp. 159–61), as well as surveillance and excessive violence, to control the movement and presence of First Peoples in towns and cities across Australia. These practices outlasted the Aboriginal "Protection" acts to persist to this day, with increasing numbers of imprisonments and Indigenous deaths in custody.[8]

Practices of displacement 2: British Mandate Regulation 119

The British administration of Palestine, granted to the UK as a mandate after 1918, implemented a punitive displacement regime unusual for the twentieth century that recalled certain ancient practices. *Defence Emergency Regulation* 119 (1945) provided for the confiscation and destruction of homes and crops. It begins with the identification of structures that may have been used as a base from which to launch insurgency, spreading to include a wide arc of collective punishment:

> Regulation 119—(1) A Military Commander may by order direct the forfeiture to the Government of Palestine of any house, structure, or land from which he has reason to suspect that any firearm has been illegally discharged, or any bomb, grenade, or explosive or incendiary article illegally thrown, or of any house, structure, or land situated in any area, town, village, quarter, or street the inhabitants or some of the inhabitants of which he is satisfied have committed, or attempted to commit, or abetted the commission of, or been accessories after the fact to the commission of, any offence against these Regulations involving violence or intimidation or any Military Court offence; and when any house, structure, or land is forfeited as aforesaid, the Military Commander may destroy the house or the structure or anything growing on the land.
>
> (2) Members of His Majesty's forces . . . may seize and occupy, without compensation, any property in any such area, town, village, quarter, or street as is referred to in subregulation.
>
> *(1)*

Since ratified by the Israeli Supreme Court,[9] this approach has formed the foundation for escalating strategies of displacement and punishment. These have been carried out under direct military orders and, increasingly, by settler vigilantes, such as the 2023 bulldozing of the West Bank village of Khirbet Zanuta near Hebron (Bergman and Mazzetti 2024). The International Court of Justice Advisory Opinion (19 July 2024, p. 14) noted that there had been almost 11,000 demolitions of Palestinian structures since 2009.

These demolitions, to the extent that they are legally ordered as punishment for particular crimes, constitute, according to the Supreme Court of Israel, an "unusual punitive action, whose main purpose is to deter the performance of similar acts".[10] It can also be seen as a form of collective punishment, since it may involve the forfeiture or destruction of the resources of a whole family or village for the crime of an individual. Displacement as collective punishment has also been ordered by the Supreme Court in deporting family members of an accused. In the Ajouri case in 2002 the brother and sister of a suicide bomber were deported from the West Bank to Gaza (International Commission of Jurists 2002). Israel's explicit use of Gaza as a place of punishment is consistent with its description as 'the world's largest open-air prison', besieged since 2007 (Chomsky 2012; Svirsky 2014, p. 182).[11]

The courts have trodden a legal path down which violent settlers stampede in their campaign to displace Palestinians. In 2018 settlers burnt around a hundred olive trees in the West Bank as revenge for the murder of a local rabbi by unknown assailants.[12] Olive trees are key resources on Palestinian lands. They are well known to take many years to reach productive maturity and can live for hundreds of years.

Sara Saleh has commented that the continuing destruction of olive trees shows a particularly brutal disrespect for the land and its resources.[13] From an Australian perspective it is impossible not to be struck by the parallels with Indigenous care for country versus settler violation. This is seen every day in Australia in open cut mining, clear felling of forests, flooding land for dams, and bulldozing for roads. Australia, after more than 65,000 years of First Nations' care and custodianship, has lost world record numbers of species and amounts of habitat in the two and a half centuries of colonisation. Displacement in its deepest sense involves the loss of economic and spiritual connections to lands, waters and the environment.

Conclusion

Republican and Christian justifications for displacement as punishment can no longer be accepted in 'post-colonial' societies. Liberal claims of land ownership, even if legally backed by appropriation by the Crown or other settlers, gain little moral traction in the face of mass displacement and the strength and persistence of the dispossessed. Attempts to justify the ongoing dispossession and oppression of the original inhabitants have produced some extraordinary justifications. This conclusion begins with some of the stories that Australians tell themselves. It finds a familiar trope, whereby the conservatives appropriate the language of their opponents. Colonisers and defeated imperialists, from Britain and Spain to Australia, adopt the mantle of victimisation that they inflicted on the oppressed. Having identified themselves as the victims then justifies continuing atrocities, as the settlers are to be "protected" from the oppressed. This argument resists rational exposition: it requires an almost Freudian ideology critique (Ricoeur 1973). So, after analysing the competition for victimhood, the chapter ends with "the return of the repressed".

Exiles, victims, and the perverse calculus of suffering

Australia celebrates its founding day, and great national holiday, on the date of the continent's first British settlement, 26 January (1788). The choice of this date, rather than (for instance) the date Australia became an independent federation some 113 years later, causes profound offence to the land's First Peoples. They and their anti-imperialist supporters refer to the day as "Invasion Day" or "Survival Day" in preference to the official "Australia Day". The debate has continued for many years and reached a low point in 2021, in the last months of Prime Minister Scott Morrison's Liberal coalition government. Responding to the usual criticisms of celebrating 26 January as the national day, Morrison said, "You know, when those 12 ships turned up in Sydney [to found the colony], it wasn't a particularly flash day for the people on those vessels either". This reference to the convicts (and perhaps their guards, too) prompted the opposition's First Nations spokesperson, Linda Burney, to respond, "Suffering is not a competition".[14]

The calculus of suffering has indeed become part of the currency of post- and neo-colonial politics. I have previously argued that in Australia the representation of suffering is a way of constituting powerlessness in the "victims" (Mohr 2010). This term is often rejected by those who have suffered, whether from crimes and historical injustices or from diseases.[15] The problem lies in tendencies to pity, or even blame, the victim. Judith Butler has argued, "The problem arises only when the discourse of victimization precludes the possibility of effective political organizing and resistance to the cause of injury". To which Athena Athanasiou responds, "We have to always make sure that the language of victimization works to address injustice, inequality, and oppression" (Butler and Athanasiou 2013, p. 115). It is therefore important to identify the crimes and responsibilities of those who have come to dominate and expropriate. "The narratives of nation", I concluded in that earlier study, "can only be effectively told if they are developed as a dialogue" (Mohr 2010, p. 139).[16] Yet when victors enter into the competition for victimhood, we see the precise opposite. Instead of reckoning with truth and justice, the oppressors mask themselves as victims. This is seen in the following instances of historical and ideological revisionism and in self-serving narratives of exile.

As empires are challenged or fail, their defenders and former beneficiaries seek to adopt the mantle of suffering of their own (former) victims. Further to the Australian example, this has been documented in Spain and Britain.

Despite the passage of time since the demise of Spain's overseas empire, it has recently been defined as a victim of its own imperialism. Maria Elvira Roca Barea claims that empires, from the Roman to the Spanish, Russian, and US empires, have inspired unjustifiable hatred, which she calls "imperiofobia" in her 2019 book of that name. "There is", she claims, "no appreciable difference in essence between imperiophobia and antisemitism or any other form of racism" (quoted Villacañas 2019, p. 34). These bizarre claims have been subject to sustained critique by José Luis Villacañas, who points out the extraordinary transference of victimhood to the imperial power, in this case the very one that "expelled the Jews in tragic circumstances and exterminated them as a most ancient people of the [Iberian] peninsula" (Villacañas 2019, p. 35).[17] The inversion is precise in Roca Barea's Spanish: the *víctima* (victim) and *victimario*[18] (executioner) exchange places; the dominators are cast as the true victims of empire.

While Roca Barea's tortuous arguments were confined to a particular book, albeit a best seller in Spain (Martínez Shaw 2019, p. 8), a similar move to injured imperial victimhood was evident in the UK during debates over Brexit. Fintan O'Toole's analysis of this debacle has likened the prevailing rhetoric to "a *Trading Places* movie in which all the complications, disappointments and restrictions of being a former colonial power can be exchanged for the exuberant victimhood of anti-colonial resistance" (O'Toole 2019, p. 100). The politics of victimhood becomes a cover and justification for maintaining or reestablishing the dominance of the victors, now painted as the victims. "Victimhood has been seen to be the currency of power—women, people of colour, ethnic minorities appeal for equality by reference to their collective suffering". It has now been coopted by the far right to declare that "Not only am I not guilty, but I am in fact a victim" (O'Toole 2019, p. 98).

In the Australian example that led this section, we saw competing narratives of exile as well as victimhood. Exile as a national founding myth goes back further than the politics of victimhood. Virgil imagined Aeneas's defeat and exile from Troy as the foundation of the Roman polity. The pilgrims, fleeing England to settle New England, are a powerful trope in US origin stories. Biblical tales of the expulsion of the Jews, reinforced throughout history by successive expulsions, pogroms and the Holocaust, underlie some Israeli claims to Palestine. There is a clear enough history of appalling Jewish suffering. Yet when this suffering is claimed to justify the expulsion, murder and untold suffering of Palestinians, and when these moves purport to weigh a calculus or competition of suffering, history turns back on itself as delusion. The factual, historical suffering, of both Jews and Palestinians, is mocked by Bible stories of exile as origin myth. Biblical origin stories don't stand up as legal, ideological, or moral justification for a contested modern nation.

Colonisation brings with it a potent mix of origin stories and myths of civilisation and salvation. The missionaries sailed with the military expeditions to Africa and the Americas to appropriate lands to create wealth for the European elites. If the imperialism of that era was justified by Christian theology, after the Enlightenment it was exonerated by reason. The "savages" that the colonisers encountered continued to be killed, converted, and expropriated, but this was now a civilising mission motivated by reason, by enlightenment. The mythology of modernity is characterised, and its actions justified, by the very denial of myth (Fitzpatrick 1992). "A modern is someone who believes that *the others* believe" (Latour 1996, p. 15, my emphasis). The modern colonial state is only "post-colonial" because its imperialist origins are cloaked in stories that are "truths", not "myths". Now the suffering of the colonisers becomes more real, as the foundation of a modern state, than the slaughter of the dispossessed. This can only be achieved in the "reversed world" of displaced suffering and official historical reason. The winners of the colonial wars—still continuing in Palestine and in Australia—claim the mantle of the dispossessed, while the dispossessed are painted as terrorists and usurpers. As in Roca Barea's *Imperiofobia*, or O'Toole's *Trading Places* movie, the executioner becomes the victim through this distorting mirror.

Punishment: the return of the repressed

Exile, displacement, and eviction have been understood, throughout most of history, as extreme punishments, a civil death almost as severe as biological death. As recently as the British transportation of convicts to Australia, or the British Mandate in Palestine, exile and eviction retained their explicitly punitive rationale. Yet punishment disappears, and suffering is reappropriated, through the magical distortions of liberal enlightenment and colonial civilising missions.

Colonialism performs its sleight of hand first, through the rationale of "saving" or "protecting" the displaced, and then a bizarre inversion of victimhood. Let me explain how the one led to the other. The removal of Australia's First Peoples proceeded from the frontier wars, continued through the Aboriginal Protection Acts and the removal of children, to the current strategies of incarceration of Indigenous people, particularly children. As discussed by Anthony (this volume, Chapter 3), incarceration involves "social death" and also, particularly for Indigenous women, children and men, physical death.[19]

First Nations people are vastly overrepresented in Australian prisons.[20] This is most stark among young people. In 2025, "about 3 in 5 (60%) young people aged 10–17 in detention were First Nations, while First Nations people in this age group make up 6.6% of the general population".[21] Australia has among the lowest ages of criminal responsibility in the world. In every state in the federation, children as young as 10 can be arrested, charged, and imprisoned.[22] Seventy-nine per cent of children aged 10–14 in detention in 2025 were from First Nations.[23] Despite some progress and campaigns such as "Raise the Age", each state election sees new policies to "get tough" on youth crime and increase penalties, particularly for young people. Since April 2024, the three most populous states in Australia have introduced draconian legislation covering 14- to 18-year-olds. New South Wales imposed restrictions on applications for bail (Wong 2024),[24] Victoria imposed adult sentences (up to life imprisonment) for violent crimes,[25] and Queensland vaunted its policy of "adult time for adult crime" also for burglary, car theft, and dangerous driving.[26] From 2021 to 2025 the rate and number of First Nations young people aged 10–17 in detention have been increasing.[27]

These policies are driven by aggressive, racially inflected moral panics in communities across Australia. News on youth crime in Google searches for particular towns brings up nearly 200,000 hits for Dubbo, NSW; 1.5 million for Townsville, Queensland; 10.4 million for Alice Springs/Mparntwe, NT.[28] Headlines scream "crisis", "crime spree", "under siege", "out of control". Each of these towns has a high proportion of First Peoples. Vigilante attacks, particularly targeting Aboriginal children, have been reported from Perth[29] to Townsville.[30] Attacks are threatened or organised through social media in towns across Australia, from Derby in Western Australia (2018)[31] to Rockhampton in Queensland (2023).[32]

The disproportionate targeting and increasing incarceration of young First Nations people amounts to an obsessive paedophobia. It prompts the question: why do children seem to cause the greatest offence to settlers? Looking to the past, Australia could purport to "smooth the dying pillow", to ease the inevitable displacement of a "dying race", a people who no longer belong (here, now). Their children could be assimilated, made White, through regimes of institutionalisation and re-education (Reynolds 2025, p. 157, p. 164). Aboriginal children today represent the future of a people who refused to die out. The continued presence of the displaced confronts the settlers with a future without displacement. Forced to see this future, their delusions are challenged by the successive new generations of the un-displaced. Groups of Aboriginal children in public places at night, Palestinian children—whether throwing stones or sheltering in a school or hospital—are terrorising the settlers. The citizenry must be protected from rampant crime, from children on the streets, from terror.

Punishing the "terrorists" returns as the legal avenue to persecute, remove, and oppress whole communities. But the motivation behind the punishment cannot be named as dispossession. This was achieved, in settler legal fantasies, decades ago. The real crime is the continuing presence of the displaced, so thoroughly erased by settler delusions that their very existence is the offence. In the imagination of the neo-colonial state, this can only be redressed by removing the racially identified "terrorists", through imprisonment or death, to protect their White settler "victims".

Coda

For the next generations

> You could not get the truth out of those street-type culturally independent kid toddlers who were preoccupied with trying to rip off their disposable nappy, or crying or screaming, and not talking properly, and generally acting tough, as

though they just wanted to be totally one with country by running amuck on the beach in the middle of the night.

Say you were sorry that you were not interested in closing the gap you naughty kids, and leave those disposable diapers on. Say that closing the gap was the net to catch all Aboriginal people so they can be saved. Say you wanted to become quick smart white and leave those diapers on, and stop wanting to go native.

– *Alexis Wright,* Praiseworthy *(2023, p. 375)*[33]

Notes

1 Sakhwil et al. v. Commander of the Judea and Samaria Region (1979).
2 *Defence (Emergency) Regulations 1945* Palestine British Mandate reg 119.
3 According to Düddul (2014), the novel "reflects a significant aspect of the Australian story—a sense of exile". I return to this issue in the first part of the conclusion.
4 Lord Shaftesbury, Annual General Meeting of the Palestine Exploration Fund, 10 June 1875, minuted in the *Palestine Exploration Fund Quarterly Statement*, 1875, 116. https://archive.org/details/quarterlystateme07pale/quarterlystateme07pale/page/n122/mode/1up?view=theater accessed 14 August 2024.
5 https://c21ch.newcastle.edu.au/colonialmassacres/map.php accessed 14 August 2024.
6 AIATSIS, Missions, stations and reserves. aiatsis.gov.au/explore/missions-stations-and-reserves accessed 6 August 2024.
7 For example the Aboriginal Protection Act 1869 (Vic), Aborigines Protection Act 1909 (NSW).
8 https://www.theguardian.com/australia-news/deaths-in-custody accessed 20 December 2025.
9 Alamarin v. IDF Commander in Gaza Strip (1992); Sakhwil et al. v. Commander of the Judea and Samaria Region (1979).
10 Sakhwil et al. v. Commander of the Judea and Samaria Region HCJ 1979.
11 While the level of collective punishment has increased by orders of magnitude since Hamas attacked Israel in October 2023, my focus here is not on open warfare or associated war crimes.
12 https://www.timesofisrael.com/settlers-filmed-destroying-100-palestinian-olive-trees-as-idf-appears-to-look-on/ accessed 6 August 2024.
13 Sara Saleh, interviewed by Colin Hesse, Radio Skid Row (Sydney), Wednesday, April 17, 2024, https://vimeo.com/936074092?share=copy Accessed 13 July 2024.
14 https://www.sbs.com.au/news/article/26-january-wasnt-particularly-flash-for-those-on-the-first-fleet-either-scott-morrison-says/5kfmmjezj accessed 14 June 2024.
15 "Survivor", as in "Survival Day", may be preferred to "victim".
16 This dialogue was decisively ended with the failure of the Australian referendum in October 2023 to give First Nations a constitutional voice to parliament, as one small, first step to constitutional justice. This, and the subsequent denial of First Nations demands by both the government and opposition parties, deprives Australia of any claim to legitimacy or mitigation in its expropriation of the land and its ongoing colonial project.
17 "Expulsó a los judíos en condiciones trágicas y los exterminó como pueblo peninsular antiquísimo".
18 From Latin, *victimarius*, who carried out sacrificial slaughter.
19 There were 33 Indigenous deaths in custody in Australia in 2024–25, the highest number since 1979. https://www.theguardian.com/australia-news/2025/dec/10/deaths-after-deaths-after-deaths-indigenous-deaths-in-custody-reach-their-highest-level-since-1980 Accessed 18 December 2025.

20 "Between 2019 and 2024, the age-standardised rate of imprisonment among First Nations adults increased 21% from 1,906 to 2,304 per 100,000 adults. Over the same period, the age-standardised rate of imprisonment for non-Indigenous Australian adults decreased 15% from 173 to 148 per 100,000 adults".
21 https://www.aihw.gov.au/reports/youth-justice/youth-detention-population-in-australia-2025/contents/first-nations-young-people accessed 2 February 2026.
22 The very small Australian Capital Territory is the only jurisdiction where the age of legal responsibility is 12.
23 https://www.aihw.gov.au/reports/youth-justice/youth-detention-population-in-australia-2025/contents/first-nations-young-people accessed 2 February 2026.
24 https://www.streetoncriminallawyers.com.au/tougher-new-bail-laws-for-nsw-youth/#:~:text=On%2012%20March%202024%2C%20the%20NSW%20government%20introduced,years%20and%20under%2018%20years%20to%20get%20bail. Accessed 12 August 2024.
25 https://www.abc.net.au/news/2025-11-12/victoria-youth-crime-laws-adult-sentencing-court/105998434 Accessed 17 December 2025.
26 https://www.qld.gov.au/makingqldsafer/adult-crime-adult-time Accessed 18 December 2025
27 https://www.aihw.gov.au/reports/youth-justice/youth-detention-population-in-australia-2025/contents/first-nations-young-people accessed 2 February 2026.
28 This sample of towns follows the "road trip" episodes of the current affairs series *The Point* from July until 6 August 2024 (Janke 2024).
29 https://www.bbc.com/news/world-australia-63467134 accessed 14 August 2024.
30 https://www.abc.net.au/news/2021-02-06/car-crash-townsville-stolen-car-thuringowa-search-jennifer-board/13128616 accessed 14 August.
31 https://www.abc.net.au/news/2018-03-25/threats-of-vigilante-violence-amid-juvenile-justice-failings/9583744 accessed 14 August 2024.
32 https://www.abc.net.au/news/2023-05-08/angry-rockhampton-locals-march-on-homes-of-alleged-offenders/102315744 accessed 14 August 2024.
33 *Praiseworthy* is set in a fictional Aboriginal town of that name. Here Wright parodies the "paedophobia" I have described, understanding the agency and connections to culture of these young people, not as victims but as links between the past and the future. ("Closing the gap" is the Australian government policy aimed at bringing statistics on a range of health, economic, etc. indicators for First Nations peoples into line with those of white communities.)

References

Cases

Alamarin v. IDF Commander in Gaza Strip (1992) HCJ 2722/92 https://versa.cardozo.yu.edu/sites/default/files/upload/opinions/Alamarin%20v.%20IDF%20Commander%20in%20Gaza%20Strip.pdf accessed 6 August 2024.

Sakhwil et al. v. Commander of the Judea and Samaria Region (1979) HCJ 434/79 (Israeli Yearbook on Human Rights, vol 10, 1980, p 345) sourced: casebook.icrc.org accessed 3 Jan 2024.

Laws and regulations

Aboriginal Protection Act 1869 (Vic).

Aborigines Protection Act 1909 (NSW).

Defence (Emergency) Regulations 1945 (Palestine British Mandate), XII Miscellaneous Penal Provisions, Reg. 119 Forfeiture and demolition of property, etc.

Books, articles, and reports

Allen, D. (2003). *Punishment in Ancient Athens*. The Stoa: A Consortium for Electronic Publication in the Humanities [www.stoa.org]. http://www.stoa.org/demos/punishment.pdf accessed 20 May 2024.

Anthony, T., Sherwood, J., Blagg, H., & Tranter, K. (2024). *Unsettling Colonial Automobilities: Criminalisation and Contested Sovereignties*. Emerald Publishing.

Bergman, R., & Mazzetti, M. (2024). The unpunished: How extremists took over Israel. *New York Times Magazine*. https://www.nytimes.com/2024/05/16/magazine/israel-west-bank-settler-violence-impunity.html accessed 6 August 2024.

Butler, J., & Athanasiou, A. (2013). *Dispossession: The Performative in the Political*. Polity Press.

Chomsky, N. (2012). *Impressions of Gaza*. https://chomsky.info/20121104/ accessed 4 August 2024.

Düddul, P. (2014). The case for David Malouf's *An Imaginary Life*. *The Conversation*, 15 July 2014. https://theconversation.com/the-case-for-david-maloufs-an-imaginary-life-28201 accessed 7 August 2024

Fitzpatrick, P. (1992). *The Mythology of Modern Law*. Routledge.

Gibney, M. J. (2020). Banishment and the pre-history of legitimate expulsion power. *Citizenship Studies*, *24*(3), 277–300.

HREOC (Human Rights and Equal Opportunities Commission). (1991). *Racist Violence. Report of the National Inquiry into Racist Violence*. Australian Government Publishing Service.

Hubbard, P., & Lees, L. (2018). The right to community? Legal geographies of resistance on London's gentrification frontiers. *City*, *22*(1), 8–25.

International Commission of Jurists. (2002). *ICJ Concerned at Israel's Use of Collective Punishment*. https://www.icj.org/israel-icj-concerned-at-israels-use-of-collective-punishment/ accessed 6 August 2024.

Janke, J. P. (host). (2024). *The Point: Road Trip*. NITV Australia. Screened 9 July—13 August 2024. https://www.sbs.com.au/ondemand/news-series/the-point

Latour, B. (1996). *Petite réflexion sur le culte moderne des dieux faitiches*. Synthélabo.

Lefebvre, H. (2009 (1967)). *Le droit à la ville* (3rd ed.). Economica/Anthropos.

Martínez Shaw, C. (2019). Contra el triunfo de la confusión. *El País*, 22 June 2019, Babelia, 8.

Mitchell, D. (2003). *The Right to the City: Social Justice and the Fight for Public Space*. Guilford Press.

Mohr, R. (2010). Responsibility and the representation of suffering: Australian law in black and white. *e-cadernos CES*, *7*, 123–146.

Mohr, R. (2020). Diversity or displacement? Housing capital and the right to place. *Oñati Socio-legal Series*, *10*(1), 147–168.

Newman, K., & Wyly, E. K. (2006). The right to stay put, revisited: Gentrification and resistance to displacement in New York City. *Urban Studies*, *43*(1), 23–57.

O'Toole, F. (2019). *Heroic Failure: Brexit and the Politics of Pain* (Second expanded edition). Head of Zeus Ltd.

Reynolds, H. (2025). *Looking from the North: Australian History from the Top Down*. NewSouth Publishing.

Ricoeur, P. (1973). 'Hermenéutique et critique des idéologies', in *Démythisation et idéologie*, ed. Enrico Castelli. Aubier Montaigne. Translation 1981 as chapter 2 of *Hermeneutics and the Human Sciences* (J. B. Thompson, Trans.) Cambridge University Press.

Samara, T. R. (2014). *Housing Demolition and the Right to Place*. Polis [Blog]. http://www.thepolisblog.org/2014/01/housing-demolition-and-right-to-place.html accessed 22 May 2017.

Svirsky, M. (2014). *After Israel: Towards Cultural Transformation*. Zed Books.

Villacañas, J. L. (2019). *Imperiofilia y el populismo nacional-católico: Otra historia del imperio español*. Lengua de Trapo.

Wong, Justin. 2024. *Tougher New Bail Laws for NSW Youth*. Streeton Lawyers. 15 March 2024. https://www.streetoncriminallawyers.com.au/tougher-new-bail-laws-for-nsw-youth/#:~:text=On%2012%20March%202024%2C%20the%20NSW%20government%20introduced,years%20and%20under%2018%20years%20to%20get%20bail accessed 12 August 2024.

Wright, A. (2023). *Praiseworthy*. Giramondo.

2

DISPATCHES FROM THE LAND OF LA LLORONA

On lives lost and the ethics of grieving in Mexico

Luis Gómez Romero

> What is a ghost? Stephen said with tingling energy. One who has faded into impalpability through death, through absence, through change of manners.
>
> James Joyce (1992 [1922], p. 188)

Introduction: the frightful senselessness of exceptions turned norms

This chapter addresses the problem of disappearance in Mexico. Its purpose is to sketch out the components of a normative structure that might enrich the legal framework surrounding this issue while accompanying those who endure its anguish—both those whose lives have vanished into its limbo and those who wait, search, and grieve in their absence. To this end, I engage storytelling—primarily through its literary forms—as a heuristic and critical tool: first, to unearth the meaning of disappearance as a phenomenon embedded in a complex political culture of violence, and second, to interrogate and expand the normative language currently available to comprehend it.

My approach draws on the insights of cultural legal studies: a mode of legal analysis that treats law not as a state-bound set of rules but as a cultural artefact produced wherever legal meaning is generated, contested, or interrogated (Giddens, Crawley & Peters 2024, p. 1). This requires opening legal inquiry to a plurality of sources and voices—including literary texts. Such a form of pluralist imagination is particularly well suited to analysing the complexities of disappearance in Mexico. Merely stating, as a matter of principle, that perpetrators violate human rights or transgress the state's formal legal order, though true, fails to capture the scale of the phenomenon. Mexico's staggering institutional ineffectiveness

DOI: 10.4324/9781003752974-4

in preventing, investigating, or punishing disappearances compels us to acknowledge, with Roderick Macdonald (2011, pp. 310–11), that law is a terrain inhabited by multiple actors who are "not just law-obeying or law-abiding" (or, in this case, law-disobeying), but essentially "law-creating".

Victims, perpetrators, and state officials are all legal agents creating legal meaning. In this sense, the perpetrators' motivations must be interpreted not just as violations of state-produced norms but as assertions of normative meaning. The norms thus created are indeed contemptibly unfair—rooted in systemic impunity and extractive violence. Their critique, however, requires acknowledging their normative nature. This tension—between formal legality and informal normativity—is central to an accurate diagnosis of the problem. In Mexico, the dialectic of violence and grief, silence and protest, drives an ongoing political struggle that law has so far failed to resolve effectively. Yet the practices of resistance by families and communities searching for the disappeared constitute new legal subjectivities, demanding that we rethink what counts as law and how it may be expressed.

For this reason, I turn to the literary critique of law. Both law and literature, when considered in functional terms, reveal a profound connection between establishing authority and producing meaning (Binder and Weisberg 2000, p. 5). Literature is intrinsic to legal meaning as law "fashions the characters, personas, sensibilities, identities, myths, and traditions that compose our social world" (Binder and Weisberg 2000, p. 18). Building on this, Desmond Manderson (2012, pp. 124–6) highlights literary polyphony as a critical heuristic for legal thought. He draws on Mikhail Bakhtin's (1981, p. 7) conception of the novel as a polyphonic form that is inherently fragmentary and dialogic, characterised by a "semantic open-endedness" and a "living contact with unfinished, still-evolving and contemporary reality". This polyphony unfolds through shifting relations—stylisation, parody, polemic—that enable literature to listen to the singularity of different voices and perspectives and to speak across silences, contradictions, and ambivalence. Manderson (2012, p. 180) thus argues that literature has "something vital to contribute to law" not by representing legal norms and institutions but rather through its commitment to "a practice, indeed an affective orientation, that is unstable, narrative, collective, polyphonic, recursive and accountable".

In this dialogic sense, law may still speak to Mexico's disappearance crisis. This methodology reorients the law—towards a rule of law that listens, understands, and transforms—rather than merely describing it. As I have previously argued (Gómez Romero 2008, p. 275 ff), literature enhances law's semantic power both internally, in its conceptual organisation, and externally, in its referential capacity to relate to the world. Literature generates social knowledge that leaves its mark on the *real world* through the affect and memory we invest in it (Maurette 2024). Though not an empirical map of social phenomena, literature nonetheless offers insight—or, to use an ancient and powerful word, *wisdom*—to name them when language falters.

This perspective engages Gabriel Gatti's (2011, p. 35) claim that disappearance is, above all, "a catastrophe of meaning".[1] Disappearance resists conceptualisation. It renders inoperative the interpretive frames we use to understand our social life, which is largely constructed through conceptual partitioning: the school, the office, the family, the state, and so on (Foucault 1966, pp. 7–16). By undermining this order, disappearance triggers a radical disruption: "anomie made norm, ambivalence made value, exception as permanent condition, abnormality as rule, perpetual mourning" (Gatti 2011, p. 37). Claudio Lomnitz (2022, p. 32) captures this reality with grave simplicity:

> From the viewpoint of family and friends, disappearance means one cannot move from loss to mourning. Without mourning, the boundary between life and death dissolves. That is why relatives of the disappeared cannot return to a 'normal' life: they inhabit a state of perpetual emergency where, paradoxically, nothing happens. Days, months, years pass, and their loved one remains missing—neither alive nor dead. Without a reunion, mourning is impossible. Without mourning, life ceases to be life.

Historically, the origin of *enforced* disappearance—an adjective that shapes the framing of the concept in contemporary law and politics—lies in late twentieth-century South American military dictatorships. This was ground zero for those Gatti (2017, pp. 13–32) calls the "original disappeared". In Argentina, for example, enforced disappearance unfolded "on the other side of the norm, beneath ordinary life, outside the boredom of the everyday", in a separate world where citizens were destroyed with no legal recourse (Gatti 2022, p. 154). The theoretical framework often used to name this phenomenon is that of the state of exception (Agamben 2012 [2003], pp. 9–43). The "original disappeared", in this view, were subjected to brutal technologies of population control deployed against political opponents who were cast as enemies of, or threats to, the state (Gatti 2011, pp. 61–65). Over time, however, the experience of enforced disappearance became narrative, discourse, testimony—a form of shared memory and institutional formation. This gave rise to the normative concept of enforced disappearance that prevails in international human rights law and the robust social and political practices surrounding it.

Mexico's case, however, requires a different conceptual grammar. Its scale, complexity, and character defy inherited meanings. As Gatti (2022, p. 154) observes, disappearance in Mexico is the rule, not the exception—the disappeared are a mass rather than a few. As of June 2025, the National Register of Missing and Disappeared Persons (RNPDNO for its Spanish initials) recorded a total of 107,554 disappearances since the 2006 onset of the country's ongoing drug wars (Secretaría de Gobernación 2025). Over half of them—56%—occurred between 2018 and 2025 (Red Lupa 2025).

These conditions compel a shift from state-centred law towards what Robert Cover (1983, pp. 4–5) calls *nomos*: a normative universe generated by narratives that confer meaning upon legal institutions and prescriptions. The crisis of disappearances in Mexico demands new stories, new structures of meaning, and new languages of grief. To that end, this chapter is divided into four sections. The first considers what Roberto González Villarreal (2022, p. 214) calls "the paradox of institutionalisation", that is, the contradiction between a burgeoning legal apparatus and the exponential growth of disappearances. To approach this problem from new perspectives, the second section revisits the myth of *La Llorona*, analysing storytelling as a normative response to political regimes that ground sovereignty in radical power imbalances. The third and fourth sections turn, respectively, to two novels by Mexican writer Emiliano Monge—*Las tierras arrasadas* (2015) and *Los vivos* (2024)[2]—exploring how literary testimony can reconfigure the epistemology of disappearance and trace ethical pathways of collective mourning and resistance. Together, they set the argument to conclude by asserting the necessity for a new form of normative (i.e. political and legal) storytelling—one that does not merely speak *about* the disappeared, but *with* them and those who carry their absence.

The 120-year forensic crisis, or the paradoxes of institutionalisation

In Mexico, disappearance has unfolded in two distinct waves (González Villarreal 2022, pp. 11–12). The first, emerging in the early 1970s, mirrored Latin American repressive technologies wielded against dissidents and political opponents. The then-authoritarian regime governed by the Institutional Revolutionary Party (PRI) used disappearance as a counterinsurgency tool—a blunt state instrument deployed to erase resistance—tied to Cold War geopolitics that dissipated with the collapse of the communist bloc in the early 1990s. The second wave, which concerns us here, is anchored not in ideological repression but in the consolidation of illegal economies that initially grew around drug trafficking and later expanded into broader domains (González Villarreal, pp. 88 ff). Coinciding with Mexico's entry into global markets through the signing of NAFTA in 1994, this shift marks a transition from political violence to market-driven necropolitics.

Mexico characterises itself as an "Estado de Derecho"—a state governed by the rule of law. This self-description is formally accurate. The country is party to both the *Inter-American Convention on Forced Disappearance of Persons* (Diario Oficial de la Federación 2002) and the *International Convention for the Protection of All Persons from Enforced Disappearance* (Diario Oficial de la Federación 2011). The latter (Art. 2) defines enforced disappearance as:

> [T]he arrest, detention, abduction or any other form of deprivation of liberty by agents of the State or by persons or groups of persons acting with the authorisation, support or acquiescence of the State, followed by a refusal to acknowledge the deprivation of liberty or by concealment of the fate or whereabouts of the disappeared person, which place such a person outside the protection of the law.

In other words, under international human rights law, *enforced* disappearance is framed as requiring the state to insert a subject—either directly or indirectly—into a category of being that is juridically unlocatable, withdrawn from the dominion of law and suspended in a zone of exception. Formally, such acts are intolerable under Mexican law. Since 2011, these international instruments and all human rights treaties have held constitutional hierarchy. Under Article 1 of the Mexican Constitution, they are directly enforceable before courts bound by the *pro persona* principle to maximally protect human rights (Castañeda Hernández 2018, pp. 51 ff).[3] Furthermore, the General Law on Enforced Disappearance of Persons, Disappearance Committed by Private Individuals, and the National Search System (Diario Oficial de la Federación 2017) penalises these acts severely. If committed by a public official or someone acting with state support, the crime carries a penalty of 40–60 years in prison (Art. 30). If perpetrated by private individuals with the aim of concealing the victim's fate or whereabouts, the sentence ranges from 25 to 50 years (Art. 34). In both cases, perpetrators also incur substantial fines.

The law mandates the creation of several protocols, procedures, and national registries—for example, for the disappeared, the unidentified dead, and clandestine graves—intended to facilitate investigation and prosecution.[4] Yet such mechanisms remain inert, devoid of effective force (Guercke 2025, pp. 199–200). Between 1976 and 1983, Argentina's dictatorship disappeared approximately 30,000 people (Duhalde 2009). In contrast, Mexico's National Search Commission reported in March 2022 that the RNPDNO held data on 99,000 disappeared persons recorded since 2006 (Azaola 2022, p. 462). The Commission noted a 98% impunity rate, with only 35–40 convictions secured (Azaola 2022, p. 462).

One month later, in April, the United Nations Committee on Enforced Disappearances (UNCED) determined that it would take 120 years to process over 52,000 unidentified human remains stored in Mexico's forensic institutions—*without accounting for the new bodies added each day* (UNCED 2022, para. 28). This figure ignores "the bodies not yet located" and "the thousands of fragments of human remains that families and search commissions collect weekly from clandestine graves" (UNCED 2022). Mexico attained independence from Spain in 1821. Eduardo Ruiz Sosa highlights the vertigo of realising that over half the country's independent life would be required merely to begin addressing the abyss of human destruction at its core. "The scale of these absences", he writes, "exceeds any narrative anchored in sanity, statistics, testimony or denunciation" (Ruiz Sosa 2022, p. 15).

On 4 April 2025, the UNCED invoked an unprecedented procedure under Article 34 of the Convention (UNCED 2025). This provision allows the Committee to act upon well-founded information of widespread or systematic disappearances. According to the Committee's Chair, Olivier de Frouville, Mexico's situation met these criteria. This mechanism—described as the Committee's "most extreme"—had never previously been applied to any State Party. It aims initially to open constructive dialogue with the Mexican government, but the gravity of the case could lead the Committee to refer the matter to the UN General Assembly via the Secretary-General.

Existing constitutional frameworks, legislation, and institutions fail to prevent disappearances or to provide meaningful redress for victims. A superficial analysis might lead one to conclude that the legal foundations are sound and that obstacles lie merely in their implementation. Yet, as González Villarreal (2022, p. 214) points out, the "unbearable reality" is the "unrestrained growth of disappearances, even during a period in which an increasingly robust institutional architecture allegedly combats them". He terms this *the paradox of institutionalisation.* Gabriel Gatti (2022, pp. 153–4) echoes this assessment:

> There are several Mexicos at play: a visible, luminous Mexico—progressive, a producer of exemplary legislation and deep reflection on human rights, a refuge and protector—that surprises with its creativity and vanguardism; and another Mexico, or others, beneath or beside it, that accumulate darkness and violence of varying origins and destinies: structural poverty . . . drug multinationals, of course, and their contested sovereignties; [and] massive migrations, cutting across everything.

Both scholars' bewilderment likely stems from the tension between the official sovereignty of the Mexican state and the competing, illicit sovereignty arising from the criminalised economies operating within its territory. Reducing the violence of disappearance to the so-called "war on drugs", however, fails to explain its political and legal mechanisms. War presupposes an enemy to be vanquished—in the drug wars, there are no victors (Lomnitz 2022, pp. 13–14). The ancient Greeks understood this well when they used the word φάρμακον (*phármakon*)—both remedy and poison—to name the ambiguous essence of drugs, as that which heals also harms (Escohotado 2021, pp. 135–7). The *phármakon,* in its ecstatic or shamanic uses, was also linked to the φαρμακός (*pharmakós*), the sacrificial scapegoat offered in rituals of collective expiation (Escohotado 2021, pp. 42–6). Though obscured by centuries, the link between these terms persists in how we deal with drugs today. For those suffering from addiction—and those who produce and sell to survive—drugs are simultaneously cure and curse: pain relief and escape, yet always shadowed by death. For the rest of society and the state, drugs become scapegoats, delaying or denying real solutions to urgent problems—foremost among them, disappearance.

La Llorona, or the narrative mirrors of negative reciprocity

Explaining disappearance via simple binary stories—a war between noble, well-intentioned state officials and a threatening cabal of vicious criminals—only legitimises violence as the sole channel used by self-defined *forces of good* to contain an evil that never dies (Smith 2021, pp. xvii–xviii). Rather, as Claudio Lomnitz (2022,

p. 34) argues, the way in which disappearance operates in Mexico expresses a new form of life, enabled by a new type of state—one not yet named. This new state is marked by a paradoxical dictum: "too much sovereignty, too little regulation of violence" (Lomnitz 2022, p. 34). It is grounded in relations of negative reciprocity reminiscent of the sixteenth-century wars of conquest—one of the bloodiest normative epochs in the history of what we now call Mexico.

Most commentators date the official start of the so-called Mexican Drug War (capitalised) to December 2006, when then-President Felipe Calderón deployed some 6,500 soldiers and federal police to Michoacán, with the aim of quelling outbreaks of criminal violence (Astorga 2015, pp. 21–30; Boullosa and Wallace 2015, pp. 95–141). As I have argued elsewhere, this marks just *one* episode in the wider global drug wars (lower case) that predate Calderón's tenure and continue to sow death and destruction today (Gómez Romero 2024, p. 391). Nonetheless, militarising law enforcement indeed triggered a surge in violence, making it more overtly visible (Durán-Martínez 2015; Silva Forné, Pérez Correa and Gutiérrez Rivas 2017, pp. 339–44). This raw violence has been read as evidence of the endemic fragmentation and weakness of the Mexican state, frequently labelled as "failed" in this regard (Morton 2012, pp. 1632–42).

Lomnitz (2022, p. 19), however, views violence in Mexico as an attribute of a new kind of state. Sovereignty obsessively underpins failed-state narratives. Yet, as Lomnitz (2022, pp. 17–18) points out—drawing on David Graeber and Marshall Sahlins's work on kingship—sovereignty does not require the monopoly of public force or the development and maintenance of an apparatus for the administration of justice. According to Graeber and Sahlins (2017, p. 73), "the question of governance . . . is not the same as the question of sovereignty" because "in its minimal sense, sovereignty is simply the recognition of the right to exercise violence with impunity". The Mexican state perfectly illustrates this tension between sovereignty and governance, having virtually abdicated its justice-administration functions without relinquishing an iota of sovereignty.

The abdication of justice is evident in the radical deterioration of policing, which has, on the one hand, been captured by illicit economies and, on the other, been entrusted to the armed forces (Lomnitz 2022, pp. 37–67, 81–91). Since 2018, under the rule of the hegemonic National Regeneration Movement (Morena), the executive has amassed faculties that have elevated its share of sovereignty to unprecedented levels (López Ayllón, Orozco Henríquez, Salazar and Valadés 2024, pp. 7–9). Although a detailed analysis of the recent concentration of power in the executive exceeds this study, two shifts in the Mexican state's legal structure exemplify this trend. First, the elimination of a merit-based judicial career service and the replacement of professional judges with popularly elected ones—often owing their appointment to Morena and its agents. This nullifies an independent judiciary, one of the few effective checks on executive power (López Noriega and Martín Reyes 2025). Second, the presidency's growing dependence on the armed forces, which symbolically stand as the quintessential representatives of sovereign power (Lomnitz 2022, p. 19).

Violence rarely fails to sink its roots into the past and extend its reach into the future. Even if these developments are not symptomatic of a loss of sovereignty, violent exchanges profoundly impact both the individuals involved and the communities in which they occur. In this regard, Marshall Sahlins (2017 [1972]), in his classic essay on exchange, distinguishes among three types of relations of reciprocity: *generalised*, where one gives without expecting an immediate return; *balanced*, where one expects something equivalent in exchange; and *negative*, which is essentially a purely self-interested seizure. "Negative reciprocity", Sahlins (2017 [1972], p. 177) writes, "is the attempt to get something for nothing with impunity, the several forms of appropriation, transactions opened and conducted toward net utilitarian advantage".

Negative reciprocity, therefore, is the cornerstone of the simplest—and most unjust—forms of sovereignty. Where impunity becomes the norm, violence exercised by those who abuse others without consequence creates a caste society. Lomnitz (2022, pp. 20–1) illustrates the sovereign reach of negative reciprocity, as manifested in caste formation, via the historical example of Christopher Columbus' encounter with the inhabitants of the Caribbean islands. Columbus describes them in his record for 16 December 1492 (Anzoátegui 1964, p. 92) as:

> They have no weapons, and are all naked and without skill in the use of arms and very cowardly, such that a thousand would not withstand three; thus they are good to command and make them work, sow, and do whatever else may be necessary, and to build villages and learn to wear clothes and our customs.

The invincibility of European arms grounded negative reciprocity because it permitted unbridled violence, tempered only by occasional restraints imposed from within the dominant group itself (Beuchot 1997; Grandin 2025, pp. 20–52). The early years of the sixteenth-century conquest thus saw the Spanish colonies in the Americas undergo an authentic holocaust that decimated Indigenous populations through warfare, plagues, and famine (Lomnitz 2005, pp. 67–72). Negative reciprocity governed the relations between conquerors and the conquered, driving the massive death of First Peoples in the territory we now identify as Mexico.

Against this backdrop, the myth of *La Llorona* emerges: the anguished spirit of a woman roaming the night to lament, with plaintive and tormented cries, her children lost in the maelstrom of the conquest wars. In some accounts, she is a spectral seeress who foretells the downfall of the Aztec Empire. Bernardino de Sahagún (2000 [1829]: Book XII, Ch. I; León-Portilla 1989 [1959], pp. 1–5) records that, shortly before the arrival of Cortés, "a woman's voice was heard in the night air crying: 'Oh, my children, we are lost'! And at other times: 'Oh, my children! Where shall I take you?'" Other versions depict her drowning her children and, cursed and repentant, wandering through rivers, towns, and cities in search of them (Morábito ed. 2014, pp. 125–6). Still others portray her as a forlorn widow grieving her orphaned children, or a desolate mother whose sons and daughters were all murdered (De Valle-Arizpe 1980 [1957], p. 23). In all tellings, however, those who cross her path either perish of terror or descend into madness (De Valle-Arizpe 1980 [1957], p. 22).

At its core, the myth centres on pain caused by absence—of children, of freedoms, of security and stability in life. Suffering is deeply disruptive; hence, those encountering *La Llorona* lose their lives or sanity. Her mythical account expresses resistance against sovereignty grounded on negative reciprocity. *La Llorona* embodies the vengeance of the dispossessed by the European conquest, offering solace in the idea that those who profited from negative reciprocity will forever be haunted by the profound sorrow incurred through unjust power. La *Llorona* thus owes her spectral existence to negative reciprocity. As colonial relationships moved beyond these exchange modalities, the spectre gradually faded, until it disappeared in the early seventeenth century (De Valle-Arizpe 1980 [1957], p. 24).

In contemporary Mexico, however, no *Llorona* haunts the perpetrators of disappearances. A new caste system is emerging from the negative reciprocity imposed on the wider population by individuals living off illegal economies—not just drug trafficking, but also criminal enterprises such as extortion and kidnapping, or the exploitation of migrants. Lomnitz (2023, pp. 104–6) suggests that the new Mexican state is shaped by a conflict between two sovereignties. One is the dominant, legally sanctioned sovereignty, entrenched in the state itself and condensed, in recent years, within the institution of the presidency and its armed wing, the military. The other is an unjust and illegitimate sovereignty imposed by participants in illegal economies, who use their capacity for violence to exploit those unable to resist. Unlike the official modality of sovereignty—fetishised in the presidency and possessing a stable political centre—the alternative sovereignty of illegal economies is spectral and unstable, as it must impose itself territory by territory. This second pole of sovereignty advances solely through negative reciprocity, including the power to take life by any conceivable means—such as disappearance.

Violence emerging from the world of illicit economies always implies something which cannot be spoken aloud—something fated to remain hidden, sealed in secrecy (Mendoza 2026). Mexican vernaculars rarely refer to those embedded in illegal economies as cartel members or part of "organised crime". Given the volatility of their domain, these figures are named in hushed tones and through ellipsis, as though they were ghouls who might appear if summoned. They are *el narco* (the narco), *la maña* (the skill), *los mañosos* (the skilled ones), or, more obliquely, *los que andan mal* (those who are on the wrong path) (Lomnitz 2023, pp. 106–7; Morín 2015). Their impunity elevates them to a kind of superior caste, able to dispose of others' bodies at will.

It is precisely here that the normative character of their conduct lies: in making violence an everyday principle and an organising norm. Juan Villoro (2010, p. 27) observes, in this sense, that *la maña* lives by "the legislation of blood" that Franz Kafka described in his short story *In der Strafkolonie* (*In the Penal Colony*). Kafka (2015 [1919]) depicts the final use of an elaborate torture-and-execution device carving the condemned prisoners' sentence onto their skin before death. Villoro

(2010, p. 27) explains that *la maña* inversely transposes juridical reasoning. Under its normative orders, violence upon bodies is not the end but the *origin* of juridical discourses—"the announcement that others may be called to 'trial'".

Disputing sovereignties might relate analytically to areas of limited statehood (ALS)—a concept prominent in human rights scholarship. The idea of ALS recognises that, within Westphalian states deemed sovereign under international law, there can be areas where they do not exercise the level of control that the legal fiction of sovereignty suggests (Guercke 2025, pp. 282–6). In other words, ALS are parts of a country in which central authorities lack the ability to implement and enforce rules and decisions because they do not command a legitimate monopoly over violence. Since I have suggested the coexistence of two sovereignties arising from the social dynamics unleashed by negative reciprocity, one might argue that such areas percolate through Mexican territory. However, as Lene Guercke (2025, pp. 286–8) notes, the Mexican state exercises a certain cunning intentionality in abandoning its justice functions, rendering it unaccountable both to citizens and to international institutions.

A detailed explanation of the complicity between the Mexican state and *la maña* lies beyond this chapter's scope. Nevertheless, since Morena's rise to power in 2018, a rhetorical convergence can be observed between the sovereignty pole embodied in the state and that represented by the fragmented groups within *la maña*. Former president Andrés Manuel López Obrador has been, since Morena's foundation, its undisputed moral leader. Here the term "moral" is key. López Obrador is a populist, and, as in all populisms (Müller 2016, pp. 100–3), his vision of the political universe is essentially moralising, dividing discourse and practice between "el pueblo bueno" (the good people), who support him, and the "neoliberales" (neoliberals) or "adversarios conservadores" (conservative adversaries), who encompass all his opponents. For López Obrador, the prime cause of violence in Mexico is poverty, which before Morena's rise to power was caused by the untrammelled greed of neoliberals and conservatives (Lomnitz 2023, pp. 192–3). *La maña* cannot be blamed, since it is part of *el pueblo bueno*, which is ontologically identical with the populist leader himself. Populism has therefore placed *los mañosos* in an ambiguous rhetorical position. In official discourses, they are now part of *el pueblo bueno*, among the many victims of neoliberals and conservatives, who—from López Obrador's perspective—plunged them into such poverty that, as Lomnitz (2023, pp. 196–7) explains, "their violent uprising can be understood and forgiven, even if misdirected by ignorance and channelled into crime rather than political transformation".

Mexico's emerging state model—one that, by abandoning the administration of justice, underpins its sovereignty through the proliferation of relations grounded in negative reciprocity—might lead to despair. Disappearances, it would seem, admit no solution. Yet the age-old myth of *La Llorona* gestures towards possible heuristic tools with which to begin thinking the unthinkable. Her mournful weeping is, after all, an expression of affect. Gabriel Gatti (2022, p. 155) warns that disappearance in Mexico cannot be analysed "from a white-coat distance" but requires "an affective approach—that is, letting oneself be affected by paradoxes and surprises, awe and passions, pains and disputes, the many forces that in Mexico pass through the worlds of disappearance". In other words, paraphrasing Gatti (2011, pp. 17–19), any attempt to make sense of disappearance must begin "from the gut", embracing suffering's unsettling force. The following two sections turn to narratives moving in this direction—embodied in the novels of Emiliano Monge.

The wretched sovereignty of the *Endriagos*

Gatti (2022, p. 155) suggests that understanding disappearance in Mexico demands allowing oneself to be marked by the field itself. The task is as affective as analytical. In his own case, this labour unfolded in three distinct moments. This section follows the first two.

The first affective moment was marked by fear and the dawning intuition that Mexico has burst the definitional bounds of *enforced* disappearance as recognised under international human rights law. The 2006 United Nations Convention imagines the disappeared person as a detainee whose whereabouts are deliberately hidden by the state or by actors operating under its instructions or with its acquiescence. This juridical frame cannot contain Mexico, where, as Gatti (2022, p. 158) writes, disappearance encompasses, among many other things:

> kidnapping, or murder, or a dismembered body, a bone fragment, a whole skeleton entangled in roots, a vat of acid in which bodies were dissolved, a discarded body abandoned to the consumption of animals and the corrosion of the elements—and it is also a raped and murdered woman in a lawless space, or slave labour.

Mexico's universe of disappearance swallows both the living and the dead, citizens and migrants alike.[5] A sense of dread descends upon researchers as they realise that, in Mexico, the disappeared are simply "all those whose whereabouts are unknown" (Gatti, p. 160)—a number that is, staggeringly, in the hundreds of thousands.

The second moment is marked by "astonishment and rejection" (Gatti, p. 155). Mexico defies the limits of language. There is no linguistic system capable of coherently naming the "encyclopaedia of horrific deaths" shaping the realm of disappearance (Gatti, p. 165). Words are lacking. Or perhaps one, close enough, has been proposed by Adriana Cavarero (2007, p. 41 ff): *horrorism*. This term seeks to capture spectacular acts of violence that threaten not only human life but also the very condition of being human. Yet even this term is too general. Law—and the social sciences—have not yet found a way to categorise or name the many faces of horror. Hence the astonishment: that our theoretical arsenal remains impotent before the facts. Hence the rejection—a revulsion, perhaps—of what Gatti (2022, p. 171) calls the "analytic cowardice" that still fails to grasp the enormity of the disappeared.

Literature offers a path out of this paralysis. Eduardo Ruiz Sosa (2022, p. 17) observes that "fiction, which is not the same as a lie but rather another kind of truth, helps us to unearth other possible truths" regarding Mexican disappearances. Emiliano Monge's work is committed precisely to this search for a new language.

The closing note of *Las tierras arrasadas* (2015, p. 342) articulates the aesthetic framework of this semantic programme. "All the italics in this novel", Monge explains, "belong to the *Divina Commedia*, or are drawn from the testimonies of Central American migrants, in transit through Mexico, heading towards the United States of America". This statement casts the migrants' journey as a descent into a Dantesque hell—a political indictment of Mexico's negative reciprocity. At the same time, by disclosing the source of these italicised fragments, Monge affirms that the migrants survived—and so were able to bear witness. As Ryan Long (2022, p. 392) argues, this paratextual citation signals the triumph of life over disappearance.

The strongest voice in Monge's novel, therefore, belongs to the voiceless: the migrants (Favaro 2019, pp. 70–3). Described as a nameless mass stripped of identity and dignity, they have no names. Like the chorus of a Greek tragedy, however, we can hear their lamentations. Their words, italicised and in first person, disrupt the narrative's cadence with a distinct metre. The form of the testimonial fragments thus transcends the typical legal uses of memory and instead draws us into a collective narration—where a plural "we" contaminates the social tranquillity that would isolate horror in the abused individual (Peña Iguarán 2019, p. 147). One testimony, for instance, reads:

> First, they punched and kicked us . . . then came the beatings with planks . . . they knocked us down with our legs open and started hitting us . . . I dream every night they're killing me . . . their planks smashing my heart . . . we stopped being ashamed to cry, we were howling dogs, animals.
>
> *(Monge 2015, p. 65)*

Yet Monge extends his narrative beyond the victims' suffering. He ventures further, unsettlingly, by granting narrative centrality to the perpetrators themselves. Displacing the victim as the focal figure—contrary to conventional human rights discourses—is another distinctive gesture in Monge's narrative (Peña Iguarán 2019, p. 143). The main characters are the leaders of a trafficking ring that kidnaps migrants to sell them into slavery. Their names—*Epitafio* (Epitaph) and *Estela* (Gravestone)—are only conceivable in a world saturated by death.

An economic cycle organises the plot, which begins and ends with the journey of two teenagers—the "chicos de la selva" (jungle boys) (Monge 2015, p. 18). They guide a group of migrants through the jungle towards a clearing where Estela and Epitafio's gang awaits them. There, they kidnap the migrants and pay the boys. The traffickers then split up and embark on labyrinthine routes to sell their captives into forced labour. Meanwhile, police, soldiers, and fellow criminals are conspiring to eliminate them and seize their power. From executioners, Estela and Epitafio will be turned into victims by the very system they inhabit. The murder of the jungle boys by those same conspirators closes the circle, ending the novel in the same jungle clearing.

Estela and Epitafio assert their sovereignty over the bodies delivered to them through degradation. Estela mercilessly mocks the migrants' dreams of reaching the United States: "Didn't you want another homeland? . . . You're going to learn what the homeland is . . . you're going to learn who the homeland is!" (Monge 2015, p. 26). Epitafio then proclaims: "I am the homeland!". In that forgotten corner of the Mexican jungle, Epitafio exercises the power of an absolute sovereign. When Estela asks what "the homeland" wants, he replies: "That they kneel" (Monge 2015). This act of supplication and humiliation becomes the symbolic gesture that inaugurates a sovereignty built on the extractive, asymmetrical relations that characterise negative reciprocity.

Monge truly plunges us into hell—at whose entrance, if Dante Alighieri (2013 [1472]: *Inferno*, Canto III, v. 9) is to be believed, we must abandon all hope. And yet, Estela and Epitafio are deeply in love with each other. Their extreme violence is repeatedly suspended by this bond, which estranges them from the world of human trafficking. Love, then, unsettles the dichotomy between victim and perpetrator. Monge, as a consummate storyteller, constructs a tragedy that compels us, while remaining firmly aligned with the victims, to problematise our normative response to the actions of their executioners.

Drawing on Oswaldo Zavala's (2018) critique of *narco* narratives, I have argued (Gómez Romero 2024, p. 391) that the stories of powerful cartels threatening Mexican state sovereignty are nothing but a myth that fuels further violence. Figures like Estela and Epitafio are indeed terrifying to those who fall into their grip. They lack, however, the means or desire to dismantle the state. They instead "cope with precarity on a daily basis" and operate "always on the edge of an abyss" (Lomnitz 2023, p. 164). The sovereignty wielded by agents of negative reciprocity is always precarious and wretched. Even "the grand lords of the criminal economy live with the abyss ever at hand" (Lomnitz 2023). This is central to the notion of dual Mexican sovereignty explored earlier.

The peculiar sovereignty arising from negative reciprocity is ultimately grounded in what Sayak Valencia (2016) calls *endriago* subjectivities. The *endriagos* are the likes of Estela and Epitafio, who submit to the extractive logics of precariousness and accumulation of "gore capitalism" (Valencia 2016, pp. 78–80)—the price the Global South pays for global capital, which is exacted in blood because "the destruction of the body becomes in itself a product or commodity" (Valencia 2016, p. 26).

In this model of political economy, some individuals are rendered disposable. Those cast out from the legal productive order—especially men—are likely to drift into making a living from terror. Valencia draws the term *endriago* from Amadís de Gaula, a chivalric sixteenth-century Iberian romance (Rodríguez de Montaño

2017). The *endriago* is a monster: furred and armoured, with eagle talons, feline limbs, vast wings, and eyes aflame. "Endowed with defensive and offensive elements sufficient to provoke fear in any adversary" (Valencia 2016, p. 100), this creature survives in our time. *Endriagos* are the offspring of thwarted desires—for recognition, for ascent—under conditions that have rendered such aspirations structurally impossible. Violence becomes the only viable path to status. *Endriago* subjects legitimise underground economies through necro-empowerment that stages spectacles of terror (Valencia 2016, p. 29). Their consumerist longings, unmet by legal means, are pursued through brutality. They manufacture a "reticular and managed terror" that moves, like a contagion, from the injured to those who fear being next (Valencia 2016, p. 118).

In *Las tierras arrasadas*, the objectification of others—both the premise and product of human trafficking—consumes those who practise it, as others rise to take their place. Yet we come to recognise how negative reciprocity also harms the perpetrators only because we have walked alongside their victims. This is Monge's gift: the insight that, to imagine a way out of hell, we must first embrace all those who dwell within it.

Disappearance in living flesh

Sorrow is the third and final affect with which Gabriel Gatti (2022, p. 155) approaches Mexico's abyss. He recounts a day conversing with families of the disappeared, when "the enormity of Mexican disappearance, the terror that cuts through life, language, the faces of those who endure it", came crashing in (Gatti 2022, pp. 171–2). As a professional scholar, he recognised the risk: social scientists and jurists demand "direct contact with *reality*, with the *thing itself*" (Gatti 2022, p. 185). Yet disappearance erases precisely that: "what occurred is no longer there" (Gatti 2022). The matter is grimmer when the disappeared are those whose story "no one tells, registers, or even considers" (Gatti 2022, p. 173)—the poor, the homeless, the migrant. Someone decided to take their life, likely with little difficulty: they were unprotected, neglected, and invisible. Before vanishing, they had already ceased to be heard.

Such erasure opens a chasm that state-sanctioned Mexican law has failed to bridge. Redress requires a shift—perhaps beginning with the kinds of questions we pose in the face of such devastation. In the aftermath of 11 September 2001, Judith Butler (2020 [2004], p. xii) observed that the realisation "that we can be injured, that others can be injured, that we are subject to death at another's whim" offers reasons for both fear and grief. She urged that, to "arrest cycles of violence", we must "ask what, politically, might be made of grief" (Butler 2020). This remains a pressing question. Mourning—the psychological and social process by which we publicly and privately recognise another's loss—reveals our vulnerability and, thereby, our shared humanity. For Butler, grief "furnishes a sense of political community of a complex order . . . by bringing to the fore the relational ties that have implications for . . . fundamental dependency and ethical responsibility" (Butler 2020, p. 22).

In dialogue with Butler—and in response to the daily experience of negative reciprocity—Mexican writer Cristina Rivera Garza (2019, p. 16) asks how to write where "the precarity of labour and the horror of death constitute the stuff of everyday life". She wonders how to sustain a creative impulse while "literally surrounded by the dead" (Rivera Garza 2019, p. 17). Her answer (Rivera Garza 2011, p. 17) is "to opt for the word", thereby activating "the critical and utopian potential of language" and, thereafter, "to grieve as one who shelters from the elements". Amid extreme violence, authentic mourning alone can restore our humanity and safeguard our communities. As she writes (2019, p. 136):

> When not only a few lives are deemed worthy of public mourning, when the obituary extends to the nameless and faceless, when, like Antigone, we are able to bury the Other—or, in other words, recognise the lived life of that Other against the edict of Creon or any ruling authority—then public mourning, by rendering us more vulnerable, will make us more human. When every life is a grievable life. This theoretical frame . . . could help us resist responding violently to the harm others inflict on us, thereby limiting the ever-present possibility of harm we inflict ourselves.

In his latest novel *Los vivos* (2024), Emiliano Monge undertakes the mourning Mexico's disappearances demand. The narrative traces first and foremost an *atmosphere*—a limbo. The reader is led into a no-place that evokes Mexico without being it outright. Here, people work, care for pets, suffer insomnia, and even quarrel with their other halves. This world shares the texture of our own, save for the waves of the *reappeared* who bear no memory of their former lives. In Monge's uncanny realm, those who vanish in one place—Mexico, perhaps—resurface in the novel's otherworld. Hence the reappeared share a singular fear: "to realise, on some random day, that one is not where one belongs" (Monge 2024, p. 58).

The pain of memory lost and recovered is central to the fable. Characters inhabit a present without past—an allegory of time framed by disappearance, frozen by the wait to confirm death or witness return. At the heart of the novel is the relationship between *Hincapié* (Emphasis) and *Vestigia* (Vestige). Their names, as in *Las tierras arrasadas*, entwine them with their world—in this case, the indefinite pause that disappearance imposes on both those who vanish and those who keep waiting for them. True to his name, Hincapié seeks to remain in the eternal present devoid of memories that is now his home. Vestigia, in contrast, feels the call of a past that is, paradoxically, the key to her future liberation. Hincapié and Vestigia are two forces equally drawn and repelled, yet bound by love: he lives consumed by fear she will vanish, she yearns to return to those she senses are seeking her elsewhere.

A soothsayer reveals Vestigia's true dwelling lies elsewhere: "Because you will be found, you will disappear", the prophecy warns (Monge 2024, p. 85). From this augury, Vestigia discerns that "we all have a place", and to find it one must "return by letting go" (Monge 2024, p. 86). "Is there anyone", Vestigia writes in her notebook, "searching for me in the place I departed from? Is my future my past?" (Monge 2024, p. 138). Hincapié, for whom the present is all, feels "hurt" upon reading these lines (Monge 2024).

Vestigia's journey thus becomes one of bridging towards that other site where she is sought, retracing her steps into the painful past of her disappearance. Being found eases "the sorrow of those who are searching there for those who continue to arrive here" (Monge 2024, p. 221). Only by being found can time resume its course, for as the soothsayer notes, "there is no other way to cure, here, a grief that does not belong here" (Monge 2024).

Vestigia reveals something we often resist, precisely because of the intimate wound it opens: part of our being is built upon the absences we endure. As Lucía—her closest friend in that limbo without a past—remarks, we are "the ghost of a former self" (Monge 2024, p. 162). Many lives dwell within our one life; every turning point leaves behind traces—absent persons, feelings, experiences—that make us who we are. To speak of this, I have no choice but to turn to the personal. I write these lines on the fifth anniversary of my mother Leticia's death. For most of my life, I was someone I am no longer: Leticia's son. But the self I now inhabit cannot be understood without that other one I once was. I am, in a sense, the ghost of Leticia's son—and it is her absence in my present that, in no small part, makes me who I am today.

As it happened with me, Vestigia's search awakens in Lucía the memory of her own mother. This leads her to the quiet realisation that mourning's work is to relearn how to speak *with* the dead:

> We are our dead. We feel them and they feel us, even if we cannot communicate with them because they have forgotten our language and we no longer know theirs . . . we speak different languages, that's all . . . I have always wanted to understand that language, I am sure it was once ours—it only needs to be found again.
>
> *(Monge 2024, p. 163)*

Monge's writing turns its gaze towards the absent through a lens that is subtly—yet profoundly—distinct. It undertakes a hermeneutic labour akin to the recovery of a forgotten language. This shift in perspective proposes a radical alternative to the dominant treatment of disappearances in Mexico. We tend to speak *of* the disappeared without compassion—parading clandestine graves, dismembered bodies, or belongings left behind in the shadows of their torment. Monge's novel resists this visual grammar by portraying the disappeared as embodied memories, anchored in the present. Only literature can offer such a vantage point. This is suggested obliquely in the novel's epigraph, which cites a fragment of a conversation between Lucía and Vestigia. Lucía often compares human beings to animals because, as she puts it, "we are their metaphor" (Monge 2024). For instance, she believes we are not a carnivorous species but perhaps scavengers, since "we eat the flesh of animals killed days or even weeks earlier"—because we are unsettled by the violence of taking a life to nourish our own (Monge 2024, p. 57). Similarly, in the epigraph, Lucía compares human literature to a frog's sight:

> Most people know that a frog's eyes are located on the sides of its head, that they bulge out, and that they can perceive some colours. But what hardly anyone knows, my friend, is that frogs can only see movement. I mean, when the world is still, they are blind. It is the wind stirring the grass, the drop that trembles the pond, the fluttering of a bug—that makes them see. That, I think, is how reading works, and how writing should work as well.
>
> *(Monge 2024, p. 9)*

Through literature, we speak *with* those who are now absent from our lives. To explain this, once again I must turn to the personal. I write these lines with tears upon my face. Leticia, who lives on in my memory, now emerges through my words. I am her absence—and I am also her remembrance. Monge's literary world, like the vision of the frog described by Lucía, provided the movement I needed to see. My mother, who died far from me, does not lie beneath the dust of a land that was once my own. I carry her within me, under my skin and deep in the roots of my being—and from that place, just as I find her, she too finds me.

But Leticia did not disappear. She died in her home, one night during the COVID pandemic. How would her memory—which lives within me, as the title of Monge's novel suggests—be shaped if I had never been able to say goodbye? If her absence were made of uncertainty and not-knowing? Her memory, I imagine, would then be an unending search. Like the frog, I needed Monge's literature to perceive the full depth of this.

In the eternal present of her limbo, Vestigia—who is sought—seeks in turn. In the early pages of the novel, we learn that, together with Lucía, she belongs to a group of *buscadoras* (searchers). One of them displays a piece of embroidery bearing the question: "*¿Y si yo lo encuentro, qué*?" (And if I find them, then what?). Around that question, "the silhouettes of four women . . . seem to be raking the ground" (Monge 2024, p. 18).

That embroidery exists in our world, too (Monge 2024, p. 243). It is the work of the artist and embroiderer Paulina Cuarón, who has graciously authorised me to reproduce it here (Figure 2.1).[6] Both the embroidery and Monge's narrative refer to an *insider joke*—of sorts—from Mexican popular culture. Early in our lives, we must learn nearly everything. Searching is no exception. In many Mexican homes (and probably throughout the world) the following scene is all too familiar: a child

FIGURE 2.1 Paulina Cuarón, 2021

or adolescent, unable to find something, blurts out "I can't find it" to the person who has walked a few steps ahead in life, and often stands in for a mother. That person—shaped through affections, shared meanings, and the nurturing of life—responds, sometimes patiently and sometimes not: "And if I find it, then what?"

Cuarón's embroidery and Monge's novel thus enter the search that, preceding us, taught us how to search.

"Searching", writes Gatti (2022, p. 162), "is the verb of Mexican disappearance". Those who search are, for the most part, women—relatives of the missing, gathered in groups and associations taking that verb as their identity. Gatti (2022, p. 162) describes their labour of mourning, longing, and hope:

> They do what they can. They work in fragments, with scraps—from rumours, bits of data, hunches, broken lines of testimony, traces and signs. They walk difficult paths, venture into the foulest corners of the country, converse with the earth to ask where the disappeared lie. They gently look for wounds—in the dusty scrubland or riverbanks—that might reveal the presence of holes hiding bits of phalanx, pieces of femur, a shred of flesh. They investigate, trace, piece together puzzles. They invent localisation systems, precarious at times, yet effective, like the diviners who once dowsed for hidden water.

In the act of searching, both the seekers and the disappeared emerge as political subjects. "And if I find them, then what?" ask the *buscadoras* of Mexico's new model of statehood—a state that has abdicated its duty to pursue justice. Their investigations exceed the law's hollow obligations to search, punish, account, and repair. And so, between mourning and search, something begins to shift. Not every disappeared person will be found, nor will every truth come to light. But something new is being built: human bonds and community reappear where only the desolation of negative reciprocity once prevailed.

Conclusion: towards a mourning law

The negative reciprocity that sustains the new model of the Mexican state is, as anthropologist Rossana Reguillo (2021) has characterised it, a *necromachine* that never sleeps. These pages do not contain the words that might halt such a machine, or begin to imagine a future Mexico beyond the routine repetition of violence. Their modest offering, at best, is to redirect our gaze towards places where the new words that are needed to speak with the disappeared might begin to form. These places are memory and mourning. And those who might lead us there are the *buscadoras*—the ones who search. As Capitán Insurgente Marcos, once spokesperson of the Zapatista Army of National Liberation (EZLN), wrote in a communiqué dated 8 August 2024:

> Search for the seekers. It occurs to me, I don't know, that maybe they are also looking for another tomorrow. And that, friends and enemies, is fighting for life.
>
> *(Marcos 2024)*

That is the first decision we, as legal agents responsible for the meanings we create in law, can take from out of grief: to choose life. And from there, law must relearn how to remember, how to grieve. Perhaps even how to weep. Only then might it come to utter the words that could soothe the abandonment in which Mexico's disappeared remain suspended—words now beginning to take shape in the literary work of writers such as Emiliano Monge.

Notes

1 All translations are mine unless noted otherwise.
2 *Las tierras arrasadas* has been translated into English by Frank Wynne as *Among the Lost* [2018, Scribe]. *Los vivos* remains untranslated at the time of writing.
3 This provision establishes: "Norms concerning human rights shall be interpreted in accordance with this Constitution and with the relevant international treaties, at all times favouring the most extensive protection of individuals".
4 Other legal instruments also address disappearances. The General Victims' Law (Diario Oficial de la Federación 2013) establishes numerous obligations, mainly concerning the immediate search or release of disappeared persons (Arts. 19, 21, 61, 73(ii), 120(xv), and 123(ii)).
5 Migrant disappearances in Mexico first gained international media attention in August 2010, after 72 migrants—most of them from Central America—were found tortured and executed in San Fernando, Tamaulipas (Turati 2023).
6 The embroidery was exhibited in Mexico City as part of the exhibition *Maternar*, held between November 2021 and July 2022 at the Museo Universitario de Arte Contemporáneo (2021).

References

Agamben, G. (2012) *Stato di eccezione*. Turin: Bollati Boringhieri.

Alighieri D. (2013 [1472]) "Divina Commedia", in I. Borzi et al. (eds.) *Dante: Tutte le opere*. Roma: Newton Compton, 31–664.

Anzoátegui, I. (ed.) (1964). *Los cuatro viajes del Almirante y su testamento.* 4th ed. Madrid: Espasa-Calpe.

Astorga, L. (2015) *¿Qué querían que hiciera? Inseguridad y delincuencia organizada en el gobierno de Felipe Calderón*. Mexico City: Grijalbo.

Azaola, E. (2022) "Estado de excepción y pandemia de violencia en México", *Korpus 21*, 2(6), pp. 455–468.

Bakhtin, M. (1981) *The Dialogic Imagination: Four Essays*. Emerson, C. & Holquist, M. (trans.), Holquist, M. (ed.). Austin: University of Texas Press.

Beuchot, M. (1997). *La querella de la conquista. Una polémica del siglo XVI*. 2nd ed. Mexico City: Siglo XXI.

Binder, G. and Weisberg, R. (2000) *Literary Criticisms of Law*. Princeton, NJ: Princeton University Press.

Boullosa, C. and Wallace, M. (2015) *Narco History: How the United States and Mexico Jointly Created the "Mexican Drug War"*. New York/London: OR Books.

Butler, J. (2020 [2004]) *Precarious Life: The Powers of Mourning and Justice*. London/ New York: Verso.

Castañeda Hernández, M. (2018) *El principio pro persona ante la ponderación de derechos*. Mexico City: CNDH.

Cavarero, A. (2007) *Orrorismo, ovvero della violenza sull'inerme*. Milan: Feltrinelli.

Cover, R. (1983) "Foreword: Nomos and Narrative", *Harvard Law Review*, 97(1), pp. 4–68.

De Sahagún, B. (2000 [1829]) *Historia general de las cosas de Nueva España*, 3 vols. Mexico City: CNCA.

De Valle-Arizpe, A. (1980 [1957]) *Historia, tradiciones y leyendas de las calles de México*, 2nd ed. Mexico City: Diana.

Diario Oficial de la Federación. (2002) *Convención Interamericana sobre Desaparición Forzada de Personas*, 6 May.
Diario Oficial de la Federación. (2011) *Convención Internacional para la Protección de Todas las Personas Contra las Desapariciones Forzadas*, 22 June.
Diario Oficial de la Federación. (2013) *Ley General de Víctimas*, 9 January.
Diario Oficial de la Federación. (2017) *Ley General en Materia de Desaparición Forzada de Personas, Desaparición Cometida por Particulares y del Sistema Nacional de Búsqueda*, 17 November.
Duhalde, E.L. (2009) "Carta de Eduardo Luis Duhalde a Fernández Meijide", *Perfil*, 4 August. Available at: https://www.perfil.com/noticias/politica/carta-de-eduardo-luis-duhalde-a-fernandez-meijide-20090804-0037.phtml (accessed 10 February 2025).
Durán-Martínez, A. (2015) "To Kill and Tell? State Power, Criminal Competition, and Drug Violence", *The Journal of Conflict Resolution*, 59(2), pp. 1377–1402.
Escohotado, A. (2021) *Historia general de las drogas*, 14th ed. Barcelona: Espasa.
Favaro, A. (2019) "Voces efímeras: el drama de la migración transfronteriza en México", *Ars & Humanitas*, 13(2), pp. 64–77.
Foucault, M. (1966) *Les mots et les choses: Une archéologie des sciences humaines*. Paris: Gallimard.
Gatti, G. (2011) *Identidades desaparecidas: Peleas por el sentido en los mundos de la desaparición forzada*. Buenos Aires: Prometeo.
Gatti, G. (2017) "Prolegómeno. Para un concepto científico de desaparición", in Gatti, G. (ed.) *Desapariciones: Usos locales, circulaciones globales*. Bogotá: Siglo del Hombre/Uniandes, 13–32.
Gatti, G. (2022) *Desaparecidos: Cartografías del abandono*. Madrid: Turner.
Giddens, T., Crawley, K. and Peters, T. (2024) "Cultural Legal Studies: Methodologies of Reflective Attunement", in Giddens, T., Crawley, K. and Peters, T. (eds.) *The Routledge Handbook of Cultural Legal Studies*. New York and Abingdon: Routledge, 1–19.
Gómez Romero, L. (2008) *El tiempo de los débiles: Garantismo y literatura*. Mexico City: Porrúa/Escuela Libre de Derecho/Universidad Carlos III de Madrid.
Gómez Romero, L. (2024) "The Myth of the Big, Bad Narco: Cinematic Jurisprudence and US-Mexican Drug Wars", in Giddens, T., Crawley, K. and Peters, T. (eds.) *The Routledge Handbook of Cultural Legal Studies*. New York and Abingdon: Routledge, 390–412.
González Villarreal, R. (2022) *La desaparición forzada en México: De la represión a la rentabilidad*. Mexico City: Terracota.
Graeber, D. and Sahlins, M. (2017) *On Kings*. Chicago: Hau Books.
Grandin, G. (2025) *America, América: A New History of the New World*. London: Torva.
Guercke, L. (2025) *Failure of the State: Organised Crime and Mexico's Disappeared*. Cham: Springer.
Joyce, J. (1992 [1922]). *Ulysses*. New York: The Modern Library.
Kafka, F. (2015 [1919]) *In der Strafkolonie*. Göttingen: De Gruyter.
León-Portilla, M. (1989 [1959]). *Visión de los vencidos. Relaciones indígenas de la Conquista*. 12th ed. Mexico City: Universidad Nacional Autónoma de México.
Lomnitz, C. (2005) *Death and the Idea of Mexico*. New York: Zone Books.
Lomnitz, C. (2022) *El tejido social rasgado*. Mexico City: Era.
Lomnitz, C. (2023) *Para una teología política del crimen organizado*. Mexico City: Era.
Long, R.F. (2022) "Those Who Recount Matter: Fiction and Testimonial in Emiliano Monge's *Las tierras arrasadas*", *Revista Canadiense de Estudios Hispánicos*, 46(2), pp. 391–412.
López Ayllón, S., Orozco Henríquez, J., Salazar, P. and Valadés, D. (2024) "Introducción al análisis técnico de las 20 iniciativas de reformas constitucionales y legales presentadas por el presidente de la República", in López Ayllón, S., Orozco Henríquez, J., Salazar, P. and Valadés, D. (eds.) *Análisis técnico de las 20 iniciativas de reformas constitucionales y*

legales presentadas por el presidente de la República (febrero 5, 2024). Mexico City: Instituto de Investigaciones Jurídicas/UNAM, 1–14.
López Noriega, S. and Martín Reyes, J. (eds.) (2025) *La tormenta judicial. Implicaciones de la reforma de 2024 en México*. Mexico City: Nexos.
Macdonald, R. (2011) "Custom Made—For a Non-Chirographic Critical Legal Pluralism." *Canadian Journal of Law and Society*, 26(2), 301–327.
Manderson, D. (2012) *Kangaroo Courts and the Rule of Law: The Legacy of Modernism*. New York and Abingdon: Routledge.
Marcos, Capitán Insurgente. (2024) "Un pico y una pala. De la solidaridad, la empatía, y la valentía", 8 August, *Enlace Zapatista*. Available at: https://enlacezapatista.ezln.org.mx/2024/08/08/un-pico-y-una-pala-de-la-solidaridad-la-empatia-y-la-valentia/ (accessed 25 June 2025).
Maurette, P. (2024) *Por qué creemos los cuentos: Cómo se construye evidencia en la ficción*, 2nd ed. Madrid: Siglo XXI Editores.
Mendoza, N. (2026) *El extravío de los signos: Ensayos sobre duelo y porvenir*. Cáceres: Periférica.
Monge, E. (2015) *Las tierras arrasadas*. Mexico City: Random House.
Monge, E. (2024) *Los vivos*. Barcelona: Random House.
Morábito, F. (ed.) (2014) "La Llorona", in *Cuentos Populares Mexicanos*. Mexico City: UNAM/FCE, 125–126.
Morín, E. (2015) *La maña. Un recorrido antropológico por la cultura de las drogas*. Mexico City: Debate.
Morton, A.D. (2012) "The War on Drugs in Mexico: A Failed State", *Third World Quarterly*, 33(9), 1631–1645.
Müller, J.-W. (2016) *What Is Populism?* Philadelphia: University of Pennsylvania Press.
Museo Universitario de Arte Contemporáneo. (2021) *Maternar: Entre el síndrome de Estocolmo y los actos de producción*. [Online]. Available at: https://muac.unam.mx/exposicion/maternar.
Peña Iguarán, A. (2019) "Vidas residuales: El arte en tiempos de guerra. *Las tierras arrasadas* (2015) de Emiliano Monge", *Mitologías Hoy*, 17, pp. 135–149.
Red Lupa. (2025) *Informe Nacional de personas desaparecidas 2025*. [Online]. Available at: https://imdhd.org/redlupa/informes-y-analisis/informes-nacionales/informe-nacional-de-personas-desaparecidas-2025/ (accessed 5 June 2025).
Reguillo, R. (2021) *Necromáquina: Cuando morir no es suficiente*. Tlaquepaque: NED Ediciones/ITESO.
Rivera Garza, C. (2011). *Dolerse: Textos desde un país herido*. Oaxaca: Sur+/Frontera Press.
Rivera Garza, C. (2019). *Los muertos indóciles: Necroescritura y apropiación*. Mexico City: Debolsillo.
Rodríguez de Montaño, G. (2017 [1508]). *Los quatro libros del virtuoso caualler Amadís de Gaula*. Mexico City: Porrúa.
Ruiz Sosa, E. (2022) *El libro de nuestras ausencias*. Barcelona: Candaya.
Sahlins, M. (2017 [1972]) *Stone Age Economics*. London and New York: Routledge.
Secretaría de Gobernación. (2025) *Registro Nacional de Personas Desaparecidas y No Localizadas (RNPDNO)*. [Online]. Available at: https://versionpublicarnpdno.segob.gob.mx/Dashboard/ContextoGeneral (accessed 23 June 2025).
Silva Forné, C., Pérez Correa, C. and Guitérrez Rivas, R. (2017) "Índice de letalidad 2008-2014: Menos enfrentamientos, misma letalidad, más opacidad", *Perfiles Latinoamericanos*, 25(50), pp. 331–359.
Smith, B.T. (2021) *The Dope: The Real History of the Mexican Drug Trade*. London: Ebury Press.
Turati, M. (2023) *San Fernando: Última parada. Viaje al crimen autorizado en Tamaulipas*. Mexico City: Aguilar.

United Nations Committee on Enforced Disappearances. (2022) *Report of the Committee on Enforced Disappearances on its visit to Mexico under article 33 of the Convention.* UN Doc CED/C/MEX/VR/1, 18 May.
United Nations Committee on Enforced Disappearances. (2025) *El Comité contra la Desaparición Forzada de la ONU aclara su procedimiento en virtud del artículo 34 de la Convención.* [Online]. Available at: https://mexico.un.org/es/292394-el-comit%C3%A9-contra-la-desaparici%C3%B3n-forzada-de-la-onu-aclara-su-procedimiento-en-virtud-del (accessed 30 May 2025).
Valencia, S. (2016) *Capitalismo gore: Control económico, violencia y narcopoder*. Barcelona: Paidós.
Villoro, J. (2010) "La alfombra roja", *Proceso*, no. 1735, 31 January, 26–29.
Zavala, O. (2018) *Los cárteles no existen. Narcotráfico y cultura en México*. Barcelona: Malpaso.

3

DISPLACEMENT IN THE COLONIAL CARCERAL ARCHIPELAGO

Voices of imprisoned Indigenous Women

Thalia Anthony

Introduction: colonial carceral controls of Indigenous women

Indigenous women are experiencing unprecedented levels of imprisonment in Australia. Between 2016 and 2025, the prison rate for Indigenous women soared by 150%. Indigenous women are 26 times more likely to be imprisoned than non-Indigenous women. For non-Indigenous women, their rate of imprisonment has slightly declined by 17% since 2016 (Australian Bureau of Statistics 2025). In NSW, where the yarning circles were conducted, Indigenous women constitute 42% of the NSW female prison population (BOCSAR 2025, Tables 1 and 2). They are 21 times more likely to be incarcerated than non-Indigenous women (Australian Human Rights Commission 2024).

The critical literature on harms of imprisonment conceives prison as a "social death" (Price 2015), brought about by degradation ceremonies and routinised shaming and dehumanisation. "Social death" marks the displacement of people from the civil world of rights and entitlements, which may be returned upon release. In the land known as "Australia", physical, psychological and fatal harms of imprisonment, notably Indigenous deaths in custody, are connected to a constellation of carceral colonial controls and harms. These controls transcend the prison gates and permeate into society.

This chapter adapts Foucault's (1991, p. 298) concept of the "carceral archipelago" to particularise its operation in Australia in the "colonial carceral archipelago" (see Anthony and Blagg 2025). This concept identifies how prison is one of the many institutions that reinforce everyday colonial control over the lives of Indigenous people. While prison is a key site of control, it is not an exclusive site.

Research conducted with Indigenous women in prisons in New South Wales (NSW), Australia, reveals that incarceration is but one node in a network of

DOI: 10.4324/9781003752974-5

controls. This chapter explores the colonial carceral archipelago through the stories of Indigenous women in prison. It shows that the pains of prison continue through oppressive state interventions in the community. Indigenous women's freedoms are inhibited through child protection matters, health services, housing, policing and social security. For imprisoned Indigenous women, the experience of displacement is a pervasive and enduring feature of colonial society.

Drawing on yarns and surveys with 164 Indigenous women in NSW prisons, this chapter explores imprisonment as an extension of colonial violence and White possession that exists across a sweeping colonial carceral archipelago. To understand the gendered aspects of dispossession, Aileen Moreton-Robinson's (2015) framework of "patriarchal white sovereignty" is invoked. The colonial violence of racism, exclusion, stealing children, over-policing, poverty and homelessness pervade the existence of incarcerated Indigenous women and their families.

This chapter contends that despite the colonial will to excise Indigenous women's sovereignty, it has not been eradicated. The stories of Indigenous women in prison bear witness to the strength, sovereignty and self-determination of Indigenous women's ontology, care and collectivism. Their shared truths about resistance and racism united their refusal to be displaced. In prisons, Indigenous women continue to speak with pride of their responsibilities and important contributions to family, community, and culture. In our research yarns they asserted: "We are strong independent black women"; "I'm the fighter of the family. So . . . when it comes to my family I'm a big protector" (quoted in Anthony et al. 2021, p. 8, 10). They maintain a strong sense of identity that ebbs against the "social death" of imprisonment and the colonial carceral archipelago to hold them upright in navigating "every day" colonialism (Watego 2021). This refusal defies the totalising effects of prison as a social death.

Defiance is layered with "refusal" (Simpson 2014) to relinquish their identities to the colonial inscriptions of criminals, prisoners and law breakers (Fanon 1986, p. 95). The refusal does not diminish the oppressive nature of colonial displacement but speaks to the tenacity of Indigenous women in resisting its force. Radical resistance is expressed through shared connections of Indigenous women in prison, their laws and cultures, as well as attempts to fulfil responsibilities to children while in prison and imagine a future of their making.

The White possessive and the colonial carceral archipelago

The colonial carceral archipelago is experienced uniquely by Indigenous women. Goenpul woman and critical Whiteness scholar Aileen Moreton-Robinson (2015, p. xii) refers to White 'possessive logics' enforcing the 'territoriality of patriarchal White sovereignty' (2015, p. xix). Moreton-Robinson (2015, p. 179) explains that this defines who is worthy of White privileges and legal entitlements. This dispossesses Indigenous women from the same benefits and privileges as White women. It seeks to extinguish their sovereignty and subvert them to White male power that is etched on the national narrative. Indigenous women, according to Moreton-Robinson (2020, p. 1), are known by White Australia as 'objects who lack agency'.

Wiradjuri Professor Juanita Sherwood and colleagues (2015) discuss how Indigenous women are typecast as offenders or victims who are characterised as lacking strengths, self-determination and expertise in their own lives. Formerly incarcerated Gunditjmara writer Tabitha Lean (2021) expressed this labelling in her poem, "The Disposable Humans":

> I am a disposable human.
> My blood courses with my grandmother's stories, every one of her fears and 232 years of her rage.
> My mother's songs are nestled in my mitochondria . . . my DNA carries all of her hopes and dreams never realised.
> The tragedy of her death is etched upon every one of my bones, scars that serve to remind me of the inevitability of my death—a memento mori, if you will.
> My spirit is restless . . . dispossessed . . . fragmented, even. I straddle two, sometimes three worlds, never quite comfortable in any.
> I am a criminal.

The disposability of Indigenous lives is not only in prisons or locked to a point in time but also coalesces with a range of colonial institutions and runs across generations. The invasion of Country saw the inception of colonial carceral archipelago as a constellation of sites to discipline and contain Indigenous bodies and minds. Ann Laura Stoler (2016, p. 108) engages the concept of "carceral archipelago" to elucidate "a politics of security" in the "policing of imperial borderlands and ambiguous frontiers". In their article "Prison as a Border", Angela Davis and Gina Dent (2001, p. 1241) argue that prisons reproduce "a social world" that is divided by "boundaries of nation-states, races, genders, and sexualities". It has distinct resonance with "colonial lives" because Indigenous people are violently subjugated to colonial property interests beyond prisons to assure expropriation, exploitation, and extraction (Bhandar 2018). The following section considers the historical and contemporary features of this archipelago in the colonial matrix of power.

Scope of the chapter

This chapter enlivens stories by Indigenous women in NSW prisons. Their stories convey the features of the colonial carceral archipelago that are not limited to prisons or even law enforcement. It demonstrates that Western concepts that valorise the penal prison overlook the continuous and contiguous features of containing Indigenous people on missions, enslaved labour sites (e.g. cattle stations), asylums, lock hospitals, orphanages and police cells (Havemann 2005, p. 59). The colonial state's treatment of Indigenous people is characterised by a persistence of purpose and practice (see Fanon 1986) rather than emancipatory gestures and breaks.

The "colonial matrix of power" and "coloniality of power", to use the concepts of Anibal Quijano (2007) and Walter Mignolo (2007, p. 156), shape institutions and relationships across colonial society. The erasure of Indigenous laws and cultures, and the usurpation of Indigenous land, labour sovereignty and children, continues to disempower and displace Indigenous women.

After addressing the oppressive, racialised and gendered practices of prisons and beyond, the chapter turns to Indigenous women's stories of strength and resistance. These are offered in this chapter as a counterpoint to state interventions to show that solutions for Indigenous women are in their empowerment. Expectations that the state will improve Indigenous women's lives rest in a blind hope, as Chelsea Watego (2021) powerfully contends, that the oppressor can also be the emancipator. Indigenous women demonstrate capacity to imagine and implement novel ways to address their own needs outside of the state and within their own communities and organisations. Finally, Indigenous women's sovereignty requires more than critical approaches to imprisonment and all the colonial carceral experiences they speak to across the research yarning circles.

Methodology and focus

The research project, which was funded by the Australian Research Council, listened to the voices of Indigenous women in prison and sought to provide support and a space for them to feel empowered within the confines of imprisonment. Pursuant to this endeavour, an Indigenous women's advisory group, sista2sista, was initially formed to guide research methodologies and provide in-prison and reintegration assistance and advocacy. With the joint organisational leadership of Gomeroi woman and researcher Alison Whittaker, we brought together Indigenous women with lived experience and those who worked with and for Indigenous women with lived experience in NSW.

The women in sista2sista are sovereign women, leaders, law holders, cultural teachers, carers, and healers and, accordingly, integral to their Indigenous communities. They came from Indigenous women's organisations such as Waminda, Mudgin-gal, Wirringa Baiya, and the Aboriginal Legal Service; government services such as Centrelink (social security) and Housing; and programmes such as the Werribee Clinic that support Indigenous women whose children have been taken by child protection authorities. The group guided the research and discussed how to care for incarcerated Indigenous women and how to give them voice in the community. I, along with the remarkable co-researchers who helped conduct the prison yarning circles, namely Wiradjuri researcher Gemma Sentance and Dharug woman Michelle Toy, provided assistance with housing, child protection interventions, and prison classifications, sentencing hearings and bail applications.

Over the course of 2019, Gemma Sentance, Michelle Toy and I spoke to 164 Indigenous women over 12 visits in six NSW prisons. We held large and small yarning circles and conducted surveys on experiences of criminal sentencing and their vision for change to facilitate reintegration. The research with the women occurred in secluded common rooms, away from the presence of correctional officers. We instigated yarning methods to diminish power imbalances between Indigenous women and researchers (Bessarab and Ng'andu 2010) and to enhance healing through "inner deep listening and quiet still awareness" (Atkinson 2002, p. 17, 96, quoting Miriam-Rose Ungunmerr). I would often sit on the floor while participants were seated in chairs and facing one another. The yarns were free flowing and would begin with yarning about mob, family and culture. Most commonly, Indigenous women talked about their community, their pride in culture and their longing to return to their children.

Researchers participated in yarns by sharing our own experiences growing up and involvement with our families, communities, activism and organising. We conveyed our solidarity with the women and left our contact details on a leaflet that sista2sista designed with Ngemba/Yuwaa-laraay designer artist Cassie Willis. We frequently knew the Indigenous women in prison or knew their families, which made it easier for us to connect and develop trust in the yarns. Individual Indigenous women also sought us out to speak privately and seek help, including ascertaining information on the whereabouts of children, how to approach their sentencing hearing, and sending cards to family. We followed up all these types of requests after each visit.

Women came readily forward to speak in the yarning circles and fill out surveys because they repeatedly said that no one listened to their truth in the legal system and they wanted their truth to guide change. We compensated women as much community services allowed ($15 per hour). Yet women noted that the payment was not the main motivation; it was wanting to help other "women in the future", including their own children, as one remarked. Another acknowledged the importance of being able to yarn with other Indigenous women:

> This is the first time since I've been here—I've been only here a few months—that we've all been in the same room [as Indigenous women].

We returned to each of the six prisons to provide preliminary feedback and seek input in the findings. Although the feedback visit was only a few months after the first visit, we noticed a dramatic change in the cohort of Indigenous women. In each prison, most of the women on our first visit had been released, and a new group of women had been imprisoned. This resonates with the trends in Indigenous women cycling in and out of period. The average period of imprisonment is 50 days for remand, 74 days for sentence only and 243 days for remand to sentence (BOCSAR 2024, p. 36). Of the Indigenous women in NSW prisons, 50% are on remand, having been denied bail in prison (BOCSAR 2024, p. 26). Approximately, 40% of Indigenous women who leave prison are not sentenced to prison (BOCSAR 2022, p. 35). The churning of Indigenous women through prisons over the course of a year means that the yearly aggregate is much higher than point-in-time statistics suggest.

The mass imprisonment of Indigenous women is significantly accounted for by victimless crimes. Driving without a licence or while under the influence of alcohol (21%) and breach of justice procedures (13%) in NSW, and disorderly conduct (18.4%) in Western Australia (MacGillivray and Baldry 2015, p. 3) constitute some of the key offences that result in the imprisonment of Indigenous women, and this coheres with Indigenous women's explanations in yarns for being locked up. The focus of this chapter is on criminalisation as an act of displacement that neglects alternative place- and strengths-based approaches. Criminal processes also fail to listen to the stories of Indigenous women and dignify their humanity.

Violence of imprisonment—displacement from social, cultural and emotional well-being

Constraints of carceralism

Imprisonment constrains Indigenous women's capacity to carry out family and community obligations, to care for Country and to sustain their cultural connections and transfer their cultural knowledges. Indigenous women in prison do not have access to healthcare and programmes that make them feel safe and well. One woman said, "they're not supporting us, that's what it is". A woman commented that some of the women "don't know any other life" other than punishment and imprisonment. Many women describe themselves as trapped in an intergenerational cycle of imprisonment due to racism. One participant noted, "my partner . . . my father, a lot of family spent time in jail" and I'm "stuck now here".

For one 35-year-old woman, who had been in prison since she was 11, the cycle of imprisonment meant she couldn't develop her strengths and interests or build up her income to support herself and her family. Despite having several Aboriginal healthcare and veterinary certifications, she was unable to gain stability in the community to pursue employment and help the community. A 37-year-old woman said she has been in prison every year since she was 17. A further woman who was in and out of prison between the ages of 12 and 25 regards herself as "a product of the system". She says,

> they should have helped me, back then. . . . Like Juvenile Justice didn't help. They didn't do nothing . . . they're not fulfilling their job, so they kind of cover up a lot. And as much as I don't want to blame the system and go, it's all on them . . . but the system's not designed to support you at all.

Health neglect and abuse

Untreated health conditions were a prolific issue raised among the Indigenous women in yarning circles. They said it's difficult to get a health appointment and "it takes so much to get medicated". Some claimed they could not get their standard medication for over six months. Others referred to receiving the "wrong medication" while in prison, or health staff giving medication that "drugged me up". Nurses were described as "really, really rude" and put barriers in the way of receiving needed treatment: "the screws here, the nurses here do not give a shit"; "they don't care" about Indigenous women's health concerns, even when "going through excruciating pain, and nearly dying". One said, "The health line's a graveyard", and people just give up and drop off.

The situation was worse in relation to mental health in prisons. There is inadequate screening and limited access to psychiatrists, psychologists and counsellors. Many women's experiences are encapsulated in this quote: "I haven't even seen mental health, nothing". Women said, "I haven't even seen mental health in here". In this case, she had been waiting for nine months for a response to her request for the service. She said that unless you are self-harming and at "crisis point", there is no response: "You have to have a break-down to get in there". In a survey, a woman wrote that her wellbeing depended on accessing "more services for example, Mental Health, Drug and Alcohol Counselling, Trauma Counselling".

Some women had tooth or ear infections that went untreated and were visibly suffering during the yarning circles, barely able to talk. In these cases, the researchers attempted to seek help. One woman said that she had to call the Ombudsman in order to have the nurses treat her infection. Others said they could not receive basic pain relief in prison when they had "really bad migraines". Women could not access their glasses on their property, contributing to visual impairment. One woman spoke about a "botched" surgery while in prison and said that the prison and health staff would not give her post-surgery pain relief. Others got panic attacks in prison because they were in confined spaces and would not be given Valium for their anxiety.

In yarning circles, pregnant women conveyed that they were not receiving regular checks. Cynically, one woman referred to the "screws" as masochistic with the prisoners, saying: "Watching us suffer, they like that. They like watching us suffer, basically". In some cases, they will be "having a good day" and will help, but there was no consistency. Another woman commented, "it feels like every time you go to ask for something, we're hassling them". Aboriginal Legal Services staff, who we also interviewed in the research project, talked about clients on remand who were pregnant and were placed on beds shackled on their backs for prolonged periods. Other Aboriginal Legal Service staff talked about Indigenous women clients who had miscarriages while in custody. They said pregnant clients would be "lucky" to see health staff "once a month", and usually it was much longer between appointments. The neglect presented a risk to the mother and baby, according to pregnant Indigenous women in prison.

Mistreatment in prisons and police cells

Poor treatment in prisons made Indigenous women feel susceptible to becoming another "death in custody" because of "the way we've been treated in the cells". This was shared by one woman who went on to state: "like we get treated like shit down in the cells, sometimes you can't even get a cup of water[,] . . . toilet paper" or "showers". The Indigenous women also spoke about how they are denied phone calls to family members to let them know that they have been "locked up" and cannot return home. Others spoke about violent treatment in police cells in the lead-up to imprisonment, including "the coppers hold me down" in the cells and restrain them for prolonged periods. While this woman was held down, "the coppers . . . search me because they thought I had drugs on me but I didn't". She stated: "they do abuse us in there with their power because they've got the power".

The Indigenous women referred to the unique difficulties on remand. One woman remarked, "It makes it hard for girls that are stuck on remand. Because we've got nothing". There are no programmes or supports to help them survive in prison and assist their reintegration into society when they are released. Many of them will be released without a conviction, and while remand periods are relatively short, the impact can be hugely disruptive. Women can lose jobs, education and training placements, homes and children through the child protection system.

To illustrate the impact on children, an Indigenous woman whose children were subject to child protection orders as a result of imprisonment required that she undertake "a safety report just to see my kids. Because they've got it down on paper to say that I'm, you know, I can hurt my babies". Another Indigenous woman considered the wrongfulness of restricting contact, noting that the woman had eight children and was a good mother. She pointed out that policing and imprisonment are not an indication of their parenting capacity and authorities should not harm the children by prohibiting their access to their mothers inside.

Lack of programmes

In women's prisons more generally, and beyond remand, Indigenous women commented on the lack of programmes. One woman noted that the inadequate provision of programmes constrained reintegration. She said, "They're not stopping us from reoffending at all, put it that way". They specifically commented on the difficulty of getting on the methadone programme. Another Indigenous woman said,

> Even in here when you try to get on the program here, you got to wait two or three weeks, nearly a month to get assessed. And then after you get assessed you got to wait another month or so to see if they're going to put you on the Methadone or on the program.

The women also spoke about the lack of work opportunities in prison. They referred to the fact that women's prisons are much smaller than men's. Even though some men's prisons are just "over the fence", women are relatively deprived of "the opportunity to successfully rehabilitate themselves". One woman lamented the fact that there was a lack of cultural programmes, noting:

> Well the boys have the best NAIDOC [National Aboriginal and Islander Day of Commemoration] day every year. We ask for shirts, we don't get them, we asked

> for beads, we don't get them, we asked to make things for the Elders that do NAIDOC day, we get no reply. Most of the things that we request get knocked back. And like no one has organised anything for NAIDOC day this year, there's nothing. So we've got a week and we've got nothing, you know what I mean?

Violence of open-air prison—every day colonial life in the community

As stated at the outset, the oppression of the prison system does not start or end at the prison gate for Indigenous women. As Wilcox asserts, prison is characterised structurally as "a set of relationships rather than locally organized institutions or architectures" (in Axster et al. 2021, p. 422). Indeed, the carceral archipelago is premised on "mobility control"—"to deport, sedentarize and discipline the mobile poor" (Axster and Danewid, in Axster et al. 2021, p. 428). This is accentuated for Indigenous people on the colony whose restricted movement was a prerequisite for colonial expansion and takeover of their land. It also assured that the state could control their lives and exploit their labour. This section outlines some of the main themes in Indigenous women's stories of life in the open-air prison of colonial society.

Child protection and stolen children

The pains of child protection authority interventions was commonly raised among Indigenous women in prison yarning circles. As one woman said, "too many of our babies are taken" by child protection authorities. This creates opportunities, she suggested, for the state to physically and psychologically abuse their Indigenous children. The deprivation of the capacity to care for their children and fears in relation to their wellbeing amounted to a form of torture, according to Indigenous women. Outside of prisons, Indigenous women said that they dreaded that their children would never be returned to them. The experience of having children stolen by the state resonated with many of their own experiences of removal as a child. One woman said:

> So, I'm a foster kid and I was taken from my parents at four. I was taken under false allegations from DoCS [Department of Community Services]. DoCS changed my name, everything.

Another woman expressed that she spoke with the other women about how this has wide-reaching impacts on their families, cultures and the wellbeing of their communities:

> We talked [in prison] a lot about closing the gap. You know how they create the gap. By taking our children away from us, they're getting put into homes where they don't care about them. No one loves their kids more than their own family. they're getting, I hate to say it, but molested and shit like that, and they're running away, and they're getting on the drugs. So, that's where the problem starts.

> I'm awfully scared for my kids. I don't want this life for them, but it's sad to say it's fucking scary. I'm well-educated. I went right through school to Year 12. Five years ago, I was a childcare teacher. I lost my son, got on drugs, and went downhill and here I am in jail.

Carcerality and restrained mobility

In the community, Indigenous women had difficulty escaping constant surveillance. Hyperpolicing continued after they were released and they felt constantly under siege by the police who targeted them. One woman remarked that she had "really bad anxiety" and "kept running from the coppers all the time". Although she had not done anything wrong, she couldn't stop running because the sight of them meant her "anxiety builds up": "You've got a wall there and you just keep running from them until they grab you, that's just how it is out there".

Even in private spaces, Indigenous women described policing due to AVOs. While these orders that are meant to protect women, they were weaponised by police to control Indigenous women. As professor Birri-Guba and Yugambeh professor Nicole Watson (2011) contends, the state perceives vulnerable Indigenous women as necessary subjects of control, while being blind to their needs. A number of women in our yarning circles were imprisoned due to breaches of AVOs. These AVOs were imposed on both parties in domestic violence incidents. One woman said, '[The police officer] knocks at the door on any day of the week at any time because there's an AVO'.

Another feature of restricted mobility was the lack of access to reliable transportation. Simply getting home from prison presented transportation issues. In everyday life, women described the costs of private transportation and the lack of public transport, especially in regional towns, as prohibiting their access to basic services and supports. It restrained access to healthcare, including paediatricians for children, courts, lawyers, community corrections, social workers, psychologists, training and Country, according to Indigenous women in prison.

Indigenous women also referred to loss of licences, due to being unable to afford fines, as hindering their ability to travel. Some of the women ended up in prison due to driving without a licence and unregistered vehicles. One woman explained that she was imprisoned for driving whilst disqualified because, "I was unregistered, unlicensed, uninsured, they were fines that went over, that's how it started". She said she was a safe driver who did not speed or drive under the influence, but nonetheless the prosecution described as a "habitual offender, she's a menace on the road". She felt that she was tarnished by the system for being an Indigenous woman, which meant "they just put you back in, there's no chances".

One woman explained that her cries for a card to use public transport in NSW (Opal Card) went unheard and this aggravated her inability to cope outside of prison:

> I couldn't cope out there, like I said, I went to my parole officer can you breach me, I'm not coping. I put my hand up for help, they're not helping. They aren't

> putting me on a program, they are not giving the help that I need . . . I need an Opal Card, they won't even help me get an Opal card.

Poverty, starvation and "stealing"

Outside of prison, Indigenous women struggled to have their basic needs met—both for themselves and their children. Some resorted to stealing, which resulted in their imprisonment: "I was just desperate when I did my crime". Another said that "shoplifting turned into robbery" in order to afford basic goods and rent. Stealing to provide for children's needs was a theme in the responses. One woman "got sentenced 15 months for [stealing] three baby jumpers". Another committed credit card fraud to "buy food" because "I've got kids". A further woman said,

> I'm stealing the meat and I'm that hungry. . . . We're hungry. We're starving. That's why we're stealing it . . . I'm starving. I told the judge this. I never ate for about three months. . . . And I tell him I'm guilty and this and that, about where I'm from and what happened to me and look at me . . . I'm hungry.

Indigenous women attributed their deprivations to colonisation. They referred to the inter-generational impoverishment of their people from 245 years of living in a settler colony "without compensation" for stolen land. They made the point that police officers who "hate" Indigenous women stealing, should confront their own stealing of Indigenous children, land and sovereignty. One woman told the judge in her sentencing hearing that she'll stop stealing "when you stop stealing from me":

> I told the judge, 'look sir, you know what?' I'm not going to stop stealing until you stop stealing from me. You stole my babies, you know you stole my responsibility. I'll be back here next month, after I get out I'll be back here, you can't stop me like you tell me that I'm barred from that shop, that's what I'm going to go back and do. . . . Well he gave me two months this month.

Summing up the unmet needs of Indigenous women who are criminalised, one woman eloquently remarks that authorities fail to consider the socio-economic circumstances for which they are subject,

> I don't feel like we look at crime the way that we should. If people are offending, like crime is just a reflection of whatever is going on in the community, the problems that aren't being faced. There's obviously a need that's not being met. I mean, every single person just wants to be happy and wants to live their life, wants to have a family or be able to provide for that family too. To be able to live and be free and whatever. If someone has crime or stealing issues, it's because they don't have something, there's a need there.

For this woman, the system should consider what Indigenous women need. She expresses: "Does that person need employment? Are there other factors involved that need to be addressed?" Importantly, she says, the problem and solutions require listening to the Indigenous community about what they need:

> Obviously, there's a huge proportion of the community that's marginalised and that portion of the community needs to be supported. But . . . if you look back in history, every different government has tried to . . . at times makes these token efforts to try and repair the damage that's been done in the past. But then it becomes a matter of them trying to dictate how that community should help itself, but the community doesn't get any voice on how that fucking should happen.

Racism and patriarchal colonialism

In broader society, like in the legal and corrections system, Indigenous women felt racism inhibited their capacity to reintegrate and live free lives. Many described experiences of racism that began as a child and throughout their schooling. Since then, they were subject to racial stereotypes in shops, the employment market, health services and with authorities. One woman said that people often "just look at us like we're a joke". Another said that "people love to label us" and treat us like criminals; like we're "tarnished". They commented that stereotypes resulted in child protection authorities "stepping in" to manage their kids. A pervasive concern was the grief, loss and trauma from having their children stolen from them, including within hours of giving birth, due to perceptions that they cannot care for their own children.

Women commented that police target Indigenous people to "cleanse" the streets: "They're going to clean the town up by locking all the Aboriginal people up". One woman summed it up as follows: "a lot of people don't have faith in us". Women mentioned that the "racial issues today" echo how it was "back in the day", with nothing mitigating the severity of the adverse treatment towards them. Police treat them as unworthy of being in public, the same as it was on the colony. One woman spoke of this feeling of inescapable persecution, "I'm tired. I'm sitting down. I'm trying to sit down. I can't sit down in my own Country". Indicative of the unequal treatment, one woman spoke with sadness about how her Indigenous mother was mistreated in a liquor store:

> They pushed my mum out of that store. Refused to sell to mum. My mum went down, falling on the ground, splitting her leg open. Stitches and all. But they sold to me because I was white skinned. How racist is that?

In the private sphere, Indigenous women spoke about having AVOs imposed on them due to police perceiving them as aggressive. Others explained having their home searched, which resulted in drug charges, while the police were supposed to be investigating domestic violence. Both the police and child protection authorities regarded the women as a safety risk due to family violence concerns that they had raised. When Indigenous women sought to escape family violence, this could escalate ongoing criminal matters. One woman explained, "I took off from my boyfriend that was bashing me" and to "protect my children", but the police thought "I was running from the law". Ultimately, her children were taken by child protection, which contributed to her downward spiral, and she was imprisoned.

Indigenous women repeatedly reported being punished when they required support. They felt that they were the least likely to get access to community supports, rehabilitation services and "parole houses". As it was put in a yarning circle: "we don't get the chances that other people get". White men and women, and even Black men, were more likely to access appropriate services. They said that any services available were too often run by "white fellas" in a way that was not appropriate for their needs and cultural safety. One woman said: "We need more black fellas dealing with us. It's a trust thing".

Structural oppression also featured as a theme in the yarning circles. Indigenous women described their precarious economic circumstances, a lack of employment opportunities and low wages. They regarded their poverty as more entrenched because they are also carers, rendering their resources more scarce. While Indigenous women felt keenly responsible for children, grandchildren, nieces, nephews, younger siblings and Elders, and were crucial as cultural teachers, their experiences of patriarchal racism in the community produced constant frustrations. One woman stated the acute impact of "patriarchal white sovereignty" (Moreton-Robinson 2015) on Indigenous women:

> especially with Aboriginal women, like I really think they're treated different to anyone else in the system because of people's opinions of mission life, of the way we live. . . . Things you can't change. Like I've got five children. Not having the tools in place to get back to where you want to be. You kind of lose hope.

Emancipatory futures

The focus of the state and professionals is on reform (with the 'master's tools')[1] to improve prison and community conditions. However, Indigenous women, as they expressed in prison yarning circles, were not waiting for the colonial-carceral 'master' to provide salvation. Their existence and resistance mitigated against 'social death' and reinforced their identities and empowerment. The women drew on their collective and inner strength to refuse coloniality and assert themselves as sovereign Indigenous women. They did this in prison by having a shared language for injustice; developing cultural connections to one another; and using humour to mock injustice, to promote inter-personal relations and to feel happy and free. As one woman said, "I always say it as it is. I'm not going to sugar coat nothing". She went on to explain the pride within herself that gave her this confidence to be herself: "I'm comfortable within my own skin".

In the absence of counsellors or support workers for Indigenous women in prison, they relied on one another to cope with hardships, especially worries about children and the difficulties of confinement. One woman pointed out that in prison it was really hard to get help for physical and mental pain, but she persisted to ask for help because of the other women and her strong sense of identity:

> People look at me because I've got all these scars on me, and I know I'm different, but I know where I stand. Right here. Right on my two feet. Right now. That's why I'm standing here with you. You know what I mean? Sitting here, telling you my story.

Indigenous women in prison formed care relationships and adopted cultural roles of Elder, grandmother, Aunt and big sister. This enabled them to care for one another, and to be cared for. They made plans to create a brighter future where their self-determination would be realised. One woman recalled,

> We talked a lot about Closing the Gap. You know how they create the gap? By taking our children away from us. You and me. Putting us behind this, they don't care about them. No one wants their kids more than their own family.

This woman went onto stress the importance of keeping children with family as a means to strengthen Indigenous families and cultures. The women inside saw their role as storytellers with lived experience who can "help young ones" stay on the right path. Another woman remarked on the need for "blackfulla" support groups that help with housing and services on the outside. She notes, "We talk about this a lot . . . we don't just sit around, we talk about what needs to be done and what we are going to do on the outside". This mutual support and collective sense of purpose kept the woman socially, emotionally and culturally "alive" and connected. They were able to better cope and remain proud and confident as sovereign Indigenous women.

Conclusion

The displacement of carceralism penetrates prison gates and can be characterised as a colonial carceral archipelago. It pivots on "patriarchal white sovereignty" (Moreton-Robinson 2015) resulting in incarcerated Indigenous women confronting a panoply of oppressive structures in the community. They are subject to a continuum of interventions that have distinct burdens due to their responsibilities to community, family and, importantly, children. Beyond the prison, the colony writ large is a process of displacement—from Country, sovereign laws, cultural practices and freedom. The ongoing colonial project to assure "state access to the land and resources" involves a process of "structured dispossession", according Yellowknives Dene scholar Glen Coulthard (2014, pp. 6–7). Penal imprisonment is merely one facet and phase of this enduring process. Indigenous women's burdens are compounded in this system where colonial patriarchal norms render infrastructure, services and programmes ill-equipped to respond to their needs in prison and out in the community.

In defiance of colonial norms and practices, Indigenous women assert their identity to resist the impact of carcerality. The collectivist approach of Indigenous women in prison contrasts the individualist, alienating model imposed by the colonial carceral system. The 'refusal' to be colonial (Simpson 2014) serves as a counterpoint to the relentless attempts of the colonial project to universalise its control. Refusal and resistance extend struggles for land and sovereignty that are antidotes to the colonial carceral archipelago (Walter 2016, pp. 89–90). Tracey McIntosh, a Ngā i Tū hoe, Professor of Indigenous Studies, states that anti-colonial prison abolition is an "emancipatory project" that involves "anti-colonial" spaces that reconsider human relations and responsibilities in all aspects of society (In Pranteau et al. 2022, p. 79). In our yarning circles with Indigenous women, it was identified how this is practiced in prison through a spirit of care and togetherness:

> You know we've only got each other when you leave. . . . We help each other in here, if we didn't have that communication in here I reckon half of us in here wouldn't be normal. They'd have a lot of trouble in jail. And it's good when you've got a good role model in here too, you've got a good mentor in here, girls to look up.

Note

1 Audre Lorde (2018) famously stated, "the master's tools will never dismantle the master's house".

References

Anthony, T. & Blagg, H. (2025). Abolition and the Colonial Carceral Archipelago. *Abolitionist Voices*.

Anthony, T., Sentance, G. & Behrendt, L. (2021). "We're Not Being Treated Like Mothers": Listening to the Stories of First Nations Mothers in Prison. *Laws*, 10(74) 1–18. https://doi.org/10.3390/laws10030074

Atkinson, J. (2002). *Trauma Trails, Recreating Song Lines: The Transgenerational Effects of Trauma in Indigenous Australia*. Spinifex Press.

Australian Bureau of Statistics. (2025). Prisoners in Australia. *Crime and Justice Releases*. 11 December. https://www.abs.gov.au/statistics/people/crime-and-justice/prisoners-australia/latest-release#aboriginal-and-torres-strait-islander-prisoners

Australian Human Rights Commission. (2024). *Statistics about Aboriginal and Torres Strait Islander Women and Girls*. 9 October. https://humanrights.gov.au/education/stats-facts/statistics-about-aboriginal-and-torres-strait-islander-women-and-girl

Axster, S., Danewid, I., Goldstein, A., Mahmoudi, M., Burak Tansel, C. & Wilcox, L. (2021). Colonial Lives of the Carceral Archipelago: Rethinking the Neoliberal Security State. *International Political Sociology*, 15(3) 415–439. https://doi.org/10.1093/ips/olab013

Bessarab, D. & Ng'andu, B. (2010). Yarning About Yarning as a Legitimate Method in Indigenous Research. *International Journal of Critical Indigenous Studies*, 3 37–50.

Bhandar, B. (2018). *Colonial Lives of Property: Law, Land, and Racial Regimes of Ownership*. Duke University Press.

BOCSAR. [Bureau of Crime Statistics and Research]. (2022). *NSW Custody Statistics: Quarterly Update, March 2022*. https://bocsar.nsw.gov.au/documents/publications/custody/nsw-custody-statistics-mar2022.pdf

BOCSAR [Bureau of Crime Statistics and Research]. (2024). *NSW Custody Statistics: Quarterly Update, September 2024*. https://bocsar.nsw.gov.au/documents/publications/custody/2024_09_NSW_Custody_Statistics_Sep_2024.pdf

BOCSAR [Bureau of Crime Statistics and Research]. (2025). *NSW Custody Statistics: Quarterly Update, September 2025*. 12 November. https://bocsar.nsw.gov.au/statistics-dashboards/custody.html

Coulthard, G. (2014). *Red Skin, White Masks: Rejecting the Colonial Politics of Recognition*. University of Minnesota Press.

Davis, A. & Dent, G. (2001). Prison as a Border: A Conversation on Gender, Globalization, and Punishment. *Signs: Journal of Women in Culture and Society*, 26(4) 1235–1241. https://doi.org/10.1086/495654

Fanon, F. (1986). *Black Skin, White Masks*. Pluto Press.

Foucault, M. (1991). *Discipline and Punish: The birth of the prison*. Trans. Alan Sheridan. Penguin Books.

Havemann, P. (2005). Denial, Modernity and Exclusion: Indigenous Placelessness in Australia. *Macquarie Law Journal*, 5, 57–80.

Lean, T. (2021). The Disposable Humans. *Infrastructural Inequalities*, 2. https://infrastructuralinequalities.net/issue-2/the-disposable-humans/

Lorde, A. (2018). *The Master's Tools Will Never Dismantle the Master's House*. Penguin Classics.

MacGillivray, P. & Baldry, E. (2015). Australian Indigenous Women's Offending Patterns. *Indigenous Justice Clearinghouse*, Brief 19, 1–12.

Mignolo, W. (2007). Introduction: Coloniality of Power and De-Colonial Thinking. *Cultural Studies*, 21(2–3) 155–167. https://doi.org/10.1080/09502380601162498

Moreton-Robinson, A. (2015). *White Possessive*. University of Minnesota Press.

Moreton-Robinson, A. (2020). *Talkin' Up To the White Woman: Indigenous Women and Feminism*, 20th Anniversary ed. University of Queensland Press.

Pranteau, S., McIntosh, T., Anthony, T. & Chartrand, V. (2022). Anti-Colonial Abolition: International Context. *Journal of Prisoners on Prisons*, 30, 26–27.

Price, J. M. (2015). *Prison and Social Death*. Rutgers University Press.

Quijano, A. (2007). Coloniality and Modernity/Rationality. *Cultural Studies*, 21(2–3) 168–178. https://doi.org/10.1080/09502380601164353

Sherwood, J., Lighton, S., Dundas, K., French, T., Link-Gordon, D., Smith, K. & Anthony, T. (2015). Who Are the Experts Here? Recognition of Aboriginal Women and Community Workers in Research and Beyond. *AlterNative*, 11(2) 177–190. https://doi.org/10.1177/117718011501100207

Simpson, A. (2014). *Mohawk Interruptus: Political Life across the Borders of Settler States*. Duke University Press.

Stoler, A. L. (2016). *Duress: Imperial Durabilities in Our Times*. Duke University Press.

Walter, M. (2016). Indigenous Peoples, Research and Ethics. In M. Adorjan and R. Ricciardelli (eds) *Engaging with Ethics in International Criminological Research*. Routledge, 87–105.

Watego, C. (2021). *Another Day in the Colony*. University of Queensland Press.

Watson, N. (2011). The Northern Territory Emergency Response—Has It Really Improved the Lives of Aboriginal Women and Children? *Australian Feminist Law Journal*, 35(1) 147–163. https://doi.org/10.1080/13200968.2011.10854464

4

CHALLENGING TRANSITIONAL JUSTICE IN COLOMBIA

Legal pluralism and Indigenous peoples

Bryan Vargas Reyes

> Law had to be "taken seriously" or one had to be sturdily "realistic" about its necessity.
>
> (Fitzpatrick 1992)

Introduction

With the promulgation of the Political Constitution of 1991, the social and legal mobilisations of the Indigenous peoples in favour of the materialisation of the Special Indigenous Jurisdiction (Jurisdicción Especial Indígenas, or JEI) have not ceased in Colombia. On the contrary, they have been strengthened by seeing how it has been ignored by officials of the judicial branch, as it seems that in the opinion of the multitude the indigenous people belong to another time (pre-modern), being the "archetypal others of the nation" (Gnecco 2023, p. 11), which would have a culture trapped in the past, and therefore it is their duty to adjust to the approaches of modern society and, with it, of modern law.

The infinite arrogance of a so-called majority and modern society has associated the indigenous with the mythological, the static and closed in the social order, while it has perceived itself as fruitfully open to the idea of progress and in opposition to all that is considered as the "other" or "others", those savages and ancestors that "we" (the moderns) have left behind. Despite this, as Fitzpatrick (1998) rightly puts it, by opposing modernity to myth, myth ends up being present in modernity to the extent that the mythology of modern identity is based on an opposition to myth-dominated "others", and, under this mythology of modernity, modern law is expressed as a "white" mythological form.

In this way, it develops against certain "others" that concentrate qualities to which the law is opposed (Fitzpatrick 1998, p. 11). This mythology of law has

DOI: 10.4324/9781003752974-6

served to validate and substantiate, in addition to its autonomous character, its capacity to be self-referential in its process of interpretation and reproduction, thus developing a struggle for the monopoly of the right to say the law, that is, to establish the correct way to interpret the law and say what it is supposed to be.

Following Bourdieu (2000a, p. 198), law, being seen as the means by which the order established within a State is consecrated, represents the form par excellence of discourse capable of producing effects under the form of "symbolic power of nomination that creates named things and, in particular, social groups". This results in the confrontation of conceptions in the legal field on how to interpret the law and on what should be the principles that govern it as a whole, opening the dispute over the authorised sources to *say* the law.

If the law carries a strong symbolic component, at the same time that it seeks to differentiate itself from everything considered "traditional/old", given its modern character, this is where we see materialised the opposition between the modern and the traditional when facing internal disputes over its capacity for interpretation.

In other words, for the sources of modern law, everything that does not correspond to this framework of interpretation is seen as "profane" (Ariza 2010), and this is where indigenous thought and the challenges it imposes on transitional justice in Colombia would come in. How do you say that spirits, ancestors, and natural phenomena such as thunder can and should be considered sources of law? How can legal decisions be based on new sources of law that the "majority society" does not possess?

That said, the objective of this chapter is to question the notions of legal pluralism and ethnic approach applied by the Special Jurisdiction for Peace (JEP). I will recover the observations made by the ancestral authorities of Northern Cauca in the framework of Macro Case 05, which proposed that the intercultural dialogue propitiated by the application of the ethnic approach take into account "the principles and rationalities of the Ethnic Peoples", or in other words, that the *derecho propio*[1] of the indigenous communities be considered as a valid source of law at the time of the legal qualification of the conducts within the Macro Case.

The relevance of analysing this Colombian case lies in exploring the possibilities that community knowledge and collective practice have to overcome the systemic failures of a country that has experienced more than 50 years of internal armed conflict, which has deepened exclusion, racism, and inequality, especially against ethnic groups.

Through their own knowledge, Indigenous peoples, especially in northern Cauca, are fighting against racism and institutional exclusion, demonstrating an attempt at bottom-up transformation on their own terms.

In order to fulfil the purpose of this chapter, first, I will proceed to explain the mythical character of law and its link with a certain idea of modernity. Second, I will show how the ability *to say* the law is further measured by the continuum of violence that Indigenous people have suffered as a result of colonialism. Last but not least, in the last part, I will show how, from the dispute *to say and interpret* the law, Indigenous peoples challenge the JEP to combat the remnants of a colonial past and try to materialise an ethnic approach in accordance with their desires and aspirations.

Law as a myth in modernity

Modernity, as a political project of universalisation, is inseparable from European concepts like citizenship and the nation-state, which attempt to project a secular vision of the human that colonisers often denied in practice (Chakrabarty 2000, pp. 4–5). Since the Enlightenment, the pursuit of progress through science and the imposition of universalist assumptions—such as Law and the State—have ignored the inherent inequalities of imperialism and geopolitics (Santos 1995).

The idea of universalism applied to law has attempted to build a place for the rule of law, either in its social attributes or through the separation and distance of these attributes from what law is or should be. Despite the attempt to invoke a certain social characteristic, the excessive search for distinction led to contradiction and the creation of a myth. This contradiction could be summarised in that law transcends society, goes beyond it, even though it is part of it (Fitzpatrick 1998, pp. 1–13). Law is the main instrument of regulation "from above", invested with a function as sacred as that of being the instrument of power and can even be confused with the function of being in turn the designer of power.

Thus, law and power are paradoxically related, while law affirms itself as neutral in relation to politics given its technical character, at the same time that it voluntarily or not conceals the representation of law as the expression of politics, understanding that the legal form can become the structure of the discourse through which power is expressed, thus becoming a common reference where the supreme political power becomes the only source of law, instituting a rigorous legal monism (Commaille 2023, pp. 45–48).

Like a deity, law creates its own world, has its own priests/custodians and interpreters of its will, has its own rituals, and the legal reality it creates results from the magical effect of invoking formulas, within the law, to which society as a whole adheres. Given these characteristics, law is perceived as autonomous, capable of standing on its own and not depending on any external reality or temporal order (Fitzpatrick 1998, pp. 57–59).

To the above-mentioned mythical contradiction of law is added, then, the contradiction between the universal approaches of law and colonial domination on which radical differentiations were made between the colonies and the metropolis.

As Santos (2023, p. 127) puts it, European colonial expansion brought with it a division between metropolitan societies and colonies, where metropolitan societies became the only terrain on which the assumptions of modernity, its fundamental rules, universal principles, and humanist ideals were to be applied. In the colonies, on the other hand, radically different logics operated, where it was not possible to apply these same principles because those who existed there had not yet reached any status of civilisation.

This division and differentiation between these two realities, expressed by Santos (2007) as an abyssal line, led to modern law being imposed by the colonisers in the colonies to ensure that the colonial enterprise developed in the best viable way. What at first operated as ignorance and incommensurability of local realities in the colonies, since there were only savages there, would later become a strategic recognition of local native or indigenous laws, only to the extent that they could serve the purpose of ensuring and expanding the proper functioning of domination (Santos 2023, p. 128).

Legal pluralism: who says and interprets the law?

The coexistence of a variety of legal norms and institutions in society calls into question two central elements of the idea of the State: first, that national legislation is supreme and has a monopoly on it within a given territory; second, that national legislation is a unified whole organised hierarchically.

Given the impossibility on the part of the state to eliminate all collectively recognised forms of law as well as internal divergences, contemporary legal systems are then characterised by being constituted through multiple institutions scattered throughout society in ways that are not closely linked to each other within monopolistic and unified hierarchies that emulate a sort of "supreme law", the source and fuel for the existence of pluralism being: the social, cultural, economic and political heterogeneity that exists in each society (Tamanaha 2021, p. 209).

Although it is not the main objective of this chapter to delve into and detail the different advances and changes within the theoretical approaches to legal pluralism, especially in the rich Latin American context, I can affirm that not only do they adopt a sufficiently broad concept of law in which everything (or almost everything) fits, but a priori, it would seem that their main concern is the effectiveness and validity of the other types of law vis-à-vis the State.

This causes the forms of cooperation or relationship of the different legal systems within the same territory to be neglected and also ignore the possibilities of syncretism that could be generated between them, even when they defend this possibility.

In the search to leave aside a rigid concept of law close to positivist traditions, legal pluralism (even that which proposes non-hierarchical relations between the different legal systems) does not delve into how the different systems could resolve their differences and mix their positions on the different sources of law for the resolution of conflicts that interest society as a whole as.

In this way, those who proclaim the existence of multiple forms of law or legal systems focus more on legal provisions than on the social order which is the set of basic social institutions (such as the family or property, for instance) that are not fixed or immutable and are constantly changing. These changes are rarely recognisable or perceptible on a day-to-day basis, but they allow us to see the impact of society on them, thus bringing us closer to the functioning of law in society (Ehrlich 1922).

Focusing the analysis on social order not only poses the challenge of understanding law as something alive and in constant movement, which permeates society and is at the same time permeated by it, but also proposes a starting point no longer centred on the existence or validity of the constellation of legal norms within the same territory. This starting point allows us to go beyond both the idea of absolute autonomy of legal thought and action, and the subjection of these as a direct reflection of existing power relations.

On the contrary, these ideas prevent us from perceiving the existence of a relatively independent social universe where legal authority is produced and exercised through symbolic representations such as language, concepts, categorical divisions.

This social universe, which could perfectly be what Ehrlich calls "social order", is defined by Bourdieu (1989) as a "social field", that is, a space of social activity determined by structured and regulated activities, as well as by the agents that participate within it.

Bourdieu (2000a, p. 159) argues that internal logic and specific power relations doubly determine the legal field, where agents compete to transform the field according to their own interests. This competition involves a division of legal labour where professionals dispute different forms of competence to impose their vision of law, eventually uniting to legitimise their acts and obscure symbolic domination (Bourdieu 2000a, p. 180).

Consequently, a boundary emerges between authorised experts and non-experts, whose common sense is marginalised by a "wise vision" that restricts conflict resolution to legally regulated debates among professionals (Bourdieu 2000a, p. 185).

It is because of this distinction that the perspectives on "what is law" are encapsulated in discussions dominated by specialised technicians who seek to defend the status quo of their prerogatives as authorised interpreters, being one of the reasons why the problems associated with legal pluralism in what refers to the coexistence between multiple legal systems end up subordinating all legal systems to official national legislation, and, even in cases where an egalitarian legal pluralism is promoted, it has not been possible to think of the syncretic possibility of breaking with certain ways of thinking and interpreting law.

The colonial time

The weight of historical colonialism generated cultural, economic, and political practices and relationships that sought to dehumanise and naturalise the exclusion of Indigenous peoples (and not only these) in the search for a Eurocentric cultural identity project (Quijano 1991).

Colonialism, seen as a system of denial of human dignity, was established as a paradigm through which the world is represented from a certain perspective, of a rational Eurocentric type, which attempts to domesticate the diversity of the world based on its scientific, social, cultural, and political self-referentials (Meneses 2018).

With the independence of Colombia from Spain, a new push for the development of the individualist economy arose, which caused society to completely distance itself from the Indigenous people, who remained faithful to the collectivist economy of the resguardos.[2]

Following the ideals of the French Revolution, the independence movement declared the Indigenous people as free citizens (at least in theory), granting them individual freedom that led to the destruction of the resguardos, since this collective way of life limited said freedom (Friede 2017, p. 175).

All the dominant classes of the republic throughout the nineteenth century then agree in delimiting the Indigenous problem as a question exclusive to the other social groups of the republic, making the will of the Indigenous people irrelevant.

For the Colombian State, the objective was the legal and peaceful destruction of indigenous "resguardos" and the liberation of a mass of indigenous workers for the sake of the progress of the nation in order to form a rural proletariat for the benefit of those who want to accumulate land, those who have it and need labour, and those who build factories and require workers (Friede 2017, p. 184).

Indigenous as a victims

After years of armed conflict in Colombia and the recognition of its impact on society as a whole, Act 1448 of 2011, known as the "Law of Victims and Land Restitution" was enacted. It established several measures for the reparation, assistance, and comprehensive care of victims of the conflict within the framework of transitional justice, so that their status as victims is recognised and they are dignified through the realisation of their rights.

This Act defines transitional justice as the processes and measures, both judicial and extrajudicial, that society uses to ensure that those responsible for violations of International Humanitarian Law or serious violations of Human Rights committed during the internal armed conflict are held accountable for their actions, thus guaranteeing the rights of the victims.

For Indigenous victims, the Act provides for a special application starting with Decree 4633 of 2011, which recognises Indigenous people as permanent victims of serious violations of their ancestral, human, and fundamental rights. In turn, it proposes that the worldview of the peoples, that is, the "derecho propio", become the frame of reference for public policy of comprehensive care, protection, comprehensive reparation, and restitution of rights for peoples and communities.

Afterwards the signing of the Peace Agreement in 2016, the panorama of transitional justice expands with the creation of the JEP. This Court being in charge of investigating, judging, and punishing the most serious crimes committed during the armed conflict, including violations of human rights and International

Humanitarian Law, thus guaranteeing justice, truth, reparation for victims, and promoting the non-repetition of said crimes.

In order to conduct the investigation, prosecution and punishment, the JEP chose to group multiple facts related to crimes committed during the armed conflict in order to address them in a comprehensive manner. In this way, macro cases arise, which allow the JEP to analyse patterns of conduct, contexts, and command structures to proceed with the prosecution of those most responsible.

Among the macro cases that have been opened so far, my focus of analysis will be number 05, which addresses violations of human rights and international humanitarian law that occurred in the region of Northern Cauca and Southern Valle del Cauca and, specifically, auto 01 of 2023 of the Chamber for the Recognition of Truth, Responsibility and Determination of Facts and Conduct (hereinafter, the Recognition Chamber or the Chamber).

To prioritise this region, it was considered that it was strongly affected by the armed conflict, with a significant presence of illegal armed groups, including the Revolutionary Armed Forces of Colombia—People's Army (FARC-EP) and various paramilitary groups. Officially opened in November 2018, it seeks to investigate crimes committed from 1 January 1993, to 1 December 2016, in the region.

When proceeding to establish the facts and conduct of Macro Case 05 attributable to the first group of defendants from the Mobile Columns (CM) Jacobo Arenas and Gabriel Galvis of the extinct FARC-EP, the Recognition Chamber proceeded to carry out intercultural dialogues with the ancestral authorities and representatives of the indigenous organisations in which the way in which the high court would work together with the indigenous ancestral authorities to clarify the events allegedly committed in the area was agreed upon (JEP Auto 01 of 2023, pp. 32–33).

After describing the determined facts and conduct, the Chamber established a relationship of the scale or magnitude of the facts that allows the classification of the patterns of conduct in the analysed territory in order to conduct the proper legal qualification.

At this point, the Court proposes to use in a harmonious manner Colombian Criminal Law, International Criminal Law (DPI), International Humanitarian Law (IHL), and International Human Rights Law (IHRL), in accordance with Act 01 of 2017 and Act 1957 of 2019 (JEP auto 01 of 2023, p. 255).

Furthermore, the Chamber relies on what was stated by the Constitutional Court in judgment C-080 of 2018 when analysing the constitutionality of Act 01 of 2017. For the Court, the JEP must base the legal qualification of the conduct on a norm existing before its commission, assessing whether such prohibition existed and ensuring that the conduct is clearly prohibited before the event occurred, whether in the Constitution, in the current Penal Code, in international human rights norms, in international norms of international humanitarian law, or in mandatory norms of ius cogens (Constitutional Court C-080 of 2018).

Unlike the other conduct, when the Court enters into the legal qualification of the damage to the territory, it states that it will apply in a complementary manner the ethnic, racial, territorial and environmental approaches, in order to integrate the anthropocentric and eco-centric perspectives of environmental protection (JEP Auto 01 of 2023, p. 424).

It is curious that only at this point is the ethnic approach used, since in the entire Auto the only close mention of it is given when analysing the illicit crops in the prior Indigenous where the Court recognises that serious spiritual effects have been caused to the communities and territories, given the important role of a sacred plant such as coca and its ancestral relationship with the indigenous peoples of the department (JEP, Auto 01 of 2023, p. 61).

The inclusion of the ethnic approach when dealing with environmental damage is striking. Do communities also not have concerns about other crimes and damages committed? If the Court's actions when implementing transitional justice trigger legal pluralism by recognising supranational norms as valid, applicable, and part of its sources of law, why does it only recognise the opinion of the communities on the environmental issue?

The dispute over saying and interpreting the law in transitional justice

In order to answer these questions, the ancestral authorities of the Indigenous communities of Çxhab Wala Kiwe, Sa't Tama Kiwe, Nasa Üus, Uh Wala Viç, Nasawe'sx Dxi'j and ORIVAC, on 24 November 2023, issued their observations regarding Order 01. Given their recognition as justice ancestral authorities in the aforementioned intercultural dialogues conducted by the JEP, the ancestral authorities make a statement of reasons why they consider that the JEP does not yet comply with the ethnic parameters recognised both in its protocols and in the regulations applicable to the exercise of jurisdiction.

For the ancestral authorities, coordination between jurisdictions should not be limited to procedures and notifications. For them, an interpretation of their own regulations would make the JEP, in its legal qualifications within Case 05, consider the "derecho propio" of Indigenous communities as a valid source of law (Autoridades ancestrales 2023, p. 5). The first observation proposed by the ancestral authorities calls to consider the principles, logic, and rationales of the "derecho propio" in such a way that it serves as a complementary way to the sources of law necessary to determine the rights violated and the most serious facts and conduct.

Given the relationship with nature and with all the beings that compose it of the Indigenous peoples, the effects of the armed conflict and the actions of its actors affected in ways that are not always intelligible for ordinary law. Therefore, the ancestral authorities proceed to explain to the JEP the way in which their way of seeing the world is constituted and what they understand by law.

Thus, through the order that Uma and Tay (Neeh, deities) make up, Uma Kiwe (Mother Earth) emerges, and it is from her that after the union with Sek (sun) Yu' (Water) emerges. Sek would be in charge of creating, together with A'te (moon), the condor, the eagle, the hawk, and the vulture. From the union of Yu' and A' (star) the Nasa would be born (Nasa Üus Yu'tx Pehnxi Fallo 007, p. 3).

It is thanks to this order that the territory is organised and the essential basis of the justice system is constituted, there personal, family, and community care is mandated through rituals, and is guided by the paths of the sun and the moon (their own calendar), constituting the obligations and responsibilities that, as Nasas, they must maintain in order to live in harmony and balance (Autoridades ancestrales 2023, p. 7).

In this way, the Nasa conceive their "derecho propio" as the experience of spiritual mandates and the norms of conduct and principles that are inscribed in the territory. This right arises from the practice of the ancestral authorities to prevent disharmonies, protect the territory and harmonise or solve the difficulties that arise in the person, the family, the community and with mother earth. It is for this reason, from the perspective of the Nasa, that the Court must recognise the importance of the Law of Origin and the "derecho propio" in jurisdictional exercises and in its considerations regarding the facts that affected their territories and communities.

With the name "derecho propio" the Indigenous communities emphasise that this law belongs to them and is based on their own cultural conceptions, different from those of national legislation. It is a deliberate effort to affirm cultural differences and exercise justice in their own way (different from that of the State), with the purpose of achieving political autonomy and exercising it internally (without interference from the State).

Through oral proceedings and indigenous justice, the facts are recounted, explained, argued, exposed, and debated, in order to preserve the sense of society and belonging. In this way, a feeling of participation in common life is generated, which is the fundamental principle of indigenous justice. Thus, it is observed that the most important thing is not the defence of the norm or the sanction of the transgression, but the objective of staying united (Gómez 2015, pp. 116–117).

This relational form of justice finds serious gaps when observing and analysing what the Court has said, since it does not consider a fundamental factor such as the ancestral relationship with mother earth. For the Nasa, one is part of mother earth, living in it from the beginning, there being a continuity between it and the community, thus giving the form, order and structure of the body as a reflection of what is found in the world (Nasa Üus Yu'tx Pehnxi, Ruling 007 of 2021).

Thanks to this continuity, the ancestral authorities argue that the Court fails to observe the territory as a complex whole where disharmonies occurred due to the armed conflict, exceeding the limits of physical space and the environment, with the body of the Indigenous victims being inseparable from the territory they inhabit and call Uma Kiwe (mother earth).

The existence of disharmony is an attack against balance and complementarity, so necessary for life and for the well-being of the community. The constant interactions and care of the relationship between the body, the territory and the material and spiritual worlds is what allows for peaceful existence and the full development of both individual and collective capacities (Autoridades ancestrales 2023, pp. 9–12).

In this way, based on their own legal system, the Nasa ask the Court to expand the legal qualification of conduct from the ethnic, gender and life cycle perspectives, including the effects on mother earth (and the breaking of the link with it), the destruction of sacred sites, and the effects on indigenous women and life cycles (Autoridades ancestrales 2023, pp. 18–30).

Additionally, the traditional ancestral authorities expand the Court's legal assessments on forced recruitment and on the persecution of Indigenous ancestral authorities based on the use of their own law as a tool of understanding to measure the impact of such conduct not only individually considered but also on the entire community.

Forced recruitment is seen not only as contrary to international and national regulations but goes beyond that, as it impacts the *kwekwe nees fxidx fxi'z* (life cycles).

Likewise, the ancestral authorities dismiss the Court's thesis on the social control of armed groups, stating that the main objective consisted of community division and fragmentation, and demonstrating how the damage caused against the ancestral authorities (*kiwe thë'j* or *thë'j Wala*)[3] implied a rupture of what was their own, disconnecting the material world from the spiritual world.

The criticism and legal dispute conducted by the ancestral authorities additionally incorporates an effort to demonstrate to the Court the existence of a new legal qualification: ethnocide. In the words of the ancestral authorities, ethnocide is understood as *Pxhu'çxa pe'banxi wee*, or "cruelly ending", which incorporates the damage caused by territorial disharmonies and which generates the cultural and physical extermination of the Nasa people (Autoridades ancestrales 2023, pp. 43–45).

Thus, these "non-experts" (the Indigenous) of the legal field rely on other social fields (such as the political one, through their long history of resistance) to dispute, using a certain type of legal technique, the power relations within the field.

It is through translation that the appropriation of constitutional and legal precepts from an Indigenous perspective arises. According to Rappaport (2003, p. 114), this translation strategy offers an indispensable tool for Nasa activists to appropriate concepts from the dominant society, reconfigure them within indigenous categories and use them in their political disputes.

Returning to Bourdieu (2000a, p. 216), I can say that the hierarchy in the division of legal work is reflected through the ranking of specialties, where, for example, the DPI or the IHL have pre-eminence in transitional justice. This hierarchy is mainly affected by the variations in power relations within the social field. This means that the possibility of an opening to other sources of law outside the dominant specialties is mediated by the place occupied in the political field by the social groups interested in this happening.

Thus, under the interpretation of the JEP, specifically of the Chamber, the sources of law applicable to judge and deal with crimes against humanity are found in supranational regulations, such as the DPI, the IHL and the IHL, under which in turn the internal regulations are oriented. This authorised interpretation of sources is also supported by the Constitutional Court and the laws passed on the functioning and procedures of the transitional court.

Despite the internal existence of guidelines for applying the ethnic approach, as well as its constant mention by the laws that give rise to and put into operation the JEP, through codified legal work (laws, rulings) that reserves exclusively for "professionals" the role of holding the legal competence to decide the applicable norms and sources of law, thus leaving to the "others", the "non-experts", the fate of suffering the force of the form, that is, the exercise of symbolic violence.

The "force of the form" sacralises what is written on the word, granting the law its specific force, its identity, and its structuring power through the relationship between law and language. This force is magnified through the construction of legal doctrine, following the search for higher legitimation.

Lawyers (law professors at universities and high court judges) try to build a body of interpretive knowledge through almost scientific reasoning, trying to show a doctrine at the service of the general interest and free and erudite research (Commaille 2023, pp. 54–56).

When observing the requests of the traditional authorities of the Nasa people, some plausibility stands out in them, since it would not be the first time that a transitional judge would be using or mentioning their cosmovision to decide a case.

As an example, the first sentences of restitution of ethnic lands under the protection of Act 1448 and Decree 4633 of 2011 were allowed to use and invoke these categories to base their decisions, so the worldview of Indigenous peoples was part of the sources of law used to decide such matters.

However, they are limited because what they request there makes necessary the existence of a legal pluralism different from that currently known in the Colombian legal system. In addition, the point of view of the authorities, and of the law itself, is a challenge, since it is not the action but its consequence that prevails in the Nasa worldview, this being the antithesis of the official legal system where it is the actions that are judged.

Is another law possible?

In order to materialise an ethnic approach and legal pluralism in accordance with the desires and aspirations of Indigenous peoples, a horizontal way of seeing and thinking about the world is necessary, rejecting the unilateral nature of the modes of social and political regulation.

The hierarchy imposed by the Law today is inapplicable in a globalised world, thus, the social representation of the status of the law under a vertical idea from which the mandates to regulate society emanate from the top down no longer finds a place thanks to the relativisation of the functions of the State.

Law has ceased to be the embodiment of reason and an order of coercion since powers separated from political power have undertaken to forge new legal institutions much more suitable for its development (Commaille 2023, pp. 227–228).

What the political resistance of Indigenous peoples in Colombia shows us is that their dynamic within the legal field has focused on how legal regulations can be used as a means to resist and challenge established power structures. In the strategic use of the contradictions inherent in the law to generate change, the "non-experts" instead of rejecting the legal system as an instrument of oppressive power, have sought to use it creatively to subvert that same power, in a delicate balance between subversion and legitimacy.

Without denying the existence of mechanisms of domination within contemporary societies, attention must also be paid to how these are analysed. Just as resistance is not full of triumphs, much less does it have the support of a large majority, domination is not absolute and there are multiple ways in which the exercise of power does not necessarily involve the exercise of symbolic violence.

It is necessary to avoid both those materialist accounts that see only power relations in the explanation of law, as well as those idealist approaches that explain it through the general recognition of the universal values that its norms conduct (García 2003).

The institutional interpretation of the Court thus reproduces the mythical character of law, separating it from society, in this case from the victims, and imposing a vision of the world that, even when it seeks to consider the ethnic approach, fails to do so given the sources on which it is based to decide what is law and how to apply it. Regardless of the use it makes of legal pluralism, it fails to recognise in Indigenous thought an applicable source from which the authority to say the law emanates.

The Court's interpretive strategy sought to consider the highest standards in terms of protection and recognition of rights, without considering that its work continued with the official logic of the entire Colombian legal system, that is, under a single possible legal science or dogma.

Through the process of interjurisdictional coordination and intercultural dialogue, the Court considers that the recognition of ethnic justice has been fulfilled, even though the documentation of the facts and the legal qualification of the determined conduct do not seem to adequately respond to the cosmology of the ethnic peoples present in the prioritised municipalities.

If we really want to think about the transformation in the way of understanding and thinking about law today, we must question the traditional legal regulations that have been centred on the State as the exclusive source of law, even in a legal system such as the Colombian one that recognises legal pluralism. This kind of relativisation in relation to the State would open space for the possibility of looking for sources of law outside the state framework without resorting to the formal sources of positive law.

As Commaille (2023, p. 236) states, thinking about law only from this perspective leads to disconnecting from its social character (understood as the dynamics and forces that emerge from societies), which has become increasingly constitutive of law, even when it is external to it.

Conclusion

Through this text I have tried to demonstrate how non-experts, in the context of their collective mobilisations, consecrate law (and justice) as an instrument in the repertoire of their collective action, using these resources as support for the defence of the materialisation of the ethnic approach within the framework of transitional justice with the aim of achieving real change in a system that has excluded them for years.

Since the promulgation of the Political Constitution of 1991, which declared Colombia a multi-ethnic and pluricultural nation, attempts have been made to establish a legal system that recognises and respects the cultural and legal diversity of the country.

However, in practice, strong resistance persists, derived from a deep-rooted model of modern law that continues to impose a monistic and universalist vision, often to the detriment of indigenous normative systems.

In the dispute over the definition of law, the confrontation between professionals and non-experts reveals the exhaustion of the traditional hierarchical structure and the insufficiency of its self-reference, thus forcing us to rethink how it can be conceived and applied, as well as the sources on which it could be based.

If we recognise the crucial importance of society as a fundamental element in the formation and development of law, we need a vision that is more connected to social reality and less to isolated theoretical constructions, which implies a meaningful change in legal theory and practice.

The relationship between modern law and indigenous legal systems is characterised by a constant tension, derived from the predominant vision in Colombian society, which associates the Indigenous with the premodern and the mythological.

This bias not only marginalises Indigenous peoples but also reinforces a legal system that is seen as autonomous, self-referential, and disconnected from the specific cultural and social realities of ethnic communities. The struggle for the monopoly of "saying the law" then becomes a field of dispute, where hegemonic conceptions of law try to prevail over other ways of understanding and applying justice.

The fragility of attempts at more open interpretations of the sources of law clashes with the structural limits of law, which, in its essence, may be designed to preserve a conservative vision of power. This dilemma is palpable in the case analysed, where non-experts of law try to challenge the system using the tools that it provides them, thus facing both the possibility of change and the risks inherent in challenging the established order.

Recognising the validity of indigenous worldviews (their own knowledge) as a source of law within the JEP is not only an act of justice, but a necessary step to dismantle the power structures that have sustained centuries of oppression, and which have been exacerbated by the ravages of the internal armed conflict.

Another type of legal pluralism, far from fragmenting the State, would have the potential to strengthen the legitimacy of the legal system as a whole by making it more inclusive and representative of the country's cultural diversity.

This approach would honour the 1991 Constitution and lay the foundations for lasting peace in Colombia by consolidating a system where all forms of *"saying the law"* find a legitimate place, contributing to reconciliation and the reconstruction of the social fabric broken by decades of conflict.

Notes

1 The concept "Derecho propio" should be read as *Indigenous law*, a concept used in the Anglo-Saxon world, specifically in the Canadian context. "Derecho propio" should be understood as the designation that Indigenous peoples in Colombia make about their legal systems.

2 In the Colombian case, the idea of "Indigenous reservations" as it exists in the North American context is not comparable since in Colombia this figure is known as "resguardos", providing greater legal protection and more rights to Indigenous peoples. Only for a better understanding the reader should understand that "resguardos" would be like an Indigenous reservation.

3 The ancestral authorities translate everything that the grandparents (spirits) have to say to the Nasa people.

References

Ariza, R. (2010). *El derecho profano. Justicia indígena, justicia informal y otras maneras de realizar lo justo*. Bogotá: Universidad Externado de Colombia.

Autoridades ancestrales. (2023). Observaciones al «Auto No. 01 de 2023 de determinación de hechos y conductas dentro del Caso No. 05 "Situación Territorial en la región del Norte del Cauca y del Sur del Valle del Cauca" frente al primer grupo de comparecientes de las CM Jacobo Arenas y Gabriel Galvis» por parte de las Autoridades Ancestrales, en ejercicio de las facultadas Espirituales, Naturales y Comunitarias orientadas por las comunidades indígenas de Çxhab Wala Kiwe, Sa't Tama Kiwe, Nasa Üus, Uh Wala Viç, Nasawe'sx Dxi'j y ORIVAC, de acuerdo con nuestros usos y costumbres reconocidos por la Constitución Política de 1991.

Bourdieu, P. (1989). Social Space and Symbolic Power. *Sociological Theory*, *7*(1), 14–25. https://doi.org/10.2307/202060

Bourdieu, P. (2000a). Elementos para una sociología del campo jurídico. In: P. Bourdieu & G. Teubner (eds.) *La fuerza del derecho*. Bogotá, DC: Siglo del Hombre, 153–220.

Chakrabarty, D. (2000). *Provincializing Europe: Postcolonial Thought and Historical Differences*. Princeton: Princeton University Press.

Colombian Constitutional Court. (2018). Judgment C-080 of 2018. Reporting Justice: Antonio José Lizarazo Campo.
Commaille, J. (2023). *L'esprit politique des savoirs. Le droit, la société, la nature*. Paris: Éditions de la Maison des sciences de l'homme.
Ehrlich, E. (1922). The Sociology of Law. *Harvard Law Review*, *36*(2), 130–145. https://doi.org/10.2307/1329737
Fitzpatrick, P. (1998) [1992]. *La mitología del derecho moderno*. México, DF: Siglo XXI.
Friede, J. (2017). [1976]. *El indio en la lucha por la tierra: historia de los resguardos del macizo central colombiano*. Bogotá, DC: Ministerio de Cultura.
García Villegas, M. (2003). Symbolic Power without Symbolic Violence? Critical Comments on Legal Consciousness Studies in USA. *Droit et société*, *53*, 137–163. https://doi.org/10.3917/drs.053.0137
Gnecco, C. (2023). Prologo. In: L. Douay et al. (eds.) *Los indios del cauca. Una construcción etnográfica (1890–1956)*. Popayán: Editorial Universidad del Cauca, 9–33.
Gómez, H. (2015). *Justicias indígenas de Colombia: reflexiones para un debate cultural, jurídico y político*. Bogotá, DC: Centro de Documentación Judicial (Cendoj).
Jurisdicción Especial para la Paz (JEP)—Sala de reconocimiento de verdad, de responsabilidad y de determinación de los hechos y conductas. Auto 01 de 2023—Auto de determinación de hechos y conductas dentro del Caso No. 05 *"Situación Territorial en la región del Norte del Cauca y del Sur del Valle del Cauca"* frente al primer grupo de comparecientes de las CM Jacobo Arenas y Gabriel Galvis.
Meneses, M. (2018). Colonialismo como violência: a "missão civilizadora" de Portugal em Moçambique. *Revista Crítica de Ciências Sociais*, Número especial | 2018, 115–140. https://doi.org/10.4000/rccs.7741
Nasa Üus Yu'Tx Phenxi. Fallo 007 del 09 de septiembre de 2019.
Quijano, A. (1991). Colonialidad y modernidad/racionalidad, *Perú Indígena*, *13*(29).
Rappaport, J. (2003). El imaginario de una nación pluralista: los intelectuales públicos y la jurisdicción especial indígena en Colombia. *Revista Colombiana de Antropología*, *39*, 105–138. http://www.scielo.org.co/scielo.php?script=sci_arttext&pid=S0486-65252003000100004&lng=en&tlng=es
Santos, B. de S. (1995). *Toward a New Common Sense: Law, Science, and Politics in the Paradigmatic Transition*. New York: Routledge.
Santos, B. de S. (2007). Beyond Abyssal Thinking: From Global Lines to Ecologies of Knowledges. *Review*, *30*(1), 45–89.
Santos, B. de S. (2023). *Law and the Epistemologies of the South*. Cambridge: Cambridge University Press.
Tamanaha, B. (2021). *Legal Pluralism Explained: History, Theory, Consequences*. New York: Oxford University Press.

PART II

Social disruption and institutional failures

5

SUPPORT FOR VICTIMS OF DOMESTIC VIOLENCE IN BRAZIL

Identification and description of the main programmes

Gabrielle Tatith Pereira and Fabrício Castagna Lunardi

Introduction

Violence against women remains one of the most severe human rights violations across societies (Alsina et al. 2024; Quispe et al. 2022; EIGE 2002; WHO 2021). United Nations Women estimates that one in three women has experienced physical and/or sexual violence at least once in her lifetime (UNWOMEN 2024). These figures are confirmed by the World Health Organization in their systematic review, which reports that 35% of women worldwide have experienced either physical or sexual violence (WHO 2021).

In Brazil, between 2011 and 2021, more than 49 thousand women were murdered (IPEA 2024). The female homicide rate reached its peak in 2017, when it reached 4.7 deaths per 100,000 women (IPEA 2024). After a drop in 2018 (4.3) and 2019 (3.5), a slight increase trend continues in 2020 (3.6) and 2021 (3.56). Of these deaths, femicide records reached, as of 2019, the level of 1.24 per 100 thousand women (IPEA 2024). In 2022, compulsory notifications of domestic and sexual violence from the Unified Health System registered 202,608 thousand women assisted (SF 2024). The National Judiciary Database (DataJud) recorded the granting of 573,220 protective and urgent measures in 2022 and 529,690 protective and urgent measures in 2023, and the police underreporting rate, in 2023, reached 61% (SF 2024). The National Survey of Violence against Women (SF 2023) shows that 30% of Brazilian women declared they have already suffered some type of domestic or family violence caused by a man.

The elimination of gender-based violence (GBV) is a goal of democratic countries, both nationally and internationally. Women are overwhelmingly the victims, and domestic is the most ordinary form of GBV (Toro-Afonso and Rodríguez-Madera 2004; Ali and Naylor 2013). Data from around the world indicates that

DOI: 10.4324/9781003752974-8

domestic violence continues at high levels, posing a persistent challenge for governments and societies seeking to reverse this reality (EIGE 2002; WHO 2021, 2013). Domesticity is deeply rooted in systemic power imbalances between women and men (Brahmachari 2021; Delgadillo 2024; Mahtab and Fariha 2022; Ovesen and Carroll 2025). It is therefore essential to evaluate continuously the effectiveness of public policies aimed at prevention, protection (breaking the cycle of violence), and redress for women (Pereira et al. 2026).

There is substantial literature on the concepts of gender-based violence and domestic violence (Toro-Afonso and Rodríguez-Madera 2004; Stewart et al. 2012; Ali and Naylor 2013; Ali et al. 2016), as well as research evaluating the effectiveness of specific public policies to prevent or redress such forms of violence (Canedo and Morse 2021; Bullinger et al. 2023; Balakrishnan et al. 2024; Valtýsdóttir et al. 2025). However, there is a gap in the literature regarding a systemic overview of public policies within each country. Therefore, research conducted in different national contexts is, therefore, important to address these gaps.

This chapter aims to identify and describe Brazilian public policies designed to prevent and redress domestic violence. The methodology used is a literature review to seek to define domestic violence, as well as its dimensions, and documentary legal-normative analysis to identify the laws or regulations that establish protection and reparation for victims of domestic violence in Brazil.

This study seeks to contribute to both scholarship and the formulation of public policies for the protection of women by identifying and conceptualising the main policies developed in Brazil, which may also be adapted and applied in other regions or countries according to local contexts.

Domestic violence against women: a theoretical approach and data on violence in Brazil

Gender-based violence (GVB) is a persistent reality across the world (Ellyson et al. 2024; Ceroni et al. 2021; Willie et al. 2023; Dengezela et al. 2024; Bullinger et al. 2023; Quispe et al. 2022; Militza 2023; EIGE 2002; WHO 2013; WHO 2021). It encompasses different violence forms that share a common gender-based characteristic, including different general forms of violence such as domestic violence and intimate partner violence, but also other forms of violence such as verbal, physical, sexual, psychological, and economic (Quispe et al. 2022).

For the purposes of this study, intimate partner violence (IPV), or domestic violence (DV), is defined as "any act of physical, sexual, psychological or economic violence that occurs between former or current spouses or partners, whether or not the perpetrator shares or shared the same residence with the victim" (EIGE 2002). The definition of "intimate partner" varies across national legislations, but most commonly encompasses both formal partnerships, such as marriage, and informal partnerships, including dating and non-marital sexual relationships (WHO 2013). It also extends to lesbian couples, as well as transgender women and bisexual women, when they are victims of violence in intimate relationships (Ovesen and Carroll 2025). The concept of domestic violence may also apply to gay couples (Toro-Afonso and Rodríguez-Madera 2004; Stewart et al. 2012).

In Brazil, domestic violence is defined as any action or omission based on gender that results in the death of a woman, injury, physical, sexual, or psychological suffering, or moral or property damage. Such acts may occur within the domestic unit (the space of permanent coexistence of individuals, with or without family ties, including those temporarily aggregated), within the family (a community formed by individuals who are or consider themselves related, united by natural ties, by affinity, or by express will), or in any intimate relationship of affection (where the aggressor and the victim have or have had coexistence, regardless of cohabitation), irrespective of sexual orientation (Article 1, Maria da Penha Law).

The most common types of domestic violence are physical, sexual, psychological, and economic (EIGE 2002; Quispe et al. 2022; Willie et al. 2023), although economic violence is not recognised to the same extent as the others. Evidence regarding the relationship between women's economic sufficiency and the prevalence of domestic violence remains inconclusive (Canedo and Morse 2021).

Indeed, there is scientific evidence that unemployment, economic instability or dependence, work-related stress, and poverty contribute to increases in DV in its various forms (Ceroni et al. 2021; Willie et al. 2023; Dengezela et al. 2024; Bullinger et al. 2023; Brahmachari 2021; Mahtab and Fariha 2022). Contrary to the expectation that economic empowerment enables women to break the cycle of violence, some studies indicate that women who participate in the labour market may experience higher rates of violence, including those in both formal and informal employment or those receiving cash transfers (Canedo and Morse 2021). These findings, however, may be influenced by specific circumstances related to economic domestic violence: women may not receive significant sums of money, so male partners may not feel economically threatened; cash transfers may be perceived by male partners as family-focused; or male partners may coerce women into surrendering the money, thereby maintaining control (Canedo and Morse 2021, p. 11).

Economic abuse may be defined as behaviour that restricts a woman's ability to acquire, use, and maintain economic resources, undermining her financial security and capacity for self-sufficiency. It typically manifests in three ways: (a) controlling the victim's access to financial resources; (b) sabotaging her ability to obtain and maintain employment; and (c) exploiting her personal financial situation (Stylianou 2018; Willie et al. 2023; Dengezela et al. 2024; Geddes and Holz 2024).

A particularly relevant aspect of economic violence is the exercise of coercive control, whereby the aggressor employs tactics to maintain power or influence over the victim, reinforcing dependency and sustained fear linked to economic resources (Willie et al. 2023; Bullinger et al. 2023; Geddes and Holz 2024). As Willie et al. (2023) observe, there is a cyclical relationship between economic domestic violence and women's financial self-sufficiency: i) economic domestic violence undermines women's capacity for self-sufficiency, and ii) reduced self-sufficiency becomes a barrier to leaving—or to avoiding return to—abusive relationships.

Brazil's Law Against Domestic Violence, known as the Maria da Penha Law, is considered one of the three most protective laws worldwide (UN 2016). When examining domestic violence and its manifestations, it is essential to consider intersectionality in order to analyse how systems of oppression and power shape experiences through structural inequities such as racism and sexism (Mortlock 2025; Willie et al. 2023; Walsh et al. 2023; Hagerlid 2023; Sorensen et al. 2025).

A study conducted in the United States (Walsh et al. 2023), focusing on Temporary Assistance for Needy Families (TANF), highlights differential treatment of White, Black, and immigrant women in relation to their continued participation in income assistance programmes. It further demonstrates that Black and immigrant women are more frequently penalised for failing to meet legally mandated conditions and that the complex relationship between income assistance and DV warrants further exploration (Walsh et al. 2023).

Public policies to prevent and repair domestic violence

In Brazil, there is a broad set of public policies designed to combat domestic violence, reflecting the severity of the problem in the country. Based on the methodological criteria established in this study, ten public policies related to domestic violence were selected: six prevention policies and four redress policies.

Using these criteria, the main public policies addressing domestic violence in Brazil are (i) emergency protective measures; (ii) specialised women's police stations; (iii) risk assessment forms; (iv) electronic monitoring devices; (v) women's service centres; (vi) comprehensive and multidisciplinary care centres; (vii) policies to break the cycle of violence; (viii) rental assistance; (ix) special pension for orphans of femicide; and (x) aesthetic reconstruction.

Following this identification, the subsequent sections present a description of these policies, considering both public policies to prevent domestic violence and public policies to provide redress for victims of domestic violence and/or their children as mechanisms for ensuring access to justice and rights.

Public prevention policies: when saving lives matters

In the following items, prevention policies designed to preserve the integrity and lives of victims are identified and analysed, considering their potential to protect and prevent episodes of violence, notably in cases of femicide.

Emergency protective measures: law and justice system

To protect women against domestic violence in Brazil, the Maria da Penha Law establishes the need for operational integration of the judiciary, the Department of

Justice, and the Public Defender's Office with the areas of public security, social assistance, health, education, work and housing.

The same law provides that the judge may impose the following urgent protective measures on aggressors (Article 22), among others: (a) suspension of possession of, or restriction on carrying of, weapons; (b) removal from the home, domicile, or place of coexistence with the victim; (c) prohibition of specific conduct, including (c.1) approaching the victim, her family, and witnesses, with a minimum distance established between them and the aggressor; (c.2) contacting the victim, her family, and witnesses through any means of communication; and (c.3) frequenting certain places in order to preserve the victim's physical and psychological integrity; (d) restriction or suspension of visitation rights to minor dependants, after consultation with a multidisciplinary care team or equivalent service; (e) provisional maintenance; (f) mandatory attendance at recovery and re-education programmes for aggressors; and (g) psychosocial monitoring of aggressors through individual counselling and/or support groups.

Judges may also impose protective measures in favour of the victim (Article 23), including (a) referral of the victim and her dependants to an official or community protection or assistance programme; (b) return of the victim and her dependants to their home after removal of the aggressor; (c) removal of the victim from the home, without prejudice to rights related to property, custody of children, and maintenance; (d) legal separation; and (e) enrolment of the victim's dependants in the closest basic education institution, or transfer thereto, regardless of the availability of vacancies.

The Maria da Penha Law is considered one of the strongest laws in the world for the protection of women against domestic violence, according to the United Nations Development Fund for Women (UN 2016; Pereira et al. 2026). Laws aimed at preventing and combating violence against women must, however, be accompanied by effective implementation and enforcement. This requires strengthening coordination among institutions and promoting education, awareness, transparency, and accountability (Dengezela et al. 2024; Brahmachari 2021).

In high-risk situations, the justice system must be capable of providing urgent protective measures. To ensure this, high-risk victims must be identifiable, and justice system responses must be effective (Brahmachari 2021). Evidence shows that specialised police units and courts that deal exclusively with domestic violence cases, when working in coordination, can reduce the incidence of non-fatal domestic violence (Arora et al. 2024).

Research also indicates that victims participating in justice-linked assistance programmes are more likely to receive outreach services, engage with prosecutors and advocates, and attend court hearings. They are less likely to drop charges, their cases are more likely to result in conviction and incarceration, and they are less likely to cohabit with the defendant six months later (Arora et al. 2024). Conversely, a lack of trust in the criminal justice system, coupled with inadequate or limited support services, such as shelters, counselling, and legal aid, discourages reporting and hinders women from leaving abusive situations (Dengezela et al. 2024).

Regarding the timeliness of judicial decisions on urgent protective measures, there is significant disparity among Brazilian courts. Although the Maria da Penha Law establishes a 48-hour deadline, most courts fail to comply with this requirement, and in some jurisdictions nearly half of the cases remain undecided after this period (Pasinato and Severi 2022).

Urgent protective measures constitute a vital instrument for women and the justice system in preventing domestic violence (CNJ, 2024). Their effectiveness, however, depends on an adequate support infrastructure and the capacity to evaluate individual cases to prevent the recurrence of violent practices. In this regard, the digitization of the Brazilian justice system (Alves et al. 2026), the possibility of holding virtual hearings (Costa et al. 2026) and the creation of virtual procedures (CNJ 2024) have facilitated the expedited processing of urgent protective measures—from the victim's initial police request to the judicial decision—especially in regions far from urban centers (Araujo Filho et al. 2024; Moraes et al. 2024; Lunardi and Moraes 2025).

Specialised women's assistance police stations

Specialised Women's Assistance Police Stations are governed by Law No. 14,541/2023 and function as Civil Police units dedicated to assisting women victims of violence on a continuous, 24-hour basis. Their objectives are to prevent, investigate, and punish crimes of domestic violence, crimes against sexual dignity, and femicides. Furthermore, these units are also authorised to request urgent protective measures, forward police investigations to the judiciary, and obtain reports from the Legal Medical Institute (IML).

In addition to their functions as specialised police and judicial police units, these stations—through agreements with the Public Defender's Office, the agencies of the Unified Social Assistance System, and the Domestic and Family Violence Courts against Women or other competent criminal courts—provide psychological and legal assistance to women who are victims of violence (Article 2).

A key provision is that assistance to women must be offered in a private room, preferably by female police officers trained to receive victims in an effective and humane manner (Article 3, §§1–2). The law also requires the provision of a telephone number or other electronic communication channel to enable immediate contact with the police in cases of violence against women (Article 3, §3).

Resources from the National Public Security Fund (FNSP) allocated to the states may be used to establish Specialised Women's Assistance Police Stations (Article 5). In municipalities without such a unit, priority must be given to ensuring that victims of domestic violence receive assistance from specialised female officers.

Risk assessment form

The Brazilian National Council of Justice created a Risk Assessment Form to be applied to women victims of domestic and family violence, with the goal of ensuring the appropriate application of urgent protective measures established under Law No. 11,340/2006, the Maria da Penha Law.

The application of this form was subsequently regulated by Law No. 14,149/2021, which established the National Risk Assessment Form

> for the prevention and confrontation of crimes and other acts of domestic and family violence committed against women, according to a model approved by a joint normative act of the National Council of Justice and the National Council of the Public Ministry.

The law specifies that the form

> aims to identify the factors that indicate the risk of women suffering any form of violence within the scope of domestic relations, in order to support the actions of public security bodies, the Public Prosecutor's Office, the Judiciary, and the bodies and entities of the protection network in managing the identified risk, while preserving the confidentiality of the information in all cases.
>
> *(Article 2 §1)*

The form is preferably filled out by the Civil Police at the time of registering the incident. If it cannot be applied at that time—for example, if the victim is unable to speak or if the report is filed by a family member or third party—the form must be administered by the Public Prosecutor's Office or the judiciary at the first point of contact with the woman victim of domestic or family violence (Article 2 §2).

There is evidence that risk assessment forms are effective in identifying high-risk cases of domestic violence and guiding the application of urgent protective and prevention measures (Arora et al. 2024). By gathering a standardised set of data, it becomes possible to identify the factors most strongly associated with increased risk of lethality in cases of violence against women.

Although research indicates that risk assessment conducted by trained specialists is more reliable than the use of algorithms (Arora et al. 2024), technological tools can support the initial screening of cases. The implementation of risk assessment forms—whether or not associated with artificial intelligence applications—has proved to be an important instrument of the justice system, enabling the prioritisation of domestic violence cases and the adoption of the most appropriate urgent protective measure. This initiative has nationwide normative force across the judiciary and also engages other entities of the justice system, including the police, the Public Prosecutor's Office, and the Public Defender's Office.

Electronic devices: "panic button" and electronic ankle bracelets

In Brazil, the most frequent urgent protective measures granted to benefit victims—and imposed against aggressors—are removal from the home and prohibition of contact and proximity to the victim and her family. To ensure compliance with these measures, and thereby safeguard women's lives and physical integrity, technologies have been developed both to monitor aggressor's behaviour and to enable victims to seek help quickly in emergencies.

Electronic monitoring, typically through electronic ankle bracelets, is another mechanism used to enforce protective measures. It consists of technical tools that restrict the freedom of individuals subject to precautionary measures or final convictions, enabling authorities to determine their exact location. This measure was established within the judiciary through Resolution No. 142 of the National Council of Justice (CNJ 2021).

Electronic monitoring allows courts to verify compliance with judicial decisions and increases victims' safety by discouraging violations of protective measures. The service uses GPS technology to track the location of monitored individuals in real time through geographic coordinates. Beyond supervision, the use of ankle bracelets has two further advantages: it reduces costs for the State and helps alleviate chronic prison overcrowding. However, electronic monitoring is not recommended when a woman is at risk of femicide. In such cases, preventive detention is the appropriate.

At the federal level, legislative proposals under discussion in the National Congress seek to expand electronic monitoring and introduce mobile security devices or applications to improve the effectiveness of urgent protective measures in cases of domestic violence.

Women's Service Centre: Call 180

The "Call 180" Women's Service Centre is an essential public service for the prevention of violence against women. In addition to receiving reports of violations, the centre forwards complaints to competent authorities and monitors the progress of cases. It also provides guidance for women in situations of violence, referring them to specialised services, an offering information about rights, current legislation, and the nationwide support and reception network for women in vulnerable situations (MDHC 2020).

These findings are consistent with both national and international research, which indicate that violence against women occurs predominantly in domestic and family settings and is most often perpetrated by current or former partners (Ellyson et al. 2024; Ceroni et al. 2021; Willie et al. 2023; Dengezela et al. 2024; Bullinger et al. 2023; Quispe et al. 2022; Geddes and Holz 2024; Militza 2023; EIGE 2002; WHO 2013, 2021). They also confirm that Black women are disproportionately affected by violence, underscoring the need for public policies to integrate an intersectional perspective in their design and implementation (Willie et al. 2023; Bullinger et al. 2023; Malta et al. 2020; Sorensen et al. 2025; Hagerlid 2023).

Comprehensive and multidisciplinary care centres and shelters for women victims of domestic violence

The Maria da Penha Law authorises the Federal Government, the Federal District, the states and municipalities to create and promote, within the limits of their competences, comprehensive and multidisciplinary care centres for women and their dependants in situations of domestic and family violence, as well as shelters for women and their minor dependants (Article 35).

Reference centres are specialised services where women are welcomed and attended by professionals (including lawyers, psychologists, and social workers) who provide reception, legal guidance, psychological support, and individualised planning aimed at empowering victims to break free from the cycle of violence.

Shelters for women victims of domestic violence provide institutional care services to women facing life-threatening situations, as well as to their underage dependants. Shelters are recommended in cases where protective measures have been repeatedly breached, where there are serious threats to life, or where aggressors are under constant surveillance. These facilities are designed as safe and confidential environments, typically offered to women through police stations or the judiciary, on an emergency basis, to safeguard the lives and physical integrity of women and children. Shelters operate continuously, providing extended stays for victims and their families, together with psychosocial assistance.

Brazilian legislation (Law No. 11,107/2005) authorises federative entities to contract public consortia to achieve objectives of common interest. This mechanism enables municipalities and states, with the support of the Federal Government, to establish assistance centres or shelters for women victims of violence.

Reparation for victims of domestic violence and/or their children: breaking the cycle of violence and looking to the future

This subsection analyses the four main policies in Brazil that focus on repairing harms caused by domestic violence.

Breaking the cycle of violence through self-sustenance: quotas for women in vulnerable situations in public contracting

This initiative originated in the Federal Senate, through the Assistance Program for Women in Situations of Economic Vulnerability as a Consequence of Domestic and Family Violence. The primary purpose of the programme is to ensure that companies providing ongoing services to the Federal Senate reserve a minimum of 2% of vacancies for women in situations of economic vulnerability resulting from domestic violence whenever the contract involves 50 or more workers and the necessary professional qualifications are met.

The programme operates through a cooperation agreement with the State Secretariat for Women of the Federal District Government, the body responsible for policies servicing women victims of violence. This agreement facilitates the selection process while safeguarding the confidentiality of beneficiaries' identities for security reasons and prohibiting any form of discrimination (Baldutti 2021).

Considering that many of these women have urgent protective measures in place against their aggressors, the Federal Senate has access to the list of women served by the programme. Confidentiality is preserved, but the measure ensures that aggressors are denied access to Senate premises (Baldutti 2021). Based on research data from the Federal Senate, it is estimated that, on the basis of the legal minimum quota, at least 30 women have benefitted annually since 2017 through December 2024.

Following the programme's positive results, the initiative was incorporated into national legislation, and its scope expanded. The Bidding and Contract Law (Law No. 14,133/2021) established that contracts with the public administration may "require that a minimum percentage of the workforce responsible for executing the object of the contract" be composed of "women victims of domestic violence" (Article 25, §9).

This law was recently regulated by the President of the Republic through Decree No. 11,430/2023, which requires that contracts for continuous services with exclusive dedication of labour must allocate at least 8% of vacancies to women victims of domestic violence, whenever the contract involves 25 or more employees (Article 3). The decree specifies that the definition of "woman" includes trans women, *travestis*,[1] and other female gender identities (Article 3, I) and that vacancies are to be allocated primarily to Black women (Article 3, II).

Other public institutions have also regulated the law. The National Council of Justice (CNJ 2023a) and the National Council of Public Prosecutor's Office (CNMP 2023) each established the reservation of at least 5% of vacancies for women in situations of economic vulnerability, including victims of domestic violence. Both norms apply to all women, regardless of sexual orientation or gender identity, with priority given to Black women (CNJ, 2023a; CNMP, 2023). These programmes have also been expanded to include women with school-age children, as well as Indigenous, quilombola, rural, refugee, migrant, and homeless women, and those recently released from the prison system.

This programme is significant because it guarantees victims of domestic violence access to stable employment rather than temporary welfare benefits. As noted in the literature review, the relationship between economic insufficiency and domestic violence can be analysed from two perspectives: the financial strain model and the bargaining model. The financial strain model holds that financial difficulties generate stress that can increase domestic violence. The bargaining model emphasises that financial dependence reduces victims' bargaining power within the relationship, making it more difficult to leave abusive households (Geddes and Holz 2024).

The inclusion of women victims of domestic violence in the labour market produces multiple positive results: it strengthens the financial security of women and their children, facilitates access to labour rights, health insurance, and training, and provides more favourable conditions for breaking the cycle of violence.

Rental assistance for victims of domestic violence in situations of economic and social vulnerability

Law No. 14,674/2023 amended Law No. 11,340/2006 (Maria da Penha Law) to establish rental assistance for women in situations of social and economic vulnerability, to be granted by a judge for a period not exceeding six months.

Expenses related to rental assistance may be covered by budget allocations from the Unified Social Assistance System, which includes federal, state, district, and municipal resources. Several states and municipalities have regulated the payment of rental assistance for women victims of domestic violence, with varying amounts and, in some cases, longer durations than those stipulated under national law.

Research indicates that rent assistance programmes help families manage their budgets and reduce stress levels, thereby lowering the incidence of severe domestic violence (Geddes and Holz 2024). In addition, financial support for victims of domestic violence strengthens their economic bargaining power, facilitating the decision to leave abusive relationships (Bullinger et al. 2023). Indeed, even not specifically directed at domestic violence victims, cash transfers and food assistance programmes have been shown to advance gender equality by enhancing women's decision-making power over household resources (Brahmachari 2021). Other studies highlight that welfare benefits improve housing and food security and reduce episodes of violence, even when underreporting obscures these effects in official statistics (Balakrishnan et al. 2024).

Special pension for orphans of femicide

There is a demonstrated relationship between domestic violence and child maltreatment. Research shows that the presence of domestic violence in the home increases risks for child maltreatment, particularly in contexts of poverty, unemployment, economic stress, and low educational attainment (Bullinger et al. 2023). Furthermore, children who grow up witnessing violence or coercion towards women in their family or community environments are more likely to reproduce such behaviour in their own relationships, perpetuating the cycle of abuse in society (Dengezela et al. 2024; Delgadillo 2024).

In cases of femicide, orphans are often left in a highly vulnerable situation: their mothers are deceased, while their fathers are imprisoned for extended periods and may themselves pose risks to the children's safety. In most cases, custody falls to the relatives of the deceased mother, who frequently face financial challenges in covering the children's subsistence and educational needs.

To address this situation, national Law No. 14,717/2023 created a special pension for children or adolescents orphaned by femicide whose per capita monthly household income is equal to or less than one quarter of the minimum wage. The benefit, set at the equivalent of one minimum wage, is paid "to all children and dependants under 18 years of age on the date of death of a woman victim of femicide" (Article 1 §1). Payments are funded by the federal budget.

The benefit is to be granted by a judge, including on a provisional basis during ongoing judicial proceedings, whenever well-founded evidence exists of the crime of femicide. The perpetrator, co-perpetrator, or accomplice is barred from representing the children or adolescents for the purposes of receiving or managing the pension.

Aesthetic reconstruction for victims of domestic violence

Domestic violence is not only a public safety issue but also a public health problem. Physical, sexual, psychological, moral, and economic violence against women have profound consequences for women's lives, their physical and mental health, their families, and society at large (Ellyson et al. 2024; Ceroni et al. 2021; Boyle 2018).

One of the consequences of domestic violence is aesthetic damage. In many cases, aggressors deliberately inflict visible injuries, motivated by a sense of ownership and the sexist, perverse belief that "if the woman is not his, she will not belong to anyone else". In other situations, women who survive serious assaults require surgical procedures that result in permanent physical and emotional consequences.

The implications go far beyond appearance. When women are confronted daily with scars and deformities, they are often forced to relive the violence they endured. Furthermore, scars can also become stigmatising markers, complicating personal, social, and professional relationships. Thus, both physical and psychological injuries perpetuate suffering.

In Brazil, a public-private partnership has been instrumental in repairing damage caused by domestic violence. The Institute for the Development of Education and Humanitarian Action (Ideah), affiliated with the Brazilian Society of Plastic Surgery, has worked to provide reconstructive procedures for victims of domestic violence with permanent physical sequelae. This philanthropic institution has signed Technical Cooperation Agreements with courts, enabling the referral of victims for aesthetic reconstruction procedures (TJDFT 2023).

The first court to sign such an agreement was the Court of Justice of the State of Goiás, which launched the project called *Recomeçar* ("Start Over"), designed to perform reconstructive plastic surgeries on women, children, and adolescents who are victims of domestic violence (CNJ 2023b).

The project requires several steps (CNJ 2023b): (1) Judicial units are contacted by the court presidency to identify victims of domestic violence who have injuries that may be repaired by reconstructive surgery; (2) identified women are contacted to confirm their interest in receiving the benefit; (3) women who opt in undergo a specialised medical assessment to determine the need for reparative procedures, based on individual circumstances; (4) if the evaluation indicates the relevance of the procedure, the woman is referred for treatment suited to her needs; and (5) upon completion, each woman who undergoes surgery is offered a professional photo shoot.

The participating doctors work on a voluntary basis. Costs are partially covered by the public budget (through Brazil's Unified Health System, SUS), and partially by the private sector.

Conclusions

Domestic violence remains a serious and persistent problem in Brazil, reflected in rise of femicides despite an overall reduction in homicides. Analysis of current public policies reveals that Brazil has developed a significant set of policies addressing domestic violence, mostly national or national-and-regional in scope, divided into six prevention policies and four redress policies.

According to this study, the main public policies to prevent domestic violence in Brazil are (i) Emergency Protective Measures; (ii) Specialised Women's Assistance Police Stations; (iii) Risk Assessment Form; (iv) electronic devices such as the Panic Button and electronic ankle bracelets; (v) the Women's Service Centre (Call 180); and (vi) Comprehensive and Multidisciplinary Care Centres and Shelters for Women Victims of Domestic Violence. The main public policies aimed at repairing harm to victims of domestic violence and/or their children are (i) measures to break the cycle of violence through self-sustenance, such as quotas for women in vulnerable situations in public contracting; (ii) Rental Assistance for women victims of domestic violence in situations of economic and social vulnerability; (iii) Special Pension for Orphans of Femicide; and (iv) Aesthetic Reconstruction for Victims of Domestic Violence.

These policies are implemented and maintained primarily by the public authorities, although some involve joint public-private initiatives. Strengthening such partnerships is a promising path in combating domestic violence.

Another important finding is that most public policies result from the joint action of executive, legislative, and judicial branches—or at least two of them—indicating that effective prevention and redress require coordinated efforts across all levels of government and branches of the state.

In conclusion: (i) the ten policies analysed are capable of achieving their intended objectives, (ii) each has already benefitted thousands or even millions of individuals; (iii) there is a need for a dedicated coordinating body or mechanisms to integrate these policies; and (iv) each policy must be periodically evaluated, particularly with respect to quantitative and qualitative measures of effectiveness. These public policies demonstrate Brazil's concrete commitment to developing a holistic approach to domestic violence and to translating international frameworks into effective national policies.

As a research agenda, it is suggested that this study be replicated in other countries, and that in Brazil, each of the identified policies be further evaluated through data collection and semi-structured interviews, in order to capture the perspectives of both policymakers and practitioners, as well as the experiences of beneficiaries.

Note

1 Translator's note: "Travesti" is a culturally specific gender identity in Brazil and Latin America, referring to people assigned male at birth who identify and live as women, often with social, bodily, and political dimensions distinct from "trans women". The term is retained in Portuguese to respect its contextual meaning.

References

Ali, P.A., Dhingra, K. and McGarry, J. (2016) A literature review of intimate partner violence and its classifications. *Aggressive and Violent Behaviour*, 31: 16–25. https://doi.org/10.1016/j.avb.2016.06.008

Ali, P.A. and Naylor, P.B. (2013) Intimate partner violence: A narrative review of the biological and psychological explanations for its causation. *Aggression and Violent Behaviour*, 18: 373–382. https://doi.org/10.1016/j.avb.2013.01.003

Alsina, E., Browne, J.L., Gielkens, D., Noorman, M.A.J. and Wit, J.B.F. (2024) Interventions to prevent intimate partner violence: A systematic review and meta-analysis. *Violence Against Women*, 30(3–4): 953–980. https://doi.org/10.1177/10778012231183660

Alves, A.L., Lunardi, F.C. and Correia, P.M.A.R. (2026) Conciliation and mediation in digital justice: Categories, dimensions and guide for future research. *Information & Communications Technology Law*, 35(1): 93–108. https://doi.org/10.1080/13600834.2025.2514384

Araujo Filho, J.G., Lunardi, F.C., Gomes, A.D.O. and Correia, P.M.A.R. (2024) Access to justice and digital inclusion in the amazon: Geographic vulnerability and riverside communities. *Virtual Economics*, 7(2): 31–49. https://doi.org/10.34021/ve.2024.07.02(2)

Arora, A., Beberman, X., Jelveh, Z. and Motta, A. (2024) Targeted interventions for high-risk domestic violence victims. *Journal of Economic Literature*, 12(4). https://crimelab.uchicago.edu/wp-content/uploads/sites/2/2024/01/UChicago-Crime-Lab-High-Risk-DV-Paper-Jan2024.pdf

Balakrishnan, S., Chan, S., Constantino, S., Haushofer, J. and Morduch, J. (2024) Household responses to guaranteed income: Experimental evidence from Compton, California. *National Bureau of Economic Research*. https://doi.org/10.3386/w33209

Baldutti, E.A. (2021) Violência doméstica: um desafio para os formuladores de políticas públicas. *Fundação Getúlio Vargas*. https://repositorio.fgv.br/items/9e446dfb-a17b-4971-8d1c-09dfa88864c5

Boyle, K. (2018). What's in a name? Theorising the Inter-relationships of gender and violence. *Feminist Theory*, 20(1): 19–36. https://doi.org/10.1177/1464700118754957

Brahmachari, D. (2021) Changing dynamics of gender inequality in the context of COVID-19 pandemic in India. *International Journal of Governance and Public Policy Analysis*, 3(1). https://doi.org/10.31357/ijgppa.v3i01.5570

Bullinger, L.R., Klika, B., Feely, M., Ford, D., Merrick, M., Raissian, K., Rostad, W. and Schneider, W. (2023) Paid family leave: An upstream intervention to prevent family violence. *Journal of Family Violence*, 39: 471–481. https://doi.org/10.1007/s10896-022-00486-3

Canedo, A.P. and Morse, S.M. (2021) An estimation of the effect of women's employment on the prevalence of intimate partner violence in Mexico. *Journal of Interpersonal Violence*, 36(19–20). https://doi.org/10.1177/0886260519876016

Ceroni, T.L., Ennis, C.R. and Franklin, C.L. (2021) The COVID-19 pandemic: Implications for intimate partner violence. *Couple and Family Psychology: Research and Practice*. https://doi.org/10.1037/cfp0000208

CNJ—Brazilian National Council of Justice (2021) Resolution 412/2021. Establishes guidelines and procedures for the application and monitoring of the electronic monitoring measure of people. https://atos.cnj.jus.br/files/original0047482021082561259334b9264.pdf

CNJ—Brazilian National Council of Justice (2023a) Resolution 497/2023. Establishes the "Transformation" Program within the national Judiciary and sets criteria for courts and councils to include reserved positions for vulnerable individuals in contracts for outsourced, continuous services. https://atos.cnj.jus.br/atos/detalhar/5048

CNJ—Brazilian National Council of Justice (2023b) Projeto Recomeçar. Authors of the project: Sirlei Martins da Costa and Carlos Alberto França. https://boaspraticas.cnj.jus.br/pratica/889

CNJ—Brazilian National Council of Justice (2024) Presença da Justiça em locais remotos e aplicativos ampliam atendimento a vítimas de violência. CNJ Agency News. https://www.cnj.jus.br/presenca-da-justica-em-locais-remotos-e-uso-de-aplicativos-ampliam-atendimento-a-vitimas-de-violencia/

CNMP—Brazilian National Council of Public Prosecutor's Office (2023) Resolution 264/2023. Establishes general parameters for the hiring of women in situations of economic vulnerability resulting from domestic and family violence within the branches and units of the Public Prosecutor's Office. https://www.cnmp.mp.br/portal/atos-e-normas/norma/9995/

Costa, R.L., Lunardi, F.C. and Guimarães, T.A. (2026) Virtual hearings, efficiency, and access to justice: A lawyers' perception survey. *Revista Direito GV*, 22. https://doi.org/10.1590/2317-6172202614

Delgadillo, M.L. (2024) The influence of femicide on criminal behavior: An empirical approach using economic complexity for crime prevention in Mexico. *Estudios Económicos*, 39(1): 121–157. https://doi.org/10.24201/ee.v39i1.449

Dengezela, T.K., Makochekanwa, A. and Moyo, S. (2024) Partner violence against women in Zimbabwe: Prevalence, forms, and implications for legislations. *Journal of Social Work in Developing Societies*, 6(1): 56–73. https://doi.org/10.4314/jswds.v6i1.3

EIGE—European Institute for Gender Equality (2002) Understanding intimate partner violence in the European Union: The essential need for administrative data collection. https://eige.europa.eu/publications-resources/publications/understanding-intimate-partner-violence-european-union-essential-need-administrative-data-collection

Ellyson, A., Adhia, A., Shanahan, S., Alsinai, A., Dimascolo, L., Reygers, M., Bowen, D. and Rowhani-Rahbar, A. (2024) Firearm restrictions in domestic violence protection orders: Implementation, vetting, compliance, and enforcement. *Criminology and Public Policy*, 23: 803–832. https://doi.org/10.1111/1745-9133.12639

Geddes, E. and Holz, N. (2024) Housing affordability and domestic violence: The case of San Francisco's rent control policies. https://doi.org/10.2139/ssrn.4871726

Hagerlid, M. (2023) Discursive constructions of race and gender in racial hate crime targeting women in Sweden. *NORA—Nordic Journal of Feminist and Gender Research*, 31(1): 49–61. https://doi.org/10.1080/08038740.2022.2076738

IPEA—Instituto de Pesquisa Econômica Aplicada (2024) *Atlas da Violência. Brasília: IPEA*. https://www.ipea.gov.br/atlasviolencia/arquivos/artigos/1504-dashmulherfinal-conferido.pdf

Lunardi, F.C. and Moraes, B.F. (2025) Access to justice for Quilombola communities, sustainability, and digital inclusion: A case study in the Remanso Quilombola community. *Veredas do Direito*, 22. https://doi.org/10.18623/rvd.v22.n2.2955

Mahtab, N. and Fariha, T.N. (2022) Pandemic within a pandemic: Gendered impact of COVID-19 in Bangladesh with a focus on child marriage and domestic violence. *In: Understanding Post-COVID-19 Social and Cultural Realities*. Singapore: Springer. https://doi.org/10.1007/978-981-19-0809-5

Malta, M., Jesus, J.G., Legrand, S., Seixas, M., Benevides, B., Silva, M.D., Lana, J.S., Huynh, H.V., Belden, C.M. and Whetten, K. (2020) 'Our life is pointless': Exploring discrimination, violence and mental health challenges among sexual and gender minorities from Brazil. *Global Public Health*. https://doi.org/10.1080/17441692.2020.1767676

MDHC—Brazilian Ministry of Human Rights and Citizenship (2020) *Violência doméstica e familiar contra a mulher: Ligue 180 e tudo o que você precisa saber*. Brasília: MDHC. https://www.gov.br/mdh/pt-br/assuntos/denuncie-violencia-contra-a-mulher/violencia-contra-a-mulher

Militza, I. (2023) Public policy and gender-based violence in the region Tumbes. *Migration Letters*, 20(1): 1222–1239. https://doi.org/10.59670/ml.v20iS1.5271

Moraes, B.F., Lunardi, F.C. and Correia, P.M.A.R. (2024) Digital access to judicial services in the Brazilian amazon: Barriers and potential. *Social Sciences*, 13(2). https://doi.org/10.3390/socsci13020113

Mortlock, A.E. (2025) Trauma, escape and claims to black metaphysical space: Black feminist engagements with 'transracialism'. *Feminist Theory*. https://doi.org/10.1177/14647001251336159

Ovesen, N. and Carroll, C. (2025) Sexual violence in lesbian and queer relationships—double invisibility. *NORA—Nordic Journal of Feminist and Gender Research*, 33(3): 329–341. https://doi.org/10.1080/08038740.2025.2492105

Pasinato, W. and Severi, F.C. (2022) Análise descritiva dos metadados de processos judiciais sobre medidas protetivas de urgência extraídos do DataJud. *In:* Conselho Nacional de Justiça. *Avaliação sobre a aplicação das medidas protetivas de urgência da Lei Maria da Penha*, 29–56. Brasília: CNJ. https://bibliotecadigital.cnj.jus.br/jspui/bitstream/123456789/548/1/relatorio-avaliacao-medidas-protetivas-lei-maria-da-penha-23082022.pdf

Pereira, G.T., Lunardi, F.C., Correia, P.M.A.R. and Vale, A. (2026) Access to justice for women victims of domestic violence in Brazil: Analysis and categorization of policies. *Societies*, 16(5). https://doi.org/10.3390/soc16050144

Quispe, A.M., Vargas, L., Sotelo, M., Rojas, Y.G., Sabaduche, J. and Navarro, C. (2022) The impact of the COVID-19 pandemic on gender-based violence and physical violence among women in Peru. *Gates Open Research*, 6: 102. https://doi.org/10.12688/gatesopenres.13749.1

SF—Brazilian Federal Senate (2023) *Pesquisa nacional de violência contra a mulher*. Brasília: DataSenado Research Institute. https://www12.senado.leg.br/institucional/datasenado/arquivos/pesquisa-nacional-de-violencia-contra-a-mulher-datasenado-2023

SF—Brazilian Federal Senate (2024) *Mapa nacional de violência de gênero*. Brasília: SF. https://www.senado.leg.br/institucional/datasenado/mapadaviolencia/#/inicio

Stewart, D.E., MacMillan, H. and Wathen, N. (2012) Intimate partner violence. *The Canadian Journal of Psychiatry*, 58(6). https://doi.org/10.1177/070674371305800601

Stylianou, A.M. (2018) Economic abuse within intimate partner violence: A review of the literature. *Violence and Victims*, 33(1). http://dx.doi.org/10.1891/0886-6708.33.1.3

TJDFT—Court of Justice of the Federal District (2023) *Projeto do TJDFT e IDEAH realiza primeira cirurgia plástica em vítima de violência doméstica*. Brasília: TJDFT. https://www.tjdft.jus.br/institucional/imprensa/noticias/2023/dezembro/projeto-do-tjdft-e-sociedade-brasileira-de-cirurgia-plastica-realiza-primeiro-procedimento-em-vitima-de-violencia-domestica

Toro-Afonso, J. and Rodríguez-Madera, S. (2004) Domestic violence in Puerto Rican gay male couples: Perceived prevalence, intergenerational violence, addictive behaviors, and conflict resolution skills. *Journal of Interpersonal Violence*, 19. https://doi.org/10.1177/0886260504263873

UN (2016) Lei Maria da Penha é referência global, segundo Banco Mundial. *UN News: Global Perspective Human Stories*, August. https://news.un.org/pt/story/2016/08/1559231

UN Women (2024) *Global Database on Violence against Women*. New York: UN Women. https://data.unwomen.org/global-database-on-violence-against-women

Valtýsdóttir, B.S. and Halldórsdóttir, B.E. (2025) Construction of gender-based violence in prevention material in the Icelandic education system: A critical discourse analysis. *NORA—Nordic Journal of Feminist and Gender Research*, 33(3): 315–328. https://doi.org/10.1080/08038740.2025.2452540

Walsh, S., Roman, J., Parker, A. and Heatling, A. (2023) A systematic review of U.S. welfare sanctions and racial equity. *Journal of Social Equity and Public Administration*, 1(2): 26–41. https://doi.org/10.24926/jsepa.v1i2.4788

WHO—World Health Organization (2013) *Global and regional estimates of violence against women: Prevalence and health effects of intimate partner violence and non-partner sexual violence*. Geneva: WHO. https://www.who.int/publications/i/item/9789241564625

WHO—World Health Organization (2021) *Violence against women prevalence estimates, 2018*. Geneva: WHO. https://www.who.int/publications/i/item/9789240022256

Willie, T.C., Alexander, K.A., Sharpless, L., Zemlak, J.L., Smith, M.V. and Kershaw, T.S. (2023) Recent economic intimate partner violence and posttraumatic stress symptoms among a racially and ethnically diverse sample of U.S. women experiencing intimate partner violence. *Journal of Interpersonal Violence*, 38(19–20): 11091–11116. https://doi.org/10.1177/08862605231178357

6

FROM VICTIM MARGINALISATION TO PERSON-CENTRED JUSTICE

Rethinking criminal justice organisation

Davide Carnevali

Introduction. The structural neglect of victims and its consequences

In countries with a tradition of liberal democracy,[1] the justice system (prosecution offices and courts)—whether under a common-law or civil-law framework—handles cases essentially in a formalistic (and ritualistic) manner and in isolated compartments. This approach frequently leads to goal displacement in judicial actions, adversely affecting those involved.[2] The consequences are especially severe for victims of crime, particularly those with specific protection needs (e.g. victims of gender-based violence-GBV, intimate partner violence-IPV, domestic and sexual violence, hate crimes, minor victims, etc.).

Judicial actions are designed to follow a procedure and produce a correct decision by law in a reasonable timeframe, but they are not practically organised to address fairness in terms of the individuals' well-being, particularly for victims—including their physical, psychological, social, and economic conditions—either before or during the proceedings. Nor does it take care to secure the substantial reconstruction of their individual rights to ensure a safe and dignified life at the end. The harmful effects of this organisational setting and operational modality are evident. Often, it results in secondary victimisation during the process and raises the risk of further victimisation for victims afterwards. Overall, these dynamics raise concerns about how the justice system fulfils its vital role in society—particularly in ensuring actual access to justice for individuals[3]—thereby also calling into question its legitimacy.

All of this occurs despite extensive international guidance and domestic reforms aimed at protecting victims' rights. In practice, however, the situation remains largely on paper, requiring a redesign of the justice service in accordance with

DOI: 10.4324/9781003752974-9

existing provisions. As we will observe, this calls for a person-centred justice system with a multi-agency organising method that links the justice system itself (prosecution offices and courts essentially) with other institutions in an 'ecosystem' also comprising police, social and health services, victim support organisations (VSOs), etc. This configuration appears better suited to handle the growing complexity of justice administration, considering the people's needs: to support and care for those involved, address each individual case more effectively, and therefore uphold and practically restore violated rights, ultimately strengthening the system's legitimacy. Of course, aside from the valuable examples we will examine, achieving lasting change through this approach remains challenging.

Repositioning the victim in the criminal proceeding

The place of the victim in criminal proceedings raises broader questions about the role and purpose of justice in the democratic system (Zedner 1994).

The growing emphasis on the guarantees for the accused as a natural progression of the rule of law, alongside the concurrent marginalisation of the victim's role in criminal proceedings, has shaped the historical development over more than four centuries, across various social and political contexts of liberal-democratic regimes (Luparia Donati & Della Torre 2021). Victims are excluded from proceedings—the so-called "theft of conflicts"—as a fundamental aspect of modern criminal justice, reflecting the assertion of state sovereignty: every crime is primarily committed against the community (Christie 1977). Therefore, the victim is not only the source of a violation of the established order that must be restored and thus of the public interest to be protected but also the person who has suffered a violation of their individual rights and who seeks judicial action to restore their effective enjoyment. These considerations have led to a cultural shift—defined as the restoration of the "personalization of the victim" (Sebba 1996)—which aims to emphasise the need for the justice system to return to satisfying the legitimate expectations of protection, information, and service for those who have suffered a crime; thereby reintegrating this perspective into criminal justice (Crawford & Goodey 2000).

The renewed attention to victims' perspectives in criminal proceedings emerged in countries with a tradition of liberal democracy, following the work of early victimology scholars in the late 1950s and 1960s. However, it was made explicitly clear only in the 1970s, with the emergence of a distinct "victim-centred approach" in academic criminology, highlighting that victims of crime—more often than not—also become victims of the criminal justice system (Drapkin & Viano 1974). In the first 1980s, a robust movement of victim support organisations—primarily feminist—continued to promote victim-centred policies. Research on this subject, based on surveys, is also expanding. Yet very few effective remedies have been implemented to address the disregard for victims by the system—particularly regarding secondary and repeated victimisation (Shapland et al. 1985). This issue was highlighted through the extensive application of specific domestic and international surveys, notably by the United Nations' International Crime Victims Survey (ICVS) in 1988, 1992, and 1996. Since the Mid-Nineties, numerous political debates occurred alongside the growth of victimology research on victim-centred issues, especially related to raising "restorative justice" practices.[4] Nevertheless, few substantial reforms of criminal procedure were undertaken in this area: concerns about the potential restriction of defendant rights have always prevailed. Some authors, in this regard, have even argued that the debate has not been a source of innovation at all, but rather has caused more harm than good (Marshall 1996).

At the same time, another significant movement has sought to draw attention back to the individuals connected to the institutions—and consequently also to the victim within the criminal proceedings—is centred on the concept of "procedural justice" (Thibaut & Walker 1975; Tyler 1990, 2006). Procedural justice refers to the notion that individuals' perceptions of fairness are profoundly influenced by the quality of their experiences in court rather than solely by the outcomes of those experiences. This highlights not only the necessity for economic compensation for victims but also the significance of fair treatment for persons involved in criminal proceedings and trials (May & Morrow 2012). Throughout the judicial process, individuals should be treated with dignity and respect, provided with adequate information, given the opportunity to express their voice, and receive decisions that are fair, transparent, and well-reasoned, regardless of whether those outcomes are favourable or not (Tyler 2003).

The "victim-centred justice" and "procedural justice" movements emphasised the importance of restoring victims' perspectives in criminal proceedings and promoting reform in that direction. This was gradually supported by an expanding body of case law from higher courts in various countries, the International Criminal Court, and the European Court of Human Rights (ECHR), which responded to ongoing negative effects observed in many nations where victims, particularly those with specific protection needs, faced secondary and repeated victimisation due to the absence of explicit legal protections (Soulez-Lariviere & Eliacheff 2007).

Such a situation raised increasing awareness among both international and domestic institutions regarding the importance of promoting specific provisions favour the active victim role in criminal proceedings, with explicit rights and means of protection. Almost all countries with a tradition of liberal democracy have enacted legislation in this direction. The United States, which renewed its focus on victims, initiated a significant process of regulatory reform starting in 1984 with the Victims of Crime Act (VOCA) at the federal level, as well as at the state level. Notably, the federal government established an office for victims of crime at the US Department of Justice, and several states followed suit. Similarly, other relevant countries have implemented measures to support victims of crime. For instance, Australia enacted the Victims of Crime Act in 1994, with additional regulations introduced at the federal and state levels commencing from 2001. New Zealand established the Victims' Rights Act in 2002, while the United Kingdom introduced the Victims' Code in 2004, building on legislation from 1994. In the European Union, this was first articulated in Framework Decision 2001/220/JHA (which was largely unheeded) and more concretely in Directive 2012/29/EU, progressively adopted by all member states. In 2015, Canada followed suit with the Canadian Victims Bill of Rights (CVBR).

In all these legal provisions, a victim is defined as a natural person who has suffered harm, including physical, mental, psychological suffering, or material damage caused directly (or indirectly, such as to the victim's family) by acts or omissions that breach criminal law. The reform process regards the crime as a violation of the individual rights of victims, as well as a socially harmful act, and therefore, the victim of the crime regains a "visibility" and active role within the criminal proceedings and the trial. It establishes that individual rights must be protected regardless of whether the perpetrator of the crime is identified, captured, prosecuted, or convicted, and regardless of the family relationship between the offender and the victim. Among the fundamental rights recognised for the victim is the right to receive clear and understandable information from the first contact with authorities, enabling participation in the proceedings. Consequently, a translation service will be provided, as well as free legal assistance if the victim cannot afford a lawyer. Furthermore, several rights of participation in the criminal process are established and must be considered in treatment during and after the judicial experience, especially for individuals with special protection needs.

Formalism in the case management: legal changes and practice failures

The reform process's focused on a legislation protecting and safeguarding the rights of crime victims essentially centres on fairness in the treatment of persons (in this case, victims) within the proceedings—emphasising "taking care" rather than merely "taking charge" of them—and on carefulness to ensure the effective renewal enjoyment of violated rights at the conclusion of the process as determined by a judge.[5] However, despite the victims' rights provisions introduced in recent decades, the structure and daily functioning of criminal proceedings still operate as if little has changed: the system mainly prioritises formal adherence to procedural rules while too often failing to effectively provide protection and support for victims, from the initial contact with the police to the period after the judgment yet (Carroll 2021).

The chain of shortcomings begins before the trial, where inadequately trained police, the absence or uneven distribution of specialised units, and weak coordination with health and social services and VSOs mean that many victims—particularly those with specific protection needs—are not recognised as such, are heard in unsuitable conditions, and face secondary and even potential repeated victimisation, especially in domestic violence cases where negligent handling can return them to the perpetrator's control (Parti 2024). The competence and coordination among related public and private services make the difference in the outcome. However, even where high-quality related services are available, they often rely on local goodwill rather than formal institutional arrangements, creating a landscape of unequal protection that conflicts with the idea of victim-centred justice promoted by law (IDLO 2023).

When the case enters the judicial phase, the victim's "invisibility" becomes structural: prosecution offices and courts tend to manage the file exclusively through the lens of procedural competence and case-flow, while the victim—who remains the same person harmed by the crime before, during and after the proceedings—experiences decisions on related civil matters, custodial measures, or release conditions as events with profound psychological and material consequences that the system scarcely considers (Kool & Verhage 2014). The ruling itself, whether aligned or not with the victim's expectations, rarely guarantees that the person can concretely recover safety and a dignified life; inadequate monitoring and insufficient integration among police, social and health services, VSOs, justice mean that conditions for secondary or repeated victimisation often persist, despite empirical evidence on the importance of continuity of support and risk management to prevent revictimisation (Tompson et al. 2021).

Inside the courtroom, interactions often remain impersonal, heightening vulnerability and secondary victimisation (Van Dijk 2013). All these elements reveal a deep mismatch between the "service" delivered by the justice system and what people expect when they seek redress: access to justice that is merely formal—affordable only in the technical sense, intelligible only to professionals, comfortable only for institutions—does not meet citizens' demand for a system that takes care of their specific situation and offers decisions that change their lives for the better before, during and after proceedings (Parti 2024).

This is primarily an institutional and organisational problem: formalistic and compartmentalised case management displaces the goal of protecting victims and addressing the harm suffered, turning persons into a "number" that moves anonymously through procedural stages, in open contradiction with the victim-centred justice paradigm provided by law and ultimately eroding confidence in justice.[6] This scenario impacts the justice system's effectiveness for the public and undermines the overall credibility and legitimacy of the judicial system (Tyler 2007)—a concern that any democratic society should not overlook.

A new paradigm emerges for justice organisation: person-centred approach and multi-agency method

Although there is now widespread legislation reinstating the victim's centrality in criminal proceedings, the harmful effects of the organisational setting of justice with formalism and watertight compartments are evident and nullify what was provided for. This is also the experience of many people who must deal with justice every day. It would be necessary to tackle this significant system failure by reshaping the justice service.

This would mean radically changing the paradigm of the justice organisation, as an intentional process aimed at altering the status quo by reshaping the form and function of a targeted system. This concept extends far beyond the idea that organisations should merely collaborate more closely (Foster-Fishman et al. 2007). It involves moving away from the sacrality of the "Temple of Law" to become a "public service", thus opening up to reorganise justice delivery around the person's needs (person-centred approach)—balancing even opposing interests of the various actors involved—and to provide integration among public services, as well as collaboration with private service and support associations (multi-agency methods) for organising justice delivery. Without this deep institutional and organisational transformation, any principle, however enshrined in strict legislation, is destined to shatter against the harsh reality of everyday life, as described earlier.

Person-centred approach

The "person-centred approach"[7] is a new cultural effort to promote the individual and their needs centrality within the public service organisation, including the justice sector.

From a theoretical perspective, it can be linked on one side to the victimological aspect of the "victim-centred" model, and on the other, to elements associated with the "procedural justice" strand, as previously described. Both strands have contributed to the development of specific legislation aimed at providing adequate protection for victims and offering overall attention and support for those engaging with the justice system. However, the person-centred approach introduces a more radical reformist spirit into the organisation of justice services, which warrants further exploration.

In the context of Welfare State theories, the science of administration has long defined justice as a public service comparable to social and health care (Cappelletti & Garth 1978). Furthermore, according to the so-called "welfarism" studies, public service must be developed explicitly in the community's interest, understood as the collective well-being of individuals (Sen & Williams 1982). In fact, it holds that the decisions and actions of public administrative services are centred on the individual and their needs to improve their life (Semple 2025). Welfarism is a prescriptive theory that determines what public administration should try to do for individuals (and not vice versa), and that such developments must, in any case, be based on analysis, evidence, and empirical data (Pilliar 2023). As regards justice, the objectives become those of improving the quality of justice for people—and therefore also its accessibility—by designing a service that places individual needs and interests at the centre (person-centred justice), primarily to protect the weakest actors in the proceedings, such as victims (Semple 2022).

However, in the judicial sphere, individual needs and interests can also be conflicting—and in many cases, they are. Therefore, a balancing act must be carried out with the awareness that, in practice, there are many elements of uncertainty and risks. This inevitably involves experimenting with solutions through trial and error and prioritising interventions for those who need it more (Holtug 2022). Ultimately, the "consequentialism" that characterises a person-centred approach even prescribes that a choice is then acceptable only when individuals have a concretely observable benefit from it (Pilliar 2023).

Multi-agency method

As previously mentioned, the need to redefine a service tailored to the interests of individuals, particularly regarding the care of victims, cannot rely solely on the justice system but requires integration across other public and private services. Public-management research views multi-agency working as a key design for coordinated, integrated responses. The methods of multi-agency working have evolved to address the diverse needs of individuals and communities by fostering collaboration among public institutions and private organisations (Sullivan & Skelcher 2002).

Model ranges based on varying levels of service integration. Initially, as a first step, there are strategic decision-making groups in which professionals from different agencies come together to discuss issues and make collective decisions, and training programmes that enhance expertise through shared knowledge without necessarily providing integrated services (Atkinson et al. 2002). Next, centre-based delivery models co-locate services at a single site, enabling efficient communication and coordination while maintaining distinct roles. Coordinated delivery involves a designated coordinator who ensures cohesive responses across agencies and links strategic planning with operational implementation. Lastly, operational-team delivery represents the most integrated model, where professionals from different agencies work together daily as a unified team to deliver seamless services directly to clients. Each model emphasises shared goals, communication, and trust while addressing challenges such as differing organisational cultures, resource boundaries, and distinct institutional missions (Atkinson et al. 2007).

The history of multi-agency methods in practice shows how collaboration has developed among organisations (both public and private) to tackle social, health, educational, and even justice issues that are too complex for any one entity to resolve. This is particularly true for the so-called "wicked issues": multifaceted, unpredictable, open-ended, intractable, and resistant to conventional solutions (Head & Alford 2015). The roots of such methods date back to the 1970s, with significant legislative and policy developments during the 1980s and 1990s in the UK for the protection of children and disadvantaged people, emphasising the importance of coordinated services. Since 2000, multi-agency working spans other public sectors such as healthcare and education, employing methods such as co-located services, coordinated delivery, and operational teams to achieve shared goals (Cheminais 2009). Effective collaboration relies on principles such as strong leadership, clear communication, trust, and regular evaluation (Atkinson et al. 2002).

At the same time, even within the justice sector, the prodromes of cooperation, inter-agency, and multi-agency methods have been tested albeit in a limited way to address specific problems related to enhancing the management of risks to public safety associated with urban and social decay in the United Kingdom at the beginning and in other countries such as Australia, Canada, and the United States shortly thereafter. This approach did not rely solely on the police to manage the problem but suggested that crime prevention should be a collective responsibility involving multiple stakeholders (Gilling 1994). This implication required implementing public policies to promote cooperation among various agencies: police, social services, and healthcare. Subsequently, this framework was expanded to include prisons in the circle of agencies concerned with correctional practices (Pycroft & Gough 2010), particularly regarding youth offenders (Souhami 2008).

However, none of these experiences foresaw the permanent involvement of the public prosecutor and the courts in the network of public services, along with the participation of private organisations, such as NGOs. This significantly increases the complexity of addressing the growing need for cooperation and integration. Nevertheless, some successful and important examples are already in place and under development, as will be discussed later.

Implementing the new paradigm: opportunities, examples, and constraints

Therefore, in countries with a tradition of liberal democracy, robust legislation has been enacted to protect victims' rights, and, more broadly, the principles of access to justice are clearly defined. Moreover, regarding the judicial political framework for their implementation, there is increasing recognition of the need to reform justice services—particularly prosecutions and courts—to uphold this legislation and its principles. Taking a person-centred approach and employing multi-agency methods in the reform process is somewhat on the political agenda. As we shall see, this is demonstrated by the growing number of international and domestic guidelines in this area. This situation creates conditions and opportunities for change. But what tangible results have been realised? Conversely, what constraints might impede this reform effort?

Opportunities

It is no coincidence that this new paradigm is acknowledged by the United Nations (Achinonu et al. 2023; Sedra 2022; UNODC 2022)[8] and more recently summed up very focused on the works of the Organization for Economic Cooperation and

Development (OECD 2021)—passing through the Council of Europe (COE & FRA 2016) and European Union (EU)[9] in the much more traditional context of the access to justice—throughout the definition of key elements a government-wide strategy for promoting people-centred justice based on multi-agency cooperation, as well as mechanisms to ensure accountability and sustainability. Drawing on analyses of some good practices, guidelines aim to encourage countries to reshape justice into more concrete and responsive systems that contribute to increasing citizens' trust in public institutions and strengthening democracies.

The main pillars of such a reform perspective include designing people-centred justice services that begin by identifying people's justice needs (in terms of information, protection, treatment, and outcomes), what works for them, and how to deliver accessible services, including for the most vulnerable groups. Then, it must provide operators, organisations, and infrastructures that can concretely and effectively address those needs. This means promoting a multi-agency method for arranging the justice service (even called "whole-of-government" or "whole-of-state" approach), in which the full group of public agencies, along with non-government agencies, involved in justice delivery work together and even structure new and more integrated institutions to resolve the problems experienced by people in the justice proceeding. According to this approach, ensuring appropriate capability development for actors involved in providing justice services—through adequate training—has an important impact on successes in this new way of service delivery (OECD 2021).

Furthermore, the justice system must not only reform itself according to these principles, but it must also provide for a permanent monitoring system to commit to learning what works from the people's perspective through rigorous evaluation, research, client surveys, user feedback, deep community engagement, and data monitoring, determining what strategies and pathways are most effective, sustainable, and appropriate for meeting some changing legal and justice needs of different groups in the community and periodically adapting the service to them. Lastly, governments must provide resources to invest appropriately in such a reform process (OECD 2021).

It all sounds promising, but how is this reflected in daily justice practice?

Experiences

An analysis of experiences within the justice system reveals that, in various countries, different experiences are progressing in this direction. However, these experiences are often linked to specific circumstances or revolve around issues concerning public information, legal aid and assistance—such as social care, healthcare, and housing—primarily within the civil sector (small claims, social security disputes, divorce, business, etc.). However, three pertinent examples of the criminal sector of so-called all-inclusive problem-solving organisations are highlighted below. The first two are more widespread globally but specialised on GBV, IPV, domestic and sexual violence; the third is an initiative unique to the Netherlands, yet it is particularly noteworthy due to its design to handle all ordinary cases.

GBV, IPV, domestic and sexual specialised courts

Specialised Family and Domestic Violence Courts in the United States, Canada, the United Kingdom, New Zealand, and Australia emerged in the 1980s and 1990s as an innovative judicial response to the complexities of such case typology (Berman & Feinblatt 2001). Traditional court systems were ill-equipped to address the unique interpersonal dynamics and safety risks in these cases, prompting reforms that prioritised victim safety and offender accountability through specialised approaches (Moore 2009). A core advantage of these courts is the development of judicial expertise. Judges dedicated to domestic violence cases acquire in-depth knowledge of abuse patterns and effective interventions, fostering more consistent and informed rulings (Koshan 2014). This consistency contrasts with traditional systems, in which family and domestic violence cases are handled by various judges with differing experience levels, often leading to uneven outcomes (Stewart 2010).

Victim safety is a key focus, with specialised courts implementing measures such as separate waiting areas, staggered arrival times, and heightened security. Early access to victim support services is prioritised, recognising that legal remedies alone are insufficient. This early intervention sustains victim engagement and supports them in prosecution and court experience, improving long-term outcomes. Additionally, offender accountability mechanisms, including regular judicial monitoring and compliance checks, ensure offenders face ongoing oversight. This approach is particularly effective with repeat offenders, as judges become familiar with recurring behavioural patterns (Robinson 2008).

Efficiency is another hallmark of specialised courts. Streamlined processes lead to faster case resolutions, reducing stress for victims while enabling timely offender intervention. Centralised expertise and dedicated case management systems prevent administrative oversights. Moreover, these courts function as coordination hubs, uniting law enforcement, prosecutors, victim advocates, and social services. This integrated response treats domestic violence as a complex societal issue, easing victims' burden to navigate fragmented systems while fostering broader community accountability (Eley 2005). Despite requiring thoughtful planning around structure, resources, and stakeholder collaboration, specialised courts demonstrably enhance judicial responses to family violence. They improve victim outcomes, manage offenders more effectively, and bolster public trust in the justice system through expertise, consistency, and comprehensive service integration (Freiberg 2001).

Spain stands out as the primary continental European country with a nationwide network of dedicated courts specifically for gender-based violence cases. These *Juzgados de Violencia sobre la Mujer*, established since 2004, number over 100 specialised courts, including detached offices, handling complaints promptly with trained judges, on-call services, and protection orders, resulting in increased reporting and improved victim protection. However, the origin and operation of these courts have sparked a more complex and controversial debate, mainly concerning the respect for values of impartiality (García-Hombrados et al. 2024). Following the provisions of the Istanbul Convention aimed at preventing and combating violence against women and domestic violence, other countries in the Council of Europe that have ratified it have established specialised sections, trained judges, and implemented specific procedures or protocols within general or family courts to handle these cases, but without creating dedicated courts.

Family Justice Centers

Family Justice Centers (FJCs)[10] in the United States, established since 2002, exemplify a comprehensive, trauma-informed approach to supporting victims of domestic violence. Designed as "one-stop" service model, these centres consolidate various essential services in one location, reducing the need for victims to navigate through the different agencies. FJCs provide a range of support, including law enforcement investigations, prosecution assistance, medical care, counselling, legal advocacy, and social services. This structure fosters collaboration among police, prosecutors, healthcare providers, social workers, advocacy groups, and nonprofits, ensuring a coordinated response to domestic and sexual violence for both adult and child survivors (Gwinn et al. 2007).

There are now over 100 centres across 45 US states, serving more than 70,000 victims annually, with approximately 300 FJCs established worldwide across 25 countries (FJCA 2025). These centres offer crisis counselling, safety planning, and case management in secure, supportive environments. On-site police can immediately facilitate protective orders and evidence collection, while prosecutors initiate cases early to improve outcomes. Ongoing legal advocacy, counselling, and court accompaniment reduce victim recantation and promote engagement, acknowledging trauma's impact on victim behaviour (Simmons et al. 2016). Pro bono attorneys assist with protective orders, custody, and immigration cases, ensuring victims navigate complex legal systems effectively. Even after court proceedings, FJCs continue to offer safety planning, shelter referrals, and long-term support, contributing to documented outcomes like reduced homicides, increased victim safety and autonomy, and decreased fear and anxiety for victims and their children (Bastomski et al. 2019).

Inspired by the US model, the *European Family Justice Centres Alliance (EFJCA)*[11] adapts this integrated approach to Europe. While many European countries maintain specialised victim support units within police departments in collaboration with social and health services, few have fully adopted the centralised model. Belgium and the Netherlands stand out as pioneers, piloting EFJC structures where services co-locate and collaborate—though prosecution offices and courts involvement remains rare (Groen et al. 2017).

ZSM Project for ordinary criminal cases

The *ZSM Project*[12] in the Netherlands represents a significant innovation in applying a person-centred approach and a multi-agency method to handling ordinary criminal cases.

Launched as a pilot in 2011 and implemented nationwide by 2013, ZSM aims to handle ordinary criminal cases quickly, ideally within a day, to reduce court backlogs and improve outcomes for both suspects and victims. It integrates police, prosecutors, victim support services, probation, and child protection agencies into one location to enable rapid, collaborative decision-making. ZSM prioritises speed, simplicity, selectiveness, and collaboration. Cases are triaged to determine whether they can be resolved immediately or require traditional court proceedings (ASAP service). Resolutions can involve penalty orders, conditional dismissals, or referrals to support programmes. Sanctions are applied immediately, ensuring direct assistance for the victim while any potential compensation is arranged simultaneously. By 2016, nearly 189,000 cases were processed this way, with the Public Prosecutor's Office settling directly around half of them (OECD-OPSI 2019; ZSM 2016).

However, ZSM is not without its criticisms. The use of penalty orders by prosecution offices—where defendants must actively contest decisions to avoid automatic convictions—raises concerns about fairness, particularly for those without legal representation. This process can lead to long-term consequences, such as a criminal record, which can impact employment opportunities. While ZSM aims to prioritise the interests of victims, the urgency to resolve cases may undermine their emotional closure and sense of justice. Victim Support Netherlands (SHN) works to ensure that victims are heard and compensated, but some still feel disadvantaged by the speed of the process (Jakobs & Van Kampen 2014). Despite these challenges, ZSM serves as a notable example of multi-agency cooperation in delivering justice. Ongoing refinements are necessary to balance the need for quick resolutions with the principle of fairness, ensuring suitable outcomes for both convicted and victims.

Constraints

Therefore, despite international guidelines and legislation in most countries emphasising the importance of addressing people's concrete needs in delivering justice services and widespread political awareness about the need for profound reforms in justice organisations in that direction, there has been no comprehensive and widespread implementation of practices in this area. Currently, development focuses on managing family and domestic violence along with related issues such as gender-based violence, sexual harassment, and abuse. This is a significant starting point, but it still requires further support, as it often remains a highly fragmented and short-lived phenomenon (Amato & Carnevali 2022).

Certainly, reforming the justice system to align with this new paradigm is challenging. The structure, functioning, rites, and ceremonies associated with the traditional concept of "justice" are difficult to alter. It focuses on compliance with legal requirements, which naturally leads to formalism and the implementation of the principle of legality, which has shaped the judicial system and its operations over time. This principle also includes the judiciary's impartiality, which has likely created a barrier due to fears of potential compromises from cooperation with other institutions or potentially could privilege victims over accused rights (Luparia Donati & Della Torre 2021). Moreover, even the affirmation of the principle of efficiency in public administration, which affected all public services and, consequently, the justice system (despite its unique characteristics), has not changed this attitude. The justice system has evolved along a relatively coherent trajectory, increasingly prioritising timeliness, effectiveness, and efficiency in its organisation and decision-making, yet often in a self-referential way. Although public-management reforms have introduced a greater emphasis on the user, this has largely been framed from a top-down perspective that privileges institutional priorities over individuals' needs, which are foundational to legitimacy. A genuinely person-centred reform, therefore, requires a deeper change, including a reconfiguration of the relationship among key justice values, such as those identified by Contini and Mohr (2008) in legality, efficiency, and legitimacy.

Furthermore, the concrete experiences associated with this potential transformation remain limited and highly specific, even given the intrinsic organisational constraints of multi-agency case management. Indeed, multi-agency case management cuts across various cultural and power dynamics, legal barriers, organisational boundaries, role ambiguity, leadership deficiencies, communication gaps, financial misalignments and limitations (Baldwin 2024). Declarations of cooperation are insufficient without structured governance, shared procedures and accountability (Webb 1991). Services based on a multi-agency organisational model must work genuinely together (Harwin et al. 1999). This requires a well-defined structure for organisation, coordination, and governance that are hard to achieve. Victims of domestic violence, for example, need fair trial, as well as security and protection—along with essential resources such as housing and living, legal aid, psychological support, job training, healthcare, even for their children—before, during, and after the criminal proceedings (Vinton & Wilke 2014).

So, even with a clearly defined structure for managing cases requiring special attention, experience shows that adopting an expert role known as a boundary-spanner is essential for facilitating integration among the different agencies. This role can guide and support victims through the complexities of this network of organisations and the challenges encountered at the beginning and throughout the judicial process. Boundary-spanners must possess comprehensive knowledge of the procedures and their impacts on the victim's life; they act as the glue that holds everything together—as coordinators, facilitators, negotiators, problem-solvers, and analysts. Their contribution to agency integration is so crucial that they can be seen as key figures in modern public service management and integration (Van Meerkerk & Edelenbos 2018).

Conclusion. Effecting victim- and person-centred reforms to enhance the legitimacy of justice

Although widespread legislation has now placed the victim of crime back at the centre of criminal proceedings, daily justice practice highlights the persistence of procedural formalism and compartmentalised case management, which leads to the displacement of justice goals for victims, particularly for those with protection needs.

The current system, primarily focused on procedural correctness and formal outcomes, often neglects the needs of victims, resulting in secondary and repeated victimisation. To address this, a paradigm shift from a system-centred approach to a person-centred one is required. The justice system must be restructured not only to deliver legal sound decisions made by a truly independent judge, with formal fairness, and within a reasonable time—this is certainly fundamental—but also to genuinely "take care", not only "take charge", of the individuals involved and their needs. This entails adopting multi-agency approaches to organise cooperation, where judicial, social, and health services work together to ensure victims are treated fairly and care, with a focus on restoring their rights in practice, which means ensuring safety and dignity for the present and for their future.

International organisations have already recognised this need, promoting people-centred justice, but implementation remains inconsistent in everyday practice. The gap between legislative provisions, international and domestic institutional efforts, and actual enforcement presents a significant challenge. While the legal framework is developing, organisational and institutional structures are lagging behind, resulting in a justice system that remains largely self-referential. To bridge this gap, systematic policy measures are necessary to integrate person-centred and multi-agency approaches across all levels of justice service delivery.

Therefore, the challenges of multi-agency work are significant but not insurmountable. Positive examples and effective organisational mechanisms exist. Experiences show that establishing collaboration rules, cooperation mechanisms, interoperable procedures, "one-stop" services, targeted pooled funding, and boundary-spanning roles can alleviate these constraints and barriers. Sustainable solutions require treating inter-organisational cooperation as a core skill. Future initiatives in the justice reform process must focus on investing in relational infrastructure across public and private institutions and on redefining success by the real impact on individuals' needs rather than agency-specific outputs.

The practical adoption of this new paradigm is essential to make the justice service effective, ensuring seamless support and care for victims and indeed for others involved in the justice experience—throughout and beyond criminal proceedings. This aligns with the proper dynamics of social relations in mature democracies, which now require justice to be recognised by people not only as legal but also as legitimate.

Notes

1 The chapter analyse countries with a tradition of liberal democracy and their justice system. In particular, it is focused mainly on studies coming from international organizations, European countries, the United States, Canada, Australia, and New Zeeland. This work was carried out using a qualitative, interdisciplinary, and comparative approach: documentary study of legislation and literature and case study analysis.

2 What Merton would describe as the classic means-ends inversion in the actions of bureaucracies (1949).

3 Access to justice is an established yet evolving concept referring to the capacity of individuals to obtain effective remedies for grievances through formal or informal justice institutions, in accordance with human rights principles. It is one of the fundamentals of the rule of law and justice legitimacy. The scientific debate framed access to justice as a condition for making rights effective, addressing social, economic, and procedural barriers to achieve fair, effective, and meaningful remedies for their justice problems through institutions and services that are accessible, understandable, affordable, and responsive to their needs (Cappelletti & Garth 1978; Tyler 1990, 2003, 2006; Sandefur 2008; Farrow 2014; Semple 2022; Pilliar 2023).

4 This contribution intentionally excludes restorative justice, as it does not operate within criminal justice system rules directly but offers an alternative or complementary approach. Restorative justice, applied voluntarily with consent, seeks to repair harm through mediation or reconciliation, requiring offenders to acknowledge responsibility, understand damage caused, pursue moral and economic reparation, and commit to preventing recurrence. Victims gain empowerment, tangible satisfaction, and reduced anxiety from offender-directed remedies. (Zahr 1990; Johnstone & Van Ness 2007; Umbreit & Peterson Armour 2011). However, it must be avoided in cases involving victims with special protection needs, as prohibited, for example, by the Istanbul and Lanzarote Conventions of the Council of Europe, to prevent secondary victimisation. Therefore, restorative justice is not discussed here.

5 This contribution deliberately excludes experiences of victims' participation in determining punishment, as they are misleading for the argument. In the United States and some South American countries, victim participation in sentencing has produced serious procedural distortions and weakened defence rights (Crawford & Goodey 2000). Some scholars, therefore, criticise the renewed centrality of victims. Yet it is not rational to let such excesses, which concern a distorted decision-making process, undermine advances in affirming victim rights before proceedings (protection), during them (treatment) and after their conclusion (effectiveness).

6 Public services have long faced similar challenges. A notable example is the healthcare system, which has been working towards a new perspective for some time. The journey towards viewing patients not merely as numbers associated with specific illnesses but as whole individuals requiring a holistic approach has been lengthy and complex (Kelley & Hurst 2006). This shift in thinking can be summarised in one key sentence: patients now expect to be treated with care rather than focused solely on their healing.

7 This approach is also defined as "people-centred", a term more appropriate for identifying a collective interest rather than an individual one. Alternatively, it is referred to as "users-centred", a phrase more frequently employed for technology-based public services.

8 See: https://digitalguides.undp.org/guide/people-centred-justice-and-security accessed Dec 1st, 2025.

9 See: https://www.europarl.europa.eu/about-parliament/en/democracy-and-human-rights/fundamental-rights-in-the-eu/ensuring-access-to-justice accessed Dec 1st, 2025.

10 See: https://www.familyjusticecenter.org accessed Dec 1st, 2025.

11 See: https://www.efjca.eu accessed Dec 1st, 2025.

12 *ZSM—Zorgvuldig Snel Maatwerrk* means well-considered, fast, and tailormade. See: https://www.om.nl/onderwerpen/veelvoorkomende-criminaliteit-zsm (Presentation in

English https://www.cep-probation.org/wp-content/uploads/2018/10/DG15Presentation-ZSM-A-S-A-P-25-11-2015-def.pdf) accessed Dec 1st, 2025.

References

Achinonu, K., A. Adeniran, M. de Langen, & D. Steven (2023). *From Justice for the Few to Justice for All: A Model for High-Ambition Action to Deliver the SDGs [Challenge Paper]*. United Nations Foundation. https://unfoundation.org/what-we-do/issues/sustainable-development-goals/a-model-for-people-centered-justice

Amato, R., & D. Carnevali (2022). The Calm after the Storm? The Tricky Path to Restoring the Enjoyment of Individual Rights in Intimate Partner Violence Cases. *Oñati Socio-Legal Series*, 12(3), 443–477. https://doi.org/10.35295/osls.iisl/0000-0000-0000-1272

Atkinson, M., M. Jones, & E. Lamont (2007). *Multi-Agency Working and Its Implications for Practice: A Review of the Literature*. CfBT Education Trust. https://www.nfer.ac.uk/media/qy5hccud/mad01.pdf

Atkinson, M., A. Wilkin, A. Stott, P. Doherty, & K. Kinder (2002). *Multi-Agency Working: A Detailed Study* (LGA Research Report 26). National Foundation for Educational Research. NFER Slough. https://www.nfer.ac.uk/publications/multi-agency-working-a-detailed-study/?utm_source=chatgpt.com

Baldwin, R. (2024). A Systems Approach Analysis of a Multi-Agency Response to Domestic Abuse. In: Adisa, O., & Bond, E. (Eds.), *Tackling Domestic Abuse and Sexual Violence*. Palgrave Studies in Victims and Victimology. Palgrave Macmillan, Cham. https://doi.org/10.1007/978-3-031-58600-2_2

Bastomski, S., A. Ricks, E. Henderson, & J. Yahner (2019). *Evaluation of the Polyvictimization Initiative at the Queens Family Justice Center.* Urban Institute. https://calio.dspacedirect.org/items/7b9cab64-aed9-46e0-8b08-d82c5db151b3

Berman, G., & Feinblatt, J. (2001). Problem-Solving Courts: A Brief Primer. *Law & Policy*, 23, 125–140. https://doi.org/10.1111/1467-9930.00107

Cappelletti, M., & B. Garth (1978). Access to Justice: The Newest Wave in the Worldwide Movement to Make Rights Effective. *Buffalo Law Review*, 2, Spring, 181–292. https://digitalcommons.law.buffalo.edu/cgi/viewcontent.cgi?article=1927&context=buffalolawreview

Carroll, C.P. (2021). The 'Lottery' of Rape Reporting: Secondary Victimization and Swedish Criminal Justice Professionals. *Nordic Journal of Criminology*, 22(1), 23–41. https://doi.org/10.1080/2578983X.2021.1900516

Cheminais, R. (2009). *Effective Multi-Agency Partnerships, Putting Every Child Matters into Practice*. SAGE Publications. https://doi.org/10.4135/9781446288269

Christie, N. (1977). Conflicts as Property. *British Journal of Criminology*, 17(1), 1–15. https://doi.org/10.1093/oxfordjournals.bjc.a046783

COE & FRA (2016). *Handbook on European Law Relating to Access to Justice*. Council of Europe (COE) & European Union Agency for Fundamental Rights (FRA). Publications Office of the European Union. https://www.echr.coe.int/documents/d/echr/Handbook_access_justice_ENG

Contini, F., & R. Mohr (2008). *Judicial Evaluation: Traditions, Innovations and Proposals for Measuring the Quality of Court Performance*. VDM Verlag Dr Mueller. https://library.ddtc.co.id/en/collections/judicial-evaluation-traditions-innovations-and-proposals-for-measuring-the-quality-of-court-performance_4303

Crawford, A., & J. Goodey (2000). *Integrating a Victim Perspective within Criminal Justice*. Routledge. https://doi.org/10.4324/9781315252179

Drapkin, I., & E. Viano (1974). *Victimology*. Lexington Books. https://scispace.com/papers/victimology-a-new-focus-volumes-i-theoretical-issues-in-3fjq6lniwg

Eley, S. (2005). Changing Practices: The Specialised Domestic Violence Court Process. *The Howard Journal of Criminal Justice*, 44, 113–124. https://doi.org/10.1111/j.1468-2311.2005.00361.x

Farrow, T. C. W. (2014). What Is Access to Justice? *Osgoode Hall Law Journal*, *51*(3), 957–988. https://doi.org/10.60082/2817-5069.2761

FJCA (2025). *Family Justice Center Framework Impact Report 2025*. Family Justice Center Alliance (FJCA). https://www.allianceforhope.org/resources/family-justice-center-framework-impact-report-2025

Foster-Fishman, P. G., B. Nowell, & H. Yang (2007). Putting the System Back into Systems Change: A Framework for Understanding and Changing Organizational and Community Systems. *American Journal of Community Psychology*, 39, 197–215. https://doi.org/10.1007/s10464-007-9109-0

Freiberg, A. (2001). Problem-Oriented Courts: Innovative Solutions to Intractable Problems? *Journal of Judicial Administration*, *11*(8), 8–27. https://www.researchgate.net/publication/292693494_Problem-oriented_courts_Innovative_solutions_to_intractable_problems

García-Hombrados, J., M. Martínez-Matute, & C. Villa (2024), Specialised Courts and the Reporting of Intimate Partner Violence: Evidence from Spain. *Journal of Public Economics, Elsevier*, 239(C). https://doi.org/10.1016/j.jpubeco.2024.105243

Gilling, D. (1994). Multi-Agency Crime Prevention in Britain: The Problem of Combining Situational and Social Strategies. *Crime Prevention Studies*, 3(8), 231–248. https://popcenter.asu.edu/sites/g/files/litvpz3631/files/library/CrimePrevention/Volume_03/08_gilling.pdf

Groen, B., P. Franck, & D. Simons (2017). *One Safe Place for Hope and Empowerment: Development of Multidisciplinary Approach of Domestic Violence, Child Abuse and Sexual Abuse in European Family Justice Centers*. Éditions Politeia SA. https://www.politeia.be/fr_BE/shop/one-safe-place-15822?search=Groen&order=name+asc#attr=613

Gwinn, C., G. Strack, S. Adams, R. Lovelace, & D. Norman (2007). The Family Justice Center Collaborative Model. *Saint Louis University Public Law Review*, 27, 79–120. https://scholarship.law.slu.edu/plr/vol27/iss1/6/

Harwin, N., G. M. Hague, & E. M. Malos (1999). *The Multi-Agency Approach to Domestic Violence: New Opportunities, Old Challenges*? Whiting & Birch. https://www.whitingbirch.net/cgi-bin/indexer?product=1861770022

Head, B. W., & J. Alford (2015). Wicked Problems: Implications for Public Policy and Management: Implications for Public Policy and Management. *Administration & Society*, 47(6), 711–739. https://doi.org/10.1177/0095399713481601

Holtug, N. (2022). Prioritarianism and Population Ethics. In: Arrhenius, G. et al. (Eds.), *The Oxford Handbook of Population Ethics*. Oxford Handbooks. https://doi.org/10.1093/oxfordhb/9780190907686.013.12

IDLO (2023). *Diverse Pathways to People-Centred Justice* (Report of the Working Group on Customary and Informal Justice and SDG16.3). International Development Law Organization (IDLO). https://www.idlo.int/sites/default/files/2023/other/documents/diverse_pathways_to_people-centred_justice_sept_2023.pdf

Jakobs, P., & P. Van Kampen (2014). Dutch 'ZSM Settlements' in the Face of Procedural Justice: The Sooner the Better? *Utrecht Law Review*, 10(4), 73–85. https://doi.org/10.18352/ulr.291

Johnstone, G., & D. W. Van Ness (2007). *Handbook of Restorative Justice*. Willan Publishing. https://doi.org/10.4324/9781843926191

Kelley, E., & J. Hurst (2006), *Health Care Quality Indicators Project: Conceptual Framework Paper* (OECD Health Working Papers, No. 23). OECD Publishing. https://doi.org/10.1787/440134737301

Kool, R. S. B., & G. Verhage (2014). The (Political) Pursuit of Victim Voice: (Comparative) Observations on the Dutch Draft on the Adviesrecht. *Utrecht Law Review*, 10(4), 86–99. https://ssrn.com/abstract=2529960

Koshan, J. (2014). Investigating Integrated Domestic Violence Courts: Lessons from New York. *Osgoode Hall Law Journal*, 51(3), 989–1036. https://doi.org/10.60082/2817-5069.2762

Luparia Donati, L., & J. Della Torre (2021). Victims of Crime in the Area of Freedom, Security and Justice. In: Iglesias Sanchez, S., & M. Gonzales Pasqual (Eds.), *Fundamental Rights in the EU Area of Freedom, Security and Justice*. Cambridge University Press. 328–349. https://doi.org/10.1017/9781108769006.019

Marshall, T. F. (1996). The Evolution of Restorative Justice in Britain. *European Journal on Criminal Policy and Research*, 4(4), 21–43. https://doi.org/10.1007/BF02736712

May, L., & P. Morrow (eds.) (2012) *Procedural Justice* (2nd ed.). Routledge. https://philpapers.org/rec/MAYPJ

Merton, R. K. (1949). *Social Theory and Social Structure*. Free Press. https://archive.org/details/dli.ernet.6060/mode/2up

Moore, S. (2009). *Two Decades of Domestic Violence Courts: A Review of the Literature*. Center for Court Innovation. https://www.innovatingjustice.org/wp-content/uploads/2009/12/DV_Court_Lit_Review.pdf

OECD (2021). *OECD Framework and Good Practice Principles for People-Centred Justice*. Organisation for Economic Co-operation and Development. OECD Publishing. https://www.oecd.org/en/publications/oecd-framework-and-good-practice-principles-for-people-centred-justice_cdc3bde7-en.html

OECD-OPSI (2019). *New Multi-Agency Collaboration: Pulling Together as a Recipe for Better Justice*. OECD-OPSI Observatory of Public Sector Innovation. https://oecd-opsi.org/innovations/new-multi-agency-collaboration-pulling-together-as-a-recipe-for-better-justice/?utm_source=chatgpt.com

Parti, K. (2024). Preventing Revictimization in Sexual Assault Investigations: Personal Security and Trauma-Informed Case Management. *Journal of Applied Security Research*, 19(1), 147–158. https://doi.org/10.1080/19361610.2022.2161799

Pilliar, A. (2023). Toward Justice Epidemiology: Outlining an Approach for Person-Centred Access to Justice. *Dalhousie Law Journal*, 46(1), 1–32 https://digitalcommons.schulichlaw.dal.ca/cgi/viewcontent.cgi?article=2218&context=dlj

Pycroft, A., & D. Gough (Eds.) (2010). *Multi-Agency Working in Criminal Justice: Control and Care in Contemporary Correctional Practice*. Policy Press. https://policy.bristoluniversitypress.co.uk/multi-agency-working-in-criminal-justice-1

Robinson, A. (2008). *Measuring What Matters in Specialist Domestic Violence Courts* (Paper 102). Cardiff University School of Social Sciences. https://orca.cardiff.ac.uk/id/eprint/25567/1/wp102.pdf

Sandefur, R. L. (2008). Access to Civil Justice and Race, Class, and Gender Inequality. *Annual Review of Sociology*, 34 339–358. https://papers.ssrn.com/sol3/papers.cfm?abstract_id=1142098

Sebba, L. (1996). *Third Parties: Victims and the Criminal Justice System*. Ohio State University Press. https://www.ncjrs.gov/pdffiles1/Digitization/176312NCJRS.pdf

Sedra, M. (2022). *A People-Centred Approach to Security* [Contributing paper]. United Nations Development Programme; Folke Bernadotte Academy. https://www.undp.org/sites/g/files/zskgke326/files/2022-06/The People-Centered Approach to Security.pdf

Semple, N. (2022). Better Access to Better Justice: The Potential of Procedural Reform. *The Canadian Bar Review*, 100(2), 344–381. https://cbr.cba.org/index.php/cbr/article/download/4772/4523/5213?utm_source=chatgpt.com

Semple N. (2025). Welfarism and Person-Centred Justice. *Canadian Journal of Law and Society*, 39(3), 580–598. https://doi.org/10.1017/cls.2024.22

Sen, A., & B. Williams (1982). *Utilitarianism and Beyond*. Cambridge University Press. https://www.utilitarianism.com/beyond.pdf

Shapland, J., J. Willmore, & P. Duff (1985). *Victims in the Criminal Justice System*. Gower.
Simmons, C. A., K. H. Howell, M. R. Duke, & G. Beck (2016). Enhancing the Impact of Family Justice Centers via Motivational Interviewing: An Integrated Review. *Trauma Violence Abuse*, 17(5), 532–541. https://doi.org/10.1177/1524838015585312
Souhami, A. (2008). Multi-Agency Practice: Experiences in the Youth Justice System. In: Green, S., E. Lancaster, & S. Feasey (Eds.), *Addressing Offending Behaviour: Context, Practice and Value* (1st ed.). Willan. https://www.routledge.com/Addressing-Offending-Behaviour-Context-Practice-and-Value/Green-Lancaster-Feasey/p/book/9781843922438
Soulez-Lariviere, D., & C. Eliacheff (2007). *Le temps des victimes*. Albin Michel. https://doi.org/10.3917/chev.027.0251
Stewart, J. (2010). *Specialist Domestic Violence Courts: What We Know Now, How Far Have Australian Jurisdictions Progressed* (Topic Paper no.20). The University of New South Wales: Australian Domestic and Family Violence Clearinghouse, University of New South Wales. http://www.adfvc.unsw.edu.au/PDF files/Topic Paper 20.pdf
Sullivan, H., & C. Skelcher (2002). *Working Across Boundaries: Collaboration in Public Services*. Palgrave Macmillan. https://doi.org/10.1007/978-1-4039-4010-0
Thibaut, J., & L. Walker (1975). *Procedural Justice: A Psychological Analysis*. Erlbaum.
Tompson, L., J. Belur, & K. A. Jerath (2021) Victim-Centred Cost–Benefit Analysis of a Stalking Prevention Programme. *Crime Sci*, 10, 21. https://doi.org/10.1186/s40163-021-00158-5
Tyler, T. R. (1990). *Why People Obey the Law*. Yale University Press.
Tyler, T. R. (2003). Procedural Justice, Legitimacy, and the Effective Rule of Law. In: Tonry, M. (Ed.), *Crime and Justice—A Review of Research* (Vol. 30). University of Chicago Press. 283–357. https://doi.org/10.1086/652233
Tyler, T. R. (2006). *Why People Obey the Law*. Princeton University Press. https://press.princeton.edu/books/paperback/9780691126739/why-people-obey-the-law?srsltid=AfmBOoqoUGyDmVhL4sVJnolwSoh4qs9nSkA_Xr3sJAfIHqjM5ekFMfUu
Tyler, T. R. (Ed.) (2007). *Legitimacy and Criminal Justice: An International Perspective*. Russell Sage Foundation. https://www.russellsage.org/sites/default/files/92860txt.PDF
Umbreit, M., & M. Peterson Armour (2011). *Restorative Justice Dialogues: An Essential Guide for Research and Practice*. Springer Publishing Company. https://doi.org/10.1891/9780826122599
UNODC (2022). *People-Centred Crime Prevention and Criminal Justice Reform* (Global Programme) United Nations Office on Drugs and Crime (UNODC) Publications. https://www.unodc.org/documents/justice-and-prison-reform/LegalAid/A2J/Global_Programme_on_People-Centred_Crime_Prevention_and_Criminal_Justice.pdf
Van Dijk, J. (2013). Victim-Centred Restorative Justice. *Restorative Justice*, 1(3), 426–429. https://doi.org/10.5235/20504721.1.3.426
Van Meerkerk, I., & J. Edelenbos (2018). *Boundary Spanners in Public Management and Governance*. Edward Elgar Publishing. https://doi.org/10.4337/9781786434173
Vinton, L., & D. Wilke (2014) Are Collaborations Enough? Professionals' Knowledge of Victim Services. *Violence against Women*, 20(6), 716–729. https://doi.org/10.1177/1077801214539857
Webb, A. (1991). Coordination: A Problem in Public Sector Management. *Policy and Politics*, 19(4), 229–241. https://doi.org/10.1332/030557391782454188
Zahr, H. (1990). *Changing Lenses: A New Focus for Crime and Justice*. Herald Press. https://archive.org/details/changinglensesne00zehr/mode/2up
Zedner, L. (1994). Victims. In Maguire, M., R. Morgan, & R. Reiner (Eds.), *The Oxford Handbook of Criminology*. Clarendon Press. http://www.paccoa.org.au/uploads/2/0/2/4/20249739/the_oxford_handbook_of_criminology__mike_maguire_rod_morgan_robert_reiner___z-lib.org_.pdf

ZSM (2016). *ASAP ZMS Den Haag*. https://www.om.nl/onderwerpen/veelvoorkomende-criminaliteit-zsm (Presentation in English https://www.cep-probation.org/wp-content/uploads/2018/10/DG15Presentation-ZSM-A-S-A-P-25-11-2015-def.pdf)

Websites

https://digitalguides.undp.org/guide/people-centred-justice-and-security
https://www.efjca.eu
https://www.europarl.europa.eu/about-parliament/en/democracy-and-human-rights/fundamental-rights-in-the-eu/ensuring-access-to-justice
https://www.familyjusticecenter.org
https://www.om.nl/onderwerpen/veelvoorkomende-criminaliteit-zsm (Presentation in English https://www.cep-probation.org/wp-content/uploads/2018/10/DG15Presentation-ZSM-A-S-A-P-25-11-2015-def.pdf)

7

VOICES OF SEPARATED MOTHERS ON FAMILY AND CHILDREN'S JUSTICE

Patrícia Branco, Paula Casaleiro, and Luciana Sotero

Introduction

Family law?

In the last decades, rapid and profound changes have reshaped family law across most Western countries. These transformations—including the displacement of marriage as the primary legal link to families and a shift towards rule-like statutory provisions (Dewar 2000)—reflect a global bearing rather than a merely local phenomenon. However, by using the Portuguese case as a lens, this chapter explores how these global tendencies create systemic challenges, highlighting the ongoing debates about gender biases and the risk of further victimisation when the pursuit of children's welfare is entangled in a rigid judicial framework.

The late transformations in what concerns family law include the displacement of marriage as the central concept linking law to families and the growth in the importance of other concepts such as cohabitation or parenthood; a reduced reliance on discretionary decision-making to more rule-like statutory provisions; and the fragmentation of the family law system itself (Dewar 2000). These transformations—including the displacement of marriage as the central concept linking law to families, a shift from discretionary decision-making towards more rule-like statutory provisions, and the increasing fragmentation of the legal system itself (Dewar 2000)—reflect a global bearing. This broader institutional landscape has given rise to a new form of institutional displacement, where the lived realities of families are often overshadowed by standardised legal procedures. Rather than being isolated incidents, these challenges represent a widespread tendency within modern justice systems to prioritise procedural efficiency over the substantive well-being and rights of those they serve. It is within this global context of shifting legal paradigms and

DOI: 10.4324/9781003752974-10

increasing institutional complexity that specific local responses must be examined. Such an analysis must simultaneously consider the ongoing debates about gender biases, the effectiveness of legal standards, and the paramount importance of children's welfare in custody decisions while uncovering how these elements may inadvertently contribute to cycles of institutional victimisation.

Outline of the chapter

This chapter thus argues that family law transformation is marked by sometimes contradictory tendencies, especially in what concerns parenthood. To do so, we will look at family law transformations in what concerns child custody/parenthood, using the Portuguese case as an example. Even though our analysis stems from the Portuguese case, we propose this should be read as an example of a broader tendency, not limited to the local context but reflecting, instead, a global bearing.

The second argument is that law, and especially courts, may be the only hope of finding common ground and breaking the conflict cycle and hence empowering families, especially mothers and their children. We hence examine the perceptions of mothers on child custody procedures and how their experiences reflect the main transformation tendencies and contradictions, identifying key challenges and potential solutions. Based on interviews with ten mothers involved in family court conflicts, the study highlights their experiences and offers suggestions for improvement. In this case, their views demonstrate that change may emerge from local reclamations that challenge institutional shortcomings and offer pathways for resolution.

Despite criticisms that legal involvement may exacerbate family disputes and that the legal system often fails to deliver meaningful justice to those who go through it—criticisms often reinforced by governments seeking to cut costs in the family justice system (Dewar 2000)—in situations of deep familial conflict, such as child-related proceedings, courts may still offer the most viable resolution.

Modern families and family law

Family dynamics in Western countries, particularly in Europe, have undergone significant change in the last decades. We have been witnessing a growing sentimentalisation, privatisation, secularisation and individualisation of families that transformed people's family lives into more plural and diverse combinations, particularly when compared with much more homogeneous models from the past (Ariès 1988; Badinter 1985; Beck & Beck-Gernsheim 2002; Shorter 1995; Singly 2006, 2011). In fact, from the 1970s onwards, demographic indicators have portrayed profound changes in family behaviours and gender relations in European countries: the decrease in nuptiality and Catholic marriages, the increase in cohabitation and the divorce rate, the fall in fertility and the increase in births outside marriage, and the growth of new forms of family organisation (e.g. same-sex parents). Portugal was no exception, marked by a late and accelerated modernisation process, compared to other Western countries, following the democratic revolution in 1974, and by the intersection between change and continuity, the modern and the traditional in family and parental relationships (Almeida 2003; Portugal 2014; Torres 2002; Wall 2005).

Alongside the transformations of family dynamics, the interconnected transformation of family and children's law has been analysed in light of, on the one hand, the tendency towards privatisation, deinstitutionalisation, and contractualisation of family relationships and the de-juridification and de-juditialisation of family conflicts between adults, and, on the other hand, the tendency towards the (re)publicisation and expansion of family law, particularly in matters concerning children's rights (Pedroso & Branco 2008; Pocar & Ronfani 2008). The state increases its intervention in the sphere of the family in the name of child protection, following a logic of social control (Donzelot 1977; Singly 2006; Théry 1989).

So how does the law currently "see" families? In many jurisdictions, the answer to that question used to lie in marriage: marriage was the chief means by which families were linked to law (Dewar 2000). Marriage conferred a status, in the sense of rights not available to others, in private and public law. There was only limited recognition of other forms of family organisation as having legal significance. Traditionally, marriage was the primary legal link to family, conferring specific rights and recognition. However, the rise of non-marital cohabitation and increasing numbers of children born outside of marriage have challenged this. This has led to an increased importance of parenthood as a legal status attributed to: a) the elimination of legal distinctions between children born from marital and non-marital relations and the concept of illegitimacy; and b) parenthood as a means for family law to maintain legal and economic ties between parents and children after separation, creating a sense of continuity despite the instability of adult relationships.

If legal parenthood is indeed becoming a more critical status, we must question its meaning in the twenty-first century. While historically anchored in biological ties within a two-parent framework, contemporary realities challenge this simplicity. Assisted reproductive technologies (ARTs) sever the direct link between genetics and legal parentage, introducing complexities like gestational surrogacy and multi-party parentage. Furthermore, culturally diverse understandings of family and child-rearing practices expose the limitations of a singular, biologically based legal model. This raises crucial questions about who can be recognised as a parent, what rights and responsibilities are entailed, and how legal frameworks can adapt to reflect the evolving landscape of family formation. And it leads to one of the fundamental and traditional questions at the heart of family law; that is, how family law and family courts determine parents' responsibilities towards children?

Discretionary decision-making to more rule-like statutory provisions

From the 1970s onwards, there was a movement towards the "best interests of the child" standard in legal decision-making concerning children (like custody, adoption, and welfare), representing a shift away from prioritising parental rights (automatic paternal right or maternal preference) towards focusing on the child's overall well-being (Neale & Smart 1997; Sottomayor 2011). Historically, legal decisions often favoured biological parents or applied rigid rules. Over time, recognition that children have independent rights and needs that should be paramount grew. The United Nations Convention on the Rights of the Child (UNCRC), adopted in 1989, solidified this principle internationally, stating in Article 3 that the best interests of the child shall be a primary consideration in all actions concerning children. This led to the development and increasing adoption of the "best interests" principle—a standard that requires decision-makers to consider a range of factors related to the child's physical, emotional, educational, and psychological needs to determine the most beneficial outcome for them.

In the last years, there have been ongoing debates and refinements regarding the "best interests" principle's application, interpretation, and the weight given to various factors in determining what truly constitutes a child's best interests. Although the underlying principle is to prioritise the child's welfare above all other considerations, and despite the apparent discretion involved, there has been a noticeable trend towards reducing or eliminating judicial discretion in family law decision-making.

The dominant paradigm is that the child's best interests require the involvement of both parents, and, consequently, the recognition of the child's "right" to contact with both parents, which led to the implementation of joint custody laws or the principle of shared parental responsibility. In Portugal, child custody proceedings are also governed by the principle of the best interests of the child, as enshrined in Article 1905 of the Portuguese Civil Code and reinforced by international instruments such as the United Nations Convention on the Rights of the Child. Portuguese law distinguishes between two primary models of parental responsibility: shared custody (*responsabilidades parentais conjuntas*) and exclusive custody (*responsabilidades parentais exclusivas*). Since 2008, the general rule, pursuant to Article 1906 of the Civil Code, is that parental responsibilities continue to be exercised jointly after the end of the couple's relationship. Exclusive custody may be granted when it is deemed contrary to the child's interests for one of the parents to participate in key decisions, typically in cases involving abuse, neglect, or extreme conflict, requiring a reasoned decision.

These developments indicate a move away from granting decision-makers (primarily judges) a legally authorised choice and towards specifying outcomes more precisely. This growing prescriptiveness is particularly evident in policies aimed at maintaining the relationship between children and the non-resident parent after separation or divorce, suggesting a strong normative push to ensure the continuation of both parental ties (Novales 2012; Boyd 2003). This shift towards reduced discretion is occurring not only as a matter of desire to maintain relations between children but also as a matter of costs. According to Dewar (2000), discretion is increasingly seen as being too costly; it makes decision-making harder and time-consuming and, therefore, more expensive to settle cases.

Research method and data collection

An exploratory qualitative research design was adopted to investigate the joint exercise of parental responsibilities from the perspective of divorced mothers. Employing a naturalistic and narrative approach, the study sought to understand the meanings individuals give to phenomena—such as actions, perceptions, and experiences—within their social contexts (Ormston et al. 2003). Data was collected using a convenience sampling strategy, implemented through snowball sampling (Clark 2017). Initial participants were recruited via personal contacts of the research team. These participants—mothers engaged in family court proceedings concerning disagreements over joint parental responsibility—were then invited to recommend other potential participants who might also be eligible and willing to participate. The initial contact was made electronically via email and included detailed information about the study, an informed consent document, and a background questionnaire. Accordingly, a sample was obtained comprising participants who were both accessible and met the following inclusion criteria (Aspers & Corte 2019): (i) divorced or separated mothers for a period of at least three years; (ii) with at least one child aged 18 or under; (iii) whose parental responsibility arrangement had been subject to judicial intervention; and (iv) who were engaged in joint parental responsibilities. The requirement of a minimum three-year post-divorce/separation period was based on evidence suggesting that, after approximately two years, negative emotions associated with the divorce and patterns of high conflict tend to decline (Maccoby & Mnookin 1992). This criterion aimed to ensure that participants were reflecting on their experiences at a potentially less emotionally intense stage, thereby safeguarding their well-being and avoiding recollections from a period of heightened conflict.

Sample and data collection

The final sample consisted of ten mothers, aged between 38 and 52 years ($M = 46.7$; $SD = 4.61$). Six participants had completed secondary education (12th grade), while the remaining four held higher education qualifications. Most mothers lived with their children; only three reported cohabiting with a new partner. Regarding the focal child in the study (i.e. aged 18 or under), the mean age was 12.8 years ($SD = 2.86$). The duration of the relationships with the children's fathers ranged from 5 to 22 years ($M = 12.0$; $SD = 5.10$), with separations or divorces occurring between 2006 and 2020.

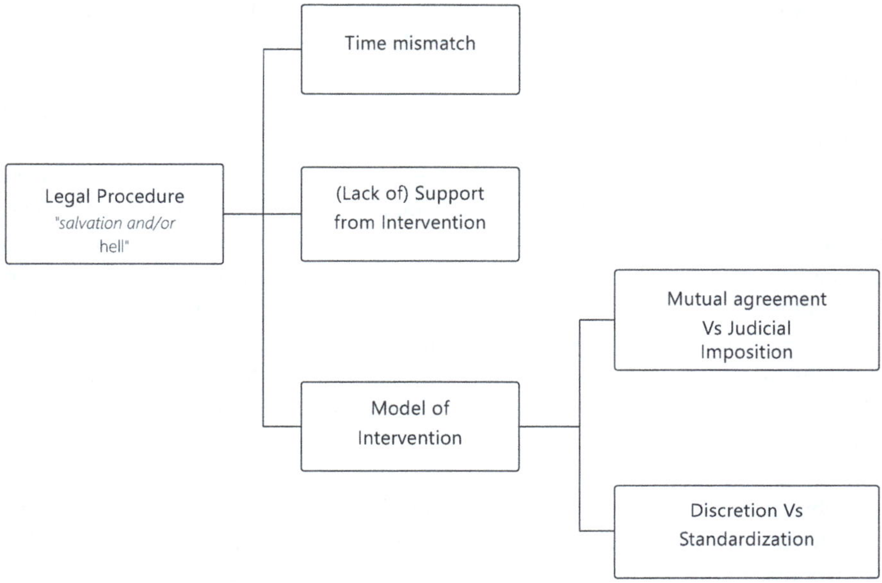

FIGURE 7.1 Map of Themes and Subthemes: Judicial Process Experience

The interview data was analysed using thematic analysis, a method that facilitates the identification, analysis, and interpretation of recurring patterns of meaning in qualitative data (Braun & Clarke 2006). In the initial phase, the research team engaged in data familiarisation through transcription and repeated readings of the interview material. Subsequently, two team members independently generated an initial set of codes. These codes were then reorganised and clustered into broader thematic categories and subcategories. The formation of themes was based on conceptual relevance rather than frequency of occurrence. This step involved the entire research team, fostering collaborative discussion, critical reflection, and refinement of the proposed themes. Finally, the themes were reviewed for coherence, and the interview transcripts were revisited to verify the relevance and accuracy of the themes and corresponding illustrative excerpts. The labels for themes and subthemes were refined through successive team meetings. This process led to the identification of four major themes that illustrate the mothers' experiences, which are visually represented in the thematic map (see Figure 7.1).

Results: mothers' voices on family justice

The Portuguese legal system approach to child custody prioritises, as we have mentioned, the child's well-being; it promotes the involvement of both parents and parental cooperation, and it integrates mediation and conciliation as fundamental tools for conflict resolution. This child-centred and conciliatory framework aims not only to foster better outcomes for families but also to alleviate the burden on judicial resources. In this section, we will explore the interviewed mothers' perspectives on these topics. In other words, we will analyse the perceptions of mothers on how the child procedures occurred and how their experiences reflect the main transformation tendencies and contradictions.

Court proceedings are seen as a last resort and experienced both as threatening and as essential. This duality echoes findings in the literature on "procedural justice" (e.g. Tyler 2006), which emphasises that perceptions of fairness often depend as much on the process as on the outcome. The emotional toll of court appearances—described by one participant as "like walking into a noose"—also resonates with studies showing that formal justice mechanisms may exacerbate feelings of anxiety and loss of control (e.g. Smart 1989; Morrison 2015). Nevertheless, the judiciary is seen not only as a decision-maker but also as a protective agent, especially for enforcing rights.

> Obviously, no one wants to go through this kind of court proceedings, because it ends up being draining, psychologically exhausting, but if I have to advise other women, I still say they should do it. It's a right of the children, and children come above everything.
>
> *[Ent.2]*

> I don't like going to court, it's horrible, I always feel like I'm walking into a noose. Because we must deal with injustice, with the possibility that it won't be fair to us or to our children. . . . But it can also be the only salvation when there's nothing else left . . . So, it's a mix of emotions—we only go to court when we've tried everything and nothing else works.
>
> *[Ent.10]*

Contrary to widespread critiques of judicial inefficiency, some participants described court intervention as timely and decisive, particularly in enforcing parental responsibilities and financial duties. They argue that the court acted swiftly, resolving disputes effectively while maintaining simplicity throughout the process. They praise the role of both the judge and the Public Prosecutor's Office, believing they fulfilled their duty to protect children's best interests.

> The response from the Court was very swift, and it forced [him the father]—that's the word—to make the required payments. . . . The divorce process itself, from submitting the documents to finalising it, was very fast. It took one month. It was a very quick process. I don't know if it's always like this, but in my case, it was very, very fast.
>
> *[Ent.2]*

> Regarding family matters, I felt supported by the Public Prosecutor's Office.
>
> *[Ent.8]*

Despite these positive experiences, other participants conveyed strong emotional distress tied to their Court's experience. The judicial environment is often described as impersonal and even intimidating, leading to a profound sense of institutional displacement that, instead of providing resolution, ends up aggravating the psychological strain of family conflict.

> The court, in fact, was frightening for me. The image I have is "Avoid court as much as possible, try to resolve things outside, or just go there to get the stamp". Because that whole process. . . . I did not have a good experience with the court.
>
> *[Ent.4]*

A recurring theme among interviewees is the paradoxical temporal experience of the justice system: while the overall duration of litigation is perceived as excessive, the actual time allocated for hearings is seen as too brief for a fair assessment.

> The ten minutes I spent inside the courtroom didn't seem enough to assess the case. I think that maybe, instead of ten minutes, if I had been there for twenty, talked a bit, seen how things worked, yes. I think the issue is the time. . . . We waited six months—it's a long time.
>
> *[Ent.1]*

> The court takes years to deliver anything, and in the meantime, people have to go on with their lives and find ways to solve their problems.
>
> *[Ent.4]*

Many linked judicial inefficiencies to systemic factors such as the overwhelming number of cases, high workloads, and disruptions caused by the COVID-19 pandemic.

> It took many years, four and a half years of litigation. . . . The hearings were constantly postponed. There was always something—either the judge went on medical leave, or it was court holidays.
>
> *[Ent.4]*

> We went to court on [5], and then on the 13th, the lockdown started, the courts closed, everything closed because of Covid, deadlines were cancelled, and a series of things were cancelled. My case was going to be cancelled too—in other words, it would be frozen as of that date, and R. was no longer required to leave the house within the forty-something days. Why? Because him leaving the house wasn't considered an urgent matter.
>
> *[Ent.8]*

Despite family courts being designed as a last resort, many parents find themselves reliant on judicial intervention. As seen above, some participants praise the efficiency and assertiveness of court rulings—particularly regarding child support enforcement or when other avenues fail. However, many also describe the judicial process as emotionally taxing, bureaucratically slow, and, at times, detached from the realities of their family lives.

Mutual consent versus judicial imposition

Portuguese family law, like many other legal systems, emphasises negotiated settlements over adversarial litigation in family disputes. The goal is to reduce conflict and reach consensual agreements, which are then subject to legal validation. However, when agreements break down or are deemed unacceptable by public authorities, judicial intervention is mandatory.

As shown in the experience of one participant, the process of obtaining official approval from the Civil Registry Office can trigger judicial proceedings. Below, ENT 1 describes how an initial agreement was refused by the civil registry office, prompting automatic referral to court:

> the request was denied at the Registry Office, then, if we don't reach an agreement within X days, it goes to the Juvenile Court of the District. . . . We waited six months [for the Juvenile Court procedure]—that's a long time.
>
> *[Ent.1]*

Thus, the bureaucratic rejection of parental agreements may unintentionally escalate conflicts by forcing parties into adversarial legal processes.

Simultaneously, while family court procedures include provisions encouraging parties to settle, namely through mandatory or suggested mediation, this mechanism appears ineffective in high-conflict cases. Participants expressed frustration with the mismatch between mediation ideals and the emotional or communicative reality of entrenched disputes:

> There was one time in court when they sent us to family mediation. It was also kind of absurd. I think that scenario could be fantastic. But when you're facing a brick wall, it's very hard, no matter who tries what. . . . Poor mediator [laughs] . . . but anyway, we went. Nothing came of it. . . . And sometimes even psychologists I went to would say, "you Parents need to get along." Sure, but that is not happening. I need help solving things beyond that scenario.
>
> *[Ent.4]*

Discretion versus prescription

Interviewees' experiences suggest growing tension between the legal principle of prioritising the best interests of the child and the increasing standardisation of judicial decision-making. Many mothers expressed concern that judicial discretion is being reduced in favour of generalised rules, particularly the presumption of shared custody, often at the expense of individual case assessment, failing to attend to the concrete needs of children and families.

Mothers expressed scepticism towards what they perceive as a de facto policy promoting shared custody—often alternating weekly residence—regardless of circumstances such as geographical distance or parental availability:

> I know that, for example, judges now always push hard for shared custody. Even if the mother doesn't want it or isn't comfortable with it, there's always pressure, always.
>
> *[Ent.10]*

> I never understood how a court granted shared custody when he was living abroad. I never understood that, I swear. I think there are, in fact, a lot of very strange judicial decisions.
>
> *[Ent.4]*

When courts are perceived as indifferent to lived realities, this leads to some scepticism regarding institutional fairness. Participants voiced doubts about the professionalism of judges and prosecutors, describing decisions as superficial and emotionally detached.

> My opinion about judges is that you have to be very lucky. . . . The court-appointed experts, too . . . it depends, some are more neutral than others. But I always felt a bit of . . . not favouritism, but my impression was that . . . they just wanted to get rid of the case. That's what I felt. Like it was an inconvenient case.
>
> *[Ent.6]*

> But the court was a nightmare in this process. I had to write a 22-page statement with dates, episodes, everything, and it's like no one read it.
>
> *[Ent.4]*

Participants also highlighted how lack of time and attention may undermine the capacity of professionals to understand the case or protect children's rights. The perception that professionals do not read case files or lack the time to understand them contributes to a sense of abandonment and dehumanisation:

> I know it's not easy, because there are surely thousands of cases and they're overwhelmed. But what I felt was that no one ever read anything. No one read the case, no one knew who I was, who he was. It was all very superficial.
>
> *[Ent.6]*

> The truth is that, since there's no time, they don't actually read the case files. And then, when they make decisions, they don't know the context. And that's very complicated.
>
> *[Ent.4]*

This sense of arbitrary or superficial decision-making is also reflected in broader criticisms of how justice is delivered. Some participants criticised the limited role played by courts, especially in verifying whether shared custody arrangements truly serve the best interests of the child. The interviewees underscored the need for follow-up mechanisms to evaluate whether the arrangement was functioning and serve the child's best interests.

> Even though, stupidly, the court granted us shared custody—not physical, but shared responsibilities. And that was it, the case ended there, and there was no further follow-up.
>
> *[Ent.6]*

> I felt the court's role was very superficial. Basically, it was just to validate an agreement that already existed—there was already shared custody, a visitation schedule. . . . There was never any attempt by the court to understand whether the conditions were appropriate. Nothing. It was just a validation.
>
> *[Ent.4]*

This tension between individualised justice and standardised procedures is not new. As Dewar (2000) noted, discretion is increasingly seen as too costly, time-consuming, and unpredictable. Several interviewees implicitly reinforce this idea by pointing out the pressure on courts to "clear files" rather than to defending children's rights:

> I think the one who represents the children there is the Public Prosecutor, but I didn't always feel they were representing the children. Not always. . . . Sometimes it felt like they were just there to sign papers.
>
> *[Ent.4]*

This generalised sense of prescription and lack of care points to a justice system that many perceive as prioritising formal closure over substantive protection of the child's best interest.

Conclusion

The legal procedures in cases involving children evoke diverse perspectives from those who experience it first-hand. The findings highlight the complexity and ambivalence of experiences in the Portuguese family justice system, particularly among parents involved in high-conflict separations. Participants express strong ambivalence towards the judiciary, simultaneously needing its intervention and distrusting some of its methods.

Participants highlight moments of institutional support—particularly from judges and the Public Prosecutor's Office—as well as systemic barriers such as delays, poor communication, and understaffing. The pandemics' effects (court closures, procedural delays) further exposed the fragility of timely justice, reinforcing broader concerns about children's access to rights and justice during crises (Branco & Casaleiro 2020).

While legal and policy frameworks promote amicable settlement and mediation, the participants' narratives suggest a dissonance between normative expectations and lived experiences. The emphasis on mediation as an alternative to litigation is a core principle in family law reform across many jurisdictions. However, mediation can be ineffective—or even harmful—when one party adopts a rigid or dominating stance. This reflects critiques in feminist legal scholarship and empirical studies (e.g. Beck & Sales 2001) that question the neutrality of mediation in high-conflict or coercive relationships. The metaphor of the "wall" used by the interviewees aptly illustrates the perception that mediation, and even judicial encouragements to "reach an agreement", are unrealistic when power imbalances or deep mistrust exist. These insights reinforce the need for a more nuanced application of mediation that considers power dynamics, echoing Parkinson's work (2010).

The emotional dimension of the testimonies—from fear and confusion to indignation and hope—reveals that justice is not merely procedural or legalistic but also deeply affective. For many participants, seeking justice was not merely a legal endeavour but a deeply moral and affective journey. Parents framed their actions not only in terms of individual rights but also in relation to broader responsibilities—especially towards their children. Expressions such as "I did it for my daughter" or "children come above everything" suggest an ethics of care that transcends the adversarial logic of litigation.

Finally, the mothers' testimonies provide ethnographic evidence of a legal culture that increasingly prefers clear rules (e.g. shared custody) over contextual discretion—a shift that risks overlooking children's actual needs. When mothers feel their agency is undermined by a bureaucratic system, they experience a profound sense of institutional displacement. This lack of recognition may act as a site of further victimisation, highlighting the urgent need for a justice system that, instead of silencing these voices, strives to give meaning and voice back to those it serves. Thus, the findings reinforce the need for reforms that prioritise sensitivity, accessibility, and individualised consideration in cases involving children. The testimonies collected in this study represent a denunciation of difficulties, but also a local reflection on justice, a way to give meaning and voice back to those who have their lives entangled with the justice system. Their views underscore the need for a more differentiated approach to family justice that accounts for the emotional, moral, and relational dimensions of conflict. Legal reforms should reconsider the blanket promotion of mediation and "amicable solutions" in cases characterised by entrenched power asymmetries or psychological abuse. Furthermore, efforts should be made to streamline procedures and reduce delays—particularly in post-separation arrangements involving children—to mitigate the emotional and financial burdens on litigants.

These testimonies not only denounce systemic failures but also offer a tangible pathway for redress. By embracing an ethics of care that prioritises the child's lived reality over standardised rules, the justice system can move from being a site of institutional displacement to a partner in breaking the cycles of family and institutional conflict.

References

Almeida, A. N. de (2003). Família, conjugalidade e procriação: valores e papéis. In J. Vala, M. V. Cabral, & A. Ramos (Eds.), *Valores sociais: mudanças e contrastes em Portugal e na Europa* (pp. 50–94). Lisboa: Imprensa de Ciências Sociais.

Ariès, P. (1988). *A criança e a vida familiar no Antigo Regime*. Lisboa: Relógio D'Água.

Aspers, P., & Corte, U. (2019). What is qualitative in qualitative research. *Qualitative Sociology, 42*, 139–160.

Badinter, E. (1985). *O amor incerto: história do amor maternal do séc. XVII ao séc. XX*. Lisboa: Relógio D'Água.

Beck, C. J. A., & Sales, B. D. (2001). *Family mediation: Facts, myths, and future prospects*. Washington, DC: American Psychological Association.

Beck, U., & Beck-Gernsheim, E. (2002). *Individualization: Institutionalized individualism and its social and political consequences*. London: Sage Publications.

Boyd, S. (2003). *Child custody, law, and women's work*. Don Mills, ON: Oxford University Press Canada.

Branco, P., & Casaleiro, P. (2020). Acesso das crianças ao direito e à justiça. In *Palavras para lá da pandemia: cem lados de uma crise*. Coimbra: CES. https://ces.uc.pt/publicacoes/palavras-pandemia/?lang=1&id=30084.

Braun, V., & Clarke, V. (2006). Using thematic analysis in psychology. *Qualitative Research in Psychology, 3*(2), 77–101.

Clark, R. (2017). Convenience sample. In G. Ritzer (Ed.), *The Blackwell encyclopedia of sociology* (pp. 1–2). Hoboken, NJ: Wiley & Sons.

Dewar, J. (2000). Family law and its discontents. *International Journal of Law, Policy and the Family, 14*(1), 59–85. https://doi.org/10.1093/lawfam/14.1.59.

Donzelot, J. (1977). *La police des familles*. Paris: Les Éditions de Minuit.

Maccoby, E. E., & Mnookin, R. H. (1992). *Dividing the child: Social and legal dilemmas of custody* (1st ed.). Cambridge, MA: Harvard University Press.

Morrison, F. (2015). All over now? The ongoing relational consequences of domestic abuse through children's contact arrangements. *Child & Family Law Quarterly, 27*(1), 35–50.

Neale, B., & Smart, C. (1997). Experiments with parenthood? *Sociology, 31*(2), 201–219. http://doi.org/10.1177/0038038597031002002.

Novales, T. P. (2012). Ruptura familiar y coparentalidad: un análise comparado. In T. P. Novales (Ed.), *La custodia compartida a debate* (pp. 45–76). Madrid: Dykinson.

Ormston, R., Spencer, L., Barnard, M., & Snape, D. (2003). The foundations of qualitative research. In J. Ritchie, J. Lewis, C. M. Nicholls, & R. Ormston (Eds.), *Qualitative research practice: A guide for social science students and researchers* (pp. 1–23). London: Sage.

Parkinson, L. (2010). *Family mediation: Appropriate dispute resolution in a new family justice system*. London: Bloomsbury Publishing.
Pedroso, J., & Branco, P. (2008). Mudam-se os tempos, muda-se a família: as mutações do acesso ao direito e à justiça de família e das crianças em Portugal. *Revista Crítica de Ciências Sociais, 82*, 53–83.
Pocar, V., & Ronfani, P. (2008). *La famìlia e il diritto*. Roma-Bari: Editori Laterza.
Portugal, S. (2014). *Famílias e redes sociais: ligações fortes na produção de bem-estar*. Coimbra: Almedina.
Shorter, E. (1995). *A formação da família moderna*. Lisboa: Terramar.
Singly, F. de (2006). *Uns com os outros: quando o individualismo cria laços*. Lisboa: Instituto Piaget.
Singly, F. de (2011). *Sociologia da família contemporânea*. Lisboa: Edições Texto & Grafia.
Smart, C. (1989). *Feminism and the power of law*. London: Routledge.
Sottomayor, M. C. (2011). *Regulação do exercício das responsabilidades parentais nos casos de divórcio*. Coimbra: Almedina.
Théry, I. (1989). "The interest of the child" and the regulation of the post-divorce family. In C. Smart & S. Sevenhuijsen (Eds.), *Child custody and the politics of gender* (pp. 78–99). London: Routledge.
Torres, A. (2002). *Casamento em Portugal: uma análise sociológica*. Oeiras: Celta Editora.
Tyler, T. R. (2006). *Why people obey the law* (2nd ed.). Princeton, NJ: Princeton University Press.
Wall, K. (2005). *Famílias em Portugal*. Lisboa: Imprensa de Ciências Sociais.

8

VICTIMISATION IN HOMICIDE IN INTIMATE RELATIONSHIPS

Challenges to the law

Madalena Duarte and Ana Oliveira

Introduction

Homicides committed in an intimate context continue to represent a concerning issue worldwide, accounting for an estimated 13.5% of all homicides (Stöckl et al., 2013). In such cases, women comprise approximately 82% of the victims (WHO, 2013), making it evident that gender inequality is a significant predictor of the occurrence of this crime (Gartner et al., 1990; Heirigs & Moore, 2018; UNODC, 2019). This data sheds light on the political significance of the concept of "femicide", as defined by Diana Russell in 1976 (Russell, 2008) and further developed by various authors to refer to the murders of women in an intimate context (Gartner et al., 1992; Smith, 2019).

In Portugal, despite several legislative amendments, official data indicates that, between 2014 and 2019, 111 women were murdered in an intimate context (Polícia Judiciária, 2020). More recently, in 2023, 22 people were murdered in similar circumstances, of whom 17 were women (PGR, 2024). Although official statistics for 2024 are not yet available, the NGO UMAR, through its Observatory of Murdered Women, which collects information based on press analysis, reports that in 2024, 16 women were murdered in an intimate context (UMAR, 2024). In six of these cases, complaints had already been filed with the police for domestic violence, and in three others, death threats had been reported (UMAR, 2024). In the light of this data, we developed a research project[1] to examine the legal response—juridical and judicial—to cases of domestic violence that have ended in homicide and homicide attempts, the most extreme scenario of violence that occurs in intimate relationships. We draw on the recommendations of the European Court of Human Rights, which, in its analysis of specific cases, has emphasised that, regardless of governments' legislative efforts, there appears to be insufficient commitment to take

DOI: 10.4324/9781003752974-11

appropriate action to address domestic violence. Therefore, it is essential that states take all necessary measures to protect vulnerable victims, including the establishment and effective implementation of a system for the prosecution of all forms of domestic violence (*Z.B. v. Croatia*, No. 47666/13, decided on 11 July 2017). The Court has underscored the crucial role of law and criminal justice practices in preventing intimate partner homicide. This is the starting point for the analysis we propose to develop in this chapter.

Drawing on a qualitative study of 163 Portuguese judicial decisions concerning intimate partner homicide, the chapter explores the hypothesis that more effective upstream legal interventions in cases of domestic violence could prevent fatal violence. Furthermore, it briefly examines which subjective factors may contribute to the existing shortcomings of the law in addressing these crimes.

Secondary victimisation and displacement

The sociology of law has long challenged the assumption that law constitutes a neutral and objective mechanism for the protection of social order. Bourdieu's (1986) conception of law as a relatively autonomous field is particularly useful in understanding how legal professionals—judges, prosecutors, and lawyers—exercise symbolic power through the interpretation of legal categories such as intent, credibility and evidence. Likewise, Foucault's (1977) analyses of punishment and disciplinary power illuminate how law functions not merely to sanction unlawful conduct but also to classify subjects, normalise behaviour and produce hierarchies of legitimacy within penal institutions. Feminist legal theories extend these insights by demonstrating how law is deeply shaped by gendered assumptions that structure both substantive offences and procedural norms. Scholars such as MacKinnon (1987) and Smart (1989) have shown that the purported objectivity of criminal law often conceals male-centred understandings of harm, consent, agency and rationality, which become embedded in evidentiary rules, prosecutorial decision-making, and judicial reasoning. These tensions are especially evident in the criminal law's engagement with gender-based violence. While the criminalisation of domestic violence, for instance, marks a significant normative shift, empirical feminist research consistently demonstrates the limits of penal responses. Lagarde's (2008) reflection on femicide in fact acknowledges the responsibility of the state and its institutions—through action and/or omission—in the persistence of these crimes.

Criminal proceedings and legal actors frequently prioritise forms of evidence and narrative coherence that are poorly equipped to capture the lived realities of gender-based violence. As a result, common features of these forms of violence, including ongoing abuse, delayed reporting, and victims' emotional ambivalence towards the perpetrator, are often misunderstood or misinterpreted. As a result, survivors are often required to translate complex experiences of harm into legally intelligible accounts that conform to narrow penal scripts, while structural patterns of inequality and power remain marginal to legal evaluation. Feminist literature thus emphasised that, in cases of gender-based violence, interaction with the justice system can generate further violence (Epstein & Goodman, 2019). Secondary victimisation manifests itself, for example, when the victim is subjected to procedures that question her morality, minimise her suffering or devalue the abuse she has suffered (Duarte, 2023). The way in which certain questions are asked—about the victim's intimate life, lifestyle, emotional choices or reputation—reinforces the idea that the victim may have contributed to the violence suffered, creating additional symbolic damage. There are several dynamics that contribute to this process. First of all, there is a lack of understanding on the behalf of legal actors regarding the dynamics of violence in intimate relationships, compounded by myths about this type of violence. These are socially available scripts of shared cultural stories, expectations, and prejudices that shape how violence against women is understood and that are reflected in the legal treatment of these cases (Bartels et al., 2012; Easteal et al., 2019). Moreover, courts and trials emerge as a symbolic act of production and reproduction of narratives and images that reflect on social gender relations (Bumiller, 1990). More specifically, the legal culture is filled with cisnormative gender stereotypes that influence how the court interprets male and female behaviour in domestic violence cases (e.g., Hunter & Cowan, 2007; Kafka et al., 2019). These stereotypes are often incorporated into legal language, the assessment of witness credibility and how the relational context is legally framed. Thus, judicial interpretation does not occur in a vacuum, or in a context of neutrality (Smart, 1989), but in a cultural environment saturated with normative expectations about femininity and masculinity. Within these scripts, the aggressor is often portrayed as emotionally fragile due to the end of the relationship, while the woman is described as unstable, provocative or morally reprehensible (Duarte, 2023). Although the victim is not formally blamed, these practices construct an implicit narrative of shared responsibility (Grembi et al., 2024; Mulla et al., 2019).

Intersectional feminist analyses further show how these narratives about gender interact with race and class to shape differential experiences of criminalisation and protection within the penal system (Crenshaw, 1991). Lugones' thinking (2007), for instance, invites us to consider how the law inherits and reproduces a colonial system that imposes rigid categories of gender, sexuality, and family. As a consequence, these scripts are also shaped by gender coloniality (Lugones, 2007), which homogenises women's experiences, presenting them as a coherent and universally oppressed group, regardless of specific historical, cultural, and socioeconomic contexts (Mohanty, 1984).

In this sense, we can speak of legal displacement as one of the central mechanisms of symbolic reproduction of gender inequality in the judicial sphere. The lived experience of violence is translated into abstract legal language, which privileges certain types of harm and specific forms of evidence, while marginalising others. In the following sections, we will seek to analyse the consequences that this displacement process can have on the lives of women who are victims of violence.

The Portuguese legal context

Public concern regarding domestic violence emerged belatedly in Portugal, compared to other European countries, as a result of an oppressive political dictatorship that curtailed women's rights in both public and private spheres. In the original version of the 1966 Civil Code, women had a status inferior to that of men, although this was presented as an indication of "greater liberalisation in the legal treatment of the married woman, reflected in the elimination of certain unfounded limitations on her capacity" (Gersão, 2006, p. 234). In what concerns gender violence, it is paradigmatic the existence, until 1976, of the 1886 Penal Code, which stipulated in Article 372, that a husband who killed his wife in flagrante delicto of adultery would only be subject to six months' exile outside the district. This mitigating circumstance was only extended to the wife if the husband's mistress was kept by him as a "permanent and maintained" guest in the marital home.

With the advent of democracy in 1974, it became clear the need to combat discriminatory norms against women in various spheres of social life. There was a growing awareness of the need for penal law intervention in areas previously closed to it, such as the private sphere, leading to the classification of the crime of "mistreatment of minors, subordinates, or between spouses" in the 1982 Penal Code. This was a significant milestone in the history of combating domestic violence, as it recognised domestic violence as a criminal offence. But it was only in 2007 that the Penal Code introduced the legal autonomisation of the crime category entitled "Domestic Violence". Despite this autonomisation, under Portuguese law, there is no specific legal category for homicides occurring within intimate relationships or the domestic sphere. The Portuguese legal system retains the concept of "Homicide" as the basic legal type for crimes against life, with the legislator asserting that it is "sufficient to characterise the essential content of the illicit nature of all crimes against life, since it concerns the same legal good: the life of another person" (Monteiro, 2012, p. 20). The law outlines mitigating circumstances that allow for the reduction of penalties in cases of simple homicide, referred to in this case as privileged homicide (Article 133 of the Penal Code), a legal figure that, for a long time, was understood as "crimes of passion", as it refers to situations in which a person kills another "due to a comprehensible violent emotion". The law also foresees aggravating circumstances. The qualification of homicide corresponds to a situation that merits greater condemnation from both the community and the legal order. Thus, although simple homicide is the basic type for other crimes against life, the Penal Code provides for circumstances that lead to an aggravation of guilt, resulting in "Qualified Homicide" (Article 132 of the Penal Code). To better understand the circumstances that reveal special blameworthiness or perversity and thus denote a higher degree of culpability on the part of the perpetrator, the Penal Code defines "standard examples", serving as guidance for what can qualify a homicide. These include, among others, the relationship of intimacy with the victim(s), coldness of spirit, premeditation, and persistence in the crime.

With the inclusion, in 2007, of the standard example specifying that homicides occurring within the context of "marital relationships and analogous situations" reveal special blameworthiness or perversity, it becomes evident that the victim–perpetrator relationship plays a significant role in determining the motivations for the crime (Dawson & Gartner, 1998), making it essential to understand the causes and dynamics surrounding victimisation.

Methodology

The study of criminal sentencing has remained a prominent area of scholarly inquiry for several decades. The 1980s and 1990s were particularly significant, marked by notable improvements in data quality, methodological rigour, and theoretical development. Research in this field has continued to flourish throughout the 2000s, with sentencing-related studies frequently appearing in leading criminology and criminal justice journals (Ulmer, 2012, p. 2). Following the sentencing studies, the study that serves as the foundation for this chapter is based on a content analysis of 163 legal cases (first-instance decisions) regarding homicides in intimate relationships, from the 23 Portuguese judicial districts. Each presiding judge in these districts was asked to provide a list of cases related to homicide, qualified homicide, and privileged homicide, occurring in intimate relationships, whether committed or attempted, that were adjudicated in the respective district court. Although the methods of case identification varied across districts and did not fully encompass the scope of this crime, the sample provided is significant. The survey of the 163 cases took place between April 2019 and April 2021. The analysis of these legal cases was carried out using a matrix with predefined categories, including not only those variables more often used in sentencing studies, such as the initial prosecution charge, the judge's final decision, the mode of conviction and the length of the sentence (Dawson, 2016), but also other elements that might significantly influence judicial outcomes (e.g., Grant, 2010). So, we also included in our analysis categories such as the characterisation of the case, the dynamics of the intimate relationship, the offender's characteristics, the victim's characteristics and the reasoning supporting the trial decision.

Taking into consideration the legal framework, one might assume that all homicides and femicides occurring in an intimate relationship would automatically be qualified. However, the standard examples were not applied automatically. Given the indeterminate nature of concepts such as special blameworthiness or perversity (Brito, 2007), the qualification depended on the assessment of the specific case by the judge, considering the guilt of the perpetrator. The case analysis showed that 38 defendants were convicted of homicide, although the Public Prosecutor had sought the legal classification of the offence as murder (qualified homicide).

As in previous studies (e.g., Agra et al., 2015; Matias et al., 2020), our analysis also points to women being more vulnerable to this crime, with men constituting the overwhelming majority of perpetrators. In fact, within the analysed cases, there were only 22 female defendants: 15 were sole defendants and seven were co-defendants. These data underscore the gendered nature of this crime, which, in our view, calls into question the adequacy of the legal term "homicide".

In all, 85 of the victims in these cases died, and in the same event, seven people related to the victims (children, partners, parents) were also killed. Additionally, 33 victims sustained serious, disabling, and permanent injuries.

The conviction rate in these cases is high, standing at 89%. It should be noted that, within the sample of cases analysed, in addition to convictions for homicide, 25% of cases also resulted in convictions for domestic violence. Regarding the penalties applied, in the 75 cases of committed homicides, the sentences ranged from 9 years (applied to one defendant) to 24 years in prison (sentence applied to two male defendants and one female defendant). In the cases of attempted homicides, sentences ranged from 2 years and 8 months to 15 years in prison.

A critical dimension observed in these legal cases was that, in approximately 40% of the cases, the victim had previously filed complaints against the aggressor—in many cases, more than once—most of which were subsequently dismissed. In 11 cases, there were multiple complaints for conduct fitting the crime of domestic violence, in a persecutory and threatening context; in 9 cases, the formalisation of the complaint occurred a few days before or on the very day of the homicide or attempted homicide; in 4 cases, the defendant had already been convicted of the crime of domestic violence (against the same victim) and was serving, at the time of the event, a suspended prison sentence, subject to compliance with duties and rules of conduct; in 4 cases, the defendant had already completed a provisional suspension of the case or was currently undergoing it; and, in at least 7 cases, the defendant was subject to coercive measures that involved restricting contact between him and the victim. Also, in the study conducted by Agra et al. (2015), in about half of the cases analysed, there were previous episodes of violence against the victim, and in about 18% of the cases, these were known to criminal police authorities. In summary, there seems to be evidence that a significant number of homicide cases (committed or attempted) are preceded by a history of violence, whether reported or concealed, which would have warranted more effective institutional intervention.

The institutional violence continuum

Liz Kelly (1987) sought to demonstrate how violence against women is part of a broader, complex and "continuum" web of abuse and coercion. The way in which these different types of violence occur in time and space is not always correctly understood by legal institutions and, as mentioned earlier, can lead to processes of revictimisation. We argue that this process is part of an institutional violence continuum.

Our empirical analysis highlights three factors that contribute to the ineffective intervention of the legal system in these homicide cases with prior formal complaints: the shortcomings in the requirement to produce evidence; the ineffectiveness of the protective measures and the penalties imposed, which failed to address the needs of both special and general prevention; and the idea of shared responsibility. In all these factors, it was possible to identify subjective factors regarding the victim and the dynamics of violence.

Lack of evidence: displacement of the victim to witness

The procedural analysis revealed that several cases of homicide (attempted or consummated) show a trajectory marked by multiple complaints from the victim (or other people/entities), many of which were dismissed or, when charges were brought, resulted in acquittals (see Case 1). According to the most recent Portuguese justice statistics (SGMAI, 2022), out of a total of 94.282 investigations into domestic violence opened between 2015 and 2021, 78.3% resulted in case closures, 16.9% in an indictment, and 4.8% in a provisional suspension of proceedings. Looking at the reasons for closing cases, it can be concluded that 79.2% resulted from a lack of evidence.

Case 1

The defendant, 47 years old, a farmer with no criminal record, and the victim, 44 years old, unemployed, had been married for 27 years. They had five children, aged between 26 and 12 years. The defendant and the victim lived with their two youngest daughters, aged 12 and 14. The defendant had problems with alcoholism, "and, when drunk, he became aggressive and violent". For some time, they had not been living together as a couple, although they shared the same house. The victim had suffered physical and psychological abuse since the beginning of the marriage, having reported some incidents to the criminal police. The case is linked to several processes and inquiries related to domestic violence or similar matters, including reports of assaults by the defendant against the victim and their eldest son, as well as reports of assaults by the victim against the defendant. Out of a total of eight criminal proceedings, all were archived, either due to the withdrawal of the complaint or because the victim and children did not provide statements.

In 2013, the police arrested the defendant in the act, and he was charged with the crime of domestic violence and attempted qualified homicide. He was placed in preventive detention and was later sentenced for attempted homicide (unqualified) to four years in prison and for domestic violence to two years and nine months. The homicide was not considered qualified, as stated in the ruling: "Although the victim was the defendant's wife, everything indicates that this was caused by the defendant's state of intoxication, in the context of yet another heated marital argument, fueled by insults from both parties, with the victim herself initiating the assault. This state and motivational context of the defendant, when interpreted from the perspective of the average man, cannot be considered irrelevant". In a cumulative sentence, the defendant was sentenced to five years in prison, suspended under a probationary regime (in this case, mandatory alcoholism treatment), and an accessory sentence prohibiting contact with the victim. Two years later, still under the suspended sentence, four new inquiries were recorded against the defendant for new violent acts against the victim.

This case shows that the collection of evidence is critical in domestic violence cases, where testimonial accounts often constitute the primary, if not the sole, source of proof, typically confined to the victim's and perpetrator's statements. As a result, the victim is frequently positioned as the central, and at times the sole, means of proof. This reliance on victim testimony has several problematic implications. First, it increases the risk of acquittal if the victim is unwilling or unable to testify at trial. As Buzawa and Buzawa (1990) observe, legal actors often struggle to understand the reluctance of victims to accuse their aggressors, despite a broad consensus that this is the victim's right and should not be subject to change. This recognition underscores the aforementioned need to establish evidentiary support through alternative sources, thereby ensuring that the burden of proof does not rest entirely on the victim.

Moreover, it creates room for greater subjectivity in assessing the credibility of testimony (Duarte, 2023), or at the very least broadens the scope of such assessment and amplifies its potential implications within the legal process. In this regard, the court decisions analysed reveal inconsistencies in how judges assess the victim's credibility. For instance, some judges value the victim's calmness, while others interpret unease as a sign of truthfulness. Likewise, some judges prioritise detailed statements, whereas others dismiss details as unimportant:

> *The victim provided a statement that seemed to us to be impartial, credible, and free from contradictions. The impartiality of her testimony was also reflected in the fact that she did not intend to give an absolutely accurate account of the events that took place (Case no. 702/06.8GBCNT, Coimbra District Court).*
>
> *The victim made statements in an impartial, objective and detailed manner, in an account and posture that made her testimony and what was reported in it deserve the full credibility of the Court. (Case no. 614/14.1TAPTM, Faro Judicial Court)*

As illustrated by these cases from the Coimbra and Faro Courts, a victim's credibility often hinges upon subjective factors, such as perceived impartiality, emotional responses, and the level of detail provided. This variability has significant implications for legal outcomes, as the interpretation of the testimony can either substantiate or undermine the case, depending on a judge's appreciation and criteria. The inherent subjectivity of the decision-making process challenges the consistency of credibility standards but, more importantly, underscores the critical role these assessments play in the legal process, particularly when victim testimony constitutes the primary basis for establishing the facts.

Protective measures and penalties: displacing protection towards insecurity

The appropriate application of coercive measures in the most diverse crimes remains one of the most pressing challenges for the justice system. From the procedural analysis we carried out, in cases of homicide or attempted homicide, 73% of the defendants were ordered to be held in custody. In around 8% of cases, the defendants were subject to the single measure of a term of identity and residence.[2] However, while pre-trial detention is the preferred measure of coercion in the vast majority of homicide cases, whether attempted or consummated, the same does not hold true for cases of domestic violence.

Protecting the victim when they report a crime of domestic violence is fundamental, because most women formally report their aggressor not only to immediately achieve a level of safety (Garcia & McManimon, 2011) but also to prevent the violence from escalating. The presence of violence in a relationship seems to be the most important risk factor for intimate partner homicide (Nicolaidis et al., 2003; Smith, 2019), irrespective of the victim's gender. Some data indicate that 65%–80% of homicide victims in an intimate relationship had previously been assaulted by the partner who killed them (Nicolaidis et al., 2003). The literature (e.g., Abrunhosa et al., 2021; Dobash & Dobash, 2015; Smith, 2019; Baldry & Magalhães, 2018) identifies several additional determining factors in assessing the risk of a situation of violence: the victim's intention/attempt/initiative to separate from the aggressor; escalation of the violence and/or its intensity; emotional/psychological instability on the part of the aggressor; the existence of a pattern of behaviours based on stalking/intimidation/control or threats of suicide; the victim's seeking of support services or reporting of the violence; among others. The procedural analysis conducted clearly demonstrated that the escalation of violence, separation, and reporting were key triggers for femicide and that the authorities failed to assess this risk effectively.

Case 2

The victim, 37 years old, worked in a café, and the defendant, 48 years old, was unemployed. He had a criminal record (offenses against physical integrity) and had already been imprisoned three times. They had been in a de facto relationship for nine months.

In the past three months, the defendant had become more aggressive. A week before the assaults at the victim's workplace, the defendant left the house where he had been living with the victim. Since then, he had been harassing her, sending her intimidating messages and seeking her out in the café, where he assaulted her three times.

The victim filed a complaint for domestic violence. Between this complaint (December 2012) and the attempted murder of which she was the victim (9 March 2013), she called the police several times. In December 2012, the defendant went to the café and punched her, restraining her and pushing her against the wall, until he was stopped by people present. During the month of January, the defendant went to the same café three more times, assaulting the victim both physically and verbally, and the police were called to the scene each time. Following these incidents, the defendant was charged and given an identity and residence order.

On 9 March 2013, the defendant returned to the victim's café with a machete. He entered the café, closed the door, removed the machete and struck the victim on the head. He then struck the victim's son (aged 18) on the head as he tried to help his mother. The police arrived, and both the victim and her son were hospitalised.

The defendant would be sentenced to eight years and six months in prison for attempted aggravated homicide, attempted simple homicide (involving the victim's son) and domestic violence.

Cases such as this underscore the imperative for risk assessments carried out by legal actors to be not only rigorous but also aligned with the victim's protection needs. Moreover, their implementation should undergo continuous monitoring throughout the legal process to ensure its effectiveness. These principles are equally critical at the sentencing stage, particularly in cases involving domestic violence and attempted murder within an intimate context, where the adequacy of legal responses can have far-reaching consequences for both justice and the prevention of further harm, as illustrated by Case 3.

Case 3

The defendant, 61 years old, and the victim, 52 years old, were married for 28 years, during which time the defendant physically and psychologically assaulted the victim. Eventually, the victim moved out and filed for divorce, which the defendant never accepted. He continuously stalked and threatened to kill her. The victim filed several complaints of domestic violence. As a result of these complaints, the defendant was convicted of domestic violence against his ex-wife, as well as aggravated threats and physical assault against their son. He was sentenced to a suspended prison term of three years and two months, along with a ban on contacting or approaching the victim within a 400-m radius, monitored via remote control (electronic bracelet). Five years after the divorce, despite wearing the electronic bracelet, the defendant shot his ex-wife's aunt, then his ex-wife, followed by their daughter and ex-mother-in-law, all of whom were in the same room. The aunt and the mother of the victim died at the scene, while the daughter and the ex-wife were taken to hospital.

In the domestic violence cases analysed, even where there was a known history of violence in the legal system, the sentence applied (when charges were brought) was often a prison sentence suspended in its execution, with or without associated conduct rules. While such a penalty might appear appropriate within the legal framework, feminist legal theories compel us to examine the broader implications. First, as Myrna Dawson (2016) contends, these crimes are frequently regarded as "common" or "normal" incidents, which results in them being perceived as less serious. This, in turn, leads to normative propositions or legal-conclusive judgements about a diminished need for the deterrent role of criminal law. The relationship between victim and offender is critical for understanding the context and dynamics of a homicide, as, in this particular case, the victim–offender relationship plays a significant role in determining the motives behind the crime (Dawson & Gartner, 1998). However, some studies clearly show that the greater the level of intimacy between offender and victim, the less severe the legal responses to the crime tend to be (Dawson & Gartner, 1998).

Second, the legal trajectory of many victims, as shown in the majority of the cases analysed with previous legal complaints, is often characterised by repeated complaints followed by withdrawals, a pattern that leads to their discreditation and portrayal as complicit in their own victimisation. As some authors have shown us in previous studies, these victims are seen by legal actors as "masochistic victims", who, through their own inaction, make it difficult for the criminal justice system to protect them effectively. In other words, legal actors believe that the victim's behaviour absolves them of responsibility (Duarte, 2023).

Shared responsibility: shifting the focus from male violence to moralising narratives about the victim

The idea that domestic violence is a crime in which the blame is shared—that something in the victim's behaviour contributed to the occurrence of the crime and therefore led to her victimisation—remains widespread among legal actors (Karmen, 2000). In several cases, the factors invoked to mitigate guilt included marital duties or even sexual conduct, as exemplified in Case 4.

Case 4

In May 2002, during an argument with the victim, to whom he had been married since 1991, the defendant took out his hunting rifle and fired two shots, hitting her in the lungs, heart, liver, and left leg. At the time, the children of both the defendant and the victim were in the house. It was proven not only that the defendant had acted out of distrust for his wife's fidelity but also that, in the last year of their marriage, he had hit her several times and insulted her in front of their children. After an appeal, the Supreme Court of Justice, while upholding the qualification of the crime, accepted the wife's failure to comply with her supposed duty of sexual submission to her husband as a mitigating circumstance of the sentence. The decision states that a mitigating circumstance would be the fact that "after the end of March 2002, when the defendant returned from France after completing a work contract, . . . [she] began not to refuse to have sexual relations with him, a circumstance which, at the very least, allows for the assertion that not only on the defendant's side was there a violation of conjugal duties, and may even help to explain the doubts that arose in that unenlightened mind about her (in)fidelity".

Such interpretations, however, reinforce deeply ingrained gender stereotypes concerning women's roles within the family and their sexuality (Schafran, 1985; Duarte, 2025b). These stereotypes align with the figure of "Eve". The scrutiny of women's sexual conduct in legal contexts has given rise to two idealised victim archetypes, extensively discussed in the literature: Eve and Mary. Within victimology studies, "Eve" embodies deeply entrenched stereotypes regarding female sexuality. In contrast, "Mary" represents a chaste woman whose profile conforms to more conservative and patriarchal gender roles, where motherhood is considered her highest fulfilment, and she is characterised by passivity (Schafran, 1985; Duarte, 2025b). In the present study, the "Eve" archetype appears across several sentences as support for the provocation theory, a defence strategy to mitigate or exclude criminal responsibility, arguing that the defendant was intensely provoked, leading to a strong emotional reaction that diminished his capacity for self-control. When accepted by the judge, this strategy can lead to the crime being classified as manslaughter and/or can be used as a mitigating factor in sentencing.

Similarly, jealousy has been found in several cases as a justification for the defendant's out-of-control behaviour (Pontedeira et al., 2020), who, in the wake of hegemonic masculinity (Connel, 1995), could not bear the jealousy, the victim's infidelity or her lack of love.

Case 5

A young university student murdered his ex-girlfriend by slitting her throat in a car park near the college where they both studied, because she refused to resume their relationship. The court considered that

> it was the victim's refusal that led to the defendant's tragic outcome. The defendant acted in response to her effective refusal to resume the relationship and did not previously plan or intend to kill her as punishment or simply out of spite for her rejection or for daring to want to follow her own path without him. . . . This is not a trivial motive, but a motive of passion
>
> *(Coimbra District Court, 29 June 2009)*

The Court acquitted the defendant of aggravated murder, sentencing him to 12 years in prison for (simple) murder. After appeal, the Supreme Court of Justice considered that "We are dealing with heartbreak, with the suffering it caused the defendant. This is not to be considered trivial or insignificant" (Supreme Court of Justice, 18 March 2010).

This interpretation, found in several sentences, legitimises the perception that certain emotions associated with love—such as jealousy—contribute to a decrease in guilt and a consequent reduction in punishment (Bandes & Blumenthal, 2012; Duarte, 2025a). This is a heteropatriarchal understanding of "romantic love", which is reflected in the legal and judicial analysis of these cases. While the personal circumstances of male defendants—such as emotional distress or "loss of control"—were often considered in sentencing decisions, female defendants rarely received comparable recognition for the constraints and vulnerabilities they experience. In fact, in none of the cases analysed were jealousy or loss of control considered mitigating factors when the murder was committed by a woman. The application of mitigating circumstances reveals a pronounced gendered asymmetry in legal reasoning. Moreover, when the court accepts explanations such as "crime of passion" or "jealousy", it reproduces this logic, transforming violence into an understandable or even inevitable emotional response. This framing contributes to the invisibility of the coercive control that precedes many femicides and prevents recognition of the systematic nature of gender-based violence. Consequently, it reinforces a discursive pattern that normalises male aggression.

Final remarks

This study, through the analysis of judicial decisions in cases of homicide within intimate relationships, revealed a troubling pattern: in many instances, the system had prior knowledge of ongoing violence but failed to implement adequate protective measures. The consequences for the victims were, in many cases, fatal. This failure reflects not merely an institutional inefficiency but also a deeper epistemological issue—the legal system's limited capacity to recognise and respond to gender-based violence in a meaningful and transformative way. In this sense, the study highlights how the legal system actively participates in the social construction of the victim and the dynamics of victimisation from a gender perspective. From a sociological and feminist perspective, the notion of "the victim" emerges not as a neutral category, but as one constituted through gendered expectations and legal discourse. The judicial emphasis on the victim's behaviour—particularly in relation to her sexual conduct or perceived emotional provocation—positions her within pre-existing moral and patriarchal frameworks that implicitly assign blame. Narratives invoking jealousy or female infidelity, even in cases where convictions occur, contribute to a symbolic exoneration, where male violence is explained, if not justified, through appeals to emotional provocation. So, when victims deviate from the figure of the "ideal victim"—by being sexually autonomous, emotionally expressive or refusing subservience—they are often repositioned within the judicial narrative as partially responsible for the violence they suffer.

Such framing results in a process of secondary victimisation, whereby the victim is subjected to renewed scrutiny and symbolic violence within the very institutions meant to offer protection. Furthermore, instead of focusing the analysis on the behaviour of the aggressor, legal discourse shifts the focus to aspects of the woman's personal life, such as decisions to separate, alleged infidelity, "inappropriate" lifestyles or supposed failures to fulfil traditional cisgender roles. That said, judicial responses often reflect a profound misapprehension of the dynamics of gender-based violence, which reproduces harmful social narratives.

A truly protective legal response must go beyond procedural reforms. It requires a fundamental shift in the epistemological foundations of legal practice—one that centres feminist and sociological understandings of victimhood, power, and resistance. Only by confronting the gendered assumptions that shape legal interpretations can we begin to imagine a justice system capable of both recognising and responding to the complexities of intimate partner violence.

Note

1 The research project IPHinLAW—Intimate Partner Homicide: Challenges to the Law, coordinated by Madalena Duarte, was funded by the Foundation for Science and Technology and was carried out at the Centre for Social Studies between 1 June 2018 and 31 May 2022. Project reference: POCI-01-0145-FEDER-030862—PTDC/DIR-DCP/30862/2017.

2 The term of identity and residence is a coercive measure that can be applied to defendants in criminal investigations. It is the least severe coercive measure and entails the identification of the defendant; the indication of the defendant's residence; the obligation to appear before the authorities; the requirement to notify any change of residence and the obligation not to leave the residence for more than five days without prior notice.

References

Abrunhosa, C., et al. (2021). Crimes against women: From violence to homicide. *Journal of Interpersonal Violence*, 36(23–24), 2973–2996.

Agra, C., et al. (2015). *Homicídios conjugais: estudo avaliativo das decisões judiciais*. Lisboa: Comissão para a Cidadania e a Igualdade de Género.

Baldry, A. C., & Magalhães, M. (2018). Prevention of femicide. In S. Weil, C. Corradi & M. Naudi (Eds.), *Femicide Across Europe* (pp.71–92). Policy Press.

Bandes, S., & Blumenthal, J. (2012). Emotion and the law. *Annual Review of Law and Social Sciences*, 8, 161–181.

Bartels, L., Bradford, S., & Easteal, P. W. (2012). Language, gender and 'reality': Violence against women. *International Journal of Law, Crime and Justice*, 40(4), 324–337.

Bourdieu, P. (1986). The force of law: Toward a sociology of the juridical field. *Hastings Law Journal*, 38, 805.

Brito, T. (2007). *Direito Penal—Parte Especial: Lições, Estudos e Casos*. Coimbra: Coimbra Editora.

Bumiller, K. (1990). Fallen angels: The representation of violence against women in legal culture. *International Journal of the Sociology of Law*, 18, 125–142.

Buzawa, E. S., & Buzawa, C. G. (1990). *Domestic Violence. The Criminal Justice Response*. Newbury Park, CA: Sage.

Connell, R. W. (1995). *Masculinities*. Cambridge, UK: Polity Press.

Crenshaw, K. W. (1991). Mapping the margins: Intersectionality, identity politics, and violence against women of color. *Stanford Law Review*, 43(6), 1241–1299.

Dawson, M. (2016). Representing intimacy, gender and homicide: The validity and utility of common stereotypes in law. In K. Fitz-Gibbon & S. Walklate (Eds.), *Homicide, Gender and Responsibility: An International Perspective* (pp. 53–77). Routledge.

Dawson, M., & Gartner, R. (1998). Differences in the characteristics of intimate femicides: The role of relationship state and relationship status. *Homicide Studies*, 2(4), 378–399.

Dobash, R., & Dobash, R. (2015). When men murder women. *Policing*, 10.

Duarte, M. (2023). *O Papel do Direito e dos Tribunais na Violência Contra as Mulheres*. Porto: Afrontamento.

Duarte, M. (2025a). Amor, género e justiça: uma análise das emoções a partir dos homicídios e femicídios em contexto de intimidade. *Revista Crítica de Ciências Sociais*, 137, 147–170.

Duarte, M. (2025b). Is a good woman hard to find? Conceptions of victim and stereotypes in judicial intimate partner violence cases. *AG-About Gender. International Journal of Gender Studies*, 14(28), 25–48.

Easteal, P., Bartels, L., & Mittal, R. (2019). The importance of understanding the victims' "reality" of domestic violence. *Alternative Law Journal*, 44, 11–16.

Epstein, D., & Goodman, L. A. (2019). Discounting women: Doubting domestic violence survivors' credibility and dismissing their experiences. *University of Pennsylvania Law Review*, 167, 399–461.

Foucault, M. (1977). *Discipline and Punish: The Birth of the Prison*. London: Penguin.

Garcia, V., & McManimon, P. (2011). *Gendered Justice*. Lanham, MD: Rowman & Littlefield.

Gartner, R., et al. (1990). Gender stratification and the gender gap in homicide victimization. *Social Problems*, 37(4), 593–612.

Gartner, R., et al. (1992). Woman killing: Intimate femicide in Ontario. *Women We Honour*, 1–36.

Gersão, E. (2006). Mulher: O longo caminho para a igualdade: memórias de uma década (os 40 anos da publicação do Código Civil de 1966). *Revista do Ministério Público*, 107, 231–259.

Grant, I. (2010). Intimate femicide: A study of sentencing trends for men who kill their intimate partners. *Alberta Law Review*, 47(3), 779–882.

Grembi, V., Rosso, A. C., & Barili, E. (2024). Domestic violence perception and gender stereotypes. *Journal of Population Economics*, 37(1), 1–32.

Heirigs, M., & Moore, M. (2018). Gender inequality and homicide: A cross-national examination. *International Journal of Comparative and Applied Criminal Justice*, 42(4), 273–285.

Hunter, R., & Cowan, S. (Eds.). (2007). *Choice and Consent. Feminist Engagements with Law and Subjectivity*. London, UK: Routledge.

Kafka, J. M., Moracco, K. E., Barrington, C., & Mortazavi, A. L. (2019). Judging domestic violence from the bench: A narrative analysis of judicial anecdotes about domestic violence protective order cases. *Qualitative Health Research*, 29(8), 1132–1144.

Karmen, A. (2000). *Crime Victims: An Introduction to Victimology*. Belmont, CA: Wadsworth.

Lagarde, M. (2008). Antropología, feminismo y política: Violencia feminicida y derechos humanos de las mujeres. In M. Bullen & C. Díez (Eds.), *Retos Teóricos y nuevas prácticas* (pp. 209–239). ANKULEGI Antropologia Elkartea.

Lugones, M. (2007). Heterosexualism and the colonial/modern gender system. *Hypatia*, 22(1), 186–219.

MacKinnon, C. (1987). *Feminism Unmodified: Discourses on Life and Law*. Cambridge MA: Harvard University Press.

Matias, A., Gonçalves, M., Soeiro, C., & Matos, M. (2020). Intimate partner homicide: A meta-analysis of risk factors. *Aggression and Violent Behavior*, 50, 1–12.

Mohanty, C.T. (1984). Under Western Eyes: Feminist scholarship and colonial discourses. *Boundary*, 2 (12–13), 333–358.

Monteiro, E. (2012). *Crime de Homicídio Qualificado e Imputabilidade Diminuída*. Coimbra: Coimbra Editora.

Mulla, M., Witte, T., Richardson, K., Hart, W., Kassing, F., Coffey, C., Hackman, C., & Sherwood, I. (2019). The causal influence of perceived social norms on intimate partner violence perpetration: Converging cross-sectional, longitudinal, and experimental support for a social disinhibition model. *Personality and Social Psychology Bulletin*, 45(4), 652–668.

Nicolaidis, C., et al. (2003). Could we have known? A qualitative analysis of data from women who survived an attempted homicide by an intimate partner. *Journal of General Internal Medicine*, 18(10), 788–794.

Polícia Judiciária. (2020). *Homicídios nas relações de intimidade—Estudo dos inquéritos investigados pela Polícia Judiciária (2014–2019)*. Lisboa: Ministério da Justiça.

Pontedeira, C., Quintas, J., & Walklate, S. (2020). Intimate partner homicides: "Passionate crime" arguments in the Portuguese Supreme Court of Justice. *International Annals of Criminology*, 58(2), 193–216.

Procuradoria Geral da República (PGR). (2024). *Homicídios em contexto de Violência Doméstica. Análise dos Indicadores*. Lisboa: PGR.

Russell, D. (2008). *Femicide: Politicizing the Killing of Females*. Strengthening Understanding of Femicide, in Opening Panel Discussion for the Meeting was Co-sponsored by the Interagency Gender Working Group (IGWG) of the US Agency for International Development.

Schafran, L. (1985). Eve, Mary, Superwoman—How stereotypes about women influence judges. *Judges Journal*, 24(1), 12–17.

SGMAI. (2022). *Relatório Anual de Monitorização de Violência Doméstica-2021*. Lisboa: Ministério da Administração Interna.

Smart, C. (1989). *Feminism and the Power of Law*. Routledge.

Smith, J. (2019). Intimate partner femicide: Using Foucauldian analysis to track an eight stage progression to homicide. *Violence Against Women*, 26(11), 1–19.

Stöckl, H., et al. (2013). The global prevalence of intimate partner homicide: A systematic review. *The Lancet*, 382(9895), 859–865.

Ulmer, J. T. (2012). Recent developments and new directions in sentencing research. *Justice Quarterly*, 29(1), 1–40.

UMAR. (2024). *INFOGRAFIA. Dados preliminares sobre as Mulheres Assassinadas em Portugal de 1 janeiro a 15 de novembro de 2024*. UMAR.

UNODC. (2019). *Global Study on Homicide: Homicide Trends, Patterns and Criminal Justice Response*. UNODC.

WHO. (2013). *Global and Regional Estimates of Violence Against Women: Prevalence and Health Effects of Intimate Partner Violence and Non-Partner Sexual Violence*. Geneva: World Health Organization.

9

"IF I GO, THERE WILL BE TROUBLE . . . AND IF I STAY, IT WILL BE DOUBLE"

The intimate partner violence victims' dilemma between danger and displacement

Rosanna Amato

Introduction

Intimate Partner Violence (IPV) victims face formidable barriers to justice. Many hesitate to come forward due to intertwined legal, economic, and social obstacles, exacerbated by gender dynamics and cultural factors. At the same time, detection and prosecution are hindered by the challenge of defining and proving sustained patterns of abuse. Evidence is often limited to victim testimony, which is frequently recanted or minimised, further weakening judicial intervention.

The harm of IPV lies not in isolated acts, but in an enduring cycle of abuse that erodes connections to both external reality and the self (Johnson 1995, 2008; Johnson & Ferraro 2000; Vlachovà & Biason 2004; Canu 2008; Garcia-Moreno et al. 2006; Bonewit & De Santis 2016; Pecorella & Farina 2018; Zara & Gino 2018; FRA 2014; EIGE 2019). Escaping this situation can feel insurmountable—and such sentiment cannot be said to be unjustified. Whether to leave an abusive milieu carries profound consequences for victims, particularly the need to secure safety for themselves and their children while rebuilding a sense of control over their lives. However, the danger does not always end with separation, as pursuing legal action against an abuser is known to potentially heighten the risk of further violence (Klein 2009; Long et al. 2010).

To protect victims from immediate danger and prevent escalation, safety plans often involve relocation to undisclosed residences. While this measure can be effective, it presents challenges (GREVIO 2022). Beyond institutional barriers—such as limited access to safe housing—it entails profound personal costs. Victims must cope with displacement, sever ties with support networks, disrupt their children's lives, and face financial uncertainty (Stylianou et al. 2021; Gezinski &

DOI: 10.4324/9781003752974-12

Gonzalez-Pons 2021). Perhaps most painfully, many experience this arrangement as unjust, forced to uproot their lives to stay safe (Amato 2024).

> Let me put it this way. You are at home when your husband is beating you. I come as a representative of the law and say: Yes, your husband has assaulted you, and you are entitled to consider yourself a victim. But now you must leave your home, because the State cannot guarantee your safety there.[1]

Alternatives to displacement exist in nearly all domestic legal frameworks. Protective measures—such as emergency barring, restraining orders, and protection orders—are available to prevent contact between victims and perpetrators, thereby reducing the risk of minimisation or withdrawal during court proceedings. However, their application remains far from ideal (SWD(2022) 180 final; SWD/2022/0179 final; SWD(2022)62 final). These measures are often weakened by lengthy procedures, high evidentiary thresholds, and reliance on legal action. Moreover, relocation is frequently preferred over their use, reflecting practical and cultural considerations (GREVIO 2022).

This chapter examines the dilemma many victims face between remaining in a dangerous relationship and accepting displacement as the price of safety. It first outlines how fear, coercion and institutional uncertainty shape victims' engagement with justice, and then considers why relocation continues to be frequently prioritised as a protection strategy despite its personal and institutional costs. It subsequently discusses why alternatives to displacement—particularly protection measures and protection orders—remain unevenly implemented despite their formal availability within domestic legal frameworks. The final part focuses on local strategies aimed at making displacement a last resort, drawing on a case study (2022–24) of the judicial handling of IPV cases in a local Italian jurisdiction to illustrate how organisational reform, coordination and specialised case management can strengthen early protection while reducing risks of secondary and repeat victimisation.

Should i stay or should i go? Introducing the IPV victim's dilemma

> Freedom is not being afraid . . . , not being afraid to leave the house, not being afraid to go to work, not being afraid for your children.[2]

If freedom means living without fear, for many IPV victims, it remains an unattainable privilege. Victims' testimonies reveal recurring patterns: anxiety and the constant fear that violence may erupt at any moment. They speak of humiliation—being forced to endure or participate in degrading acts while remaining silent. They recount being compelled to work even when ill, to compensate for their partners' spending, yet never gaining control over their own earnings. Their voices evoke a fear of death—pinned against walls, a hand clasped around the throat, as each breath becomes elusive.

In these stories, a prevailing emotion is resignation, rooted in the belief that any attempt to escape may lead to more severe consequences. The psychological toll of violence erodes victims' self-worth and autonomy. Over time, many come to perceive abuse as "normal" or as part of their expected role as a wife or partner (Amato & Carnevali 2022). This distorted perception is not only instilled by the abuser but reinforced by societal attitudes—including those within the family. Dysfunctional relational patterns may sustain victim-blaming narratives and gendered expectations that assign women primary responsibility for preserving family unity. When such expectations extend to motherhood, victims who leave abusive relationships involving minor children may be placed in a double bind: they can be scrutinised either for an alleged failure to protect their children from harm or, conversely, for being perceived as disrupting the children's relationship with their father (Barnett 2001; Koepsell et al. 2006; Flood & Pease 2009; Miyaoi 2016; Shreeves & Prpic 2019).

The possibility of such scrutiny may heighten victims' concerns, as these assumptions do not remain confined to the social sphere; they may also shape legal reasoning in family law proceedings, particularly in decisions on custody and visitation. As a result, violent behaviour within an intimate relationship can be treated as analytically distinct from parental capacity, reducing the weight given to abuse-related risks in assessments of the child's best interests.

> After a week, I filed a complaint against my ex-husband, and there I met the social worker who was very nice to me. I immediately asked her, "Do you take my son from me?" . . . . I kept asking her for a long time every time I met her. The night after the complaint, I cried all the time; I couldn't sleep or breathe.[3]

The cumulative effect of these challenges may act as a deterrent to leaving abusive relationships, contributing to a perception that viable alternatives are limited or unattainable. Such perceptions can persist over time, delaying action until circumstances become intolerable. Importantly, however, this dynamic cannot be understood solely in terms of individual resilience or decision-making. It raises a broader institutional question: whether justice systems are equipped to offer credible pathways to safety and emancipation for those seeking to exit violent relationships (Amato 2024).

For IPV victims, protection from further abuse is often a central consideration when deciding whether to engage with legal processes. This concern is grounded in evidence suggesting that seeking justice may, in some cases, be associated with an increased risk of repeated abuse, serious injury or even lethal outcomes

(Klein 2008; Long et al. 2010). Awareness of these risks may weigh heavily on victims' choices, contributing to delays in seeking assistance or initiating legal action (Stubbs 2008; Johnson 2008). These concerns may be further compounded by experiences of disengagement or disappointment in interactions with law enforcement and judicial authorities, particularly following emergency interventions or during the initial stages of proceedings. In some instances, reports of violence may be framed as private family matters, with reconciliation—explicitly or implicitly—encouraged in the interest of preserving family unity (Amato & Carnevali 2022). Even when institutions intervene, responses may be perceived as slow or procedurally burdensome, limiting their capacity to provide the immediate, effective protection necessary for legal remedies to function as intended.

Protect by displacing

When preventing contact between perpetrators and victims is essential to ensuring safety, the prevailing practice has long been—and largely remains—relocating victims to shelters. Beyond providing secure, round-the-clock accommodation, shelters offer essential forms of support, helping victims navigate complex challenges, rebuild self-esteem, and develop the skills needed for independent living. Victim relocation is widely regarded as an effective protective measure and can be implemented even in the absence of a formal complaint. It often remains crucial throughout criminal proceedings, particularly when an arrest in *flagrante delicto* is not possible due to evidentiary constraints. Relocation may be necessary, for example, when the victim's living environment poses risks—such as when the perpetrator's family lives nearby or in the same building (Amato 2024).

Despite its advantages, this process remains complex, requiring multi-stakeholder coordination and placing financial strain on already overburdened institutions. Shelter availability is often inadequate, meeting only a fraction of national needs, with particularly severe consequences for vulnerable groups who frequently fall outside eligibility criteria (GREVIO 2022). Beyond these structural constraints, displacement carries high emotional and practical costs. While many IPV survivors report initial relief upon entering safe housing, they also experience fear, grief, and uncertainty (Fisher & Stylianou 2019; Glenn & Goodman 2015). Emergency shelters, though essential, can be deeply isolating, as limited social contact, restrictions on visitors, barriers to employment, and housing instability undermine autonomy and reinforce a sense of disconnection (Bonomi et al. 2009; Hadeed & El-Bassel 2006; Haaken 2010; Goodman & Smyth 2011; Katerndahl et al. 2013; Clough et al. 2013; Pajak et al. 2014; Thomas et al. 2015; Gezinski & Gonzalez-Pons 2021; Stylianou et al. 2021). Although emergency relocation saves lives, it is often experienced as an unjust burden, with consequences that extend well beyond the conclusion of court proceedings or the completion of a sentence, as the absence of sustained case management and institutional support leaves survivors in ongoing uncertainty and risk.

> Even after the trial came to an end and he was released, I still have extreme difficulty walking downtown. The anxiety is overwhelming. It's a fear that you can't control, that pervades you all the time, and it continues until you lock the world out by staying inside your car.[4]

Given this context, it is unsurprising that justice can be seen as a "last resort". Faced with the dilemma "should I stay or should I go?", many victims may opt to endure a known hell rather than engage in a judicial process perceived as lengthy, painful, and uncertain in its outcome (Amato & Carnevali 2022). Beyond instituting mechanisms that yield fair and effective outcomes within reasonable timeframes, delivering justice requires understanding and addressing victims' needs and legal interests. In cases of violence within intimate relationships, safety is a central concern shaping victims' engagement with the justice system. While displacement can be effective and is sometimes necessary, it raises critical questions about its underlying rationale and long-term impact. By shifting the burden of protection to victims rather than to aggressors, it challenges principles of fairness and strains public resources, casting doubt on its long-term sustainability (Amato 2024).

Alternatives to displacement: why does implementation remains an uphill battle?

Since the 1970s, protection orders (POs) have been introduced across many legal systems to restrict or prevent contact between victims and perpetrators, either temporarily or permanently (Römkens 2010; van der Aa 2014; Cerrato et al. 2017). These measures typically prohibit or regulate (a) access to specific locations or areas where the protected person resides or visits; (b) any form of contact—such as phone, electronic communication or written correspondence; or (c) physical proximity, by imposing a minimum distance from the protected person. POs constitute a key safeguard for IPV victims, who face an elevated risk of post-separation abuse, harassment, and, in some cases, lethal violence (EPRS 2017).

POs may be applied in different legal contexts. In civil proceedings, restraining orders primarily serve a preventive function, seeking to avert further harm. In criminal proceedings, they may operate as an alternative to pre-trial detention or be incorporated into a judicial sentence. In addition, emergency barring orders can be issued rapidly to provide immediate protection in situations involving imminent risk (Sellier & Weyembergh 2018). Taken together, these measures offer a prompt way to reduce ongoing victimisation and can help victims regain a sense of safety.

Accessing them, though, is not always guaranteed. In some countries, emergency barring orders involve cumbersome procedures or require excessively high evidentiary thresholds. Similarly, restraining and protection orders are often limited to cases formally classified as IPV or domestic violence. As a result, if there is insufficient evidence at the outset to establish IPV, these protections may not be granted. Moreover, the issuance of these orders is frequently tied to the initiation of legal proceedings. This further restricts their accessibility since many victims are hesitant to take legal action, whether pressing charges or filing for divorce (GREVIO 2022).

What remains striking is the inconsistent use of these measures, including in legal systems not marked by evident procedural gaps. This suggests that the difficulty lies less in the availability of legal tools than in how risk and victim vulnerability are assessed and operationalised in practice. Preventing repeat violence requires close attention to the specific circumstances and needs of individual victims, particularly in the early stages of proceedings, when timely and tailored interventions are most likely to be effective.

In this regard, the initial interaction between victims and professionals is often decisive, both for addressing immediate safety concerns and for shaping subsequent judicial action. It is at this stage that evidence is first identified and documented, sometimes in ways that later influence prosecutorial decisions and legal outcomes. Also, shortcomings in how this phase is managed may increase the risk of further victimisation. Managing this phase is inherently complex. IPV cases involve multiple actors in evidence collection, and specialised skills and procedures are not evenly available at the local level. Law enforcement officers, for example, may not always recognise when a reported incident forms part of a broader pattern of abuse, leading to partial interpretations of the crime scene or limited guidance to victims on evidentiary needs. Similar challenges may arise in medical settings, where professionals may lack the training required to detect patterns of violence or to document injuries in ways that support possible legal action. Referral pathways to judicial authorities or specialised support services are not consistently activated, further narrowing opportunities for timely intervention. During on-site interventions and emergency room visits, documenting isolated episodes of violence may be insufficient if they are not situated within a broader pattern of coercion and control. Limited understanding of IPV dynamics can lead to the omission of relevant contextual details, potentially weakening subsequent investigations and indictments. Moreover, the way victims are received and questioned at this stage can directly affect the evidentiary record, as their engagement with the legal process may depend on how the interaction unfolds. This becomes particularly evident when allegations of abuse arise alongside civil proceedings and risk being reframed as elements of relational conflict.[5]

> If someone goes to report the theft of a car, unless something unusual has happened, their account is not questioned. It is passed on to the Public Prosecutor, who then takes the appropriate steps. . . . If, however, a woman goes to report violence—whether rape, stalking, or abuse by a partner—this does not happen automatically.[6]

These shortcomings, however, cannot be attributed solely to individual limitations—such as gaps in empathy or professional expertise—but reflect structural weaknesses. A critical issue concerns the absence of clearly defined guidelines at both European and national levels for conducting individual assessments[7] (COM/2020/187 final; SWD(2022)180 final): who should conduct these assessments? How should they be carried out? And, which actors should be involved? Also, even where formal assessment protocols exist, they are seldom integrated into a wider multi-agency framework (SWD(2022)180 final; GREVIO 2022). These challenges are compounded by the limited availability of systematic and mandatory training for professionals on key issues such as power and control dynamics, the distinction between violence and conflict, and post-separation violence. This can further weaken risk assessments and limit justice professionals' ability to fully appreciate the preventive role of POs in interrupting the cycle of violence (Pecorella & Farina 2018). Ultimately, the effectiveness of risk assessment continues to depend on local contexts and the capacity of local actors to coordinate their efforts and develop appropriate safety plans (Amato & Carnevali 2022; SWD(2022)62 final—Annex 5, p. 168).

Local strategies to make displacement a last resort

Protecting victims from repeat victimisation continues to present significant challenges. POs may offer an effective and financially sustainable alternative to displacement and can help reduce the risk of secondary victimisation. In practice, however, their implementation remains uneven, including in well-established legal systems, often reflecting cultural and institutional constraints.

Against this background, this chapter explores how existing legal provisions can be translated into more concrete forms of protection through targeted organisational strategies. It draws on a case study from the Public Prosecutor's Office at the Court of Tivoli (Rome judicial disctrict), where, since 2017, a structured case management approach grounded in standardisation and professional specialisation has been developed, contributing to a more consistent handling of IPV cases.

Methodological note

This research employed a mixed-method approach, combining qualitative empirical research with desk-based legal and documentary analysis, as well as direct observation.

The desk analysis encompassed different types of sources. In order to ensure a proper legal framing of the study, supranational and national legislation was examined. This included the most recent developments introduced into the Italian legal system by Law No. 168 of 24 November 2023 on combating violence against women and domestic violence, as well as developments at European Union level, with particular attention to the legislative process leading to Directive (EU) 2024/1385 of 14 May 2024 on violence against women and domestic violence. In addition, soft law instruments and organisational documentation produced at district level were analysed, together with data elaborated by the Tivoli Public Prosecutor's Office (PPO). These materials were essential to gaining a comprehensive understanding of the ongoing reorganisation process, providing detailed insight into the practices adopted and their impact. The analysis of this documentary development also made it possible to assess the degree of progression of the reorganisation process, highlighting the gradual consolidation of practices developed through a bottom-up approach.

Qualitative analysis constituted the core of the research and was essential for achieving the objectives of the project. The study relied on in-depth, open-ended interviews with key informants, conceived in a manner close to a joint inquiry approach. This form of inquiry, conducted in dialogue between researchers and practitioners, created opportunities for exchange with professionals directly engaged in combating violence against women and preventing escalation. Interviewees were not treated as mere providers of information, but as interlocutors invited to contribute reflections and to take part in moments of feedback on the research findings.

The interviews aimed to identify and understand the solutions adopted at local level, exploring the reasons behind their introduction, their structural and operational features, their development trajectory, and the results achieved. They also made it possible to investigate professional orientations and cultural aspects not readily accessible through documentary analysis. Eleven interviews were conducted via videoconference (Microsoft Teams) between January and June 2022. In accordance with GDPR requirements and academic research ethics procedures, participants were fully informed about the purpose of the research and the use of the information collected, and informed consent—including consent to recording where applicable—was obtained prior to each interview. Participation was entirely voluntary and without incentives.

Finally, research material was also collected through direct observation. A site visit to the PPO premises (20 June 2023) enabled observation of the building, spatial organisation, and file classification systems, and provided an opportunity for follow-up discussions with staff on interim findings and future developments. Research results were subsequently consolidated in a final report validated in April–May 2024.

Drivers and dimensions of organisational change

Organisational reform at the Tivoli Public Prosecutor's Office was driven by a combination of evolving legal mandates, increasing caseloads and growing social awareness of the impact of intimate partner violence. Supranational developments,[8] including the Istanbul Convention[9] and the case-law of the European Court of Human Rights, have clarified that failures to ensure timely protection for victims may contribute to structural gender discrimination and perpetuate cycles of violence (Prechal 2019). Within this framework, judicial authorities are increasingly required to account for underlying power imbalances and their implications for case management. Italian legislation has progressively aligned with these standards, placing greater emphasis on prompt judicial intervention where POs are necessary to prevent further harm. At the same time, the volume and complexity of IPV cases—particularly those involving precautionary measures—highlighted the limits of existing organisational arrangements. Such cases demand specialised investigative approaches and close coordination to reduce the risk of repeat victimisation. Within the Tivoli PPO, these pressures were accompanied by a growing institutional awareness that effective enforcement of protective measures constitutes not only a legal obligation but also a broader responsibility towards victims.

In response, the reorganisation was implemented incrementally across two interrelated levels. At the macro level, reforms focused on redistributing workloads, clarifying responsibilities and strengthening coordination with judicial police and judges. A specialised working group on violence against women was established, supported by targeted training and dedicated resources, alongside the creation of an internal judicial police unit to enhance investigative capacity and cooperation with external law enforcement agencies. Additional measures included priority case management, upgrades to information systems, and new coordination mechanisms to promote more consistent investigative practices, particularly in cases involving POs. Standardised instructions for the judicial police further clarified the procedural framework for victim interviews and the preparation of precautionary requests. At the micro level, the reform introduced training initiatives and operational tools designed to support professional judgement and specialisation. These included integrating an informational vademecum into investigative protocols and increasing specialisation within the judicial police to ensure that victims receive accurate information about their rights. Taken together, these measures supported improved listening practices, earlier risk assessment and closer alignment between investigative activity and the applicable protective framework (Keilitz et al. 1997).

Requesting and applying protection orders: an organisational model

As part of a broader organisational reform, the Tivoli PPO has developed a structured approach to the requesting, enforcement and monitoring of pre-trial protective measures in IPV cases. Rather than focusing on individual tools in isolation, the reform addresses the entire lifecycle of POs, from the initial intake of complaints to judicial decision-making and follow-up. Interventions at both the macro and micro levels have aimed to streamline procedures, reduce fragmentation and ensure that protective measures can be applied in a timely and consistent manner, in line with victims' protection needs.

From first contact to evidence: standardised and specialised intake

Central to this model is the specialisation and standardisation of preliminary law enforcement procedures, which are designed to balance the need for timely intervention with careful case management and procedural fairness. This initial phase plays a critical role in early risk assessment, the identification of protection needs and the handling of situations involving ongoing violence.

One of the challenges addressed by the reform concerns the persistence of biases, stereotypes and subjective interpretations that may weaken investigative activity and judicial outcomes. In practice, failures to adequately recognise the seriousness of intimate partner violence have at times led to sustained abuse being framed as a "quarrel" or "family conflict", obscuring the structural power imbalances inherent in such cases. To mitigate these risks, law enforcement officers are required to operate within a clearly defined procedural framework supported by practical tools, including vademecums, checklists and standardised sets of questions, aimed at promoting more consistent and accurate reporting.

The protocol is activated from the first point of contact. During emergency calls, operators follow structured guidelines to provide safety information and collect essential details to support an effective response. On-site procedures emphasise objective documentation of the crime scene, including an assessment of the incident's circumstances, the condition of those involved and the surrounding environment. Where possible, photographic or video material is collected to support subsequent case assessment. When reports originate in healthcare settings, particularly emergency departments, officers are instructed to coordinate with medical staff in order to obtain clinical documentation and information relevant to identifying potential patterns of abuse.[10] At its core, this intake framework emphasises respectful and non-judgmental interaction. By fostering a supportive environment, it seeks to facilitate communication, ensure that victims' accounts are accurately documented and support the early identification of protection needs.

Victim interviewing and risk assessment as case-management tools

Given that victim testimony often constitutes the primary source of evidence in IPV cases, particular attention has been paid to how victims are received, questioned and how their statements are recorded. At the same time, gathering information from victims can present specific challenges. Some individuals may struggle to recognise certain behaviours—such as financial control or subtle forms of dominance—as coercive, while others, even when aware of the abuse, may not yet feel ready to engage with legal proceedings or to fully grasp their implications. Levels of cooperation may therefore fluctuate over time, sometimes resulting in hesitation or the withdrawal of allegations. As one practitioner observed:

> you have to bear in mind that you are not simply dealing with a stolen car or a missing wallet; you are being entrusted with the story of a life that has been shattered, . . . a life in pieces.[11]

To support staff, particularly those with limited experience, the Tivoli PPO has adopted a trauma-informed approach to victim interviewing. This includes a standardised set of questions designed to enhance the reliability of the information collected and to foster victims' awareness of abusive dynamics. A separate assessment tool is used to evaluate the risk of recidivism, helping prosecutors identify situations where precautionary measures may be warranted. Judicial police are also encouraged to audio- or video-record interviews using available technology, including smartphones, enabling magistrates to review both the content of victims' statements and the conduct of the interview more closely.

Taken together, these practices have been associated with several practical benefits, such as facilitating investigations, shortening procedural timelines and limiting the risk of case downgrading or withdrawal. They also allow follow-up interviews to focus on essential issues only, thereby reducing the likelihood of secondary victimisation. Beyond procedural efficiency, this approach may help create conditions in which victims feel better able to participate, articulate their needs and develop greater confidence in the justice system.

Prosecutorial continuity and judicial coordination

The approach developed by the Tivoli PPO is best understood as a specialised case management model rather than as a set of isolated protective tools. Its core feature lies in the reorganisation of internal units and procedures, designed to ensure continuity, specialisation and timely intervention in IPV cases. Under this model, the receipt of a crime report activates a structured and expedited workflow in which IPV cases are prioritised from the outset. Each case is immediately registered in the system, allowing relevant information—such as indicators of gender-based violence, previous victim interviews and urgent precautionary needs—to be systematically recorded and assessed at an early stage.

Responsibility is assigned on the same day to a prosecutor from the Specialised Group through the "Gender Violence Weekly Shift" system, which ensures that experienced prosecutors handle new cases on a rotating basis while maintaining continuity of oversight throughout the proceedings. Once assigned, the prosecutor follows the case from the investigative phase through trial, enabling informed decision-making and contributing to preventing secondary victimisation.

Within this framework, requests for protective measures are embedded in a broader assessment of risk and case progression. Depending on the circumstances, prosecutors may request a range of precautionary measures from the Judge for Preliminary Investigations (GIP), including custodial and non-custodial restrictions, removal of the alleged perpetrator from the home, or restraining orders. Where risk indicators warrant additional safeguards, electronic monitoring may also be sought as one component within the overall protective strategy. Standardised protocols support the preparation of these requests and aim to facilitate timely enforcement.

This operational model interacts with a legal setting in which precautionary measures require judicial authorisation by the GIP and may be reviewed, if denied, by the Review Court (Tribunale del Riesame). In the Tivoli experience, applications—particularly those involving electronic monitoring—have at times reflected different assessments of evidentiary sufficiency and risk, especially during the early phases of implementation. Subsequent review by the Tribunale del Riesame has frequently contributed to clarifying interpretive standards, and a substantial proportion of contested decisions have reportedly been revised on appeal. Over time, this iterative process appears to have supported a more structured dialogue between prosecutors and judges and greater convergence in the practical understanding of protective measures in IPV cases, within a broader institutional context that has coincided with a substantial increase in proceedings against known IPV perpetrators and in recorded gender-based violence offences in the district between 2016 and 2020—trends that may be consistent with reduced tolerance for such conduct and greater engagement with judicial institutions (Procura della Repubblica presso il Tribunale di Tivoli 2023).

Conclusions

Victims of IPV face unique barriers to seeking justice, shaped by fear, emotional strain and practical constraints. The decision to leave an abusive relationship may appear daunting, not without reason, as it can entail exposure to retaliation, uneven protection and uncertainty regarding the capacity of institutions to ensure safety. Experiences of disengagement or perceived inadequacy during initial contacts with law enforcement or judicial authorities—particularly in emergency situations—may further undermine trust and discourage early recourse to legal remedies. Addressing these concerns is therefore central to justice systems that aim not only to deliver timely decisions but also to respond to victims' primary interest in personal safety. In this sense, the difficulties faced by IPV victims cannot be reduced to individual hesitation or resilience but are closely connected to how protection and risk are institutionally organised.

Institutional responses have traditionally relied on forms of "protection by displacement", most commonly through placement in shelters. While often lifesaving, this approach may entail challenges for the institutions involved and, more importantly, high emotional and practical costs for victims. Faced with the dilemma of "should I stay or should I go?"—where "staying" means remaining in a harmful situation, and "going" means entering an uncertain process of relocation—many delay or avoid engaging with the justice system, which is consequently perceived as a measure of last resort rather than a pathway to protection and autonomy. The systematic transfer of the burden of safety onto victims, rather than onto perpetrators, reflects a broader pattern identified in international monitoring and policy frameworks, where protection is frequently secured at the cost of displacement, disruption and loss of autonomy for those subjected to violence.

POs, introduced in various legal systems from the 1970s onwards, were intended to provide an alternative by restricting contact with the alleged perpetrator at an early stage. When applied consistently and enforced effectively, such measures can strengthen confidence in legal institutions, facilitate access to justice and reduce the risk of repeated violence. In practice, however, their availability and impact have varied, often limited by gaps in implementation, uneven institutional coordination and differing levels of professional expertise. Approaches that centre on victims' safety and recognise structural power imbalances are therefore critical to limiting repeated victimisation and reducing reliance on displacement-based solutions. These implementation gaps do not primarily stem from the absence of legal instruments, but from how vulnerability, risk and credibility are assessed and operationalised within everyday institutional routines.

Against this background, this chapter explores how legal provisions can be translated into more tangible forms of protection through organisational reforms and routines. Drawing on a case study of IPV case management in a local Italian jurisdiction, it examines how the restructuring of internal units and workflows, enhanced coordination among institutional actors, and closer alignment with domestic and supranational policy frameworks can strengthen judicial responses. This case study neither claims representativeness nor seeks to advance generalisable conclusions; rather, it offers a situated point of observation on how forms of injustice widely recognised at the supranational level are experienced, negotiated and addressed within a specific local context.

These changes appear particularly relevant in the earliest stages of proceedings, when timely protective measures may prevent further harm and support longer-term engagement with the justice system. Key elements of the model include a dedicated case management structure, professional specialisation and the use of standardised practices in pre-trial investigations. Attention to reducing bias, improving interactions with victims and reinforcing inter-agency cooperation has contributed to broadening the protective capacity of the justice system. Read within the broader debate on global injustice and local responses, the experience examined here suggests that locally embedded organisational practices can play a crucial role in mitigating the unequal distribution of risk and responsibility that continues to characterise institutional responses to IPV.

Notes

1 Excerpt of the interview carried out on 6 June 2022 with the staff of the Tivoli PPO, as part of the case study presented in this chapter. The full research findings have been elaborated in Amato (2024).

2 Excerpt from the reportage 'The voices and stories of women victims of violence', by F. Mannocchi, aired on 24/11/2023 at https://www.la7.it/propagandalive/video/le-voci-e-le-storie-delle-donne-vittime-di-violenza-il-reportage-di-francesca-mannocchi-25-11-2023-515561 accessed March 23, 2026.

3 Excerpt from the article *Donne uscite dalla violenza: una testimonianza*, in Save the Children blog, 30 November 2020. Available at https://www.savethechildren.it/blog-notizie/donne-uscite-dalla-violenza-una-testimonianza accessed March 23, 2026.

4 Excerpt of an IPV victim interview given to RSI. Available at https://www.rsi.ch/info/ticino-grigioni-e-insubria/"Gli-ho-chiesto-di-smetterla-mi-ha-riso-in-faccia"—1997643.html
5 See Italian Corte di cassazione: S.C. sent. nn. 19847/2022, 21174/2022, 3377/2023, 39578/2022.
6 Excerpt of the interview carried out on 6 June 2022 with the staff of the Tivoli PPO, as part of the case study presented in this chapter.
7 Directive 2012/29/EU, arts. 22 and 23.
8 Legge 4 aprile 2001, n. 154; Legge 29 marzo 2001, n. 134; Legge 23 aprile 2009, n. 38; Legge n. 77 del 2013; Decreto-Legge n. 93 del 2013; Legge n. 69 del 2019 (c.d. codice rosso); Legge n. 134 del 2021; Legge n. 53 del 2022; Legge 24 novembre 2023, n. 168.
9 Council of Europe, Convention on preventing and combating violence against women and domestic violence (Istanbul), 2011. Critical legal developments have also been introduced with Directive 2012/29/EU; Directive 99/2011/; Regulation 2013/606/EU; Directive 2024/1385/EU.
10 In Italy, health facilities are required to adhere to social and healthcare protocols for women who experience abuse, including notifying authorities when medical reports are suspected to be linked to violent incidents (Decreto del Presidente del Consiglio dei Ministri del 24 novembre 2017, GU n.24 del 30-1-2018). However, these protocols are rarely implemented in practice.
11 Excerpt of the interview carried out on 6 June 2022 with the staff of the Tivoli PPO, as part of the case study presented in this chapter.

References

Amato, R. (2024). La gestione giudiziaria dei casi di violenza nelle relazioni di intimità (IPV): Dall'organizzazione effimera a un sistema specialistico di case-management (CNR-DSU Working Paper 2). CNR-Dipartimento di Scienze Umane e Sociali, Patrimonio culturale.

Amato, R., & Carnevali, D. (2022). The calm after the storm? The tricky path to restoring the enjoyment of individual rights in intimate partner violence cases. Oñati Socio-Legal Series, 12(3), 443–477.

Barnett, O. W. (2001). Why battered women do not leave, part 2: External inhibiting factors—Social support and internal inhibiting factors. Trauma, Violence, & Abuse, 2(1), 3–35.

Bonewit, A., & De Santis, E. (2016). The Issue of Violence against Women in the European Union (PE 556.931). March. Study, Policy Department C: Citizens' Rights and Constitutional Affairs European Parliament.

Bonomi, A. E., Anderson, M. L., Reid, R. J., Rivara, F. P., Carrell, D., & Thompson, R. S. (2009). Medical and psychosocial diagnoses in women with a history of intimate partner violence. Archives of Internal Medicine, 166(1), 22–30.

Canu, R. (2008). La violenza domestica contro le donne in Italia e nel contesto. Cagliari: La Riflessione Davide Zedda.

Cerrato, Cerrato, E., et al. (2017). European Protection Order, European Implementation Assessment. Brussels: EPRS Study.

Clough, A., Draughon, J. E., Njie-Carr, V. P. S., Rollins, C., & Glass, N. (2013). Having Housing Made Everything Else Possible": Affordable, Safe and Stable Housing for Women Survivors of Violence. Qualitative Social Work, 2014, 13(5), 671–688.

European Institute for Gender Equality (EIGE) (2019). Police and Justice Sector Data on Intimate Partner Violence against Women in the European Union. 12 June. Vilnius: EIGE.

European Union Agency for Fundamental Rights (FRA) (2014). Violence against Women: An EU-Wide Survey: Main Results. Vienna: FRA, 64–67.

Fisher, E. M., & Stylianou, A. M. (2019). To stay or to leave: Factors influencing victims' decisions to stay or leave a domestic violence emergency shelter. Journal of Interpersonal Violence, February, 34(4), 785–811.

Flood, M., & Pease, B. (2009). Factors influencing attitudes to violence against women. Trauma, Violence, & Abuse, 10(2), 125–142.

Garcia-Moreno, C., Jansen, H. A. F. M., Ellsberg, M., Heise, L., & Watts, C. H. (2006). Prevalence of intimate partner violence: Findings from the WHO multi-country study on women's health and domestic violence. The Lancet, 368(9543), 1260–1269.

Gezinski, L. B., & Gonzalez-Pons, K. M. (2021). Unlocking the door to safety and stability: Housing barriers for survivors of intimate partner violence. Journal of Interpersonal Violence, 36(17–18), 8338–8357.

Glenn, C., & Goodman, L. (2015). Living with and within the rules of domestic violence shelters: A qualitative exploration of residents' experiences. Violence against Women, 21(12), 1481–1506.

Goodman, L. A., & Smyth, K. F. (2011). A call for a social network-oriented approach to services for survivors of intimate partner violence. Psychology of Violence, 1(2), 79–92.

Hadeed, L. F., & El-Bassel, N. (2006). Social support among Afro-Trinidadian women experiencing intimate partner violence. Violence against Women, 12(8), 740–760.

Haaken, J. (2010). Hard Knocks: Domestic Violence and the Psychology of Storytelling. Routledge.

Johnson, M. P. (1995). Patriarchal terrorism and common couple violence: Two forms of violence against women in U.S. families. Journal of Marriage and Family, 57(2), 283–294.

Johnson, M. P. (2008). A Typology of Domestic Violence: Intimate Terrorism, Violent Resistance, and Situational Couple Violence. UPNE.

Johnson, M. P., & Ferraro, K. J. (2000). Research on domestic violence in the 1990s: Making distinctions. Journal of Marriage and Family, 62(4), 948–963.

Katerndahl, D., Burge, S., & Ferrer, R. (2013). Differences in social network structure and support among women in violent relationships. Journal of Interpersonal Violence, 28(9), 1948–1964.

Keilitz, S. L., Hannaford, P. L., & Efkeman, H. S. (1997). Civil Protection Orders: The Benefits and Limitations for Victims of Domestic Violence. National Institute of Justice.

Klein, A. R. (2009). Practical Implications of Current Domestic Violence Research: For Law Enforcement, Prosecutors and Judges. U.S. Department of Justice.

Koepsell, J. K., Kernic, M. A., & Holt, V. L. (2006). Factors that influence battered women to leave their abusive relationships. Violence and Victims, 21(2), 131–147.

Long, J., Mallios, C., & Murphy, S. (2010). Model Policy for Prosecutors and Judges on Imposing, Modifying and Lifting Criminal No Contact Orders: The Battered Women's Justice Project. Washington, DC: Aequitas.

Miyaoi, K. (2016). Developing Policy and Legal Frameworks for Ending Violence against Women: International Experiences. Minsk: United Nations Population Fund (UNFPA) Belarus.

Pajak, C. R., Ahmad, F., Jenney, A., Fisher, P., & Chan, L. M. (2014). Survivor's costs of saying no: Exploring the experience of accessing services for intimate partner violence. Journal of Interpersonal Violence, 29(14), 2571–2591.

Pecorella, C., & Farina, P. (2018). La risposta penale alla violenza domestica: un'indagine sulla prassi del Tribunale di Milano in materia di maltrattamenti contro familiari e conviventi (art. 572 c.p.). A Quarterly Review for Criminal Justice, 2, 190–208.

Prechal, S. (2019). The European Union's accession to the Istanbul convention. In: K. Lenaerts et al., eds., An Ever-Changing Union? Perspectives on the Future of EU Law in Honour of Allan Rosas. Oxford University Press, 279–292.

Römkens, R. (2010). Legal Protective Provisions or POs. Document Prepared for the Ad Hoc Committee on Preventing and Combating Violence against Women and Domestic Violence (CAHVIO). 21 May.

Sellier, E., & Weyembergh, A. (2018). Criminal Procedural Laws across the European Union—A Comparative Analysis of Selected Main Differences and the Impact They Have over the Development of EU Legislation. Study. Policy Department for Citizens' Rights and Constitutional Affairs.

Shreeves, R., & Prpic, M. (2019). Violence against Women in the EU: State of Play. European Parliamentary Research Service (EPRS).

Stubbs, J. (2008). The criminal justice response to domestic violence. Social & Legal Studies, 17(4), 423–439.

Stylianou, A. M., Counselman-Carpenter, E., & Redcay, A. (2021). "My sister is the one that made me stay above water": How social supports are maintained and strained when survivors of intimate partner violence reside in emergency shelter programs. Journal of Interpersonal Violence, 36(13–14), 6005–6028.

Thomas, K. A., Goodman, L. A., & Putnins, S. (2015). Deliberate self-presentation in help seeking by survivors of intimate partner violence. Psychology of Violence, 5(2), 129–138.

van der Aa, S. (2014). The right to protection. In: Superior Council of Magistracy of Romania, Strengthening Judicial Cooperation to Protect Victims of Crime: Handbook (JUST/2012/JPEN/AG/294). Superior Council of Magistracy of Romania, 112–127.

Vlachovà, M., & Biason, L. (2004). Women in an Insecure World: Violence against Women—Facts, Figures, and Analysis. Geneva Centre for the Democratic Control of Armed Forces.

Zara, G., & Gino, S. (2018). Intimate partner violence and its escalation into femicide: Frailty thy name is "violence against women". Frontiers in Psychology, 9.

Reports, institutional documents, and guidelines

Commission Staff Working Document Evaluation of Directive 2012/29/EU (SWD(2022) 180 final).

Commission Staff Working Document, Evaluation of Directive 2012/29/EU establishing minimum standards on the rights, support and protection of victims of crime, and replacing Council Framework Decision 2001/220/JHA (SWD/2022/0179 final).

Commission Staff Working Document, Impact Assessment Report Accompanying the Proposal for a Directive on combating violence against women and domestic violence (SWD(2022)62 final).

European Parliamentary Research Service (EPRS)—ex-post Evaluation Unit, 2017. Directive 2012/29/EU: European Implementation Assessment. PE 611.022.

Group of Experts on Action against Violence against Women and Domestic Violence (GREVIO), 2022. Mid-term Horizontal Review of GREVIO baseline evaluation reports.

Procura della Repubblica presso il Tribunale di Tivoli, 2023. Direttiva n. 2/2019: protocolli investigativi e buone prassi per la Polizia Giudiziaria in materia di reati di violenza di genere (Last update, 21 November 2023).

Report from the Commission to the European Parliament and the Council on the implementation of Directive 2011/99/EU of the European Parliament and of the Council of 13 December 2011 on the European Protection Order (COM/2020/187 final).

PART III

Contemporary drivers of victimisation and displacement

Climate and algorithms

10

DISPLACEMENT BY LOSS OF HOME AND COUNTRY

Global warming, climate change, and environmental degradation as drivers of trafficking

Jocelynne A. Scutt

Introduction

Displacement is occurring on a massive scale globally. A major cause—up to the present time possibly the foremost cause—is war, the last 50 years including the Viet Nam war, Afghanistan, the Gulf, Iraq, Syria . . . , plus African states of Rwanda, the Congo (DCR), South Sudan, Libya (Mishra 2025; ISS | PSC Report 2022), and the enduring and more recently intensified conflict in Israel/Gaza, the West Bank and Lebanon. Atop this, family disputation including criminal assault at home and other forms of domestic violence generates ongoing displacement within countries and internationally. The Hague Convention (Hague Conference nd; Hague Convention nd; Attorney-General's Department, nd), designed to address removal of children from their homebase to the country of origin of one parent against the wishes of the other is under review (Tetley 2012).[1] Surrogacy has gained traction as a growing source of displacement of children from the birth-mother's country to the country of commissioning couples, exacerbated by the Russia-Ukraine war (Bolton 2025; Pringle and Klein 2022; Klein 2019). Forced and "arranged'" marriages is another wellspring of transportation—displacement from Pakistan to China has considerable coverage (News Human Trafficking 2019; News World 2019), with other countries figuring regularly in the "paid for" brides stakes—for example Thailand and the Philippines to Australia, the United Kingdom, Germany, the United States, Canada . . . , with numerous sites advertising "mail order" brides (Lee 2024: Zare and Mendoza 2012; Epstein 2009), and Russia and eastern European countries adding to the exoticism and vulnerability of those trafficked.[2]

Climate change or global warming is rapidly becoming an equally urgent fount of displacement, destined (unless effective action intervenes) to eclipse other sources. Emergency motions are passed by national governments and local authorities

DOI: 10.4324/9781003752974-14

emphasising environmental degradation and damage to biodiversity on an expanding scale, emphasising the need for local, national and global action. Commitments agreed at successive UN Conference of the Parties (COP) meetings are touted as addressing nation states' responsibilities (UN Climate Change 2024d, 2024a, 2024b, 2024c; and see Scutt forthcoming). Yet such actions belie the Global North's continued reliance on fossil fuels and disproportionate dependency on modes of transport and manufacture generating dangerous levels of carbon dioxide (CO_2) and methane (CH_4) emissions. They also ignore the Global North's shift of production to the Global South, meaning that China, India and Bangladesh, countries in Africa and more recently South America (with rising manufacturing costs in China particularly driving this move), resulting in a commensurate shift of CO_2 and CH_4 emissions from (principally) the United Kingdom, United States and the EU (Scutt 2024). Harms to health, food security, loss of livelihoods and rising sea levels threatening dwellings are swelling the growth of trafficking. This becomes an inevitability when people are forced from their homes or live precarious lives exacerbated by global warming, with climate change increasing the vulnerability of already vulnerable groups, particularly women and children. Pelizzon (2025) canvasses the development of an ecological jurisprudence based in law aimed at reclaiming a global ecological balance, yet whether the law can drive or accelerate positive action rather than merely legal declarations, court opinions, or empty undertakings remains in question.

Global Warming Driving Displacement

The role of transport

That displacement through climate change requires transport of those trafficked is ironic, as transport is one of the major drivers of global warming, whether on land or sea. Suzanne Greene of MIT observes that trains, ships, planes, and trucks transport "billions of tons of cargo . . . around the world each year", constituting 8% of greenhouse gas emissions globally, and "as much as 11% if warehouses and ports are included" (Greene 2023). She confirms that road transport disproportionately contributes to emissions, the breakdown in 2023 being:

Air—303 billion of tonne-kilometres moved annually, generating 155ku millions of tonnes of CO_2 emissions

Rail—10,842 billion of tonne-kilometres moved annually, generating 170 million of tonnes of CO_2 emissions

Road (mainly trucking and urban deliveries)—26,807 billion of tonne-kilometres moved annually, generating 2,230 million of tonnes of CO_2 emissions

Sea and inland waterways—101,486 billion of tonne-kilometres moved annually, generating 657 million of tonnes of CO_2 emissions

Greene concludes that as "nearly all freight transportation runs on oil and gas", with Asia, Africa and Latin America "expected [by 2050] to triple global demand for freight . . . [this is anticipated] to double freight's greenhouse gas emissions" (Greene 2023, citing International Transport Forum 2021). This continues despite alternative forms of energy (Evans 2007).

For the United Kingdom and Australia, the figures on road versus rail transport are compelling. Road moves twice as much freight as does rail, yet the damage to the environment and contribution to global warming far outweigh any rail freight environmental damage or global warming contribution. Both countries embrace road versus rail, hence contributing disproportionately not only to their respective country's environmental degradation and threatened eclipse of biodiversity, but globally too. Here, the polluting nature of road transport through exhaust fumes (even with de-leaded petrol) and the extraordinary cost of road maintenance due to heavy vehicle traffic also add to the equation.

Why this reliance on expanded road transport over rail? In 1963 the British Railways Board published its Report No 1, the first Beeching Report (British Railways Board 1963). Beeching's recommendations for rationalising the rail system were based on duplication of routes by private companies that developed and initially ran railways, with varying gauges not only disallowing integration but rendering it impossible without major adjustment. Following the second world war, railway nationalisation produced some rationalisation and proposals for improving profitability. However, by the 1960s railways were designated as continuing to fail, with car travel and road freight predominating. The 1962 Transport Act introduced changes, including Beeching's appointment to the British Railways Board to lead reorganisation, including downgrading coverage of the UK by rail, "rationalising" passenger services and limiting freight transport. Many passenger services were transferred from trains to buses, seen as more accessible, reliable and responsive to changing needs for transport to and from varying locations. The freight question focused on increased road carriage and perceived rail transport problems. Smaller goods transport was addressed primarily by turning this freight over to highway carriage and, where retained by rail, introducing container transport. This was prescient, bearing in mind the now universal ship to truck freight carriage in containers (with efficient handling and transfer between transport modes), which could equally well serve transport by rail. The first Beeching Report undercut this potential, however, recommending that the major focus of freight by rail would be on bulk commodities, principally minerals and coal (British Railways Board 1963, pp. 141–148 , Appendix 2). This inevitably led to even greater concentration of freight transport by road, and consequent impact on climate change through the exponential growth of emissions and pollution.

For Australia, vast distances mean freight transport is essential on a large scale. That more freight is carried along highways by truck transport rather than on railways by freight trains, with greater negative impact on the environment, is a direct result of government policy. Transfer from rail to truck occurred later for Australia than the UK, freight transport by rail remaining pre-eminent until in the 1970s transfer to highways began on a significant scale. One company, Linfox, run by one man, Lindsey Fox, has been the major player. Son of a truck driver, Fox began his working career delivering coal from one location to another using his sole asset, a truck purchased on time payments (RTH nd). Born in 1937, Fox and his place in the Australian financial firmament is a measure of the lucrative nature of the trucking industry. In 2023, referencing Thomson's article "Celebrating 30 years of the Rich 200" (2013) based on the BRW Rich 200 (the Financial Review's annual listing of Australia's 200 wealthiest individuals and families, according to personal net worth), Bailey and Sprague (2023) in the Australian Financial Review noted that since 1984 Fox was one of ten Australians appearing in every Financial Review "Rich List". The Financial Review assessed his net worth in 2019 as A$3.72b, with Forbes assessing it for that year as US$3.50b (updated in 2025 as US$2.75b listed as "logistics"), this wealth gained through his business interests—principally the trucking industry (Karmali 2025).

Because road transport runs on oil and gas, if freight continues via this route at today's levels, by 2050 estimates set it as "the highest emitting sector", 65 percent of emissions being driven by road vehicles. Greene observes that although ships and trains carry freight:

> Most ships burn fossil fuels and emit carbon, but they carry large amounts of freight at the same time, making them the most efficient way to move cargo. Road freight, however, can emit more than 100 times as much CO_2 as ships to carry the same amount of freight the same distance. Road transport is also a fast-growing sector—80% of the global increase in diesel consumption can be attributed to trucks. E-commerce and home delivery are two reasons for this growth.
>
> *(Greene 2023; see also Emanuel 2024)*

Further, CO_2 and CH_4 are not the only environmentally damaging emissions attributable to road and highway transport. Car and truck exhaust pipes spew carbon into the atmosphere, exacerbating breathing disorders and polluting the air (CRECA 2025). Greene observes:

> Transportation equipment emits over 20% of the world's black carbon, a powerful short-lived climate pollutant. If you have ever seen a black plume of smoke coming from a truck's tailpipe—you've seen black carbon. These emissions can cause serious health problems if they happen where people live, as with home delivery or communities near ports. Black carbon is also tied to the fast melting of ice-covered areas, like glaciers or sea ice, where the dark particles from black carbon cause hotspots that lead to melting
>
> *(Greene 2023).*

Melting is, of course, a significant reason for rising sea levels, a principal force behind displacement and trafficking.

Further, exacerbation of environmental harm and biodiversity destruction by road transport lies not only in emissions and pollution directly associated with and emitting from vehicles. It arises from the damage to infrastructure requiring constant road and highway maintenance and repair, themselves producing CO_2 and CH_4 emissions and pollution, and adding to the mutilation of ecological growth and animal life skirting domestic thoroughfares, freeways and major arteries. Australia spends annually, across all levels of government, A$30b on roads and highways. Laird (2023) reports that reconstruction of "the entire Hume Highway (Melbourne to Sydney), bringing it up to modern engineering standards'" was funded by federal grants amounting to A$20b, with "a similar sum . . . spent on reconstructing most of the Pacific Highway (Sydney to Brisbane)". Without the massive trucks pounding up and down the highways environmental damage would be vastly lessened and such expenditure and road maintenance would be unnecessary, their contribution to global warming and hence displacement of populations would be eliminated.

The impact of war and defence spending

Climate change as a driver of human trafficking must also factor in war and defence spending: their impact is crucial not only as to direct displacement through bombing and rocket attacks destroying homes, buildings and communities, but in driving increased ecological harm leading to displacement. Despite estimates of global militaries as "some of the largest carbon polluters on the planet" (Neimark 2024), precise assessments are impossible. The 1997 Kyoto Protocol exempted military emissions reporting and, 18 years later, the 2015 Paris Agreement incorporated no requirement for inclusion of the impact of defence industries and war into participating countries' reduction of emissions programmes. Yet in reviewing various estimates of military affect, Jack Johnson (2021) reports that 20% of all environmental degradation globally is consequent upon military-related activities, with a 2020 Scientists for Global Responsibility (SGR) and Declassified UK finding that the UK military-industrial sector "produced the equivalent of 6.5 million tonnes of carbon dioxide", this being "greater than the CO2 emissions of 60 other countries":

> Meanwhile, the United States' Department of Defence (DOD) is the world's largest institutional consumer of petroleum and the world's largest institutional producer of greenhouse gases (GHG), producing over 3,685 million metric tonnes of CO_2 between 1975 and 2018. . . . In a similar fashion to the UK, US military emissions alone are consistently larger than the entire output of other industrialised nations, with the Pentagon's greenhouse gas emissions outweighing that of Sweden, Denmark and Portugal and GHG emissions from the DOD are also greater than all CO_2 emissions from US production of iron and steel.
>
> *(Johnson 2021, citing Angus 2016; Crawford 2019; Parkinson 2020a, 2020b, 2020c; and see also Verjauw 2019)*

Furthermore, emissions resulting from military action and defence production "are not limited to the Anglosphere". Rather, it appears that globally "the combined militaries of the world contribute to 6% of the global carbon footprint total, with China, Saudi Arabia, Russia and India being likely large contributors, [although being far] less transparent on their statistics" (Johnson 2021).

Crawford (2024) sets out six "known unknowns" crucial to setting baselines to determine the amount of GHGs (greenhouse gas) emissions necessary to cut if global temperature increase is to be limited below 1.5C° (34.7 F°), the "politically and scientifically" agreed necessary level:

- What are the total GHG emissions (CO_2e) of every country's military?
- What are the emissions of overseas installations (e.g. the US has approx. 800 bases in 80 countries);
- What are the radiative forcing (RF) effects of water vapour (contrails), black carbon and sulphates due to military aerial operations?
- What are the emissions of local military industries?
- How much fuel is used to defend sea lanes so that fossil fuels can be transported from the Persian Gulf?
- To what extent have "drop-in'" biofuel blends, or 100% biofuels, replaced petroleum-based fuels for naval, ground and air operations?

Kinney (2024) reports that the Conflict and Environment Observatory (CEOBS), an organisation "working to reduce the harm to people and ecosystems from armed conflicts and military activities" reports the launch of the "Military Emissions Gap" in 2021 to "track and analyse military emissions data" simultaneously with advocating for "accountability for the military's contribution to the climate crisis". The CEOBS and Scientists for Global Responsibility estimates that "everyday military activity" may account for "around 5.5% of global missions. If equalling countries' emissions with emissions of the world's militaries, the militaries would be the fourth largest emitter in the world" (Parkinson and Cotterell 2022; see also CCPI 2025).

A contrast between defence funding and funding for support and preservation of biodiversity highlights the difference in how these sectors are viewed, with defence spending and the military resources being favoured more than disproportionately over the latter. Co-founder of the Invasive Species Council and "expert on introduced species", Tim Lows "believes biosecurity is a growing threat" that has become "increasingly complex to prevent, detect and intercept" (Alwakal 2026). Yet the Australian Department of Agriculture, Fisheries and Forestry cites the Australian Department of Defence budget measured at "almost A$ 60 billion a year", whilst funding for biosecurity "is $AUS 935 million" with an estimated decline to A$ 889 million in 2028–2029. From Lows' perspective, biosecurity is "underfunded" and "should be valued as highly as defence" (Alwakal 2026). Factoring all this into analysis of displacement through global warming is essential, as is the recognition of vulnerable groups and communities not only in displacement into trafficking through wars and conflict, but when it comes to susceptibility and exposure to climate change and trafficking.

Climate change exacerbating vulnerability

CEDAW people's tribunal identifies sex-based inequalities and climate change

Demographic vulnerability and comparative defencelessness in the face of climate change is evidenced by research and reports on global warming. In the UK CEDAW People's Tribunal held in on 21–23 June 2021 climate change and its impact on women and girls formed a comprehensive section of the Report (CEDAW People's Tribunal 2021). The Report referenced UN CEDAW Committee GR (General Recommendation) 37, adopted on 13 March 2018 by 15 countries, including Argentina, Australia, Columbia, Egypt, Greece, Guatemala, Jordan, Malta, Mauritius, Mexico, Norway, Peru, the Russian Federation, Switzerland, and Trinidad and Tobago. GR 37 addresses risk and disasters, recognising that these are not limited to environmental degradation, but simultaneously acknowledging that "increasing frequency and severity of weather and climate hazards' aggravate and intensify risk and disaster impacts, heightening vulnerability of communities to those hazards" (UN OHCHR 2018). Human rights are affected through "political and economic instability, growing inequality, declining food and water security and increased threats to health and livelihoods" (UN OHCHR 2018). Whilst climate change "affects everyone", the effects on women and girls, men and boys are different, "with many women and girls experiencing greater risks, burdens and impacts" (UN OHCHR 2018; see also Wahono and Tobin 2024).

This results from existing sex-based inequalities and intersecting forms of discrimination, prompting a particular vulnerability to displacement and trafficking: not only does sex-based discrimination narrow the capacity for control over decision-making, including decisions about how to address global warming and its consequences, but limits "access to resources such as food, water, agricultural input, land, credit, energy, technology, education, health services, adequate housing, social protection and employment" (UN OHCHR 2018; see also UN Women 2025). This means in turn that women and girls "are more likely to be exposed to disaster-induced risks and losses relating to their livelihoods" whilst their adaptability to alterations in climactic conditions is less fluid. Discrimination underpinning or promoting structural barriers can leave women and girls with limited or no opportunities for alternative employment or opportunities for livelihood, meaning they must look elsewhere. Opportunistically, traffickers are on the watch, ready and waiting.

The CEDAW People's Tribunal Report recounted evidence from witnesses focusing on the need to combat neglect of attention to women and girls living under negative environmental and ecological conditions, examples including:

- Farmers—the typical image is of a male farmer, yet in many parts of the world, in particular sub-Saharan Africa and Asia, women are over 75% of the agricultural workforce so women are disproportionately affected by droughts or flash floods, with crops decimated, harvests lost and families going hungry, and women affected as producers of food and as carers and feeders of families . . . food insecurity is one of the primary effects of climate change, deepening hunger and poverty, in turn leading to greater dislocation and internal and international migration: the UN has projected numbers of climate migrants as well into the hundreds of millions;
- Cultural norms—women and girls can be more vulnerable to floods and drowning in parts of the world such as South Asia, impacted by cultural norms regarding modesty, clothing and physical activity—here, witness Melina Mehra noted the campaign Teach A Girl to Swim (Mehra 2021);
- Great East Japan Earthquake & Tsunami of 2011, with the rise of climate-related disasters including floods, hurricanes, fires and drought highlighted the essential need to improve understanding of gendered impacts to enable targeted investment in prevention and capacity building, involving women in the chain from community organisers to first responders, planners and ministers, thereby setting a good model for investment and capacity building (CEDAW People's Tribunal 2021, para 5).[3]

Tribunal witness Melina Mehra observed that not only food security, but water security "is a major climate risk, with public health implications and (impacting on food production and wellbeing) lack of irrigation" (CEDAW People's Tribunal 2021, para 5).

Global warming displacement and trafficking linkages

By 2018, warnings were sounding of the link between global warming and trafficking. Gerrard (2018) drew attention to deficiencies in implementing the objectives for limiting global increases in temperature set out in the 2015 Paris Climate Agreement, and limitations in international agreements and domestic laws designed to address human trafficking. Noting that human trafficking globally victimises "at least 21 million people . . . typically involving either sexual exploitation or forced labour", Gerrard concludes that the number is "possibly many more" and it is "highly uncertain whether [measures directed to combatting human trafficking] will be adequate to cope with the scale of the problem likely to occur as a result of climate change" (Gerrard 2018).

In July 2022 the US Department of State presaged that climate change had the potential "to become one of the main drivers of population displacement, internally and across international borders" (Office to Monitor and Combat Trafficking in Persons 2022). Listing "climate changing events" including "wildfires, droughts, flooding, extreme weather conditions, heat waves, environmental degradation, and rapid ice loss" as causing "hundreds of thousands of lives and billions of dollars in damages", the "negative repercussions on women and children" in particular, and their vulnerability to trafficking, was noted as a major concern. Food (in)security is one of the key factors, intensified by damage from drought and flooding, increases in destruction or harm to crops, and rising temperatures. As women are heavily invested in farming and agricultural food production on a domestic scale, the resultant decrease in crop productivity disproportionately affects them and their livelihoods (Office to Monitor and Combat Trafficking in Persons 2022). The International Labour Organisation (ILO) sees direct links between this and increased sex and domestic labour trafficking in women and children (IOM UN Migration 2019).

The 2024 UN Global Report on Trafficking in Persons found that women and girls "continue to make up the majority of victims detected worldwide", with "displacement, insecurity and climate change . . . exacerbating the vulnerability of Africans to being trafficked" (UNODC 2024). For the number of trafficking victims detected on a global level, the UN Office on Drugs and Crime (UNODC) reported a 25% increase over and above 2019 pre-pandemic rates, with forced labour between 2019 and 2022 "surging" by 47%. Causes were listed as "conflicts, climate-induced disasters and global crises", with children accounting for 38%of victims detected:

> Criminals are increasingly trafficking people into forced labour, including to coerce them into running sophisticated online scams and cyberfraud, while women and girls face the risk of sexual exploitation and gender-based violence.
> *(UNODC 2024)*

Legal action—potential for addressing displacement?

In light of this, legal action is at last beginning to nudge the attention of governments and private sector. Taking various approaches, lawyers highlight the impact of global warming on health and cultural rights, with rising sea levels, drought and floods interfering with food security, and damaging or rendering insecure housing and habitat, displacing populations and increasing traffickers' opportunities for exploiting their vulnerability.

Exemplar: Island States in the UN International Tribunal for the Law of the Sea (ITLOS)

In 2023 island nation states—Niue, Palau, St Lucia, Vanuatu, Saint Vincent and the Grenadines, Saint Kitts and Nevis, and The Bahamas—took their claim under the Convention on the Law of the Sea (CLOS) to the UN International Tribunal for the Law of the Sea (ITLOS) for a determinative opinion (International Tribunal for the Law of the Sea 2024). The dispute related to the responsibility—or not—of "first world" nations polluting sea levels, drowning the islands or at least cutting into the landmass and despoiling the land remaining. Island nation states are susceptible to the emissions, pollution, environmental degradation and narrowing of biodiversity imposed upon the world as a consequence of "first world" nations industrialisation generating climate change and global warming. On 21 May 2024 the tribunal determined the scope of the law of the sea under CLOS (decision (International Tribunal for the Law of the Sea Year 2024 (ITLOS) 2024). That the decision was ground-breaking is evident in legal commentary and the response of the international community. The OCHCR reported immediately ITLOS' conclusion that nation states are obligated to "protect the marine environment from climate change impacts and ocean acidification". Greenhouse gas emissions are, said ITLOS, "a form of marine pollution'" (OHCHR 2023). The World Economic Forum weighed in, observing that ITLOS had held the Paris Agreement inadequate to advance the rights of these island nation states, and "first world'" countries must institute better action to remedy the wrong and to prevent further degradation of both sea and land (World Economic Forum 2024).

Precised by the OCHCR, the claimants' case:

> analysed how international human rights obligations are applicable to the protection of the marine environment from climate change, including preventing disproportionate impacts on those in vulnerable situations, particularly in Small Island Developing States.
>
> *(OCHCR 2023, para 258)*

In its landmark decision delivered on 21 May 2024 (International Tribunal for the Law of the Sea Year 2024 (ITLOS) 2024), ITLOS "made the unprecedented recognition that greenhouse gas emissions are a form of marine pollution" (World Economic Forum 2024). ITLOS held that states parties to CLOS have a duty beyond the 2015 Paris Agreement to protect the marine environment "from climate change impacts and ocean acidification". This duty includes:

> designing mitigation measures to minimise, to the fullest extent possible, the release of toxic substances into the marine environment and exercising strict due diligence to ensure that non-State actors comply with mitigation measures.
>
> *(World Economic Forum 2024)*

That is, the duty extends beyond nation states exercising responsibility in relation to its own actions and design and implementation of mitigation measures, to taking whatever action they can to control or implement measures impacting on corporations which states have a duty to regulate effectively.

As to cooperation between states in applying obligations under CLOS Article 194, ITLOS judges were not unanimous. The dispute was, however, as to scope rather than the fundamental question of duty. The majority held that international cooperation went beyond states' duty in respect of the ocean within its own boundaries. According to the majority, this meant that CLOS imposes upon states "a particular obligation applicable to the transboundary setting in addition to the obligation to prevent, reduce and control pollution from anthropogenic GHG emissions". States must, thereby:

> take all measures necessary to ensure that anthropogenic GHG emissions under their jurisdiction and control do not cause damage to other States and their environment, and that pollution from such emissions under their jurisdiction or control does not spread beyond the areas where they exercise sovereign rights.
>
> *(ITLOS 2024, para 258)*

This obligation is stringent because it is designed to address transboundary pollution.

In respect of displacement the decision is significant in going to, amongst other matters, food security. Small nation states are reliant upon fishing for sustainability. Oceanic pollution directly impacts on their ability to survive. Food security goes beyond "what is in the ocean", to the incursion of the sea onto land and interference with agriculture and other food sources. This aspect arose, together with additional impacts of climate change on populations and interference with their right to remain on their own territory, in a case brought by Torres Strait Islanders against Australia.

Exemplar: Torres Strait Islands in the UN Human Rights Committee

A year before action was initiated in ITLOS, in 2022 the UN Human Rights Committee held Australia liable for failure to take adequate steps to support Torres Strait Islanders in maintaining their cultural heritage, food production, health (particularly of the children) and land (from disappearing under the sea) (Daniel Billy and Ors (represented by counsel Client Earth) v Australia 2022; see also OHCHR 2022b). The case was fought by reference to the International Covenant on Civil and Political Rights (ICCPR) (OHCHR 1966a; OHCHR.org (nd). Alleged violation of Article 6 of the ICCPR was dismissed on the basis that the evidence did not disclose loss of life or imminent loss of life due to climate change, albeit that might lie in the future:

Article 6

1. Every human being has the inherent right to life. This right shall be protected by law. No one shall be arbitrarily deprived of his life.

Nevertheless, the UN Committee determined that Australia had violated ICCPR Articles 17 and 27 (OHCHR 1966a), meaning there was no need for it to go on to consider violation (or otherwise) of Article 24 (1) (OHCHR 1966b).

Rights of the claimants breached were, therefore:

Article 17

1. No one shall be subjected to arbitrary or unlawful interference with his privacy, family, home or correspondence, nor to unlawful attacks on his honour and reputation.
2. Everyone has the right to the protection of the law against such interference or attacks.

> ### Article 27
>
> In those States in which ethnic, religious or linguistic minorities exist, persons belonging to such minorities shall not be denied the right, in community with the other members of their group, to enjoy their own culture, to profess and practise their own religion, or to use their own language.

The case was brought by Australian citizens being inhabitants of the Torres Strait islands, variously living on four of the approximately 274 islands comprising Torres Strait Islands, namely Boigu (Stanley Marama and Keith Pabai), Masig (Yessie, Genia, Ikasa, Awara, Santoi Mosby and Baimop Mosby, and Nazareth Warria), Warraber (Daniel Billy and Ted Billy, and Kabay and Tyrique Tamu) and Poruma (Nazareth Fauid). The claimants or authors of the application to the UN Human Rights Committee were agreed to be residing "in low-lying islands, [and therefore] are among the populations most vulnerable to the impact of climate change" (Daniel Billy and Ors v Australia 2022).

An Australian government body, the Torres Strait Regional Authority (TSRA), was cited as stating:

> the effects of climate change threaten the islands themselves as well as marine and coastal ecosystems and resources, and therefore the life, livelihoods and unique culture of Torres Strait Islanders. [Further,] even small increases in sea level due to climate change will have an immense impact on Torres Strait communities, potentially threatening their viability [and] large increases would result in several Torres Strait islands being completely inundated and uninhabitable.
>
> *(*Daniel Billy and Ors v Australia *2022, para 2.2)*

Flooding and erosion of Boigu, Masig, Warraber and Poruma was evidenced as occurring already, with "higher temperature and ocean acidification [producing] coral bleaching, reef death and the decline of seagrass beds and other nutritionally and culturally important marine species". The TSRA confirmed that in the Torres Strait region, "sea level has risen at the rate of approximately 0.6 cm per year from 1993 to 2010 (compared with the global average of 3.2 mm per year)" (Daniel Billy and

Ors v Australia 2022, para 2.3). However, this difference did not lessen the urgency of the claimants/authors' concerns.

The case was brought on four bases:

(a) Health—particularly for the children, accepted in the outcome to be particularly susceptible to the effects of climate change and global warming, because their age means that they will—if fortunate—live longer during increasing impacts (it is accepted that some will die from the impacts and many will suffer health consequences);
(b) Food—not only is land for cultivation disappearing, but the incursion of sea water is affecting the viability of growing produce;
(c) Culture—rising seas are sweeping away graves and ancestors, grandparents and parents buried in graveyards that are vital to the maintenance of history and continuity of culture and lifestyle;
(d) Land swallowed up—land is disappearing with the prospect of the claimants/authors losing their homes and habitat entirely—some homes are already at risk.

Evidence provided to the Committee observed:

> the village on Boigu, one of five communities particularly vulnerable to inundation, is flooded each year. Erosion has caused the shoreline to advance and has detached a small area from the island. On Masig in March 2019, a cyclone caused severe flooding and erosion and destroyed buildings. The cyclone resulted in the loss of three metres of shoreline. Approximately one metre of land is lost every year. . . . On Warraber, high tides and strong winds cause seawater to flood the village centre every two to three years. On Poruma, erosion has washed away much of the island's sand over the past few decades.
>
> (Daniel Billy and Ors v Australia *2022, para 2.4)*

On food (in)security, the claimants/authors' evidence was that the rising sea-levels "caused saltwater to penetrate the soil of the islands, [resulting in] areas previously used for traditional gardening [being unable to] be cultivated". Rising sea levels on Masig had "caused coconut trees to become diseased", rendering them unable to produce "fruits or coconut water, which are part of the authors' traditional diet". This created reliance on "expensive imported goods", often beyond the claimants/authors' income capacity. The unpredictability arising from climate change and global warming interfered with seasonal and wind patterns that "play a key role in ensuring the authors' livelihoods and subsistence" meaning that these are no longer dependable. Additionally:

> Precipitation, temperature and monsoon seasons have been subject to change, making it harder for the authors to pass on their traditional ecological knowledge.

> Seagrass beds and dependent species have disappeared. While crayfish is a fundamental source of food and income for the authors, they no longer find crayfish in areas where coral bleaching has occurred.
>
> (Daniel Billy and Ors v Australia *2022, paras 2.4–2.5)*

> In addition to the interference with passing on "traditional ecological knowledge", family graves have been destroyed by "a tidal surge . . . scattering human remains".
>
> (Daniel Billy and Ors v Australia *2022, para 2.5)*

Thus, internal displacement is already in view of the Islanders, with the looming spectre of having to abandon their island homes altogether. The people are immediately vulnerable to traffickers and trafficking.

Although reports of traffickers descending upon the Torres Strait islands are so far lacking, the potential is there, just as it is hitting other island nations and low-lying countries impacted by sea levels rising and suffering the consequences of global warming and climate change driving trafficking. This follows, too, for loss of inland habit experiencing rising water tables. In the US, Alaska is already experiencing loss of houses and townships due to emerging sinkholes, with entire villages drowning through a combination of falling land set against rising water tables (Schwing and Adams 2025).

Displacement by interventions of traffickers and trafficking

Trafficking in human persons is defined by the OCHR as:

> the recruitment, transportation, transfer, harbouring or receipt of persons, by means of the threat or use of force or other forms of coercion, of abduction, of fraud, of deception, of the abuse of power or of a position of vulnerability or of the giving or receiving of payments or benefits to achieve the consent of a person having control over another person, for the purpose of exploitation.
>
> *(OHCHR 2021)*

Exploitation is defined to include, at a minimum, "exploitation or the prostitution of others or other forms of sexual exploitation, forced labour or services, slavery or practices similar to slavery, servitude or the removal of organs" (OHCHR 2021).

According to the OHCHR, "millions of people continue to be trafficked each year, in all regions and in most countries of the world" (2021). The UNODC relates that almost every country in the world "is affected by human trafficking", whether as "point of origin, transit or destination". Women make up two-thirds of the world's trafficked victims, one in five victims are children, and "victims from at least 127 countries" are reported as "exploited in 137 States" (UNODC 2024). This involves domestic trafficking—within a country, or international trafficking—across borders. Purposes vary from "forced and exploitative labour in factories, farms and private households", to exploitation through sexual "services", forced marriage, or removal of organs for transplantation or experimentation. Because it is carried out in secret, or at least this is the endeavour of those engaged in the trade, determining with any certainty exacting how many millions of victims—and how many victim/survivors—traffickers procure and exploit is difficult. The OHCHR cites statistics from the Walk Free Foundation and Global Estimates from the International Labour Organisation (ILO) putting the trade at "25 million people . . . subjected to forced labour and sexual exploitation in 2016 worldwide". According to the 2020 Global Report from UNODC (again cited by the OHCHR 2021) women and girls are again in the forefront:

- About one-third of total detected victims were children, both girls and boys, while 20% were adult men;
- The remainder—approximately 50%—were women;
- Most victims (50%) were trafficked for the purpose of sexual exploitation, while 38% were trafficked for forced labour.
- Concerning the shares of types of exploitation:
    - Girls: 72% trafficked for sexual exploitation, 21% for forced labour, 7% for other forms;
    - Boys: 23% trafficked for sexual exploitation, 66% for forced labour, 11% for other forms;
    - Women: 77% trafficked for sexual exploitation, 14% for forced labour, 9% for other forms;
    - Men: 17% trafficked for sexual exploitation, 67% for forced labour, 1% for organ removal, 15% for other forms.

Vulnerability through "denial of economic and social rights" and poverty gives rise to desperation leading some who are subjected to this discrimination to "take risks and make decisions" which would not have been so if they had access to freedom of choice, and real choices. Vulnerability also arises through age—obviously children are more vulnerable, and girls can be sold into marriage by families whose lack of access to "basic needs" propels them to abandon their daughters to traffickers—often on the baseless promise of "a better life". In 2002, recognising these factors led to the UN Convention Against Transnational Organized Crime being supplemented by the Protocol to Prevent, Suppress and Punish the Trafficking in Persons, especially women and children (United Nations 2000).

Increasingly climate change and global warming are being recognised as factors in and leading to an increase in trafficking. In July 2022 the UN Special Rapporteur on trafficking in persons, especially women and children, reported on "heightened risks'" of trafficking due to climate change, these being:

> rooted in existing and persistent inequalities, in poverty, in racism, and in discrimination [arising] from policy failures, failures of political will and failures of international cooperation and solidarity.
>
> *(United Nations 2022a; see also United Nations 2022b)*

Disasters that are "climate-related" and can be slow in their effect (such as loss of land to rising sea levels, interference in food cultivation through salination of the soil, or slow onset health conditions affecting parents so that children are orphaned and hence vulnerable) but lead to displacement, migration and trafficking.

Academic and "on the ground" research reveals climate change and global warming as increasingly responsible for vulnerability and the growth of predatory marketeers. This includes research into Cambodia farming communities (Phon and Price 2024) rising temperatures in China (Zhu and Fan 2021), extreme weather events endangering citizens of Pacific Island nations (Mahany and Keim 2012; Rumsey et al. 2014), India, Thailand, Sir Lanka and Indonesia suffering population displacement through the "tsunami shock" (Migration Policy Institute 2005). Focusing on the 2005 tsunami, following tidal wave flooding and devastation, "thousands of children" were left "orphaned or separated from their families". The extent of displacement is illustrated in that more than 35,000 children in Aceh were estimated as having lost one or both parents. Trafficking was already high in these areas, and warnings were rife of children in particular being trafficked "from Aceh to Medan" with "a mobile phone text message [being] sent widely around Asia advertising the sale of 300 Aceh orphans" and reports of child-trafficking to Malaysia and Jakarta in the first days after the tsunami's impact. Loss of jobs and the need for long-term recovery meant that adults, too, were at risk (Migration Policy Institute 2005).

Court action illustrates the concerns prompting efforts by island nations and developing countries to fight back against the disproportionate impact of climate change they are suffering. Legal actions are instituted on the domestic front, too, including claims of governments' duty of care towards their populations (Urgenda Foundation v State of the Netherlands 2015; Juliana v United States 2020; Kelsey Cascadia Rose Juliana et al. v United States of America et al. 2024; Mason 2025; Environment Council of Central Queensland Inc v Minister for the Environment (No 2) 2023; Living Wonders 2024; Equity Generation Lawyers 2025), and corporate liability for generating climate change through manufacturing, mining and other capital intensive activities (Friends of the Earth Netherlands (Milieudefensie) v Shell Plc (Shell) 2021;[4] Verdict climate case 2021; Commune de Grande-Synthe v France 2021a; Commune de Grande-Synthe v France 2021b; Lavrysen 2021; Climate Law Accelerator 2022). One of the consequences is displacement and the struggle to survive, which is driving increased trafficking—mistreatment through sexual imposition, slave labour and domestic exploitation.

Conclusion—trafficking and displacement by climate change and global warming

These legal interventions raise the question whether law can end or at least alleviate this new realm of displacement, a direct result of industrialisation of developed countries beginning with the UK then the US and Europe. "Modern slavery" is to some extent, at least, being addressed through legislation criminalising traffickers—including for example the Modern Slavery Act 2015 (UK), Modern Slavery Act 2018 (Cth) (Department of Attorney-General 2018) and Modern Slavery Act 2018 (NSW). These legislative initiatives address trafficking once it has been undertaken and people arrive through "slave chains"—usually from less well-off or "developing countries" into "first world" states. Yet the real question is: how can displacement generating the need for action under "modern slavery" statutes be addressed before "modern slavery" intervenes? Further, what compensatory regime can be introduced and implemented to save land from sea immersion and other forms of environmental and biodiversity destruction, ensuring real alternatives to displacement and trafficking can be achieved or, indeed, maintained or ended?

In recounting the development of an ecological jurisprudence working to displace the "anthropocentric worldview" historically anchoring both common and civil law systems, Pelizzon (2025) mounts an argument that the law can be reconfigured to address climate change in the interests of the natural world itself, in turn advantaging the humans who are wreaking destruction on the planet. He argues that the "explicit emergence of an environmental and ecological consciousness and ethics" can presage this change (Pelizzon 2025, p. 3; see also Pringle 2024). The aim is to make environmental damage—already scientifically visible, "the effects of these damages engender[ing] a high degree of scientific consensus" and scientifically agreed as "caused by human activities"—both legally visible and legally relevant (Pelizzon 2025, p. 3). Thereby the "rights of Nature" would inform judicial decision making (Pelizzon 2025, pp. 265–320). This would mean that human beings—humanity—would benefit, as the environmental destruction that is at the core of current political-social and economic organisation determined by governments and private sector operatives would be ended. In undermining the causes of global warming and climate change, this, in turn, would end trafficking through displacement.

Reflecting on the direction of contemporary case law, perhaps law and legal process are working to shift traditional jurisprudence into a new dimension that could alleviate conditions promoting an increase in human trafficking through climate change. Yet is the shift, if it is there, sufficient? In the end, the crisis confronting the world is whether global warming has gone too far. If displacement is inevitable, legal action too late or too little, are (some) human populations destined to a future of being "saved" through trafficking?

Notes

1 An Australian review of the Hague Convention is described as "tinkering" without sufficient attention paid to the "best interests of the child" (Wyeth 2023; Gray and Kaye 2023). Nonetheless it introduced a potentially firmer direction by enabling judges to refuse to order repatriation in light of child sexual abuse and exploitation allegations. This approach appears to be on the ascendent elsewhere—see, for example, *SD v AD* [2023]; Skilling 2023; *H v B Family Division* [2022]; Family Law Experts 2025.

2 These marriages not infrequently generate court action, including family law disputes, applications for intervention or non-molestation orders, and criminal cases involving violence including unlawful killing: Scutt (1983, 1990) (particularly update chapter). That this source is some 35 years ago makes little difference: if anything, statistics have increased (Epstein 2009; Joseph 2023).

3 Note that during the 2004 Tsunami in Thailand "more women than men died because they stayed back to look for children and relatives . . ., and because they did not know how to swim and climb trees as the men and boys did" (PreventionWeb 2019; and see also Mehra 2021).

4 Friends of the Earth won in the first instance, with duty of care sustained on appeal, but that part of the decision setting an emissions target was overturned, the appellate court holding that the Netherlands government has no power to impose a specific target of reduction of emissions, so long as no scientific consensus exists of the necessary reduction in a specific sector and country (Commentary 2024).

References

Reported cases

Commune de Grande-Synthe v France [2021a] 20201119_Not-Yet-Available_decision-3.pdf (accessed 5 May 2025) (interim decision in English).

Commune de Grande-Synthe v France [2021b] Commune de Grande-Synthe v. France—Climate Change Litigation (accessed 5 May 2025).

Daniel Billy and Ors (represented by counsel Client Earth) v Australia, 21 July 2022, docstore.ohchr.org/SelfServices/FilesHandler.ashx?enc=6QkG1d%2FPPRiCAqhKb7yhstmouIju%2F14z6o8I4G3YTJP7zTkztF46bmE3ilRFbvidB3GXW8LzKWzG4gM9vziil3%2FVQX4dUpqqHLnHGa78RQVA%2BPD28AmHIJR3lQH3kdJA-flpXokfgXMyYfyHhgXJNrw%3D%3D (accessed 21 September 2024).

Environment Council of Central Queensland Inc v Minister for the Environment (No 2) [2023] FCA 1208.

Friends of the Earth Netherlands (Milieudefensie) v *Shell Plc (Shell)*, Verdict-climate-case-milieudefensie-shell-26-may-2021.pdf (accessed 5 May 2025).

H v B Family Division [2022] EWHC 526 (Fam) Judge Judd J, Capcha | CaseMine (accessed 2 May 2025).

International Tribunal for the Law of the Sea (ITLOS), 'List of Cases', *Webcast Archives: Case No 21*, Request for an advisory opinion submitted by the Sub-Regional Fisheries Commission (SRFC) (itlos.org) (accessed 21 September 2024).

International Tribunal for the Law of the Sea Year 2024, Request for an Advisory Opinion Submitted by the Commission of Small Island States on Climate Change and International Law Advisory Opinion, List of cases: No. 31, 21 May 2024, C31_Adv_Op_21.05.2024_orig.pdf (itlos.org) (accessed 21 September 2024).

ITLOS, C31_Adv_Op_21.05.2024_orig.pdf (itlos.org) (accessed 21 September 2024).
Juliana v United States 947 F 3d 1159 (9th Cir 2020), Juliana v. United States | Juvenile Law Center (accessed 2 May 2025).
Kelsey Cascadia Rose Juliana et al v United States of America et al Docket for 24–645 (accessed 2 May 2025).
SD v AD [2023] CSIH 17, AD AGAINST SD | [2023] CSIH 17 | Scottish Court of Session | Judgment | Law | CaseMine (accessed 2 May 2025).
Urgenda Foundation v State of the Netherlands [2015] HAZA CX/09/00456689, Urgenda Foundation v. State of the Netherlands—Climate Change Litigation (accessed 2 March 2024).

Statutes

Modern Slavery Act 2015 (UK), Modern Slavery Act 2015 (legislation.gov.uk) (accessed 21 September 2024).
Modern Slavery Act 2018 (Cth), C2018A00153REC01.pdf (accessed 2 May 2025).
Modern Slavery Act 2018 (Cth), Federal Register of Legislation—Modern Slavery Act 2018 (accessed 21 September 2018).
Modern Slavery Act 2018 (NSW), Modern Slavery Act 2018 No 30—NSW Legislation (accessed 2 May 2025).

Articles, book chapters, reports and texts

Alwakal, Yassmine (2026). 'An invasive species': How an Australian marsupial took over this remote Bitish island', *Dateline*, 11 January, How an Australian marsupial took over this remote British island | SBS Dateline (accessed 11 January 2026).
Angus, I. (2016). *Facing the Anthropocene: Fossil Capitalism and the Crisis of the Earth System*, Monthly Review Press, New York, NY.
Attorney-General's Department (n.d.). Hague Convention on the Civil Aspects of International Child Abduction | Attorney-General's Department (accessed 21 September 2024).
Bailey, Michael and Sprague, Julie-anne (2023). 'The 200 richest people in Australia revealed', *Australian Financial Review Magazine*, 25 May, AFR Rich List 2023: Australia's 200 wealthiest people are revealed (accessed 2 March 2024).
Bolton, Maja von (2025). Chapter 9 'Surrogacy: A question of women's right to self-determination or exploitation of women's bodies?', in J. A. Scutt (ed.), *Women, Power and Autonomy—Rights, Respect and Representation in Law and Society*, pp. 243–271, Palgrave Macmillan, London.
British Railways Board (1963). *The Reshaping of British Railways*, Part 1, HMSO, London, 'The Beeching Report', BRB_Beech001a.pdf (accessed 2 September 2024).
CCPI (2025). *Climate Change Performanc Impact*, Impact | Climate Change Performance Index (accessed 1 January 2025).
CEDAW People's Tribunal (2021). (296) CEDAW People's Tribunal—YouTube (accessed 2 March 2024).
CEDAW People's Tribunal Report (2021). available from the author.
Climate Law Accelerator (2022). 'Casebook—*Commune de Grande-Synthe v France*—vulnerable coastal municiplaity successfuly challenges the French government's climate inaction', *NYU Law*, Commune de Grande-Synthe v. France—CLX—Climate Law Accelerator Toolkit (accessed 21 November 2024).
Commentary (2024). 'Landmark climate change case overturned . . .', *Insights*, 13 November, Landmark Climate Change Case Overturned: The Hague Court of Appeals Overturns Ruling Ordering Shell to Reduce CO2 Emissions | Insights | Jones Day (accessed 5 May 2025).

Crawford, Neta C. (2019). *Pentagon Fuel Use, Climate Change and the Costs of War*, Brown University, Providence, RI.

Crawford, Neta C. (2024). 'Known unknowns: Big questions around military and military industiral emissions', in Benjamin Neimark, Nita C. Crawford, Oliver Belcher, Stuart Parkinson, Linsey Cotterell, Frederick Otu-Larbi, Lennard de Klerk, Reuben Labi, Lin Kali, Michaelowa Ho-Chih, Heidrich Axel, Rajaeifar Oliver, Depledge Mohammad, Santos Duncan, Bell Tamiris, Bigger Karen, Rogaly Partick, Khem and Nico Edwards (eds.), *Confronting Military Greenhouse Gas Emissions—Interactive Policy Brief*, London, UK, Confronting-military-greenhouse-gas-emissions,-Neimark-et-el,-Interactive-policy-brief-(2024)-[Print].pdf (accessed 1 January 2026).

CRECA (2025). Health impacts of diesel vehicles suspected of using prohibited defeat devices in the EU and UK—Centre for Research on Energy and Clean Air (accessed 28 May 2025).

Department of Attorney-General (2018). 'Modern slavery', *A-G's Department, Australian Government*, Modern slavery | Attorney-General's Department (ag.gov.au) (accessed 21 September 2024).

Emanuel, Kerry (2024). 'Climate science, risk & solutions', *MIT*, Updated for 2024, Home—Climate Science, Risk & Solutions (accessed 24 April 2025).

Epstein, Daniel (2009). 'Romance is dead . . .', *Buffalo Journal of Gender Law and Social Justice*, vol 17, 1–35, Romance is Dead: Mail Order Brides as Surrogate Corpses by Daniel Epstein:: SSRN (accessed 2 February 2025).

Equity Generation Lawyers (2015). 'Parents v EnergyAustralia . . .', 15 May 2025, Equity Generation Lawyers | Parents v EnergyAustralia (Offsets Greenwashing)—Equity Generation Lawyers (accessed 15 May 2025).

Evans, Robert L. (2007). *Fueling Our Future: An Introduction to Sustainable Energy*, Cambridge University Press, Cambridge.

Family Law Experts (2025). 'Court refuses to return child . . .', *Southgate Solicitors*, 12 May, Court refuses to return child to his father under Hague Convention—southgate solicitors (accessed 12 May 2025) (England).

Gerrard, Michael B. (2018). 'Climate change and human trafficking after the Paris agreement', *University of Miami Law Review*, vol 72, no 2, Symposium Climate Wrongs and Human Rights, Climate Change and Human Trafficking After the Paris Agreement (accessed 2 March 2024).

Gray, Annabelle and Kaye, Miranda (2023). 'Redressing the balance . . .', *International Journal of Law, Policy and the Family*, vol 37, no 1, Redressing the balance: How Australia's approach under the Hague Abduction Convention is still endangering victims of domestic violence | International Journal of Law, Policy and the Family | Oxford Academic (oup.com) (accessed 21 September 2024).

Greene, Suzanne (2023). 'Explainer—Freight transportation', *Climate Portal*, 3 February, Freight Transportation | MIT Climate Portal (accessed 2 September 2024).

Hague Conference on International Law (n.d.). HCCH | Child Abduction Section (accessed 21 September 2024).

Hague Convention (n.d.). HCCH | #34—Full text (accessed 21 September 2024).

International Transport Forum (2021). 'OECD Regional, rural and urban development', *ITF Transport Outlook 2021*, Regional, rural and urban development | OECD (accessed 2 September 2024).

IOM UN Migration (2019). 'Ending child labour . . .', *IOM Publications Platform*, Ending child labour, forced labour and human trafficking in global supply chains | IOM Publications Platform (accessed 2 March 2024).

ISS| PSC Report (2022). 'African conflicts to watch . . .', *PSC Insights*, 17 December 2021, African conflicts to watch in 2022 | PSC Report (issafrica.org) (accessed 21 September 2024).

Johnson, Jack (2021). 'The impact of militaries . . .', *University of Birmingham*, The impact of militaries on climate change—University of Birmingham (accessed 2 March 2024).

Joseph, Wendy (2023). *Unlawful Killings*, Transworld Publishers, London.

Karmali, Naazneen (2025). 'Australia's 50 richest', *Forbes 2025*, Australia's 50 Richest 2025 (accessed 12 March 2025).

Kinney, Ell (2024). *Conflict and Environment Observatory*, 14 November 2024, Guest Article: CCPI x Military Emissions Gap—How Military Emissions Impact Global Warming | Climate Change Performance Index (accessed 1 January 2025).

Klein, Renate (2019). 'A Cry from the heart . . .', *CBC*, 22 August, A cry from the heart: Surrogacy scandals in Ukraine—The Center for Bioethics & Culture Network (accessed 2 March 2024).

Laird, Philip (2023). 'Australia's freight used to go by train . . .', *The Conversation*, 19 December, Australia's freight used to go by train, not truck. Here's how we can bring back rail—and cut emissions (2 March 2024).

Lavrysen, Luc (2021). 'The French climate case: Legal basis and broader meaning', *IUCN Nature* 2030, 11 February, The French Climate Cases: Legal Basis and Broader Meaning | IUCN (accessed 5 May 2025).

Lee, Kolline (2024). 'How to find and bring a Thai bride . . .', *Asian Women Blog*, 16 May, How to Find and Bring a Thai Bride to the UK?—Asian Women Blog (asiawomen.net) (accessed 21 September 2024).

Living Wonders (2024). 'Legal updates: Living wonders in the full federal court', *Living Wonders*, 17 July, Legal updates: Living Wonders Full Federal Court appeals—Living Wonders (accessed 2 May 2025).

Mahany Mollie J. and Keim, Mark E. (2012). 'Challenges and strategies for climate change adaptation . . .', *Disaster Medicine and Public Health Preparedness*, vol 6, no 4, 415–423, December, Challenges and strategies for climate change adaptation among Pacific Island nations—PubMed (nih.gov) (accessed 25 September 2024).

Mason, Larry D. (2025). 'U.S. Supreme Court ends youth climate change suit . . .', *Environmental Law Monitor*, 28 March, U.S. Supreme Court Ends Youth Climate Change Suit—Environmental Law Monitor (accessed 2 May 2025).

Mehra, Melina (2021). *Teach a Girl to Swim*, 2022, Teach a Girl to Swim (accessed 19 July 2021).

Migration Policy Institute (2005). 'Assessing the Tsunami's effects . . .', 1 April, Article: Assessing the Tsunami's Effects on Migration | migrationpolicy.org (accessed 25 September 2024).

Mishra, Vibhu (2025). 'Civilians trapped and terrorised . . .', *UN News—Global Perspective Human Stories*, 22 May, 'Civilians 'trapped and terrorised': UN sounds alarm over collapse of critical protections | UN News (accessed 22 May 2025).

Neimark, Benjamin (2026). 'We cannot cut what we do not know', in Benjamin Neimark, Nita C. Crawford, Oliver Belcher, Stuart Parkinson, Linsey Cotterell, Frederick Otu-Larbi, Lennard de Klerk, Reuben Labi, Lin Kali, Michaelowa Ho-Chih, Heidrich Axel, Rajaeifar Oliver, Depledge Mohammad, Santos Duncan, Bell Tamiris, Bigger Karen, Rogaly Patrick, Khem and Nico Edwards (eds.), *Confronting Military Greenhouse Gas Emissons—Interactive Policy Brief*, London, UK, 2024, Confronting-military-greenhouse-gas-emissions,-Neimark-et-el,-Interactive-policy-brief-(2024)-[Print].pdf (accessed 1 January 2026).

News Human Trafficking (2019). 'More than 600 Pakistani girls . . .', 5 December, More than 600 Pakistani girls 'sold as brides' to China | Human Trafficking News | Al Jazeera (accessed 21 September 2024).

News World (2019). 'Pakistani investigators say hundreds of girls and women . . .', *Associated Press*, 4 December, Pakistani investigators say hundreds of girls and women being sold to China—but neither country will act | CBC News (accessed 21 September 2024).

Office to Monitor and Combat Trafficking in Persons (2022). 'The climate crisis: Exacerbating vulnerabilities and the looming increase of exploitation', *US Department of State*, July, https://www.state.gov/wp-content/uploads/2022/07/The-Climate-Crisis-Exacerbating-Vulnerabilities-and-the-Looming-Increase-of-Exploitation-.pdf (accessed 2 March 2024).

OHCHR (1966a). International Covenant on Civil and Political Rights | OHCHR (accessed 21 September 2024).

OHCHR (1966b). Articles 17 and 27, International Covenant on Civil and Political Rights | OHCHR (accessed 21 September 2024).

OHCHR (1966c). Article 24 (1) International Covenant on Civil and Political Rights | OHCHR (accessed 21 September 2024).

OHCHR (2021). *Report of the Special Rapporteur on trafficking in persons, especially women and children, Siobhán Mullally*, United Nations General Assembly A/HRC/47/34, Document Viewer (accessed 2 August 2025).

OHCHR (2022a). 'Law of the sea . . .', Law of the sea tribunal's judgment on marine environment and climate change underscores obligations, say UN experts | OHCHR (accessed 21 September 2024).

OHCHR (2022b). 'Australia violated Torres Strait Islanders' rights . . .', 23 September, Australia violated Torres Strait Islanders' rights to enjoy culture and family life, UN Committee finds | OHCHR (accessed 21 September 2024).

OHCHR (2022c). 'About trafficking in persons and human rights', *OHCHR and Trafficking in Persons*, About trafficking in persons and human rights | OHCHR (accessed 21 September 2021).

OHCHR (2023). 'Law of the sea tribunal's judgment on marine environment and climate change underscores obligations, say UN experts', Law of the sea tribunal's judgment on marine environment and climate change underscores obligations, say UN experts | OHCHR (accessed 2 August 2026).

OHCHR.org (n.d.). UN Treaty Body Data Base, tbinternet.ohchr.org/_layouts/15/treatybodyexternal/Download.aspx?symbolno=CCPR%2fC%2f135%2fD%2f3624%2f2019&Lang=en (accessed 21 September 2024).

Parkinson, S. (2020a). *The Carbon Boot-Print of the Military*, Scientists for Global Responsibility, Lancaster, The carbon boot-print of the military | SGR: Responsible Science (accessed 21 September 2024).

Parkinson, S. (2020b). *The Environmental Impacts of the UK Military Sector*, Scientists for Global Responsibility, Lancaster, SGR-DUK_UK_Military_Env_Impacts.pdf (accessed 21 September 2024).

Parkinson, S. (2020c). *Will the UK Reduce Its Military Carbon Emissions?* Rethinking Security, 2 July, Will the UK Reduce its Military Carbon Emissions? (accessed 21 September 2021).

Parkinson, S. and Cotterell, L. (2022). *Estimating the Military's Global Greenhouse Gas Emissions,* Scientists for Global Responsibility/Conflict and Environment Observatory, SGRCEOBS-Estimating_Global_Military_GHG_Emissions_Nov22_rev.pdf (accessed 2 August 2026).

Pelizzon, Alessandro (2025). *Ecological Jurisprudence—The Law of Nature and the Nature of Law*, Springer Nature Link, Open Access, Ecological Jurisprudence: The Law of Nature and the Nature of Law | Springer Nature Link (accessed 2 January 2026).

Phon, Puthborey and Price, Rumi Kato (2024). 'Climate change, forced migration and trafficking in persons . . .', *Journal of Human Trafficking*, 8 February, pp. 361–367, Climate Change, Forced Migration and Trafficking in Persons: Risk of Young Women in Rural Cambodia: Journal of Human Trafficking: Vol 10, No 2—Get Access (tandfonline.com) (accessed 25 September 2024).

PreventionWeb (2019). 'Women may be more vulnerable to climate change but data absent', *UNDRR*, 1 July, Women may be more vulnerable to climate change but data absent | PreventionWeb.net (accessed 11 July 2021).

Pringle, Helen (2024). 'The voice of the trees in the law of armed conflict', *Denning Law Journal*, vol 33, no 1, 129–144, The Voice of the Trees in the Law of Armed Conflict | The Denning Law Journal (accessed 2 August 2026).

Pringle, Helen and Klein, Renate (2022). '"Collateral damage" . . .', *ABC—Religion & Ethics*, 8 March, '"Collateral damage": The invasion of Ukraine reminds us of the cost of surrogacy, and who pays the price—ABC Religion & Ethics (accessed 2 March 2024).

RTH (n.d.). 'Lindsey Fox', *National Road Transport Museum*, Lindsay Fox—National Road Transport Museum (accessed 2 March 2024).

Rumsey, Michele, Fletcher, Stephanie M., Thiessen, Jodi, Gero, Anna, Kuruppu, Natasha, Daly, John, Buchan, James and Willetts, Juliet (2014). 'A qualitative examination of the health workforce needs . . .', *Human Resources for Health*, vol 12, no 9, 12 February, A qualitative examination of the health workforce needs during climate change disaster response in Pacific Island Countries—PubMed (nih.gov) (accessed 25 September 2024).

Schwing, Emily and Adams, Ash (2025). 'What went wrong with the climate relocation . . .', *Washington Post*, 29 May, What went wrong with the climate relocation of Newtok, Alaska?—The Washington Post (accessed 29 May 2025).

Scutt, Jocelynne A. (1983/1990). *Even in the Best of Homes—Violence in the Family*, Penguin/McCulloch, Melbourne.

Scutt, Jocelynne A. (2024). 'Exporting environmental human rights abuses—where does responsibility lie?', *Denning Law Journal*, pp. 259–294.

Scutt, Jocelynne A. (2025). Chapter 20 'Barbie meets a very poor thing silenced by the lambs—feminist filmmaking (en)counters masculine renditions of the female', in J. A. Scutt (ed.), *Women Power and Autonomy—Rights Respect and Representation in Law and Society*, pp. 561–596, Palgrave Macmillan, London.

Scutt, Jocelynne A. (forthcoming). 'Climate change as threat to indigenous peoples' rights: A role for SDGs and UNDRIP?', in Sarah Sargent (ed.), *The SDGs and the Rights of Indigenous Peoples*, London.

Skilling, Mitchell (2023). 'Inner House allows appeal . . .', *Scottish Legal News*, 17 April, Inner House allows appeal of order to return children to USA on basis of grave risk defence | Scottish Legal News (accessed 12 May 2025) (Scotland).

Tetley, Carmen (2012). 'The Hague convention . . .', *Children Australia*, vol 37, no 4, 135–141, The Hague Convention: Who is Protecting the Child? | Children Australia | Cambridge Core (accessed 21 September 2024).

Thomson, James (2013). 'Celebrating 30 years . . .', *BRW. Financial Review*, 22 May, Celebrating 30 years of the Rich 200 (accessed 2 March 2024).

UN Climate Change (2024a). *What Is the Kyoto Protocol—UNFCCC*, What is the Kyoto Protocol? | UNFCCC (accessed 2 March 2024).

UN Climate Change (2024b). *Paris Agreement—UNFCCC*, The Paris Agreement | UNFCCC (accessed 2 March 2024).

UN Climate Change (2024c). *Documents—UNFCCC*, Documents | UNFCCC (accessed 2 March 2024).

UN Climate Change (2024d). *Conference of the Parties*, 2024, Conference of the Parties (COP) | UNFCCC (accessed 2 March 2024);

UN OHCHR (2018). *Documents—General Comments and Recommendations, GR 37*, General recommendation No.37 (2018) on gender-related dimensions of disaster risk reduction in a changing climate | OHCHR (accessed 2 March 2024).

UN Women (2025). 'How gender inequality and climate change are interconnected', *Articles—Explainer*, 21 April, https://www.unwomen.org/en/articles/explainer/how-gender-inequality-and-climate-change-are-interconnected (accessed 2 May 2025).

United Nations (2000). *Human Rights Instruments—Universal Instrument*, 15 November 2000, General Assembly resolution 55/25, Protocol to Prevent, Suppress and Punish Trafficking in Persons Especially Women and Children, supplementing the United Nations Convention against Transnational Organized Crime | OHCHR (accessed 21 September 2024).

United Nations (2022a). *Global Report on Trafficking in Persons*, Trafficking in Persons, 'Special Points', GLOTIP24_special_points_final.pdf (accessed 2 March 2025).

United Nations (2022b). *Topics—Special Rapporteur on trafficking in persons, especially women and children.* 2022-12-14-eom-statement-south-sudan-sr-trafficking.pdf (accessed 2 August 2026).

UNODC (2024). *UNODC Global Trafficking Report*, 11 December (accessed 2 March 2025).

Verjauw, Ria (2019). 'Climate change and the responsibility of the military', *ICBUW – International Coalition to Ban Uranium Weapons,* CLIMATE CHANGE and the responsibility of the Military | ICBUW (accessed 2 August 2026).

Wahono, Arimbi and Tobin, Katie (2024). 'Towards economic and climate justice: A feminist analysis of critical trends', *Feminist Action Nexus for Economic and Climate Justice*, ActionNexus_TrendsReport2024_EN_v4.pdf (accessed 2 May 2025).

World Economic Forum (2024). 'New ruling gives power . . .', New ruling gives power to small island nations in climate fight | World Economic Forum (weforum.org) (accessed 21 September 2024).

Wyeth, Grant (2023). 'Australian lawmakers tinker . . .', *The Diplomat*, 30 August, Australian Lawmakers Tinker Around Hague Convention Flaws—The Diplomat (accessed 21 September 2024).

Zare, Bonnie and Mendoza, S. Lily (2012). '"Mail-order brides" in popular culture . . .', *International Journal of Cultural Studies*, vol 15, no 4, 365–381, 'Mail-order brides' in popular culture: Colonialist representations and absent discourse—Bonnie Zare, S. Lily Mendoza, 2012 (accessed 2 February 2025).

Zhu, Mingan and Fan, Bihang (2021). 'Exploring the relationship between risking temperatures . . .', *International Journal of Environmental Research on Public Health,* vol 18, no 2, 745, 16 January, Exploring the Relationship between Rising Temperatures and the Number of Climate-Related Natural Disasters in China—PubMed (nih.gov) (accessed 25 September 2024).

11

THE REMNANTS OF USERS' RIGHTS AND ACCESS TO JUSTICE IN VERY LARGE ONLINE PLATFORMS

Are embedded ODR mechanisms becoming neo-feudal courts?

Elena Alina Onțanu

Introduction

Technology is part of our everyday life. Many online activities are taking place through platforms, for example: buying or selling goods on Amazon, posting news feeds on X, sharing the latest holiday photos on Instagram, commenting on posts and photos on Facebook, communicating, booking holiday accommodation, or selling transport services on the Uber platform. At first sight, platforms facilitate users' and businesses' activities, expedite transactions, speed access to information, and connect parties. At times, platform-based activities may lead to struggles for private or business users who rely on these systems. One might wonder in what way?

For a number of years, there have been reports that platforms may unexpectedly lock their providers or users out of their systems. This can happen without any prior warning or contact if a breach of contractual terms or wrongful activity is suspected. The consequences for businesses, especially small and medium-sized ones, can be serious, including paralysing their operations, making it impossible to contact their clients and to pay their employees or providers. An example in this regard is the experiences of sellers on the Amazon platform whose accounts were suspended. In several cases sellers were suddenly locked out without misconduct towards a client, due to administrative arrangements related to product listings, or even without any clear information on why they were locked out of the platform. The follow-up consequence was that their merchandise and funds became unreachable for any professional activity during their account suspension. Sometimes accounts were suspended for several weeks. This had significant consequences for their workers and cash flow (Premack 2019). Amazon could even keep the funds permanently if the account was not reinstated and the merchant was deemed a bad

DOI: 10.4324/9781003752974-15

actor (Hodgson 2024). Another similar dynamic involved the X platform. Profile holders were banned from the platform without having violated any rules or terms of their membership contract because the platform's automated algorithm flagged their activity as spam and blocked profiles that saw a sudden increase in activity or number of followers (Goryashko 2024). In both examples, the decisions appeared to be algorithm-led, without clear human control, resulting in actual unfair treatment (Hodgson 2024).

While the above-mentioned examples may seem minor issues at first, their impact on a business's life and viability may be significant. Without cash flow, the business may need to send its employees home for several weeks or force them into redundancy. The same applies to individuals' livelihoods and identities within the community, especially if they are influential persons. Their financial independence, moral standing, and the community's perception of their activities as wrong or misleading because of being banned from a platform may affect their position within society, the possibility to voice their dissent and point to violations, and, ultimately, to their livelihoods. Both situations can even have a snowball effect on the community these individuals are part of, leading to a lack of trust and avoidance of these businesses or for persons to lose their voice and standing. Further, this affects business activities and income. Users are not only excluded from a digital marketplace or social media. They are also faced with what can appear similar to a social death (*morte civile*) (see Chapter 1 in this volume). Their platform user activities get paralysed – doing business, contacting clients, voicing concerns, losing access to their user profile and/or reputation data. They can be legally and socially annihilated, with difficult avenues of appeal. Although the platform's initial exclusion decision can be challenged and the profile or business activity reinstated, this process takes time and can become costly if a court or arbitration proceeding is required. The platform's automatic evaluation decision is not part of an ex officio review process and can remain final if not challenged. Interested parties must request a review, challenge the decision, and wait for an outcome.

In this, the platforms start to resemble feudal lords and their courts (Mazzucato 2019, 2025). They have a business interest in the activities carried out on their platforms, they monetise and collect rent from the activities carried out online by users and third parties, they regulate and control the activities taking place on their systems, and if they assume there is any wrongdoing or breach, they have the power to decide and impose sanctions and expulsion. In-person or digital forms of court justice are unable to keep pace with the speed and effectiveness of the digital environment (Abrantes Geraldes 2022; OECD 2021). Arbitration and certified alternative dispute resolution (ADR) mechanisms in the EU are also not well equipped to handle these types of cases and, above all, their enforcement. They cannot manage the high volume of online disputes resulting from digital transactions, platform bans, social media activities, and online purchases (Koulu 2016, 2018). The platforms' offered mechanisms – online dispute resolution mechanisms, or ODR-Ps – are the only real solution for businesses and users to regain access to their activities and profiles, lift bans, and access quick solutions and enforcement. ODR-Ps seem to respond to a societal demand for rapid dispute resolution and can process extraordinarily large numbers of cases internally – in the range of millions, at high speed, and at a very low cost (if any) for users (Katsh & Rabinovich-Einy 2019; Ortolani 2023).[1] In this, the platform's review or dispute resolution scheme is without the safeguards and transparency of traditional judicial processes. The platforms' embedded dispute resolution bodies are not subject to the same boundaries and diversity of requirements the other two justice paths, certified ADR and courts, have. They can apply their own private terms and conditions to govern any user disputes or content moderation brought through their internal online dispute resolution mechanisms.

ODR-P mechanisms are providing relief to users in a broader sense, but given platforms' economic interest, ODR-Ps' outcomes should not be at variance with users' rights as guaranteed by substantive law or come at the expense of weaker parties in their relationship with the online platform. One of the EU's latest legislative actions – the 2022 Digital Service Act (DSA)[2] – is acting in this sense. The DSA provisions are setting some guarantees and require a certain degree of due process in relation to various forms of ODR-P mechanisms that the platforms offer to their users for dealing with disputes and content moderation requests. Procedural guarantees for ODR-P mechanisms promoted by the DSA follow a flexible, incremental approach with less stringent requirements than in certified ADR mechanisms[3] or traditional court procedures. One could argue that this choice is in line with the online platforms' role in society as private parties. Nonetheless, this can be somewhat problematic when the parties' only viable option to obtain redress is the platforms' ODR-P mechanisms.

While the concept of access to justice is being remodelled towards a more flexible format that can be accommodated by private sector providers, the question is whether this approach offers the "appropriate" mix of guarantees and flexibility. The chapter uses the DSA as an example to examine whether flexible procedural guarantees and a gradual redress model can mitigate the risks of concentrating adjudicatory power in the hands of the same private actors that also regulate online activities and have economic interest in the outcome.

The chapter is structured in four main sections that progress from traditional justice standards to contemporary regulatory solutions of dispute resolution provided by private platforms. Section "Access to Justice and Online Dispute Resolution Mechanisms" reflects on the traditional procedural requirements embedded in Article 6 of the European Convention of Human Rights (ECHR) and their relevance for various court and ADR procedures. Section "Platforms' Complaint Procedures: A Neo-Feudal Approach to Justice" examines platform complaint procedures through the lens of neo-feudal justice, arguing that platform ODR-P mechanisms resemble medieval feudal courts in important structural aspects. The neo-feudal justice concept offers a structural analogy supporting the analytical analysis. Section "The DSA Framework: A European Response to ODR-Ps Issues?" focuses on the DSA example as a regulatory attempt to respond to the dangers of neo-feudal dispute resolution models, assessing whether its gradual ODR-P approach can balance efficiency with fundamental justice principles. The last section concludes by moving from the perspective of traditional standards, through a critique of current practices, to an evaluation of potential future solutions.

Access to justice and online dispute resolution mechanisms

Traditionally, in Europe, access to justice is guided by Article 6 of the European Convention of Human Rights (ECHR) and, for a couple of decades, by Article 47 of the Charter of Fundamental Rights (the Charter). These provisions rely on two sets of key requirements: institutional and procedural. The institutional requirements are centred around the idea of a legally established tribunal with independent and impartial judges assessing claims. Procedurally, access to justice requires fair, adversarial proceedings, equality of arms, evidence-based and reasoned decisions, public hearings, and proceedings of reasonable length.

When it comes to ADR, the European Court of Human Rights recognised that the principles of Article 6 ECHR are subject to certain limitations, provided such restrictions serve efficiency objectives and do not compromise the fundamental essence of the procedural right (ECtHR, *Stanev v. Bulgaria* 2012; ECtHR, *Naït-Liman v. Switzerland* 2018; Tjong Tjin Tai & Frenken 2023). However, in practice, there is hardly any guidance as to the actual application of Article 6(1) ECHR/Article 47 Charter procedural standards in various ADR mechanisms (Onţanu & Tjong Tjin Tai 2025). Table 11.1 maps the procedural standards that various available instruments aim to promote and which partially mirror the principles established by Article 6(1) ECHR and Article 47 Charter. This is more closely the case for the certified ADR bodies and more loosely followed or even dispersed by ODR-P mechanisms.

TABLE 11.1 An overview of procedural standards applying in-court and out-of-court procedures

Online Non-Binding Private Schemes of ODR-P	*Certified ADRs*	*Public Courts*
No legal rules No fees Platform (human or machine) No motivation or publication of decisions Short timeframe Enforcement by platform Courts as a fallback option	Fairness (and legal rules) Small fee Procedural standards and Trained personnel Decisions motivated and published Relatively short timeframe Enforcement with court and/or professional support	Legal rules (Variable) Court fees Full procedural justice (Art. 6 ECnHR etc.) and independent judges Decisions motivated and published Extended timeframe Enforcement with court/or professional support

While certified ADR mechanisms have been around for longer, the ODR-Ps are the latest mechanisms added to a broader process initiated by Cappelletti and Garth in the 1970s: to encourage the use of ADR to facilitate access to justice. In this ongoing process of building an access to justice approach by offering more substance-oriented justice for parties, users have to accept differences in procedural and institutional guarantees compared to the regular court system. This involves different decision-makers and mechanisms, other than the regular court system, to forward and deliver an effective access to justice (Cappelletti 1976). Nevertheless, additional instruments should offer sufficient guarantees for the parties to be integrated in a multifaceted procedural framework providing effective access to justice (Mak 2012).

Platforms' complaint procedures: a neo-feudal approach to justice

Platforms generally resolve complaints and disputes in which they have a direct or indirect economic interest. These disputes may arise either between platform users and the platform or among users operating within the platform environment.[4] In this ODR-Ps mechanisms provide a broad form of private redress.

The ODR-Ps are an integrated part of platforms and are designed for very specific, closed-number types of disputes related to the activities carried out on or by the online platform they belong to. The ODR-Ps manage through 'technology-augmented dispute resolution' mechanisms to deal with 'low value, high volume e-commerce cases, which typically do not pass the relatively high threshold for litigation and enforcement through public courts' (Koulu 2018) or concern content moderation decisions. The mechanisms used combine web forms or filing platforms with different technical means (e.g. expert systems, AI) leading to a redress decision. However, the form of technology platforms employ for ODR-Ps is not always clearly disclosed.

As a general approach, the platform's system is guiding the user through the ODR-Ps' highly simplified procedural interfaces. At times, the platform itself may even identify the potential dispute and suggest possible actions (Velicogna 2022). Regardless of the stages of the procedure or the parties involved – disputes between platform users or among the platform and its users – all steps of ODR-Ps are designed to facilitate easy access for the parties in a dispute. Overall, this guided process makes ODR-Ps easier to access compared to traditional court procedures and even certified ADR alternatives.

ODR-Ps mechanisms are characterised by four main features: a small number of clear procedural steps, limited or non-visible direct costs, short duration, and effective online enforcement (Onţanu & Tjong Tjin Tai 2025; Tjong Tijn Tai & Frenken 2023; Koulu 2019; Hörnle 2009).[5] Compared to courts, the platforms are always able to intervene and enforce their ODR-P decisions on their own.

ODR-P systems transform dispute resolution not only because they introduce a variety of digital solutions; they transform the process itself. They categorise and cluster claims with similar patterns along strictly technology-driven paths and user options. Only specific types of disputes can be filed through the ODR-Ps predetermined algorithmic-based structure, and the information that can be provided is often guided and/or limited. The platforms propose solutions to disputes through ODR-P mechanisms, utilising their own data about the parties involved,[6] and their own rules. Often, dispute procedures are initiated by users in response to a platform's decision that regards them, and that was taken unilaterally and without input from the concerned user. The ODR-Ps decision-making process is often entirely opaque, and the decision taken by the ODR-P is not supported by a meaningful explanation or motivation of the outcome.[7] In the ODR-Ps, the technology-led systems are the "new judges" whose function is to deliver relief, but the way this is carried out appears to move closer to an accountant's function rather than that of a traditional judge (Millar 1923–1924).

The technology-supported rules governing ODR-Ps are not unrelated to the platforms' economic interests and profits. The economic interest, combined with the possibility of delivering dispute resolution relief, and subsequently enforcing these solutions on the platforms system or through systems under their control (e.g. providing parties with access to carry out online activities, limit users' activities through temporary blockings or exclusions from the platform, access to customers or funds) brings platforms closer to a feudal approach to justice. Generally, ODR-Ps propose to users a mode of justice in which there is no clear separation between the provider of online marketplace or social media and the adjudicator of disputes. While providing "a seamless experience to the user who is not required to look for a solution to a dispute outside the platform's environment" (Velicogna 2022), users can oftentimes also continue their online activity.

Moreover, the speed of dispute solving can give users a false sense of security while actually further entrenching platforms power over their users, influencing their actions and guiding their behaviours into patterns users can accept (Varoufakis 2023). The "neo-feudal" approach to justice prioritises efficiency and commercial interests over traditional justice values such as transparency, impartiality, and fundamental procedural rights. ODR-Ps are not a mere technical innovation. They are part of the power construction platforms put in place. Online platforms fulfil multiple roles and exercise attributes of all three state powers – legislative, executive and judiciary (Van Loo 2021; Klonick 2018). There is no clear separation of powers between the platforms and the ODR-P mechanisms they propose to their users. When considering their powers and activities, platforms resemble feudal lords, who ruled over domains in medieval times. Their relationship with the parties using their platform system is contractual – based on standard-form contractual arrangements – and hierarchical. The activity rules are designed and imposed unilaterally by platforms on a take-it-or-leave-it basis. If users want to maintain access to the marketplace or social media accounts, they have to accept the conditions imposed or modified by the platform, and, at times, even compliance is not sufficient. Examples include cases in which the same European Commission was banned from activities on X (Cress 2025) because of an alleged abuse of the use of the platform's ads function in a post announcing a fine applied to X for illegal online activity, or Meta's activity of removing users' accounts on Facebook because its algorithm identified personal accounts as not being genuine and assimilated them with spam accounts although this was not the case (Cuthbertson 2025).

The users, as platforms' serfs, gain access to the markets or activities carried out on the platform's system through licences or private contracts. The payment they make for this is not only monetary, but also to a certain extent in kind, like in medieval times, not in work or going to war for the lord, but through the use and gathering of their private data, patterns of activities the platforms can use to their own advantage to further shape their policies and rules (see Varoufakis 2023).

For their dispute resolution function, the ODR-Ps are only accessible to the platform's users and in relation to their activity on the platform's marketplace. Further, the ODR-P mechanism is available on the same platform as the marketplace. The platform's justice is delivered through its domain in accordance with the "lord's custom" – the platform's private rules and contractual terms. The rules regulating the activity on their online environment, sanctions, and dispute resolution are internal and private to the platforms. The dispute resolution process has limited (or even lacking) transparency, and the decision process is opaque in the way the platform rules are applied or used in the delivery of the dispute resolution outcome (Hodgson, 2024). The analogy is that, as in feudal relations among feudal lords and serfs, the governed parties often lack both a clear understanding of the applicable rules structuring their obligations and an ability to independently consult them.

The possibility of taking the claim to a public court remains open if an ODR-P mechanism is used, but platform users seldom use this option. Thus, the platform's decision, although non-binding, often opaque, with no *res judicata* effect (Ontanu & Tjong Tjin Tai 2025),[8] and benefiting from a weak accountability due to the platform's dual role of provider and adjudicator, ends up becoming a binding and final outcome. The platform is hardly held accountable if its ODR-P decision is flawed. The ODR-Ps are very effective in providing a remedy, and oftentimes, they are the only remedy users consider or are forced by circumstances to rely on to unblock their activity, funds, data, and profile. The platforms providing the ODR-P mechanisms handle the financial flows and the parties' access to the marketplace; thus, enforceability is immediate as they are able to directly act on the parties' financial means and/or activities and their data, as well as apparently "keeping costs of the proceedings out of the users' pockets" (Ontanu & Tjong Tjin Tai 2025; Varoufakis 2023), and supporting their own economic activity by building and maintaining "trust" with the platforms' users.

The outcome of this technology-driven dispute resolution, whose awarding criteria is not actually clear, may appear like some form of "justice on steroids", driven by economic activities and gains rather than any clear justice principle, law, or ethical consideration (Hegel 1967 [1821]). There is a danger that platforms potentially treat their users however they like (Varoufakis 2023), or come up with any good reason for a permissible action done with an easy conscience. This can lead to a structural private subtraction of the public authority from social and economic life. Having guarantee mechanisms in place also for ODR-Ps is important because platform users – business or private parties – are often trapped in their choice. They are generally limited in their options where they can take their activities next (e.g. switch from eBay to Amazon or Alibaba), are in a weak position in comparison with the platforms, or may not survive in their activities outside internet platforms, given the highly connected world we live in.

The DSA Framework: a European response to ODR-Ps issues?

With the adoption of the 'Digital Services Act (DSA)' (DSA 2022), the European legislator recognised the need to establish specific transparency measures for online platforms' dispute resolution mechanisms. The rules aim for "a safe, predictable and trusted online environment . . . in which fundamental rights enshrined in the Charter, including the principle of consumer protection, are effectively protected" (Article 1(1) DSA).

The DSA ODR-P framework is based on a three-stage format with specific guarantees for each stage. The first stage of seeking redress is an internal notice and action mechanism that can then escalate to an internal complaint system. The latter can then proceed to an out-of-court dispute settlement, and ultimately, to a court procedure.

The entire ecosystem created by the DSA seeks to limit the powers of online platforms over their users and infuse different degrees of institutional and procedural requirements that are a reminder of Article 6 ECHR. Additionally, the third stage, the certified out-of-court dispute settlement bodies are third parties in relation to platforms.

In the first phase of ODR-P resolution, based on Article 16 DSA, the notice and action mechanism, online platforms are required to have an "effective" (Van Gelder & van Duin 2021) internal complaint handling system that is "easy to access and user-friendly" as well as decisions being taken in "timely, diligent, non-arbitrary and objective manner". This internal complaint system has to "facilitate the submission of sufficiently precise and adequately substantiated notices" by platform users (DSA 2022, art 16(2)).

The next stage of ODR-P redress, if the dispute escalates, is the platform's internal complaint-handling system (Article 20 DSA). This has to be available for parties for a period of six months following a first notice and action decision and has to be "easy to access, user friendly and enable and facilitate the submission of sufficiently precise and adequately substantiated complaints" (Article 20(3) DSA). The DSA also seeks to reinforce the procedural justice requirements for this stage of ODR-P systems (see Table 11.2).[9] This additional ODR-P-type mechanism can reverse earlier ODR-P decisions to remove, disable access, restrict visibility, suspend or terminate the provision of service, or suspend, terminate or otherwise restrict the ability to monetise information.

TABLE 11.2 Procedural requirements of DSA online dispute resolution mechanisms

Notice and Action Mechanism	*Internal Complaint-Handling System*	*Out-of-Court Dispute Settlement*
No legal procedural, but substantive rules (illegal/incompatible with Terms and Conditions) No fees Sufficiently substantiated explanation of reason why content is illegal Platform decision (human or machine-based) Statement of reason for restriction decisions (legal/contractual ground use and explanation) Information on possibility of redress Timely, diligent, non-arbitrary and objective Platform enforcement	Fairness (timely, non-discriminatory, procedure) No fees Complaints submissions to be sufficiently precise and adequately substantiated Decisions motivated and taken by qualified staff (not solely automated means) Timely, non-discriminatory, diligent, non-arbitrary Possibility to reverse earlier notice-based decisions Platform enforcement	Fairness (and legal rules) Small fee/no fee Trained personnel in the area of dispute Decisions motivated and published Relatively short timeframe Contest decisions or complaints not resolved by internal complaints-handling system Impartial and independent providers Online procedure Relies on supporting documents Enforcement with court and/or professional support

The third stage allows parties to select any out-of-court dispute settlement mechanism certified as ODR/ADR body to resolve disputes regarding decisions taken or complaints that have not been resolved in prior internal ODR-Ps. Again, interested parties should be provided access to this information in an "easily accessible . . . , clear and user-friendly" format (Article 21(1) DSA) (see Table 11.2). Online platforms participation in this type of certified ADR is not mandatory, and the outcome is not a binding settlement. The online platform can refuse to engage with such an out-of-court dispute settlement body if a dispute has already been resolved and concerns the same information and the same grounds of alleged illegality or incompatibility of content (Article 21(2) DSA). This ODR-P stage has to lead to a decision for the parties within a reasonable period – no later than 90 calendar days after the receipt of the complaint, and no more than 180 days in highly complex disputes (Article 21(3) DSA). If the out-of-court dispute settlement body decides the dispute in favour of the recipient of the service, including the individual or entity that has submitted a notice, the provider of the online platform bears the fees of the process and has to reimburse the other party for any reasonable expenses the party has paid in relation to the dispute settlement (Article 21(5) DSA). Alternatively, if the dispute is decided in favour of the online platform, the counterparty will not need to pay the costs of the dispute settlement process unless it acted in manifestly bad faith. The fees charged for the out-of-court dispute settlement should not exceed the costs incurred by the body, be reasonable, and transparently made available to the recipients of the service.

Compared with the pre-DSA situation, in which no specific requirement governed the statement of reasons of the information to be provided in the process such as the notice and action mechanism, the DSA establishes a clearer set of elements that have to be observed by the platform user submitting a notice (e.g. reasons of why content is alleged illegal, location of the content, information about the party making the notice) and by the system (technology-based or not) delivering the decision (e.g. statement of reason for restricting decision, grounds on which decision is taken, redress mechanisms) (see Table 11.2). Although the decision process can potentially remain a strictly pre-determined algorithm-based one, where the information provided in the process is guided and/or limited, the DSA seeks to address some of ODR-Ps opacity concerns through regulatory means. For example, when ODR-Ps use automated means for processing or decision-making, the platform has to include such information in the notification, offering information on the possibilities for redress in respect of the automated decision (Article 16(5) – (6) DSA). This brings some transparency on how this type of ODR-Ps function and the way they use technology in dispute settling. Another OPD-P characteristic DSA seeks to address is the lack of adequate statements of reason in the notice and action decisions. Article 17(3) – (4) DSA sets some transparency and accountability benchmarks: (1) the type of decision taken – removal, disabling access to, demotion of or restriction of the visibility of the information, or the suspension or termination of monetary payments, and, if relevant, the territorial scope of the decision and its duration; (2) the facts and circumstances relied on in taking the decision and whether the decision was taken based on a notice submitted by a person, the identification of the notifier, or whether the platform proceeded based on its own initiative; (3) the use of automated decision-making means in taking the decision, including if it concerned content detected or identified using automated means; (4) the legal ground or contractual ground relied on and the explanation why information is considered to be illegal and as to why the information is considered to be incompatible with the provider's terms and conditions; and (5) clear and user-friendly information on the possibilities for redress regarding the decision taken by the platform ODR-P mechanisms and judicial redress. These requirements shed some light on the neo-feudal ODR-P decision-making processes, and the grounds on which such decisions or proposals of relief are taken. The DSA therefore pushes these neo-feudal forms of decision-making towards more accountable grounds and infuses some procedural characteristics that are more aligned with familiar justice values rather than continuing on a path where dispute solving is or can be motivated by purely economic gains or business interests of the platform owner.

The next stage of ODR-P mechanism provided by online platforms is their internal complaint-handling systems that has to reassess the situation. Given the platforms' economic interests and the absence of any separation of powers, it can be doubtful whether the "non-arbitrariness" of the decision can be secured in practice (Article 20(4) DSA; Table 11.2). A certain independence could potentially be better envisaged if we consider that the first ODR-P stage, the notice and action mechanism, is carried out in an automated manner with the support of technology and/or AI, and this second stage of ODR-P is an ADR mechanism where human oversight is used to control the initial technology-based decision. This does not eliminate the underlying concentration of power: both algorithms and human reviewers may be biased, and both remain embedded in the same institutional and economic structure. Nevertheless, human review may contribute towards guaranteeing a clearer oversight. The procedural requirements for the decision to be taken swiftly ("without undue delay") (Article 20(5) DSA), by qualified staff ("not solely on the basis of automated means") (Article 20(6) DSA), communicated as an outcome of the internal complaint system, containing the reasons for which it was taken, and giving information on the possibility to continue with an out-of-court dispute settlement process address some of the concerns related to opacity of ODR-Ps mechanisms, the lack of separation of powers between the ODR-P, and the economic interests of the online platforms. Additionally, the decision issued by an internal complaint-handling ODR-P mechanism has to contain the reasons for which it was taken and give information on the possibility for a user to continue with an out-of-court dispute settlement process.

Online platforms should cooperate with ADR bodies to settle disputes (Article 21 DSA) as a last resort dispute resolution mechanism. Different from the first two stages, Article 21(3) DSA requires the certified out-of-court dispute settlement mechanisms to be impartial and independent (including financially) from the online platforms and the service recipients (including those who have submitted notices). The DSA seeks to create an institutional separation between the online platform and the ADR/ODR adjudicating body. The certified out-of-court members have to have specific expertise in the areas the body has to issue decisions, and their remuneration should not be linked to the outcome of the procedures. The mechanism offered has to be easy to access through ICT means and allow initiating the dispute settlement and submission of the supporting documents online. The certified out-of-court dispute settlement body has to carry out its activities in accordance with clear and fair rules of procedure that are easily and publicly accessible, and comply with applicable law (Article 21(3) DSA). This last stage of ODR-P framework attempts to move further away from the neo-feudal approach compared to the previous two stages, although certain discussed points related to the way technology could be used in the decision-settlement process, the data that is employed or can be submitted in the settlement process, who has access to the data and how this is used can remain relevant. This outcome looks more problematic if the parties to the dispute decide that the outcome proposed by the out-of-court system is binding. Although the platform user can always contest the platform's ODR-Ps decisions before a court in accordance with the applicable law (Article 21(1) DSA), it is well-known that for most types of disputes related to online platform activities there will be seldom a court claim filed. Platform users opt consistently for the platforms' offered mechanisms. The volumes of disputes ODR-Ps handle are proof of this outcome. This changes the perspective, importance, and legal relevance of the activities such private body performs in justice delivery.

If we apply the key requirements of access to justice to the analysed ODR-P mechanisms, the following picture emerges (Figure 11.1):

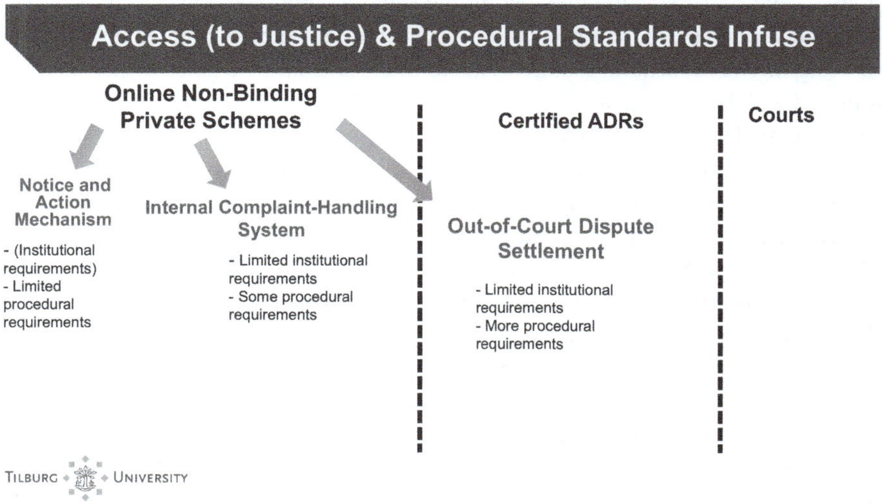

FIGURE 11.1 Access (to Justice) and Procedural Standards Infuse

This figure shows that the DSA initiative injects into ODR-P mechanisms some limited institutional requirements that can be a reminder of the principles of independence and impartiality closely guarded in court proceedings. It also seeks to secure that decisions are substantiated and/or non-arbitrary, objective, and motivated. From a legislative standpoint, this can be seen as a welcomed improvement and guarantees for parties that otherwise have no alternative viable solution to challenge the platforms' activities and decisions or that of other users on the platform.

Looking at the DSA ODR-P framework, the question remains whether the institutional and procedural requirements can be actually guarded by platforms given that they are also directly interested and affected by the activities and complaints of their users. The platforms are designing and offering dispute resolution mechanisms to their users, but how are they to maintain their objectivity and non-arbitrariness in the whole picture? Or are out-of-court dispute settlement bodies, also private entities, sufficiently independent and procedurally sound option towards securing a fair access to justice approach? And how is society to maintain transparency over a process of seeking and delivering justice that is becoming increasingly private? The DSA is not going to bring back the hard-won approach of open courts and public justice that is seen to be done. Together with limiting significantly the amount of transparency of the process, private justice is also touching upon aspects of democracy, power balances, and collective responsibility. A significant amount of power will remain concentrated in the hands of private parties – the platforms owners – who are delegated the task of solving an important volume of disputes, but at the same time retain important economic interests in the outcome of the process.

Conclusion

The digital transformation of dispute resolution has created contradictory outcomes. While online platforms have developed extraordinarily efficient mechanisms capable of handling millions of disputes annually with unprecedented speed and apparent cost-effectiveness, these ODR-P mechanisms have simultaneously risked recreating the very inequalities and power imbalances that modern procedural justice sought to eliminate. The comparison to medieval feudalism is not merely metaphorical – platforms exercise quasi-judicial authority over their digital domains, governing user disputes through opaque, economically motivated processes that bear uncomfortable resemblance to the discretionary justice and lack of separation of powers of feudal lords. Having available procedures for parties to rely on is only the first step. The ODR-Ps mechanisms have to offer users not any solution, but solutions that are fair, observing the provisions of the law, and leading to effective enforcement.

The European Union's Digital Services Act is an important legislative response seeking to address some of the ODR-P identified concerns. The DSA is attempting to inject procedural safeguards and transparency requirements into platform-based dispute resolution mechanisms. Through its three-tiered framework – notice and action mechanisms, internal complaint-handling systems, and certified out-of-court dispute settlement – the DSA seeks to bridge the gap between the efficiency demands of digital commerce and the fundamental principles of fair procedure enshrined in Article 6 ECHR and Article 47 of the Charter. At the same time, the DSA's approach reveals inherent tensions in attempting to reconcile private commercial interests with public justice values. While the regulation introduces welcomed procedural improvements – requiring reasoned decisions, transparency about automated processes, and independent oversight mechanisms – it stops short of fully addressing the fundamental power asymmetries that characterise platform-user relationships. The graduated approach to procedural guarantees, while pragmatic, raises questions about whether such flexibility can genuinely protect users' rights or merely provides an appearance of legitimacy to what remains essentially a private process.

The critical challenge is ensuring that these mechanisms serve justice rather than merely efficiency. The risk of "justice on steroids" – dispute resolution driven by algorithmic logic and economic optimisation rather than legal principles and ethical considerations – remains substantial. The concentration of dispute resolution powers in the hands of private actors with direct financial interests in the outcomes threatens to undermine the principle of fair trial, moving dispute resolution away from public scrutiny and accountability towards privatised, commercially motivated processes.

Moreover, the practical reality that most platform disputes will never reach public courts due to cost, complexity, and value considerations means that ODR-P mechanisms often represent the users' only viable avenue for redress. This reality transforms these private systems from mere alternatives to public justice into functional substitutes to what has traditionally been considered a core state function.

While the DSA's framework can be appreciated in its attempt to introduce procedural safeguards, it cannot fully resolve these fundamental tensions. The regulation's success will ultimately depend on implementation and enforcement, on whether platforms can genuinely maintain objectivity and non-arbitrariness while retaining significant economic interests in dispute outcomes, and whether society can maintain meaningful oversight over increasingly privatised justice processes.

Looking forward, the challenge is not simple: develop new procedural models that can accommodate the realities of online marketplaces and platforms while preserving the essential values of fairness, transparency, and accountability, and ultimately the rule of law and democracy. This may require more radical approaches, including greater public oversight of private dispute resolution systems, mandatory participation in certified ADR mechanisms, or even the development of public digital courts specifically designed to handle high-volume, low-value online disputes generated by online platforms.

The question of whether embedded ODR-P mechanisms in general are on a path to maintain neo-feudal court characteristics cannot be answered definitively at this moment in time. Vigilance is required to ensure that the pursuit of efficiency does not continue to come at the expense of fundamental justice principles. The remnants of users' rights in very large online platforms are not merely technical legal questions. They are fundamental issues of democratic governance, power separation, and the social contract in the digital age.

As we move forward, the challenge will be to preserve the undeniable benefits of platform-based dispute resolution while preventing the emergence of a two-tiered justice system where the quality of procedural protection depends on the commercial interests of private actors. The DSA represents an important first step, but the ultimate test will be whether these mechanisms can genuinely serve justice or whether they will remain sophisticated instruments of commercial control.

For the future, the stakes could not be higher. In an increasingly digital world where platform-mediated interactions constitute a growing share of economic and social activity, the quality of ODR-P mechanisms will significantly influence the extent to which individuals can meaningfully enforce their rights and access justice in a broader sense. In this, the efficiency gains of digital dispute resolution should not come at the cost of the hard-won principles of procedural fairness and equal access to justice that define modern legal systems.

Notes

1 For example, eBay can handle 60 million disputes a year, and Alibaba a hundred million annually. Facebook takes approximately 300,000 content moderation decisions per day.
2 Regulation (EU) 2022/2065 of the European Parliament and of the Council of 19 October 2022 on a single market for digital services and amending Directive 2000/31/EC (Digital Services Act). (2022). Official Journal of the European Union, L 277, 1–102.
3 Articles 5–11, Directive 2013/11/EU on alternative dispute resolution for consumer disputes and amending Regulation (EC) No 2006/2004 and Directive 2009/22/EC (Directive on consumer ADR), OJ L 165, 18.6.2013, p. 63–79.
4 The users can be product and/or service providers and/or individuals purchasing goods or services or carrying out online activities on the online platform.
5 Execution can be effective because the platform often has direct access to the funds stored with the platform. Thus, it can easily return a payment to the consumer by simply freezing the account of the seller or service provider and taking the amount.
6 Online platforms have direct access not only to data related to the dispute but also much more data about their users such as purchase records, opinions users agreed with or not, preferences, what their users read or watch, where their users were at a certain moment in time, ID codes and payment information, type of claims previously made, and outcomes of disputes the user accepted or not.
7 None of the provisions that arose out of eighteenth- and early nineteenth-century demands for justice to be open to the scrutiny of the people – "justice seen to be done" (Millar 1923–1924; Hegel 1967) – seem to apply to platform-based ODR. Furthermore, the DSA database classifies the decisions by ODR-Ps falling within its scope based on the "statement of reasons" criteria.
8 ODR-P procedures do not seem to fulfil the principal goal of traditional forms of dispute resolution. They also oftentimes do not even refer to their mechanisms as a procedure.
9 On a critical perspective for quite vague requirements despite the DSA's promise to offer a "procedural turn" in platform governance, see Ortolani (2023).

References

Abrantes Geraldes, A. S., (2022). A judge's perspective: Guarantees of a fair trial and online dispute resolution. In D. Moura Vicente, D. Oliveira, & F. de Almeida (Eds.), *Online dispute resolution: New challenges* (p. 22). Nomos.

Cappelletti, M., (1976). Access to justice: Comparative report. *RabelsZ*, *40*, 669–717.

Cress, L., (2025). Elon Musk's X bans European Commission from making ads after 120m fine. *BBC*. https://www.bbc.com/news/articles/c0589g0dqq7o

Cuthbertson, A., (2025). Facebook deletes millions of accounts in 'heartbreaking' purge: Meta ban wave also impacting Instagram accounts, with users blaming AI. *Independent*. https://www.independent.co.uk/tech/facebook-delete-accounts-meta-ban-wave-b2792734.html

Goryashko, S., (2024). X reinstates Navalny's widow after 'mistakenly' suspending account. *Politico*. https://www.politico.eu/article/yulia-navalnaya-suspension-x/

Hegel, G. W. F., (1967 [1821]). *Hegel's philosophy of right* (T. M. Knox, Trans.). Oxford University Press.

Hodgson, C., (2024). Amazon crackdown on sellers spawns new legal industry. *Financial Times*. https://www.ft.com/content/64f01bfe-39b9-49f6-86eb-be96374539cf

Hörnle, J., (2009). *Cross-border internet dispute resolution*. Cambridge University Press, 38–43. https://doi.org/10.1017/CBO9780511576102

Katsh, E., Rabinovich-Einy, O., (2019). The U.S. administration in transition and the impact of technology: The case of pre-dispute arbitration. *Revue Française d'Administration Publique*, *170*(2), 455.

Klonick, K., (2018). The new governors: The people, rules, and processes governing online speech. *Harvard Law Review*, *131*(6), 1598–1670.

Koulu, R., (2016). *Dispute resolution and technology: Revisiting the justification of conflict management*. University of Helsinki Conflict Management Institute, 186. https://doi.org/10.31885/9789515182661

Koulu, R., (2018). Improving consumer protection through technology: The challenge of compliance. In I. Barral Viñals (Ed.), *La resolución de conflictos con consumidores: De la mediación a las ODR* (p. 176). REUS Editorial.

Koulu, R., (2019). *Law, technology and dispute resolution: The privatisation of coercion*. Routledge, 73–78. https://doi.org/10.4324/9781315149479

Mak, C., (2012). *Rights and remedies: Article 47 EUCFR and effective judicial protection in European private law matters* (Centre for the Study of European Contract Law Working Paper No. 2012-11). Amsterdam Law School. http://dx.doi.org/10.2139/ssrn.2126551

Mazzucato, M., (2019). Preventing digital feudalism. *Project Syndicate*. https://www.project-syndicate.org/commentary/platform-economy-digital-feudalism-by-mariana-mazzucato-2019-10

Mazzucato, M., (2025). Resisting digital feudalism. *Project Syndicate*. https://www.project-syndicate.org/commentary/ai-digital-feudalism-inevitable-unless-policymakers-step-in-to-shape-markets-by-mariana-mazzucato-2025-02

Millar, R. W., (1923–1924). The formative principles of civil procedure. *Illinois Law Review*, *18*(1), 1–36.

OECD, (2021). *OECD framework and good practice principles for people-centred justice*. OECD Publishing. https://doi.org/10.1787/cdc3bde7-en

Onţanu, E. A., Tjong Tjin Tai, E., (2025). Digital technology and procedural justice: Towards a geography of justice. *Tilburg Law Review*, *30*(2), 96–119. https://doi.org/10.5334/tilr.422

Ortolani, P., (2023). The resolution of content moderation disputes under the Digital Services Act. *Giustizia Consensuale*, *2*, 533–573. http://dx.doi.org/10.2139/ssrn.4356598

Premack, R., (2019). Amazon's suspended third-party sellers aren't receiving the 30-day notice period they thought Amazon inked. *Business Insider*. https://www.businessinsider.com/amazon-sellers-suspended-no-notice-policy-2019-9

Regulation (EU). (2022/2065). Regulation (EU) of the European Parliament and of the Council of 19 October 2022 on a single market for digital services and amending Directive 2000/31/EC (Digital Services Act). (2022). Official Journal of the European Union, L 277, 1–102

Tjong Tjin Tai, E., Frenken, P., (2023). Procedurele rechtvaardigheid bij platformprocedures. *Tijdschrift Civiele Rechtspleging*, *3*, 56–66.

Van Gelder, E., van Duin, A., (2021). In de schaduw van het recht: Over Paypal's resolution centre en kwaliteitsstandaarden voor cODR op online platforms. In *Digitalisering en conflictoplossing* (p. 136). Wolters Kluwer.

Van Loo, R., (2021). Federal rules of platform procedure. *University of Chicago Law Review*, *88*(4), 832.

Varoufakis, Y., (2023). *Technofeudalism: What killed capitalism*. The Bodley Head, 78–128.

Velicogna, M., (2022). Cross-border dispute resolution in Europe: Looking for a new "normal". *Oñati Socio-Legal Series*, *12*(3), 574. https://doi.org/10.35295/osls.iisl/0000-0000-0000-1303

12

TECHNOLOGIES OF VICTIMISATION

Unravelling the Horizon IT system and the Post Office scandal in the UK

Marco Velicogna

Introduction: technology, accountability, and the fragility of justice

Technologies designed to improve accuracy and efficiency increasingly mediate the production of "truth" (Lanzara 2009a). Databases, algorithms, and automated evidentiary systems now participate in decisions once reserved for human judgement (Kallinikos 2011). Yet when these systems malfunction and produce errors, and their authority remains unchallenged, those errors can become institutional facts. The Post Office Horizon scandal, now widely acknowledged as one of the gravest miscarriages of justice in modern British history, allows us to explore how sociotechnical infrastructures can both enable and obscure accountability.

In brief, the Horizon scandal unfolded through a series of identifiable phases. Horizon (a nationwide computerised accounting system developed and operated by Fujitsu for Post Office Ltd) was rolled out nationally from 1999 as the Post Office's accounting infrastructure, and discrepancies were soon reported at the local branch level. Through the 2000s and early 2010s, these discrepancies were routinely framed as local responsibility, triggering debt demands, suspensions and prosecutions. From 2012 to 2015, a review commissioned by Post Office Ltd from Second Sight Support Services Ltd. produced reports documenting persistent system and process problems, yet the organisation continued to defend Horizon's robustness. The dispute then escalated into group litigation, culminating in a sequence of High Court judgments in 2019. Finally, from 2021 onward, convictions began to be quashed, and compensation schemes were expanded. At the same time, the statutory public Inquiry consolidated the evidential record and examined institutional responsibility. Its first final report, *Post Office Horizon IT Inquiry: Final Report—Volume 1*, was published on 8 July 2025, while the remaining phase findings and

DOI: 10.4324/9781003752974-16

overall recommendations were deferred (Williams 2025). Crucially, the scale of the problem became fully visible only when third-party actors aggregated dispersed cases and reframed them as a systemic pattern, forcing disclosure into the open.

Across the most intensive period of enforcement (1999–2015), hundreds of sub-postmasters (self-employed individuals contracted to operate local branches) were suspended, bankrupted, prosecuted, and, in several cases, imprisoned for alleged accounting shortfalls recorded in Horizon data and then pursued as evidence through Post Office investigative and managerial processes. Despite early evidence of system faults, the organisation repeatedly asserted that Horizon was "robust" and treated its digital outputs as incontrovertible evidence of theft or false accounting.

Two institutional reckonings later destabilised this narrative. In 2019, in *Bates & Others v Post Office Ltd (No. 6)*, Justice Fraser found that earlier versions of Horizon contained numerous defects and could not be treated as inherently reliable (Bates & Others v Post Office Ltd (No. 6) 2019). The 2025 Post Office Horizon IT Inquiry likewise found that Post Office and Fujitsu knew or should have known that Horizon could produce false data, yet "maintained the fiction that its data was always accurate" (Williams 2025, para. 1.4), conduct described as "wholly unacceptable behaviour" (Williams 2025, para. 1.9).

Seen through this lens, the scandal also exemplifies digital bureaucratic harm: injury produced through ordinary routines (recording, auditing, and enforcement) intensified by automated infrastructures that appear neutral and authoritative. Eubanks' work on automated decision systems shows how data-driven tools can profile, police, and punish in ways that are punitive and difficult to contest (2018). In Horizon, the technology did not merely "support" governance; it actively reconfigured it, embedding enforcement and judgment inside technical systems and institutional workflows in what Yeung terms "algorithmic regulation" (2018). Framing Horizon as victimisation therefore clarifies that the core wrong is not simply error, but the routinised production and management of harm through a sociotechnical assemblage that can discipline individuals while insulating the centre. Here, "victimisation" refers to the institutionally produced process by which harm is inflicted and normalised through routine sociotechnical and legal practices, while those harmed are positioned as culpable or denied recognition as victims.

This conceptualisation sharpens the chapter's theme of displaced accountability. The socio-political mechanism was not simply that accountability shifted onto individuals. Rather, organisations were able to preserve confidence in a contested system by directing blame towards proximate human actors who had the least power to interrogate design choices, data provenance, or institutional incentives. The scapegoating was facilitated by loss-recovery and reputational incentives, and by limited external scrutiny until MPs, courts and the Inquiry compelled disclosure. It was also sustained by information asymmetries: the Post Office and Fujitsu controlled knowledge of faults, access to logs, and the system's remote-intervention features of Horizon.

Hood's "blame game" captures how institutions protect themselves under pressure by structuring narratives and procedures that make individual fault the path of least resistance (2010). Elish's "moral crumple zone" is especially apt for Horizon: when complex systems fail, a nearby human operator can become the absorbent surface for legal and moral responsibility, regardless of their actual control over the system's behaviour (2019). The result is layered victimisation (material and reputational harms, compounded through investigatory and prosecutorial processes) while design choices around auditability and change control determine who can meaningfully contest a record.

More broadly, the scandal arose from interlocking technical, organisational and legal failures that accumulated over two decades. Problems in Horizon's operation and data were compounded by weak audit and escalation processes and by an institutional context that treated system outputs as authoritative. Drawing on sociomaterial perspectives (Latour 1993; Lanzara 2009b), the Horizon case can be analysed as a sociotechnical assemblage (technical infrastructure, contractual relations, managerial routines, courtroom procedures and judicial decisions). They translated situated transactional practices into durable evidentiary traces that travelled across organisational and legal arenas with their authority intact, while the conditions of their production remained opaque, hence functioning as Latourian inscription devices. In this setting, credibility migrated from human testimony to computational records, and the dynamic was reinforced by a legal–institutional backdrop that made reliability challenges harder to sustain and by the Post Office's dual role as commercial party and private prosecutor (see the Section "Legal and Institutional Failures, and the Reconstruction of Contestability"). As Lanzara (1998) suggests, once institutionalised, these arrangements resist corrective feedback; in Horizon, that rigidity meant the more the system failed, the more vigorously its infallibility was defended.

The ethical dimensions of this institutional behaviour have become central to scholarly analyses. Marshall (2022) frames the episode as an "intersection of law, ethics, and politics" in which managerial imperatives overrode professional duties of disclosure, while Moon (2024) describes a culture of defensive governance and procedural compartmentalisation. In Lanzara's (1998) terms, the case illustrates an institutional drift in which compliance displaces responsibility and accountability is shifted away from decision-makers and onto frontline workers.

The human consequences were profound, including widespread psychological distress and social and financial harms among affected sub-postmasters (Growns et al. 2024; Day et al. 2025). The Post Office Horizon IT Inquiry's Final Report (Volume 1) foregrounded this impact, noting that "many hundreds of people have been convicted, wrongly, of criminal offences, and many thousands . . . held responsible for losses which were illusory" (Williams 2025, para. 1.9). The scandal thus not only exposes a breakdown of justice but also generates a crisis of trust in the institutions through which justice is produced.

Against this institutional configuration (and its consequences for harm and recognition) four questions guide the analysis:

1) How did technological design and operation enable false yet authoritative evidence?
2) What organisational and professional routines sustained confidence in Horizon and with what consequences for the recognition of harm and victim status?
3) How did legal and evidentiary frameworks, together with governance incentives and information asymmetries, enable accountability to be displaced from institutions (Post Office Ltd and Fujitsu) to sub-postmasters and local branch staff?
4) What reforms could strengthen contestability, oversight, and enforceable accountability in the governance of digital infrastructures, including robust disclosure duties and independent technical assurance?

By addressing these questions, the chapter argues that the Horizon case is a *warn*ing about the governance of sociotechnical systems and the structural fragility of legal justice systems. Digital infrastructures can generate evidentiary authority without evidentiary responsibility: they produce "facts" that shape legal reality and command obedience even when their provenance is opaque. When law, management and technology align around such authority, error becomes systemic rather than exceptional.

Methodologically, this chapter adopts an explanatory case-study design (Yin 2018), treating the Horizon scandal as a single case with embedded units of analysis: (i) the technical system (architecture, operations, defects, remote interventions and data provenance), (ii) organisational/governance configurations (contracting, training, escalation/complaints and disclosure), and (iii) evidentiary/legal treatment (admissibility, disclosure, appeals and Inquiry findings). Evidence is assembled exclusively from public documents with a maintained chain of evidence: High Court group-litigation judgments (Bates & Others v Post Office Ltd) and appellate decisions; the *Post Office Horizon IT Inquiry Final Report-Vol. 1* (Williams 2025) and evidence-portal materials (witness statements, transcripts and exhibits); commissioned/internal reviews (e.g. Second Sight); and peer-reviewed scholarship on computer evidence, disclosure and governance. The analysis combines doctrinal analysis, document/process tracing and pattern matching, leveraging independent court and Inquiry fact-finding plus external expert reports. Validity is supported by converging indicators (defects, system losses, disclosure practices), rival explanations, and analytic generalisation from Horizon to the governance of digital evidence.

The discussion proceeds in five parts. Section "The UK Post Office and the Horizon System: Technological and Organisational Context" sets out the institutional and technical context of the Post Office and the Horizon system, how it was designed, deployed and operated, and how discrepancies arose in practice. Section " The Victimisation of Sub-Postmasters: Technology, Law, and Power Asymmetry

(1999–2009)" examines how organisational governance and the justice system configuration (contracting, oversight, disclosure, and the use of private prosecutions) translated system anomalies into individual blame, unfair proceedings and wrongful convictions. Section "Collective Mobilisation, Litigation, and Institutional Reckoning" reviews the legal aftermath, including group litigation, appellate decisions and quashed convictions, compensation schemes and the statutory public inquiry, and reflects on how evidentiary rules for computer-generated records shaped outcomes. Section "Technology, Law, and Digital Governance" distils lessons for digital governance, focusing on technical assurance, organisational accountability and evidentiary standards to reduce the fragility of justice in data-driven systems. The conclusion synthesises the argument and outlines implications for policy and future research.

The UK Post Office and the Horizon system: technological and organisational context

An introduction to the UK Post Office

The organisational trajectory of the UK Post Office from the late 1990s to the 2020s reflects a shift from a public utility to a state-owned but increasingly commercial organisation shaped by managerial and technological rationalisation. In 2001 it became part of the government-owned Royal Mail Group, and reforms under the Postal Services Act 2011 completed its separation from Royal Mail in 2012. Royal Mail was later privatised, while Post Office Ltd remained state-owned but expected to be financially self-sustaining; these changes formally separated commercial operations from policy/regulatory oversight and reflected an institutional configuration consistent with New Public Management priorities (efficiency, performance metrics, and contractual governance).

A central element of this model was the expansion of a franchise network operated by self-employed sub-postmasters. Contracts (later scrutinised in the High Court's Common Issues judgment) gave Post Office Ltd wide powers of suspension and termination and facilitated recovery of alleged shortfalls with limited practical avenues for dispute resolution (Bates & Others v Post Office Ltd (No. 3) 2019). Although sub-postmasters were formally independent contractors, they bore de facto strict liability for losses recorded in branch accounts, while the Post Office retained centralised control of accounting through Horizon without equivalent transparency or access for sub-postmasters to verify reliability (Bates & Others v Post Office Ltd (No. 3) 2019). After 2012, financial self-sufficiency pressures, functional silos, and weak internal information flows further entrenched opacity around Horizon issues. Together, concentrated technical control and limited independent oversight created conditions in which individuals could be held responsible for discrepancies they could neither explain nor meaningfully contest.

The deployment and function of Horizon software

Horizon emerged in the 1990s from efforts to digitise public service delivery. Developed within the Benefits Payment Card (BPC) programme by ICL Pathway (later Fujitsu) to support welfare payments, it was repurposed for retail accounting after the BPC scheme was abandoned in 1999, carrying design choices into a new operational and evidentiary setting. Legacy Horizon (c. 2000–2010) operated as a layered platform linking branch terminals to central data centres via a wide-area network. Transactions were captured locally, transmitted centrally, and processed through back-office workflows for reconciliation and reporting across a large branch network and multiple external service relationships. As services and interfaces proliferated, the system's end-to-end transaction pathway became harder to reconstruct, making discrepancies difficult to diagnose and attribute. The transition to Horizon Online (HNG-X) from 2010 shifted transaction persistence away from branches and made network connectivity a precondition of completion, increasing system-wide coupling so that updates, faults, or outages could affect multiple branches simultaneously (Williams 2025).

For governance and contestability, the key feature was the concentration of auditability and control outside the branch. Sub-postmasters lacked direct access to audit extracts or other independent means to test the provenance of disputed records, while reporting and audit requests depended substantially on Fujitsu's cooperation. The High Court found that both Post Office and Fujitsu could access Horizon data remotely; and that Fujitsu could, in some circumstances, insert or alter branch transactions in ways that could occur without the sub-postmaster's knowledge and might not be identifiable as having been done remotely (indeed, it could appear as though the sub-postmaster had performed the transaction), a position clarified only late in the litigation after earlier assurances that branch records were immutable were accepted to be wrong (Bates & Others v Post Office Ltd (No. 6) 2019).

Taken together, Horizon's evolution is best captured by three analytically relevant features: (i) the production and verification of "truth" (including auditability) largely sat outside the Post Office local branch; (ii) contestability depended on disclosures by the supplier and Post Office; and (iii) tighter central coupling meant defects and changes could propagate across the network—enabling monitoring at scale while entrenching power asymmetries in evidential access (Williams 2025).

Early discrepancies and the institutional response

Following the system's rollout in 1999, sub-postmasters reported unexplained shortfalls and transaction anomalies (often involving substantial sums), but these signals of potential system error were routinely reframed as user fault or dishonesty. The Post Office "routinely and strongly insisted" that criticisms of Horizon's accuracy were unfounded and that losses shown in branch accounts reflected "carelessness or dishonesty" by sub-postmasters (Bates & Others v Post Office Ltd (No. 6) 2019, para. 518).

On that basis, the Post Office pursued both civil claims and criminal private prosecutions, with Horizon outputs treated as authoritative and sub-postmasters effectively required to disprove the accuracy of their own accounts—an onerous burden within a regime tilted towards the institution (Bates & Others v Post Office Ltd (No. 3, No. 6)). The pattern was reinforced by frontline processes: frequent calls to the Network Business Support Centre (NBSC—the Post Office's helpline/support centre for branches) indicated recurring anomalies, yet call logs were non-verbatim and substantial sets were not disclosed to defence teams. Telecommunications disruptions could also trigger "transaction recovery" routines, where clerks' completion decisions could themselves generate discrepancies later imputed to branch error (Second Sight 2015).

Technical records and expert evidence later established documented defects across Horizon's iterations, capable of producing illusory losses in branch accounts (Bates & Others v Post Office Ltd (No. 6)). Remote access and centrally managed updates further complicated any straightforward inference from shortfall to culpable conduct (Christie 2022; Bates & Others v Post Office Ltd (No. 6) 2019). Nonetheless, Post Office Ltd maintained a narrative of system reliability and resisted disclosure of material relevant to assessing that reliability, a posture criticised as creating a closed evidentiary loop (Christie 2022; Moorhead et al. 2023).

Many prosecutions resulted in convictions for theft or false accounting, while the scale of investigative and disclosure failures became clear only later on appeal (see the Section "Appeals, Quashed Convictions, and Institutional Reckoning (2020–2025)"). Organisational mechanisms amplified harm: transaction corrections and accounting adjustments allocated losses to individual branches while keeping error mechanics opaque; escalation routes were weak, complaints handling defensive, and communication between technical and legal functions poor (Christie 2022; Second Sight 2015). External scrutiny was limited until the Second Sight review raised concerns about bugs, data integrity, and auditability, before access was curtailed and the engagement ended in 2015 (Christie 2022; Mason 2021). In parallel, potentially corroborative helpline material was withheld on the basis that disclosure would overwhelm defence teams.

NBSC entries were designed for incident resolution, not evidential reconstruction: they recorded problem categories and outcomes, but not the screen prompts, contemporaneous narratives, or system-state information needed to reconstruct disputed events after the fact. The issue, therefore, was not simply a malfunction, but a systemic limitation built into the ordinary operation of NBSC incident handling. Where connectivity between the branch terminal and Horizon's central system failed mid-transaction, Horizon's "transaction recovery" process could prompt branch staff to confirm whether a transaction had completed; depending on the failure point, an incorrect confirmation could duplicate, reverse, or mis-post an entry, later surfacing as an apparent branch shortfall.

This created two distinct but related disclosure problems: the evidential record generated through NBSC incident handling was inherently thin, and the additional reliability-relevant material that did exist—such as helpline records, technical logs, and defect information—was not disclosed in a way that permitted effective adversarial scrutiny. This approach conflicted with the prosecutor's disclosure duty (the obligation to disclose material capable of undermining the prosecution case or assisting the defence, applicable to private prosecutors as well as the CPS). It preserved narrative control (Hyde 2023) by foreclosing system-based explanations, entrenching a presumption of Horizon's reliability, and sustaining the individualisation of blame. The result was an enduring technical, informational, and legal asymmetry in which contested records were read as human fault rather than systemic artefact, and meaningful challenge depended on external actors forcing disclosure and evidential leverage that internal governance could not supply (Christie 2022; Moorhead et al. 2023).

The victimisation of sub-postmasters: technology, law, and power asymmetry (1999–2009)

From system error to criminal blame

Building on Section "Early Discrepancies and the Institutional Response", the Horizon cases show how technical anomalies were converted into criminal blame through a distinctive institutional configuration. Post Office Ltd combined the roles of commercial counterparty and private prosecutor, enabling it to control investigation, charging decisions, and access to core digital records. Following the 1999 reform of the law of evidence, which generally treated computer output as reliable unless credibly challenged, Horizon data entered proceedings with a strong presumption of reliability, thereby placing a substantial practical burden on sub-postmasters to challenge alleged discrepancies in their branch accounts. The High Court later characterised this as an onerous burden within a contractual and evidentiary regime tilted towards the institution (Bates & Others v Post Office Ltd (No. 3, No. 6)).

That burden was compounded by disclosure practices: logs, defect information, and helpline material that could contextualise anomalies were difficult to obtain, limiting adversarial testing (Second Sight 2015; Hyde 2023). The result was a prosecution pipeline in which organisational authority and informational asymmetry made system-generated discrepancies legible as dishonesty rather than fallibility, reinforced by routinised loss-recovery and investigative defaults.

As the litigation unfolded, the High Court held that Legacy Horizon was "not remotely robust" and that the robustness of HNG-X was questionable and did not justify the Post Office's confidence in its accuracy (Bates & Others v Post Office Ltd (No. 6) 2019, para. 975–978). It also documented long-known bugs and defects evidenced in Fujitsu's incident records (Bates & Others v Post Office Ltd (No. 6)

2019, para. 925), consistent with independent analyses of fault pathways and centrally managed interventions capable of producing apparent shortfalls (Second Sight 2013, 2015; Williams 2025).

Digital presumption and the collapse of evidentiary safeguards

The legal environment amplified these harms in predictable ways. Before 1999, section 69 of the Police and Criminal Evidence Act 1984 (PACE) created a statutory "reliability gateway", requiring the party relying on computer-generated records to show that the system was operating properly when the data were produced. That safeguard was removed by section 60 of the Youth Justice and Criminal Evidence Act 1999 (YJCEA), which repealed section 69 without replacement. The repeal followed the Law Commission's 1995 consultation paper and its 1997 recommendation to abolish section 69, grounded in the view that special hurdles for computer evidence were unnecessary as digital systems had matured (Law Commission 1995, 1997; De Silva 2024). Reliability therefore shifted from a condition of admissibility to a matter of weight, supporting a general presumption that computers operate properly unless the defence raises credible doubt (Moorhead et al. 2023; De Silva 2024).

Computer scientists and safety-critical engineers have long cautioned that such presumptions are evidentially hazardous because complex sociotechnical systems work and eventually fail in non-obvious, context-dependent ways. Ladkin et al. (2020) argue that presuming reliability misconceives software behaviour in real deployments and invites courts to over-credit outputs that are neither transparent nor independently verifiable. In short, the doctrinal shift removed a front-end check in precisely the domain where back-end verification is hardest.

In the Horizon case, this presumption became an institutional blind spot. Defence requests for technical disclosure were often characterised as "fishing expeditions", while proprietary control over logs, error reports, and back-end records restricted meaningful adversarial testing (Moorhead et al. 2023). The combined effect was easier admission and harder contestation: machine-generated records could be treated as de facto neutral facts even when the materials needed to test them were inaccessible to the accused.

Once Horizon convictions began to be revisited by the appellate courts in 2021, patterns dispersed across individual cases became visible as systemic (see the Section " Appeals, Quashed Convictions, and Institutional Reckoning (2020–2025)"). The lesson is clear: where law presumes reliability in complex digital systems, and institutions control the evidence needed to test that presumption, adversarial safeguards can fail at precisely the point where they are most needed.

These risks are compounded where prosecutions are private. When the complainant controls the investigation and the relevant data environment, it also controls what is recorded, retained, and disclosed. Although disclosure duties apply to private prosecutors, incentives and information asymmetries can skew outcomes:

technical logs, error reports, and remote-intervention records are generated and curated within the prosecutor's own systems, leaving defence and court without independent access or context. The CPS has powers to take over and discontinue a private prosecution, but intervention is discretionary rather than routine, typically triggered only once concerns are raised.

Prosecution without oversight: the power of the Post Office

Post Office Ltd's hybrid role as commercial counterparty and private prosecutor meant it could investigate, accuse, and prosecute while controlling access to the evidence base on which its cases depended. This created a pronounced power asymmetry: the Company acted as the primary producer, curator, and interpreter of Horizon data even as it advanced those data as proof of wrongdoing in court (Williams 2025). In practice, the Post Office became both gatekeeper and advocate for machine-generated "facts", narrowing opportunities for independent scrutiny (Christie 2022; Moorhead et al. 2023). Limits on disclosure (especially regarding bug records, audit trails/auditability, remote-intervention records, and helpline materials) further constrained adversarial testing (see the Section "Legal and Institutional Failures, and the Reconstruction of Contestability").

Behind the scenes, the Second Sight review documentation catalogued multiple categories of "transaction anomalies", but the capacity to validate causes rested largely with Post Office and Fujitsu rather than with independent access to underlying audit evidence (Second Sight 2015). The net effect, as Christie (2022) argues, was a self-validating evidence loop: the Post Office generated and curated the digital traces it then mobilised against defendants while resisting broader disclosure that could have contextualised or undermined them (see also Williams 2025).

Human consequences inflicted by digital bureaucracy

Beyond the legal and technical detail, the harms were intimate and enduring, affecting the health and wellbeing of sub-postmasters and branch staff. Empirical work with affected sub-postmasters documents very high rates of clinically significant post-traumatic stress (67%) and depressive symptoms (60%), irrespective of case outcome, alongside stigma, financial collapse, and relationship strain (Growns et al. 2024). Qualitative and clinical accounts similarly describe cumulative psychological and social harms, including suicidal ideation, amplified by delay, opacity, and the continuing struggle for redress (see also Deahl & Foster 2024).

These outcomes reflected structural conditions of organisational denial and secrecy; legal deference to machine-generated records; and an information architecture that shielded core evidence from independent testing (Christie 2022; Bates & Others v Post Office Ltd (No. 6) 2019). Crucially, these were not passive system effects: managerial and legal strategies repeatedly leveraged Horizon's opacity to protect the organisation and shift exposure onto frontline operators. Helpline records and internal "anomalies" papers illustrate how transaction corrections and recovery routines could allocate losses to individuals while obscuring upstream mechanics (Second Sight 2015). When an independent review was commissioned, Second Sight raised concerns about systemic flaws from a user perspective, but access to materials was restricted and the engagement ended in 2015, limiting the corrective effect of external scrutiny (see the Section "Early resistance and the emergence of dissent (2009–2015)"). These harms were often amplified by organisational denial, delay, and defensive handling, a pattern consistent with institutional betrayal (Smith & Freyd 2013).

Because contested records were hard to interrogate and harder to challenge, individuals carried the burden (financially, socially, and psychologically) of discrepancies they could not explain or contest.

Collective mobilisation, litigation, and institutional reckoning

Early resistance and the emergence of dissent (2009–2015)

For almost a decade after Horizon's deployment, complaints were largely individualised and interpreted as local error, and the scandal became visible at scale only through external mobilisation. Collective resistance coalesced in 2009 with the Justice for Subpostmasters Alliance (JFSA), which aggregated cases, systematised recurring discrepancy patterns, and pressed for disclosure through media and parliamentary channels (Mason 2021). Under mounting political pressure, Post Office Ltd appointed Second Sight Support Services Ltd. in 2012 to review cases under a mediation scheme. Second Sight's interim work (2013) and its 2015 briefing documented recurring anomaly patterns and warned that, in some circumstances, Horizon was "systemically flawed from a user's perspective", urging "professional scepticism" (Second Sight 2015, para. 26.8–26.9). At the same time, internal Post Office materials acknowledged categories of transaction anomalies while repeatedly attributing causation to branch error or procedural non-compliance (Second Sight 2015).

Rather than widening access to system evidence, Post Office Ltd narrowed the review: requests for historic Post Office helpline and Fujitsu Horizon Service Desk datasets were deemed disproportionate, and investigators reported difficulties accessing legal files, email archives, and other relevant datasets (Second Sight 2015). In parallel, substantial helpline material was not disclosed in subsequent litigation (Hyde 2023). The cumulative effect was a defensive governance posture in which reputation management and narrative control took precedence over investigating reliability concerns (Christie 2022).

By March 2015, as the mediation scheme collapsed, Second Sight recorded that its findings remained incomplete and reiterated concerns about systemic flaws and insufficient support to branches (Second Sight 2015). These developments set the stage for collective litigation.

The High Court Group Litigation (2017–2019)

A decisive shift came with High Court group litigation under a Group Litigation Order (GLO) brought by 555 sub-postmasters in 2017. The GLO consolidated dispersed claims into a single evidentiary forum, enabling systematic fact-finding, revealing recurring defect patterns, and creating judicial leverage to compel (at least partial) disclosure. In a sequence of 2019 judgments, Fraser J addressed both the contractual framework and Horizon's reliability in *Bates & Others v Post Office Ltd (No. 3) and (No. 6)*. In the Common Issues judgment (No. 3), he held that the relationship bore features of a relational contract with an implied duty of good faith and criticised governance and training arrangements that placed sub-postmasters at a structural disadvantage. In the Horizon Issues judgment (No. 6), he found documented defects and rejected the Post Office's long-standing "robustness" narrative, including by addressing disputes concerning remote access and the scope of issues requiring trial.

The judgments sharpened the evidential stakes: not merely whether defects existed, but whether they could generate apparent discrepancies and how far Post Office and Fujitsu could insert, edit, or rebuild transactions without the sub-postmaster's knowledge (Bates & Others v Post Office Ltd (No. 6) 2019; Christie 2022). Concerns about Fujitsu witness evidence were also referred to the DPP, given the potential implications for earlier prosecutions (Mason 2021). Although the litigation settled in December 2019 on confidential terms and many claimants received limited net compensation after costs, the judgments established the factual and legal foundation for subsequent appeals and the wider public reckoning.

Appeals, quashed convictions, and institutional reckoning (2020–2025)

Following the High Court findings, Horizon-related cases were revisited through the Criminal Cases Review Commission (CCRC) referral process. The CCRC referral process exists to independently review suspected miscarriages of justice by investigating applications, obtaining new material, and assessing whether a conviction or sentence may be unsafe. If it concludes there is a "real possibility" the conviction or sentence would not be upheld, it refers the case back to the appropriate appeal court (typically the Court of Appeal), effectively reopening the route to appeal. In Hamilton and Others v Post Office Ltd (2021), the Court of Appeal quashed 39 convictions in a single judgment, criticising cumulative investigative and disclosure failures and the uncritical reliance on Horizon data. Further decisions followed, and by 17 April 2025 officials reported 595 individuals in England and Wales with at least one conviction quashed, amounting to 2,135 convictions in total (Ministry of Justice 2025). These figures are reported in the Ministry of Justice's management-information series tracking convictions quashed under a case-specific legislative intervention, the Post Office (Horizon System) Offences Act 2024. Compensation schemes were introduced both for those with quashed convictions and for those who suffered substantial financial losses without prosecution, but implementation proved complex and uneven, prolonging distress (Moon 2024; Williams 2025). By early 2026, redress was being channelled increasingly through administratively managed schemes, each with its own published procedures, targets, and deadlines. Most visibly, the Horizon Shortfall Scheme closed to new applications on 31 January 2026, although it continued to process claims already received (Post Office 2025). This underlined the gap between legal exoneration and practical restoration: formal acknowledgment of injustice did not itself deliver redress, which remained dependent on separate administrative processes.

Alongside the appellate process, criminal investigation progressed. The Metropolitan Police opened an investigation in January 2020 following a referral from the Director of Public Prosecutions, and it remains ongoing, including potential offences such as perjury and perverting the course of justice. A published update in December 2025 provides the most recent public metrics on the investigation's scale and progress. As of December 2025, the Met Police Operation Olympos reported an investigation team of around 111, a review set of about 7.5 million documents, eight named suspects (with a wider pool of persons of interest), and five interviews under caution, with further interviews planned in 2026 (Metropolitan Police Service 2025).

Public scrutiny also intensified through the Post Office Horizon IT Inquiry, converted into a statutory inquiry in 2021 with powers to compel evidence and testimony. The Inquiry record documents disclosure failures, board-level visibility of reliability concerns, and a sustained organisational tendency to frame anomalies as local fault rather than systemic risk (Williams 2025). It also raises governance questions for a state-owned enterprise, including the role of shareholder oversight, given evidence of senior attention to litigation, disclosure, and reputational strategy (Christie 2022). In October 2025, the Government published its response to the Inquiry's Volume 1 recommendations, signalling an executive commitment to implementation alongside the continuing criminal and appellate processes (Hansard 2025). Separately, in December 2025 the Metropolitan Police's Operation Olympos appealed for affected individuals who had signed non-disclosure agreements with the Post Office to come forward, stating it had written confirmation that such NDAs would not be enforced (Metropolitan Police Service 2025).

Taken together, the post-2019 phase shows how technological opacity, organisational defensiveness, and weak evidentiary safeguards can combine to produce—and then belatedly expose, systemic injustice (Williams 2025; Christie 2022).

Technology, law, and digital governance

The risks of overreliance on technology

The Horizon litigation and Inquiry illustrate why complex digital systems should not be treated as self-proving evidence of real-world states. In the Horizon litigation, the court rejected a single, timeless answer to "robustness", finding that the system contained defects and that reliability could not be assumed from its data alone (Bates & Others v Post Office Ltd (No. 6) 2019). The Inquiry likewise records that liabilities were imposed for losses that did not, in fact, exist (Williams 2025). Together, these findings undermine any presumption that computer-generated records faithfully represent reality. A safety-oriented approach treats reliability as something to be engineered and demonstrated through assurance practices—change control, traceable auditability, and governance arrangements that make failures detectable and explainable rather than discoverable only after harm occurs (Leveson 2011).

Horizon also demonstrates how the gravest risks may lie less in the existence of defects than in diagnosability: the practical difficulty of reconstructing how disputed records were produced in a complex operational environment. Layered processing, incomplete or opaque audit trails, and remote intervention capabilities can make end-to-end reconstruction difficult or impossible, especially for frontline users without access to system logs, defect histories, or diagnostic tools (Second Sight 2015). This is due also to a structural information asymmetry: institutions and suppliers can frame discrepancies as user fault while restricting access to material that would support system-based explanations (Christie 2022; Moorhead et al. 2023).

Generalising, technical complexity must not translate into evidential advantage for the party asserting reliability. Technical assurance should therefore be paired with contestability: affected users need workable routes to challenge outputs, supported by transparent auditability and timely access to reliability-relevant technical material (Hyde 2023; Second Sight 2015).

Horizon's core failure was not that software can be defective, but that operational opacity and asymmetric access to provenance/audit material allowed disputed outputs to function as authoritative "facts" even when they could not be independently tested (Williams 2025, paras. 1.4, 3.26–3.29; Bates & Others v Post Office Ltd (No. 6) 2019, paras. 526–527, 976–978). Accountability in data-driven systems therefore depends on countervailing institutions—collective voice, independent review capacity, and courts able to compel disclosure.

Legal and institutional failures, and the reconstruction of contestability

As discussed above, the Horizon case shows that technical defects became legally consequential because evidential and institutional safeguards were too weak to expose them in time. Once reliability ceased to function as an admissibility threshold, computer-generated records were often treated as presumptively trustworthy, while disclosure failures and the Post Office's hybrid role as investigator, prosecutor, and controller of the evidential environment made effective challenge exceptionally difficult (Moorhead et al. 2023; De Silva 2024; Hyde 2023). The key issue, then, was not only technical error, but the institutional conditions under which such error could be identified, scrutinised, and challenged.

These vulnerabilities were compounded by the Post Office's use of private prosecutions. In many cases, the organisation alleging loss also directed the investigation, shaped charging decisions, relied on supplier-linked technical expertise, and controlled what was recorded and disclosed. Although disclosure duties applied to private prosecutors, Horizon shows how incentives and information asymmetries could blunt those safeguards when the evidential environment was owned and curated by a party with a direct stake in the outcome (Christie 2022; Moorhead et al. 2023). Formal "safety valves" existed, notably CPS powers to take over private prosecutions, and later appellate and review mechanisms, but these were discretionary and were typically activated only once concerns could be articulated and evidenced, after significant damage had already been done.

What ultimately made Horizon contestable, therefore, was not internal governance but the construction of external counter-power: mechanisms able to aggregate dispersed experiences, validate them, and compel access to records that were otherwise institutionally held. The Justice for Subpostmasters Alliance (JFSA) performed the initial aggregation and advocacy function, converting individual disputes treated as "local errors" into a pattern visible through media and parliamentary channels (Mason 2021). Independent review capacity also mattered: although constrained, Second Sight documented recurring anomaly patterns and urged scepticism about Horizon records, helping to legitimate concerns that had previously been dismissed (Second Sight 2015).

Litigation and appellate scrutiny then converted those concerns into an evidential record with institutional traction. High Court fact-finding—particularly on defects, limits on user auditability, and remote access—produced findings that could no longer be reduced to anecdote (Bates & Others v Post Office Ltd (No. 6) 2019). That record enabled safeguards outside the Post Office to operate at scale: the CCRC and the Court of Appeal could revisit convictions in light of systemic defect and disclosure patterns that had not been realistically testable in first-instance proceedings (Hamilton and Others v Post Office Ltd 2021). The statutory Inquiry further consolidated the account by compelling evidence and assessing responsibility across organisational and supplier boundaries (Williams 2025).

Horizon shows that effective contestability is not an automatic by-product of adversarial procedure, but a governance capability that must be designed and maintained. In digital-evidence environments, this depends on at least three conditions: technical contestability, in the form of auditability and workable access to relevant logs or audit extracts; procedural contestability, through disclosure practices that make systemic material practically obtainable; and institutional contestability, through credible external review and escalation routes that do not depend solely on organisational willingness. Without such counterweights, information asymmetries are likely to persist, and correction may arrive only after severe harm has already been done.

Conclusion: towards a just technological society

The Horizon scandal is not simply the story of defective software. It is a case of how machine-generated records can acquire institutional authority and, when coupled with institutional and bureaucratic self-protection, be used to allocate blame, liability, and criminal responsibility at scale. In Horizon, technical anomalies were converted into stable organisational "facts" through the interaction of system design, information asymmetries, governance choices, and legal procedure, until courts and the Inquiry could compel disclosure, consolidate the record, and make reliability contestable.

Read through a sociomaterial lens, Horizon's outputs functioned as inscription devices: they translated situated counter transactions into portable records that travelled across organisational and legal arenas with their authority intact, while the conditions of production remained opaque (Latour 1993; Lanzara 2009b). Lanzara's account of institutional rigidity helps explain why corrective feedback failed: once the "robustness" narrative was embedded in routines, litigation strategy, and governance incentives, the organisation resisted error signals rather than learning from them (Lanzara 1998).

A three-step escalation dynamic captures the mechanisms through which things went wrong. First, complex digital systems can generate false or misleading outputs through ordinary failures and human–machine interaction. Second, the most consequential risk often lies in opacity and diagnosability: even when problems exist, layered processing, incomplete audit trails, and remote interventions make end-to-end reconstruction difficult, especially for frontline users without access to logs, defect histories, or diagnostic tools. Third, those asymmetries can be actively exploited: in Horizon, Post Office management and legal teams (working with supplier expertise) sustained a presumption of user fault, restricted access to system-based explanations, and (through private prosecution and litigation strategy) carried a curated evidential picture from internal discipline into criminal proceedings with limited effective challenge.

The legal system did not merely "receive" this evidence neutrally. After the repeal of the statutory reliability gateway for computer records, reliability disputes were pushed into the adversarial arena, where defendants were least able to mount them. In first-instance proceedings, Horizon outputs were often treated as routine proof, and disclosure failures narrowed the courts' capacity to test provenance and reliability, frequently within prosecution-led evidentiary frames that judges and juries were not equipped to verify independently. Only when litigation and appellate review consolidated dispersed cases did systemic patterns of defect and non-disclosure become visible and actionable.

Horizon therefore shows that the governance of high-stakes digital infrastructures depends on effective contestability, supported by auditability, meaningful disclosure, and independent review. Viewed through victimisation scholarship, the case also shows how ordinary system users can be recast as presumptive wrongdoers while the harms they suffer are denied recognition and accountability is displaced elsewhere.

References

Articles, books and reports

Christie, J. (2022). The Post Office IT scandal—why IT audit is essential for effective corporate governance. Digital Evidence and Electronic Signature Law Review, 19, 42–85. https://doi.org/10.14296/deeslr.v19i0.5425

Day, S., Nokes, K., Moorhead, R., & Helm, R. (2025, May). Understanding the impacts of the Post Office scandal (Working Paper 10). Evidence-Based Justice Lab, University of Exeter. The Post Office Project.

De Silva, S. (2024, August 12). Post Office scandal: Understanding computer evidence in cases. https://www.bcs.org/articles-opinion-and-research/post-office-scandal-understanding-computer-evidence-in-cases/

Deahl, M., & Foster, P. (2024). Mr Bates and the Post Office: The implications of the UK Post Office scandal for the taxonomy of trauma. JRSM Open, 15(12). https://doi.org/10.1177/20542704241304573

Elish, M. C. (2019). Moral crumple zones: Cautionary tales in human-robot interaction. Engaging Science, Technology, and Society, 5, 40–60. https://doi.org/10.17351/ests2019.260

Eubanks, V. (2018). Automating inequality: How high-tech tools profile, police, and punish the poor. St. Martin's Press.

Growns, B., Kukucka, J., Moorhead, R., & Helm, R. (2024). The Post Office scandal in the United Kingdom: Mental health and social experiences of wrongly convicted and wrongly accused individuals. Legal and Criminological Psychology, 29(1), 17–31. https://doi.org/10.1111/lcrp.12247

Hood, C. (2010). The blame game: Spin, bureaucracy, and self-preservation in government. Princeton University Press.

Hyde, J. (2023, September 22). Solicitor for Post Office defends failure to disclose Horizon helpline calls. Law Society Gazette. lawgazette.co.uk

Kallinikos, J. (2011). Governing through technology: Information artefacts and social practice. Basingstoke: Palgrave Macmillan. https://doi.org/10.1057/9780230295148

Ladkin, P. B., Littlewood, B., Thimbleby, H., & Thomas, M. (2020). The Law Commission presumption concerning the dependability of computer evidence. Digital Evidence and Electronic Signature Law Review, 17, 1–14. https://doi.org/10.14296/deeslr.v17i0.5143

Lanzara, G. F. (1998). Self-destructive processes in institution building and some modest countervailing mechanisms. European Journal of Political Research, 33, 1–39. https://doi.org/10.1023/A:1006850820973

Lanzara, G. F. (2009a). Reshaping practice across media: Material mediation, medium specificity and practical knowledge in judicial work. Organization Studies, 30(12), 1369–1390.

Lanzara, G. F. (2009b). Building digital institutions: ICT and the rise of assemblages in government. In F. Contini & G. F. Lanzara (Eds.), ICT and innovation in the public sector: European studies in the making of e-government (pp. 9–48). Palgrave Macmillan.

Latour, B. (1993). We have never been modern. Harvard University Press.

Law Commission. (1995). Evidence in criminal proceedings: Hearsay and related topics (Consultation Paper No. 138). HMSO.

Law Commission. (1997). Evidence in criminal proceedings: Hearsay and related topics (Law Com No. 245; Cm 3670). The Stationery Office.

Leveson, N. G. (2011). Engineering a safer world: Systems thinking applied to safety. MIT Press.

Marshall, P. (2022). Scandal at the Post Office: The intersection of law, ethics and politics. Digital Evidence and Electronic Signature Law Review, 19, 12–28. https://doi.org/10.14296/deeslr.v19i0.5395

Mason, S. (2021). The Post Office Horizon scandal: A brief chronology. Digital Evidence and Electronic Signature Law Review, 18 (Documents Supplement). https://doi.org/10.14296/deeslr.v18i0.5390
Moon, C. J. (2024). The Post Office scandal: Implications for Management, Leadership, and Governance. Proceedings of the 20th European Conference on Management, Leadership & Governance, 719–722.
Moorhead, R., Nokes, K., & Helm, R. (2023). Independent review, miscarriages of justice, and computer evidence: Brian Altman KC's General Review and the Post Office scandal. Digital Evidence and Electronic Signature Law Review, 20, 96–119. journals.sas.ac.uk
Second Sight Support Services Ltd. (2013, July 8). Interim report (incorporating the preliminary results of four spot reviews) [Unpublished report prepared for Post Office Ltd].
Second Sight Support Services Ltd. (2015, April 9). Initial complaint review and mediation scheme: Briefing report—Part Two (Inquiry exhibit POL00029849 Independent review report prepared for Post Office Ltd). Post Office Horizon IT Inquiry, Evidence Portal.
Smith, C. P., & Freyd, J. J. (2013). Dangerous safe havens: Institutional betrayal exacerbates sexual trauma. Journal of Traumatic Stress, 26(1), 119–124. https://doi.org/10.1002/jts.21778
Williams, W. (2025). Post Office Horizon IT inquiry: Final report—Volume 1 (HC 1119). The Stationery Office. https://www.postofficehorizoninquiry.org.uk/volume-1-post-office-horizon-inquirys-final-report
Yeung, K. (2018). Algorithmic regulation: A critical interrogation. Regulation & Governance, 12(4), 505–523. https://doi.org/10.1111/rego.12158
Yin, R. K. (2018). Case study research and applications: Design and methods (6th ed.). SAGE Publications.

Case law

Bates & Others v Post Office Ltd (No. 3: Common Issues), [2019] EWHC 606 (QB).
Bates & Others v Post Office Ltd (No. 6: Horizon Issues), [2019] EWHC 3408 (QB).
Hamilton & Others v Post Office Ltd, [2021] EWCA Crim 577 (CA (Crim Div), 23 April 2021).

Websites

Hansard. (2025). Post Office Horizon IT inquiry report: Government response to volume 1 recommendations volume 773: Debated on Monday 13 October 2025. https://hansard.parliament.uk/
Metropolitan Police Service. (2025). Operation olympos. https://www.police.uk/pu/operation-olympos/
Ministry of Justice. (2025, July 24 update). Quashed convictions management information: 24 April 2025. https://www.gov.uk/government/publications/post-office-horizon-system-offences-act-2024-quashed-convictions-management-information/quashed-convictions-management-information-24-april-2025
Post Office Ltd. (2025). The Horizon shortfall scheme. https://www.onepostoffice.co.uk/scheme

13

JUSTICE FOR ALGORITHMIC INJUSTICE

Courts, communities, and redress

Francesco Contini and Anne Wallace

Introduction

Automated decision-making is a growing presence in public service delivery. The technology used varies from relatively simple systems of data-matching to artificial intelligence (AI). Its promise of objective, fast, and efficient decisions made with limited or no human supervision makes it appear the perfect tool for a seamless implementation of public policies. In this paper, we examine two examples of automated decision-making in public service delivery that illustrate the risks associated with these systems. "Robodebt" in Australia and the Toeslagenaffaire, the "Child Welfare Scandal" in The Netherlands involved the use of automated systems in the investigation, calculation and collection of welfare overpayment debts from citizens. In both cases, the systems asked for and forced the collection of money that was not due. People affected by forced money collections were pushed into poverty, forced to sell property, and suffered stress and trauma that damaged their physical and mental health, families and social ties. Both systems have been blamed for some deaths, including suicides, and triggered controversies, outcry, and investigative commissions.

These two cases have been analysed by non-government organisations, journalists, investigative commissions, courts and a growing body of academic work focusing on technological, sociological, political and legal perspectives.[1] Building on these analyses, this paper offers a comparative assessment of Robodebt and the Dutch welfare scandal. We examine the development, implementation and operation of these two schemes to identify the factors that were implicated in their discriminatory outcomes, in bringing them to light and providing redress for victims. As previous studies show, these two cases illustrate the need for measures to prevent this type of outcome at the design level (of policies and techno-legal

DOI: 10.4324/9781003752974-17

systems). Furthermore, they highlight the potentially critical role that courts can play in investigating and providing remedies for individuals who are discriminated against or otherwise unlawfully victimised by algorithmic and other automated decision-making systems. We investigate this issue by identifying the features of technology-assisted decision-making and analysing how they weaken the effectiveness of judicial proceedings as a means of redressing injustice, discrimination and inequalities. Finally, we identify measures to make judicial decision-making more effective in these cases, including steps to support the role that intermediate bodies as NGOs and unions can play in empowering people to access judicial remedies to combat algorithmic injustice.

Case histories—"Robodebt" and the "Toeslagenaffaire"

Robodebt

> Robodebt was a crude and cruel mechanism, neither fair nor legal, and it made many people feel like criminals. In essence, people were traumatised on the off-chance they might owe money. It was a costly failure of public administration, in both human and economic terms.
>
> (RRC, 2023 Vol 1. p.xxix)

What became known as "Robodebt" originated in 2015 as a cost-savings measure proposed in Australia's Commonwealth government budget. A conservative government elected in 2013 had signalled budget control and cost reduction as priorities, and an intention to investigate methods of recovering debt owed by citizens to government agencies. In 2015, a newly-appointed Social Security Minister described his intention to be "a strong welfare cop on the beat" to ensure individuals did not "rort the system"[2] (Morton, 2024 pp.75–76; RRC, 2023 p.xxiii).

Under his leadership, the Department of Human Services (DHS), responsible for the delivery of social welfare benefits payable under the Social Security Act (Cth) 1991 ("the SSA"), developed a package of measures for the 2015 budget that projected savings of AU$1.7billion over 5 years, largely drawn from an "Employment Income Matching" measure designed to recover overpayments from incorrect declarations of income by welfare recipients. Begun as a pilot project in 2015, the scheme was fully rolled out in 2016 and progressively expanded in subsequent budget years to operate for a total of 4 years (RRC, 2023 pp.xxiv–xxv).

The centrepiece of this project was an automated system of data-matching that compared data obtained from employers' returns to the Australian Taxation Office (ATO) of income paid to welfare recipients with the amounts of income that those recipients had declared to DHS. If a discrepancy was identified and the recipient did not respond to an invitation to explain or contest that discrepancy, their employment income would be averaged across a period of time using the data supplied by the employer. Through a process of income "averaging" or "smoothing" the amount declared by the employer would be divided equally and allocated into the number of fortnights in that time period. If that averaged amount exceeded the amount a recipient was entitled to receive in that fortnight (before their benefit was reduced), that would give rise to an overpayment which would be recovered either as a debt or by way of deductions from their current benefit (RRC, 2023 p.xxiv).

DHS in-house lawyers raised concerns at the outset that this process of income averaging conflicted with the income calculation provisions of the SSA which stated that entitlement to benefit depended on the recipient's *actual* fortnightly income. Employers reported to the ATO yearly, so it could not be assumed on the basis of that data that a recipient had worked every fortnight during that year or earned the same amount each fortnight (Morton, 2024 pp.272–274; RRC, 2023 pp.xxiv–xxv). The advice that legislative change—potentially contestable and likely to delay the implementation of the scheme—would be necessary to implement the income-matching scheme was downplayed by senior public servants who saw their role primarily as facilitating the government's agenda, and was ignored by the relevant minister (Morton, 2024 pp.84–88, 91–92).

In Robodebt's most fully automated phase, there was a complete absence of any process or intervention to check the accuracy of the data supplied and, as there had been no proper testing of the pilot scheme, problems identified in its initial manual operation had not been fully addressed: "The system sometimes deleted details of previously declared income; there were failures in employer name matches which led to wrong duplication of earnings; particular allowances and payments were wrongly treated" (Rinta-Kahila et al., 2024 p.166; RRC, 2023 p.xxvi). This led to many debts being raised on the basis of incorrect information (RRC, 2023 pp.477–478). At this point the system operated as "a system of business rules with no ability to move outside of specific and defined action on the basis of the data received" (RRC, 2023 p.472) and, in effect, "complex fact-finding and data-entry functions were offloaded to the citizen" (Rinta-Kahila et al., 2024 p.166) who bore the onus of contesting the calculated debt.

Their ability to do so was impaired by an on-line interface that had not been user-tested, was difficult to use and subject to "crashing" (Morton, 2024 pp.142–143; Rinta-Kahila et al., 2024 p.166; RRC, 2023 p.xxvi). Those recipients who managed to access it and confirmed the ATO employment data presented to them were not told that this data would then be used to average their income over that yearly period and potentially calculate a debt against them; others either did not receive the notifications or did not understand what they needed to do (Rinta-Kahila et al., 2024 p.166; RRC, 2023 p.xxvi).

By the end of 2016, there was heavy public criticism of the scheme. Daily media included reports of individuals with clearly erroneous debts raised against them pursued by debt collection agencies, others struggling financially, and even a suicide (Morton, 2024 n2, pp.11–12; 158–174; Rinta-Kahila et al., 2024 p.167; RRC, 2023). In response, the government went on the attack, defending the system. An investigation into the scheme by the Commonwealth Ombudsman found that, despite some technical problems in the online interface, the scheme was raising accurate debts (Carney, 2018 p.6; RRC, 2023 p.xxvii). This finding was influenced by a further in-house legal advice provided by DHS to the Ombudsman which, contrary to the earlier advice, advised that the scheme was in accordance with the legislation (RRC, 2023 p.xxvii).

Meanwhile, some recipients who had a debt raised against them exercised their right to seek a review from the Level 1 of the Commonwealth Administrative Appeals Tribunal ("AAT"). The AAT made a number of decisions setting aside debts on the basis that "averaging, of itself, could not provide evidence of actual income or, it followed, overpayment and debt" (RRC, 2023). Although DHS took steps to rectify the individual cases in accordance with these decisions, in a deliberate strategy it took no steps to exercise its right to appeal the legal findings (Carney, 2018 p.7; Morton, 2024 p.270). This was despite a practice between DHS and the Department of Social Services ("DSS")—the department responsible for content and policy of the SSA—that required DHS to refer AAT decisions to DSS where there was a significant error of law, a significant issue of policy or administrative practice, or the matter had attracted or was likely to attract media or parliamentary attention (all issues that were potentially applicable in these cases) (RRC, 2023 p.xxvii). The government's failure to act on the systemic implications of these decisions was obscured because outcomes of decisions made by Level 1 of the AAT were published only to the parties, not to the general public (Carney, 2018 p.7; Morton, 2024 p.270).

Although Section 8(f) of the SSA also requires DSS to apply government policy with due regard to relevant decisions of the AAT, DSS took no notice of the AAT findings concerning the lawfulness of the method of income-averaging until mid-2018 when it sought advice from a private law firm. A draft legal advice obtained from the firm confirming that the income average method was unlawful was never finalised, and the department took no action in respect of it.

Problems with the system and questions about its legality continued to attract public and media attention, assisted by an online activist movement #NotMyDebt[3] (Rinta-Kahila et al., 2024 p.166). The government was also experiencing pressure from social welfare and community organisations, including the Australian Council for Social Services, as well as the political opposition (RRC, 2023 Ch.8). However, only when the issue reached the Federal Court in 2019, in two applications for judicial review, did DSS finally seek legal advice from the Commonwealth Solicitor-General who confirmed that the income-averaging method was unlawful (RRC, 2023 pp.xxviii–xxix). The government then announced that debts would no longer be raised solely on the basis of averaged income (RRC, 2023 p.xxix). A class action was then instituted in the Federal Court which was settled by the Government in 2020 with the announcement that all debts raised in whole or part through averaging would be reduced to zero (Morton, 2024 p.327; RRC, 2023). A formal apology from the then prime minister, the former DSS minister, followed (RRC, 2023 p.v.).

A Royal Commission into the scheme established in August 2022 presented its final report to the government on 7 July 2023 (RRC, 2023). In addition to detailing the horrendous and traumatic impact on individuals wrongly charged with debts, the Commission comprehensively detailed the failures—technological, managerial and legal—that had been responsible for their victimisation and made a series of recommendations designed to address them.

Toeslagenaffaire: the Dutch child welfare scandal

Official data shows that nearly 70,000 people applied for compensation as victims of the Dutch childcare benefits scandal.[4] Many were wrongly labelled as fraudsters, resulting in poverty, debt, homelessness, and suicides. Ultimately, the scandal led to the resignation of the government in January 2021. At its core was a harsh and punitive legal framework requiring administratively perfect applications enforced by a rule-based computer system, and the use of a machine-learning algorithm, *Systeem Risico Indicatie* (SyRI), to identify fraudulent claims.

Since 2005, child welfare scheme had provided subsidies to parents to cover part of the costs of purchasing preschool and out-of-school childcare services from registered providers. The reimbursement was paid in advance. A subsidy control scheme was implemented in the 2009 General Act on Income-Related Schemes (AWIR) and related anti-fraud regulations. Parents were required to submit digital applications, using their Digital ID, inputting and regularly updating personal data and the contributions received (Peeters & Widlak, 2023 p. 874). Such an error-prone procedure was made critical by an "all or nothing" principle established by AWIR, stating that even minor errors, such as a wrong digit in a date of birth, resulted in a demand to repay the full benefit.

Although commercial agencies (*gastouderbureaus*) could assist, parents remained responsible for accurate submissions and documentation (Peeters & Widlak, 2023). There was no hardship clause which would have enabled the debt to be reduced or cancelled where it would result in an excessive burden on the debtor; exceptions were considered "sand in the wheels" that would complicate control procedures (POK, 2020 p.13; van den Berge & Gaakeer, 2025). This strict approach was enforced by a digital system built to automatically check applications and identify errors to facilitate a streamlined automatic check of the benefits paid out (POK, 2020 pp.35, 53).

Appeals to the administrative courts against demands for repayment initially met with some success; however, in 2012, the Judicial Division of the Council of State confirmed that the "all or nothing approach" was lawful.[5] This decision gave the green light to the request for full clawback of benefits paid in case of formal mistakes and bound the administrative courts' judgements in subsequent appeals. The Council of State subsequently re-confirmed the strict approach several times, even in case of a minor formal error (Bouwmeester, 2023 p. 29).

Meanwhile a series of frauds received widespread media publicity. Some childminding agencies committed fraud by applying for childcare benefits without securing the required client contribution (POK, 2020). In another scandal, ringleaders organised Bulgarian citizens to briefly register at Dutch addresses and retrospectively claim benefits (Berends, 2021). At the time allowances were paid immediately and eligibility checked afterwards, when applicants had already left the Netherlands (Peeters & Widlak, 2023).

These scandals triggered a stricter fraud prevention policy endorsed by the House of Representatives in 2013. New control measures included the creation of a Fraud Management Team, including top officials within the Tax and Customs Administration (TCA) and the Combi Team Approach Facilitators (CAF) investigating suspicious childcare centres and childminding agencies.

CAF's work was assisted by SyRI, a new AI-based system designed to discover frauds, developed under the 2013 SUWI decree that enhanced the pre-existing anti-fraud information system through data mining and machine learning (Bekker, 2021). It analysed extensive personal data (processed pseudo-anonymously) collected in State managed databases, including identity, employment, taxation and housing, to identify "high-risk" welfare beneficiaries (Chiusi et al., 2020; van Bekkum & Zuiderveen Borgesius, 2021).

High-risk flags prompted further scrutiny often leading to TCA and police involvement. However, rather than examining individual cases, authorities flagged entire groups as "high fraud risk" based on aggregated indicators without case-specific evidence (pilp.nu, 2020). This approach disproportionately targeted residents of low-income areas, applicants with foreign backgrounds, and clients of intermediary agencies suspected of fraudulent activity (UN Special Rapporteur, 2019; van Bekkum & Zuiderveen Borgesius, 2021 pp.332–333).

Despite opinions from the Council of State and the Data Protection Agency that expressed concern about its disproportionate intrusion on privacy and lack of transparency (Autoriteit Persoonsgegevens, 2014; Raad Van State, 2014), SyRI became operational in 2014. Between 2014 and 2019, 9,631 families were involved in CAF investigations and 1,300 had their benefits suspended before any individual investigation (Auditdienst Rijk 2020, pp.23–24). An estimated 200 CAF-related cases were referred to the prosecution service, resulting in 15 convictions and 8 settlements (Storp, 2020).

The issues with the welfare anti-fraud policy, including SyRI, eventually became a scandal thanks to a 2017 report by the National Ombudsman criticising the TCA's harsh approach in one of the fraud cases and recommending compensation to the parties affected (de Nationale Ombudsman, 2017). Investigations by media outlets (RTL Nieuws and Trouw) published in 2018 and 2019 placed the government under further media and societal pressure.

In this climate, on 23 October 2019, in two decisions, the Administrative Division of the Council of State made a U-turn, expressing the opinion that the principle of proportionality established by the General Administrative Law Act (AWB) could be applied, in the absence of a hardship clause in the AWIR, to mitigate the strict "all or nothing" approach.[6] This reversal was later justified by the President of the Division on the basis that it was required to solve an issue that the Government and Parliament should have solved through legislative changes (van Ettekoven, 2021).

Meanwhile, in 2018, non-government organisations, unions and legal experts had filed a case in the Hague District Court, arguing that SyRI breached Article 8 of the European Convention of Human Rights (ECHR) (privacy) and Article 22 of the EU General Data Protection Regulation (GDPR), prohibiting fully automated decisions with legal effects. The UN Special Rapporteur on Extreme Poverty and Human Rights filed an Amicus Curiae in the proceeding highlighting the suspected discriminatory use of SyRI (UN Special Rapporteur, 2019). The judgment found SyRI unlawful due to violation of Article 8 (lack of transparency and disproportionate surveillance, leading to its suspension in 2020.[7]

Similar roads towards discrimination

Examination of these two case studies reveals a number of common features in the way their technologies were developed, implemented and operated that created the conditions in which they harmed citizens, and delayed or impeded the detection, investigation and remediation of those harms. We discuss these before considering the role played by judicial systems in each case with reference to the questions we posed at the outset of this paper.

The catalytic role of the media and civil society

In both Australia and the Netherlands, concerns about real or perceived welfare fraud formed part of the public discourse against which these schemes were developed. In both countries, the media and civil society also played a prominent role in bringing their failures to light.

As outlined above, in the Netherlands, the background to the development and use of SyRI included several large, well-documented and well-publicised frauds committed on the child welfare system which triggered a strong political reaction. While there was no *actual* fraud scandal available to justify the political-governmental reaction that resulted in Robodebt in Australia (RRC, 2023 p. 180)[8] there was a high level of public and media concern about undetected welfare fraud, arguably, fuelled by the government (RRC, 2023 pp.xxiv–xxv). According to the Royal Commission, "It was well known that there was often conflation of the concepts of welfare fraud and inadvertent overpayment in the media" (RRC, 2023 p.141) and concern about welfare payment was often based on political rhetoric that stigmatised welfare recipients as inherently dishonest (RRC, 2023 pp.330–331).

In both cases, there appears to be a common political approach. First identify (or create) a scandal. Then identify and stigmatise the "enemy"—welfare applicants (the poor) or immigrants. Next, start a political campaign, and find a "solution" that involves stronger investigative and or remedial measures, using the media to both publicise the scandal and promote the "solution".

However, in a democratic society, access to the media and publicity is not confined to the organs of the state. In both the Netherlands and Australia, public criticism, amplified through the media, as well as the work of investigative journalists, played a major role in bringing the deficiencies of these schemes to light. Civil society—trade unions, non-government organisations, international organisations—also played an important role in these public campaigns, requesting investigation and action by the relevant government (Venice Commission, 2021 p.6). They were also significant players in the strategic litigation—the cases in the District Court in the Hague and the Federal Court of Australia—that played a significant role in forcing government action.

Disproportionate investigative approach

The background to SyRI and Robodebt also evidenced the use of investigative approaches in both countries that were increasingly heavy-handed and operated on the basis of adverse assumptions about welfare recipients. The notorious CAF case "Hawaii" (the name of the childminding agency) was carried out despite a previous investigation that resulted in a court ruling that acquitted the defendants of the accusation of fraud. A subsequent enquiry found CAF had operated on the assumption that 80% of the clients were fraudsters, despite a lack of actual evidence to that effect (Auditdienst Rijk, 2020; Venice Commission, 2021 p.5).

The Royal Commission into Robodebt in Australia found that the scandal was, in part, the result of a similar trend in investigating welfare fraud, that included data-matching and the presumption of debt. This included requiring welfare recipients to provide their Tax File Number (TFN) to the department administering their benefits to enable their declared employment to be cross-checked with income declared to the Australian Taxation office (ATO). Where a discrepancy appeared to indicate an overpayment of benefit, the recipient would be given 21 days' notice and an opportunity to contest the debt (RRC, 2023 pp.11–12). Later, the department began matching information provided by employers to the ATO under Australia's Pay as You Go (PAYG) income tax deduction scheme with income declared by benefit recipients, under a protocol that was not made publicly available (RRC, 2023 pp.13–14).

One of the significant respects in which Robodebt differed from the previous approach to detecting and investigating welfare fraud in Australia was that reliance on data provided by the ATO and the application of "income-averaging" gave rise to a presumption of over-payment. This means that, in common with the practice of the Dutch CAF relying solely on SyRI, repayment notices issued to welfare recipients were based simply on the calculations performed by the technology, without any detailed investigation into the individual facts and circumstances. This, in effect, presumed the correct operation of the technology and placed a "reverse onus" on recipients to contest it. At the height of the scheme this could only be done by interacting with the department online, requiring the recipient to locate and upload past employment and pay records that disproved the correctness of the automated calculation (RRC, 2023 p.xxiv).

In the Netherlands, a welfare beneficiary who believed they had been wrongfully issued with a notice of overpayment could appeal that decision, firstly by lodging an objection that was reviewed internally by the agency and, if unsuccessful, to the administrative courts. In both cases, the onus was on the recipient to show that they did not commit errors. In practice, this was a difficult onus to discharge, given the strict "all or nothing" approach and the finding that it was mandated by law, and an assumption at both the internal review and by the courts that the TCA systems worked properly and lawfully.

At a broader level, in the Dutch case, the presumption that 80% of cases signalled by SyRI involved fraud, turned the presumption of innocence into a presumption of guilt at the investigation stage. Similarly, the design of Robodebt assumed the existence of a large number of welfare recipients deliberately defrauding the system who had hitherto remained undetected.

In both cases, then, fundamental principles intended to protect the citizens against the power of the State—the onus of proof on the State and the presumption of innocence—were disregarded. This is a significant change in the approach to welfare provision, from a beneficence that is designed to facilitate access to rights to a more rigid system that is designed to make it more difficult for users to maintain and justify their entitlements.

Technological discriminations and managerial failures

Both Robodebt[9] and the Dutch case used rule-based automated systems that matched data to find errors. SyRI differed in that it was an AI based stochastic system, evolving due to its embedded machine-learning architecture, that provided statistical risk indicators. These features create a relevant difference at the level of deployment and piloting.

During the piloting stage, data matching applications are typically tested against actual data and deployed once their correct functioning is assured. Apparently, this was the case with the Dutch matching system since no malfunctions were reported. As noted earlier, Robodebt was deployed in a rushed fashion, with apparent disregard for normal evaluation processes, so it at times relied on inaccurate data while its operation was also marred by technical errors.

Piloting a system like SyRI is a more complex process than that involved in testing a system like Robodebt. It requires thoughtful and time-consuming examinations, particularly when checking risk profiles against actual fraud, which must be done on a case-by-case basis. The risk that the system identifies false positives (or negatives) is very high, as is the risk of bias and discrimination. Despite numerous official inquiries, it remains unclear whether SyRI was piloted, which could have helped identify bias and discrimination early on.

In both cases, there also was a lack of transparency in relation to the way these systems operated. This appears both at the level of information given to individual users and to the public generally. Robodebt users were not given full information about the consequences of responding or not responding to the ATO employment data presented to them. In the Dutch case, users were not properly informed about the consequences of any errors, even minor, committed while entering an application. Furthermore, SyRI remained totally black-boxed: the Dutch authorities never disclosed its working when requested in litigation or by the subsequent parliamentary commission. This was echoed, in Robodebt, by a reluctance to disclose the details of how the data matching process worked, when requests were made for that information under Freedom of Information legislation (Morton, 2024 p.23; O'Donovan, 2021 pp.37–38).

Other commonalities emerge when studying the way in which the two schemes were implemented and managed by the bureaucracy, particularly when concerns emerged. In the Dutch case, the lack of a standard approach and business rules addressed to achieve a homogeneous approach to SyRI risk assessment led to inconsistent risk management and incorrect recording and use. There was also virtually no feedback mechanism to process the assessment of a risk signal. Similarly, many of the failures of Robodebt resulted from an administrative and managerial environment that was not "conducive to instances of careful consideration, well-reasoned decision making, and proper scrutiny and supervision" (RRC, 2023, p. 28).

Administrative and managerial actions also appear to have been more addressed to fulfilling desires and goals of politicians than to implementing a sound rule-based policy or providing independent and objective advice and support. This imperative appears to have led those responsible for the schemes' development to ignore relevant expert opinion and advice that would have delayed or prevented their full implementation. While the nature of these concerns varied between the two cases, the concerns expressed in each implicated fundamental aspects of the scheme.

In the case of Robodebt, legal advice that the scheme did not accord with the provisions of the governing legislation was repeatedly ignored or tailored to suit the alternative view. The systemic implications of tribunal decisions that found the scheme to be based on illegality were also disregarded. In the case of SyRI the concerns raised in 2014 by the Council of State and the Dutch Data Protection Agency, were disregarded. An internal 2017 memo by TCA's Chief Legal Advisor, pointing out serious problems in the childcare benefit system, was not added to the relevant file as it should have been, and it took until December 2020 for the full memo to be received by Parliament (Venice Commission, 2021 p.6).

The consistency with which relevant advice was ignored, downplayed, or, in some cases, withheld, suggests a systemic failure in what has, traditionally, been seen as a fundamental component of liberal democracy, that is, a professional, career, independent public service that provides informed, impartial advice to the executive (Peters & Pierre, 2022 p.632). A decline in the political independence of the public service has been observed in many countries in recent decades (Peters & Pierre, 2022 pp.633–634). These examples further illustrate the way in which a failure to provide frank and fearless advice to a Minister, the deliberate disregard of advice received, or the withholding of relevant information from the legislature, risks a civil service becoming complicit in a political agenda that unbalances and undermines the rule of law.

In both cases, the government response to public criticism of the scheme was initially characterised by defensiveness and delay. Once the scale of institutional discrimination was clear, there was a retraction and apology. Ultimately, in The Netherlands example the government was forced to resign, an outcome which arguably should also have occurred in Australia.

Judicial remedies

In both Robodebt and the Dutch welfare scandal safeguards to avoid public policies and administrative action that damaged and discriminated against citizens were ignored in order to fulfil political objectives, and large-scale investigative commissions were ultimately required to identify the complex factors implicated in their failure. Judicial remedies in the form of strategic litigation also played a key role in forcing the two governments concerned to acknowledge and begin to address the problems associated with these schemes: the 2019 class action in the Federal Court of Australia and the case at the Hague District Court for breach of art. 8 ECHR.

Of course, earlier recourse to judicial remedies was sought in both instances. In the case of Robodebt, it was, in part, appeals by individual recipients which drew attention to the problems with the scheme, although initially the government and the bureaucracy took no steps to address the systematic implications of these decisions. In the Netherlands, the path to administrative review was slower, and until 2020, the first instance administrative courts were bound by the "all or nothing" approach enforced by the Council of State decision.

In both these cases, then, the judicial solutions arrived late in the story and required extraordinary efforts, in the form of strategic litigation and a jurisprudential U-turn of a higher court. This suggests that the work of courts can be more difficult in litigation implicating algorithmic systems, potentially rendering judicial proceedings less effective as a means of redressing injustice. Our analysis identifies several factors connected to the features of technology-based decision-making and its interaction with judicial proceedings that contribute to this.

Judging algorithmic systems in courts

Challenging the outcome of technological decision-making often involves surmounting a reverse onus of proof, since governmental technologies implementing the State's regulations tend to be considered correct by default. In the case of Robodebt, not all applicants to the AAT were successful in having debts raised by the method of income-averaging over-turned. In 114 of the 558 cases that went to the AAT in which that method was potentially an issue over the period 2016–2022, the tribunal appears to have simply assumed that income averaging was lawful.[10]

The complexity and cost involved in challenging algorithmic systems may be out of reach for a single applicant (O'Donovan, 2021 p.50), a difficulty compounded when technologies used in administrative decision-making are "black-boxed" systems with internal processes, rules, or decision-making mechanisms hidden or not transparent to users, their legal representatives, or external observers and hence difficult to investigate. In addition, courts and lawyers are generally not equipped to undertake such investigations which may require expert knowledge. For these reasons, they may go unchallenged (Ombudsman New South Wales, 2021). An added difficulty, as the Australian and Dutch cases illustrate, can be reluctance and resistance by government to unbox these systems and disclose the basis of the systems' operations in litigation-related requests, and even in official investigative commissions. Governments' resistance may be made on grounds such as commercial confidence (where the design of systems is outsourced to commercial organisations), or based on arguments that may enable fraudsters to devise ways to work around or manipulate the system, so detracting from the ability to detect and investigate fraud (Jesse, 2020 p.33; O'Donovan, 2021 pp.34–41 for case examples in the Australian context).

Additionally, discrimination often emerges only as statistical analysis showing that similar cases have been treated differently, or different groups have received different treatment. This makes it difficult to build individual cases, and appeal rights can only be exercised in individual cases. These difficulties are compounded by the fact that the work of courts is usually structured on a case-by-case basis, making it difficult to identify systemic problems (Ombudsman New South Wales, 2021 p. 80) a task that is not normally seen as one for the courts. Since people in the same group are treated similarly, systemic algorithmic discrimination is unlikely to be revealed in judicial proceedings in individual cases.

In addition, these factors do not work in isolation. Complexity, black-boxing, government resistance to disclose biases and the invisibility of discrimination other than at a statistical level reinforce each other, making the onus of proof even harder, and forcing judges to decide cases without having a comprehensive understanding of relevant facts.

Empowering the effectiveness of judicial remedies

Ensuring that courts effectively identify and remedy algorithmic discrimination and protect citizens' rights requires the fulfilment of several fundamental conditions. While individually these measures may have some impact, we argue they are likely to be most effective in combination.

The first is guaranteeing effective access to legal and judicial information. This step extends beyond the mere publication of judgments, although, as the example of Robodebt demonstrates, this is an essential first step. It also requires mechanisms that allow meaningful analysis of case law to uncover patterns of discrimination or other systemic issues. To take one example, anonymised judgments, while protecting privacy, can obscure critical details that would otherwise help in detecting and addressing discriminations. The Dutch case shows how only underprivileged suburbs were targeted by the SyRI investigations; hence, the lack of information about applicants' residency can make it hard to discover that specific discrimination.

However, access to information alone is insufficient; the community needs to be empowered in order to effectively identify discriminations and the systemic issues arising in litigation. Intermediary bodies—such as labour unions, universities, NGOs, research institutions, the media, legal aid agencies and civil society—can play a role in analysing court data, identifying discriminatory trends and organising reactions. These organisations serve as a bridge between raw legal information and actionable insights and also enable advocacy and support for victims of discrimination.

There is a role, also, for technology. Coupling data with data analysis, using tools provided by AI and data analytics can further enhance the ability to spot discrimination. AI-driven tools can aggregate and compare similar cases, detect whether bureaucracies and courts are treating similar cases alike, and identify deviations that may indicate bias.

Moreover, we suggest that there is a role for courts themselves to draw to the attention of the public systemic issues and discriminations that appear to be arising in litigation that is coming before them. While individual judges should remain neutral, courts as institutions can highlight recurring legal issues, for example through their annual reports.

By combining increased transparency, the involvement of intermediary bodies, and the strategic use of technology, legal systems can improve their ability to detect and address discrimination. In particular, the role played by the intermediate bodies and their capacity to transform individual issues into a collective problem and then search for remedies, is pivotal. However, it is also essential to make it easier for the courts to investigate discrimination, by opening the "black box". The requirement to make such systems reviewable by courts (and other agencies) should be legislated.

Conclusions

Notwithstanding some differences between the Dutch and the Australian cases, their many similarities capture the blueprint for a new style of neo-liberal reforms in which digital technologies play a role in implementing government policy. Our comparison of these systems' development, functioning, and oversight shows that the use of these technologies in administrative decision-making requires careful development, rule-based automation, accurate data, respect for data protection, legal rules and expert opinion. The failures of Robodebt and SyRI demonstrate how political and socio-environmental factors can override these requirements, leading to legal and human rights violations, and that existing oversight mechanisms may fail to identify and protect against harm.

We examined whether courts and the legal system can address automated injustice, drawing on the experience in these two cases. We identified the importance of strategic litigation in both cases in forcing governments to concede. However, such litigation is only possible after much injustice has occurred. To maintain confidence in the rule of law we suggest it is critical to ensure that courts—as the independent, third-party arm of government—are able to exercise oversight and provide earlier, more effective remedies. Identifying those factors associated with algorithmic injustice that may make it more difficult for courts to carry out this task is the first step in investigating how we can achieve this; we hope our paper has made a start on this important task and in making some suggestions as to how they may be overcome.

Further, at the core of this discussion is the role of intermediate bodies. In both cases where public institutions failed, civil society, NGOs, labour unions, media outlets, and, to some extent, political opposition groups (which are not the focus of this work) took action. They contributed to revealing the magnitude of the scandals, their impacts on the people, and supported access to strategic litigation. Ultimately, they transformed individual victims into communities of persons sharing problems and remedies, reducing the isolation that makes it impossible to address discrimination and injustice at the individual level.

This reveals how organising individuals and community building are also essential in counterbalancing the risks and damages of algorithmic discrimination. The growing relevance of algorithms and digital technologies in any sphere of private and public affairs requires more than technical and legal measures to regulate design and use, to guarantee technological accountability and strengthen the work of courts. Critically, the expansion of algorithmic decision-making in public policy implementation requires the balancing provided by community empowerment, which emerges as a primary means for protecting the rights of the people against possible technological abuses.

Notes

1 The study is based on documentary analysis of these sources. Those primary sources, available only in Dutch, were translated into English through automatic systems.
2 "Rort" is Australian slang meaning "to defraud".
3 https://www.notmydebt.com.au/ Accessed the 16 of January 2025.
4 https://herstel.toeslagen.nl/dashboard-kinderopvangtoeslag/ Accessed the 16 of January 2025.
5 ECLI:NL:RVS:2012:BY6772
6 ECLI:NL:RVS:2019:3535 and ECLI:NL:RVS:2019:3536.

7 ECLI:NL:RBDHA:2020:865.
8 A brief to the relevant minister at the time "revealed that fraud accounted for 0.1 per cent of the debt raised [by the Department of Social Security] in the 2015–16 financial year, and just 1.2 per cent of the outstanding debt base as of 30 June 2016".
9 At the height of its operation—subsequently modified to provide some human oversight when complaints started attracting media attention.
10 In the remaining 13 cases decisions that did not consider the merits of income averaging because the Applicant conceded the debt (RRC, 2023 p. 555).

References

Auditdienst Rijk. (2020). *Toeslaggerelateerde CAF-zaken Investigation into CAF-related childcare benefit cases*. Retrieved from https://informatiepuntkinderopvangtoeslag.rijksoverheid.nl/publicaties/9ebc0f244fb97cc58dbe3fb626e92a82/27214onderzoeksrapport-toeslaggerelateerde-caf-zakenpdfpdf.pdf

Autoriteit Persoonsgegevens. (2014). *Advies conceptbesluit SyRI*. Retrieved from https://autoriteitpersoonsgegevens.nl/documenten/advies-besluit-syri

Bekker, S. (2021). Fundamental rights in digital welfare states: The case of SyRI in the Netherlands. In O. Spijkers, W. G. Werner, & R. A. Wessel (Eds.), *Netherlands Yearbook of International Law 2019* (pp. 289–307): Springer.

Berends, S. (2021). *Dutch child benefit scandal: Origin and latest developments*. Retrieved from https://ec.europa.eu/social/BlobServlet?docId=24723&langId=en

Bouwmeester, M. (2023). System failure in the digital welfare state: Exploring parliamentary and judicial control in the Dutch childcare benefits scandal. *Journal Recht der Werkelijkheid*, *44*(2), 13–37. https://doi.org/10.5553/RdW/138064242023044002003

Carney, T. (2018). Robo-debt illegality: The seven veils of failed guarantees of the rule of law? *Alternative Law Journal*, *44*(1), 4–10. https://doi.org/10.1177/1037969X18815913

Chiusi, F., Fischer, S., Kayser-Bril, N., & Spielkamp, M. (2020). *Automating society report 2020*. Retrieved from https://automatingsociety.algorithmwatch.org

de Nationale Ombudsman. (2017). *Geen powerplay maar fair play* (2017/095). Retrieved from https://www.nationaleombudsman.nl/system/files/onderzoek/Rapport%202017-095%20Geen%20powerplay%20maar%20fair%20play_0.pdf

Jesse, F. (2020). Tienduizenden gedupeerden, maar geen daders: zo ontstond de tragedie achter de toeslagenaffaire. https://decorrespondent.nl/. Retrieved from https://decorrespondent.nl/10628/tienduizenden-gedupeerden-maar-geen-daders-zo-ontstond-de-tragedie-achter-de-toeslagenaffaire/0f71ac81-d117-0d12-23a4-89513b0bb824

Morton, R. (2024). *Mean Streak: A moral vacuum, a dodgy debt generator and a multi-billion-dollar government shake down—the powerful story of robodebt from the award winning author of One Hundred Years of Dirt*. 4th Estate.

O'Donovan, D. (2021). Evaluating automation: The need for greater transparency. In J. Boughey & K. Miller (Eds.), *The automated state: Implications, challenges and opportunities for public law* (pp. 31–51): The Federation Press.

Ombudsman New South Wales. (2021). *The new machinery of government: Using machine technology in administrative decision-making—a special report under section 31 of the Ombudsman Act 1974*. Retrieved from https://cmsassets.ombo.nsw.gov.au/assets/Reports/The-new-machinery-of-government-special-report_Front-section.pdf

Peeters, R., & Widlak, A. C. (2023). Administrative exclusion in the infrastructure-level bureaucracy: The case of the Dutch daycare benefit scandal. *Public Administration Review*, *83*(4), 863–877. https://doi.org/10.1111/puar.13615

Peters, B. G., & Pierre, J. (2022). Politicisation of the public service during democratic backsliding: Alternative perspectives. *Australian Journal of Public Administration*, *81*(4), 629–639. https://doi.org/10.1111/1467-8500.12561

pilp.nu. (2020). System Risk Indication (SyRI). Retrieved from https://pilp.nu/en/dossier/system-risk-indication-syri/#:~:text=SyRI%20is%20a%20risk%20profiling,and%20assets%2C%20pension%20and%20debts.

POK. (2020). *'Ongekend onrecht' ('Unprecedented injustice')*. Retrieved from https://www.houseofrepresentatives.nl/sites/default/files/atoms/files/verslag_pok_definitief-en-gb.docx.pdf

Raad Van State. (2014). *Ontwerpbesluit houdende regels voor fraudeaanpak door gegevensuitwisselingen en het effectief gebruik van binnen de overheid bekend zijnde gegevens (Besluit SyRI), met nota van toelichting*. Retrieved from https://www.raadvanstate.nl/adviezen/@63143/w12-14-0102-iii/

Rinta-Kahila, T., Someh, I., Gillespie, N., Indulska, M., & Gregor, S. (2024). Managing unintended consequences of algorithmic decision-making: The case of Robodebt. *Journal of Information Technology Teaching Cases*, *14*(1), 165–171. https://doi.org/10.1177/20438869231165538

RRC. (2023). *Report of the royal commission into the Robodebt scheme*. Retrieved from https://robodebt.royalcommission.gov.au/publications/report

Storp, J.-H. (2020, December 24). Toeslagenaffaire: Commissie-Donner trok conclusies in strijd met eigen onderzoek. *Follow the Money*. Retrieved from https://www.ftm.nl/artikelen/toeslagenaffaire-wob-commissie-donner?share=o8UjHrGa6ZgZtP5ND2HNsgRasCL%2BMgYdy0URQO0GLJ2ojd%2FyYgL8ygM0Arbi0wQ%3D

UN Special Rapporteur. (2019). *Brief by the United Nations Special Rapporteur on extreme poverty and human rights as Amicus Curiae in the case of NJCM c.s./De Staat der Nederlanden (SyRI) before the District Court of The Hague (case number: C/09/550,982/HA ZA 18/388)*. Retrieved from https://www.ohchr.org/sites/default/files/Documents/Issues/Poverty/Amicusfinalversionsigned.pdf

van Bekkum, M., & Zuiderveen Borgesius, F. (2021). Digital welfare fraud detection and the Dutch SyRI judgment. *European Journal of Social Security*, *23*(4), 323–340. https://doi.org/10.1177/13882627211031257

van den Berge, L., & Gaakeer, J. (2025). Rereading Kafka's the trial: Responsibility, reflection, and the case of the Dutch childcare allowance scandal. *SSRN*, 1–22. https://dx.doi.org/10.2139/ssrn.5178474

van Ettekoven, B. J. (2021, January 15). Tussen wet en recht. *Nederlands Juristenblad*, 98–107.

Venice Commission. (2021). *The Netherlands: Opinion on the legal protection of citizens*. Retrieved from https://www.coe.int/en/web/venice-commission/-/cdl-ad-2021-031-e

14

GLOBAL INJUSTICE, GLOBAL RESPONSES

Rosanna Amato, Patrícia Branco, Francesco Contini, and Richard Mohr

Introduction

At first glance, the phenomena examined in this volume—colonial violence, failures of justice systems, algorithmic discrimination, and climate-related harm—may appear distinct in their causes, scales, and forms. Yet read together, they point to a shared problem. Common to all of them is the way harm and discrimination persist through the actions and processes of *institutions*. Institutions name, classify, and manage suffering in ways that render it administrable, often detaching it from lived experience and redistributing its consequences onto those most affected. Institutions, then, do not merely respond to harm; they also play a role in shaping its very form. What may appear to be neutral management can thus turn out to contribute to the perpetuation of harm.

This volume is concerned with how these institutional processes operate and with the forms of harm they produce, stabilise, and carry forward. The three parts reflect this concern by tracing different modalities through which harm is processed and stabilised across contexts. Part I addresses the conjunction of material and symbolic violence in colonial settings, showing how law and myth operate together to render coercion intelligible, legitimate, and repeatable over time. Part II shifts the focus to contemporary justice systems, where the issue is how harm is operationalised within institutional routines—through procedures, evidentiary thresholds, and organisational practices that can remain formally compliant while nonetheless reproducing vulnerability. Part III examines contexts in which harm is mediated through technology and climate. In cases of algorithmic discrimination and climate-related harm, classification, decision-making, and responsibility are increasingly distributed, opaque, and difficult to contest, while institutional authority is reinforced through claims of technical objectivity.

DOI: 10.4324/9781003752974-18

Across these different sites, the chapters show that harm is rarely an "accident" of misfortune or a neutral by-product of social change. It is more often the predictable outcome of classificatory practices, institutional routines, and legal or quasi-legal techniques that render suffering administrable.

One recurring effect of these processes is the production of displacement and victimisation as mutually reinforcing conditions. Displacement appears not simply as movement across space but as a broader condition in which individuals and communities are removed—from land, from rights, from recognition, or from the capacity to contest institutional decisions—while victimisation is simultaneously normalised, fragmented, or administratively managed. In this sense, the work collected here traces the ways in which institutional arrangements organise who can be displaced, how victims are recognised, and how displacement and victimisation are made to endure.

The book's subtitle foregrounds local responses as an analytic and practical claim. The chapters repeatedly show that injustice materialises through ordinary institutional operations, while meaningful responses emerge when actions or re-actions are re-situated locally, relationally, and in context—close to lived experience and attentive to how vulnerability unfolds over time rather than as a single event. More than an unquestionable necessity, local responses emerge from the specific circumstances of many of the cases discussed. Even when global efforts are in place to address phenomena like global warming or intimate partner violence (IPV), local responses emerge as a means to fill the huge gaps between policy statements and legal frameworks on one side and the lives of people on the other.

The question, then, is not only what produces global injustice but what kinds of institutional designs, normative languages, and community practices can break cycles rather than reproduce them. Before addressing these solutions, we identify common themes across the work collected here.

Each of the chapters, in its own way, shows that violence does not endure by force alone. It must be processed—named, narrated, categorised, and made legal—so that it can be carried forward as ordinary governance. In analysing how violence and suffering are processed, we must not lose sight of the normal, unexceptional, production, and legitimation of extensive suffering under contemporary social, political, and economic arrangements (Veitch, 2007). These processes of production and legitimation are based on a set of symbolic devices that can be broadly categorised as law and myth. In the following discussion of these operations, law is seen to be the institutional language through which categories harden, and violence is translated into institutional normality. Myth, meanwhile, is not treated as the opposite of reality, but as a malleable register through which suffering, loss, and domination are made intelligible, transmissible, and contestable.

Colonial injustice: law, myth, and strategies of resistance (Part I)

Each of the chapters in Part I deals with some aspects of colonisation. At the fundamental level, colonisation is a process of displacement and appropriation through physical violence. Gómez calls this process, of murder and conquest by the invincible European arms, extractive violence, or "negative reciprocity". This is the economic and material driver of imperialism. Anthony and Mohr (Chapters 3 and 1) explore the ways this violence is subsequently manifested in prisons, judicial and police violence, while Gómez (Chapter 2) refers to extrajudicial disappearances.

Each chapter then deals with the symbolic or linguistic dimensions of these conflicts, the institutional and communicative devices used to process violence. These devices can be broadly categorised as law and myth. Law is woven into the material reality of violence, through declarations and statutes as well as the institutional structures of courts and enforcement. Myth justifies and tells stories about the colonial process itself: the nature of colonisers and colonised, founding myths of heroism or conquest, "civilising missions", and moral or supernatural justifications for expropriation.

While law is overdetermined as an administrative process, myth is a highly malleable (or floating) signifier. This indeterminacy operates in the hiatus between the word or the sign and its interpretation. The two come together—or law floats off into myth—in the "mythology of modern law" (Fitzpatrick, 1992). Self-referential European law is defended as transcendent—the rule of law, and not of men—at the same time and by the same forces that deny mythic status. The "mythic" is meant to signify only the laws and cultures of the colonised, as in legal decisions described by Vargas. This serves to subjugate First Nations law, while formally "recognising"—or misrecognising—it. A similar leap of interpretation is found in Mohr's observation that the prisons, missions, indeed the whole apparatus that Anthony describes as the open-air prison of the colony, were fenced around by the laws of the "Aboriginal protection acts". This very wording alerts us to the mythology of genocide.

In the field of law, the symbolic contest plays out in the creation of legal meaning discussed by Gómez or, as Vargas puts it, the legal naming conferred by the state's "monopoly to say the law". Yet the very notion of a monopoly is another of modern law's myths. Indigenous law competes on unequal terms in the Colombian courts, sustained as they are by the excessive sovereignty of the state, noted also by Gómez in Mexico. Yet the First Peoples persist and resist. We see this in Anthony's cultural practices and sovereign law;[1] in Alexis Wright's "un-displaced", culturally independent children (discussed by Mohr): in "indigenous worldviews as a source of law" (Vargas), and even in Gómez's Llorona, as a personage who has entered legend from the suffering of the colonised.

Formal law can be changed by a stroke of the pen, if that pen and the ones wielding it are properly authorised. Application of the law is not so straightforward. It must be processed by other people and through other institutions with their own traditions and cultures. This is sometimes a drag on the implementation of progressive laws, as is seen in Part II. Yet cultures can carry laws with them through many generations of repression, even under colonisation.

Centuries after the initial imperial conquest, the First Nations have preserved their ancient laws, in counter-hegemonic practice and memory, in Country and in

Culture. The ancient law lives in the Land, always ready to emerge when the time is right.[2] Vargas illustrates both sides of this tension between formal and informal law. The struggles of the First Nations in Colombia to preserve the environment enabled pre-colonial law to emerge from the Land to claim its right to protect and nurture it. Though this was enabled under amendments to the Colombian constitution, the power of the formal law nonetheless struck back from within its own springs of culture and jurisprudence, to frustrate the intent of the recognition of Indigenous law. Even in Australia, with only limited concessions to traditional law (by granting and subsuming land rights under the formal common law), the First Nations persist by resisting. Mohr's recognition of un-displaced children and Anthony's of incarcerated women demonstrate the power of culture and alternative laws.

So while the drag of culture can be a hindrance to progressive law reform, it can also hinder colonial oppression. The law of the Land is not something that can be switched on and off by the hand of the legislator, nor does it change course by acts of parliament. It is nurtured, remembered, preserved, and built in communities, even those that are demonised and incarcerated. In the same way, changing the formal law, even when that is achieved by massive Indigenous, feminist, or progressive efforts, is just the beginning. As the First Nations of Colombia or Australia demonstrate, the work continues in practising traditional law and culture. This is a communal struggle that continues on Country and on the streets, in the courts and the colonial prisons.

Reading these chapters together, it is impossible not to be struck by the proximity of *la Llorona* to the First Nations women of Anthony's study. Not only has imprisonment removed them from their own children, but their stories are filled with generations of stolen children. These women do not haunt the colonisers as spectres of vengeance (though studies like Anthony's and further truth-telling surely threaten that). Instead, they survive through their collective resources and their cultural practices. By telling their stories to each other, by bearing witness to their shared injustices, and by forming their own communities, they persist not in a mythic realm but in the hard reality of prison and colonial policing. In this, their practice is not far from the remedy glimpsed by Gómez: through mourning and memory we can revive life.

Vulnerability and institutional design: the limits of contemporary justice and ways forward (Part II)

The chapters gathered in Part II deal with how justice systems respond to situations of conflict and violence, placing the experiences of the individuals involved at the centre of the analysis. They begin with an overview of the main support programmes for victims of domestic violence in Brazil (Chapter 5), analysing how these services are structured, implemented, and coordinated and highlighting both their strengths and their limitations; they then move to a broader critical reflection on how criminal justice tends to marginalise victims, proposing more person-centred approaches (Chapter 6); the discussion subsequently turns to family justice, showing how legal proceedings in cases of separation may exacerbate conflict and negatively affect children (Chapter 7); it further addresses violence within intimate relationships, up to cases of homicide, highlighting the shortcomings of institutional responses (Chapter 8); finally, it explores the issue of protecting victims of domestic violence, with particular attention to the dilemma between remaining in a dangerous situation or leaving and the significant personal and social costs associated with such decisions (Chapter 9).

While grounded in different jurisdictions and legal domains, they all converge on a common insight: the persistence of vulnerability cannot be explained primarily by the absence of legal norms. Across criminal law, family law, and public policy frameworks, the formal recognition of individuals' rights and safeguards has significantly expanded. Yet, as the contributions illustrate, political and legal recognition does not automatically translate into effective protection (Cappelletti & Garth, 1978). As Fineman highlighted, "institutions—the structures and arrangements . . . can almost invisibly produce or exacerbate existing inequalities" (Fineman, 2008, p. 21).

What emerges, then, is a tension between formal guarantees and their effective enjoyment, pointing less to flaws in legal design than to the way justice is operationalised across institutional settings. The issue is not one of blatant misapplication, but the fact that formally correct and ostensibly neutral applications may nonetheless generate substantively discriminatory outcomes and further victimisation (Pound, 1910; Tamanaha, 2001). From this perspective, Part II examines how formal guarantees are translated into practice across different analytical angles and levels of abstraction. It does not advance a single explanatory model; rather, it identifies recurring points at which institutional practice shapes—and often constrains—the translation of formal guarantees into concrete protection.

The global injustice discussed here is understood as the widespread presence of violence and relational conflicts across national contexts and the recurrence of similar constraints in how legal systems approach vulnerability. Across the different chapters, analogous difficulties arise: high evidentiary thresholds for inherently difficult-to-document phenomena; graduated interventions that delay protection; fragmentation across jurisdictions; and the application of formally neutral categories in domains marked by relational asymmetry. Taken together, these elements show how institutional practices shape the processing, evaluation, and prioritisation of relational harm, thus highlighting patterns of recurring constraints in evidentiary assessment, timing of intervention, and coordination across authorities (Lipsky, 1980).

The activation of protective measures, then, may be contingent on how individuals articulate harm in institutionally acceptable forms through timely complaints, coherent narratives, demonstrable cooperation, and sufficient evidentiary support. Delay and graduated responses, along with procedural safeguards, while justified in terms of prudence and balance, may nonetheless delay intervention and produce asymmetric exposure to risk. Also, similar dynamics may surface in family law, where the operationalisation of the "best interests of the child" principle may lead institutions to recast safety concerns as manifestations of conflict.

If the injustices described reveal recurrent constraints, local responses appear as attempts to organise how protection operates in practice. They cannot be reduced to approaches or to a collection of "good practices", since they constitute situated configurations in which norms, professional practices, and inter-institutional relationships combine to shape responses. Three core dimensions emerge.

First, the local level is an organisational space. The Italian case study (Chapter 9), for instance, shows that the effectiveness of protective measures depends on the conditions under which they can be activated. The local reform redefines protection as a continuous process rather than a single judicial act, reorganising the management of time, risk, and evidentiary assessment. This produces a shift from a reactive episodic-based arrangement to an early-intervention and follow-up model. Where organisational routines prioritise continuity, early risk assessment, and follow-up, intervention is less likely to fall exclusively on victims' relocation. In this sense, organisational design directly affects timing, consistency and effectiveness of protection.

Second, the local level is a space of integration or fragmentation. The Brazilian case (Chapter 5) illustrates this in two ways. The creation of specialised courts combining civil and criminal competences represents an effort to centralise decision-making and reduce fragmentation in judicial responses. At the same time, the broader ecosystem includes comprehensive preventive and reparative instruments, operating across different sectors and administrative levels, whose effectiveness should not be taken for granted. Indeed, it depends on the capacity to ensure that institutional redesign and multi-sector instruments function as a coordinated pathway rather than as parallel interventions.

Third, the local level is a cultural and interpretative space. The Portuguese chapters (Chapters 7 and 8) show that judicial decisions are shaped by how legal categories are interpreted in practice. Assumptions about victimhood, family, parenthood and conflict influence how claims are assessed and risks are evaluated. In this context, changes in legal and factual interpretation can alter outcomes without requiring new legal instruments. These include assessing complaints cumulatively rather than in isolation; recognising violence as patterned; integrating risk into decisions concerning parental responsibility; and critically examining narratives that minimise aggression. Such a shift affects how facts are established, how credibility is assessed, and how responsibility is attributed in judicial decision-making.

Therefore, the chapters show how the effectiveness of protective measures depends on the capacity to intervene early, ensure continuity of response, integrate risk assessment into decision-making, and monitor outcomes over time. Local responses emerge as configurations that combine organisational structure, coordination across actors, and interpretative practices. The local level is therefore not simply a site of implementation, but the context in which protection is operationalised through concrete institutional practices.

Algorithmic discrimination and climate change as a global injustice (Part III)

The third part of the book focuses on two diverse forms of institutional discrimination and harm: global warming and algorithmic injustice. Yet despite the clear differences, there are some deep-seated commonalities that help explain how these new global injustices unfold.

Across all these cases, technology reshapes how institutional discrimination is understood, attributed, and contested. Standard theory holds that digital systems increase accountability (Wong & Welch, 2004), but algorithmic discrimination clearly contradicts this (Bartlett et al., 2021; Kroll et al., 2017). Technical complexity, multilayered systems, incomplete documentation, and restricted system access reduce accountability. Even developers and institutional adopters may not fully understand or control these systems (Lanzara, 2009). Welfare algorithms and Horizon used layered architectures that obscured outcomes, and ODR-P systems are, by default, inaccessible. As a consequence, those affected by such systems are shielded from scrutiny by their complexity and opacity.

These dynamics reveal an institutional form marked by uneven visibility, control, and accountability. When outputs cannot be traced or explained, affected individuals often lack the means to challenge decisions, uncover mistakes, or reveal discrimination (Eubanks, 2018). Institutions may continue to rely on these systems, citing their trustworthiness, as in all the cases of algorithmic discrimination discussed. Thus, opacity not only obstructs explanation; it also reinforces power asymmetries.

This pattern is reinforced because algorithmic systems often create the same categories that trigger institutional actions (Alaimo & Kallinikos, 2022). Automated classifications help produce institutional facts, shaping who is seen as trustworthy, suspicious, or exposed to harm. Risk scores, discrepancies, and rule violations become administrative or quasi-judicial consequences. Once such signals are seen as credible indicators, resulting sanctions appear as routine rule application rather than contestable decisions. Human judgement, organised around these outputs, can become an automatic, data-driven deduction.

A related dynamic appears in climate injustice. Here, opacity comes less from code than from the complex link between technological development and environmental harm. Fossil-fuel dependence creates effects over long timescales, across places, and through complex causal chains. Converting local evidence into broader responsibility requires data and scientific analysis that can link specific harms to larger systems and then lead to climate litigation and court decisions (Pelizzon, 2025). For a long time, this complexity delayed understanding and weakened accountability. It still provides ways to deny causation or delay responsibility.

In both domains, when harms or failures are alleged, organisations rarely open their systems to scrutiny. Systems owned by corporations are inaccessible due to contractual obligations (as in ODR-p) or strategic blocks (as in Horizon). Public systems involved in welfare scandals should be open to external scrutiny. Still, system owners obstructed access, as when the Dutch government refused to disclose its risk system to Parliament. Similarly, climate denial and institutional inaction use strategies that separate technology from harm, minimise findings, or claim uncertainty to avoid responsibility (Lamb et al., 2020). In each case, opacity is increased by strategic closure. As a consequence, technology-induced opacity feeds a broader politics of irresponsibility: institutions maintain authority and restrict contestation, leaving the vulnerable to carry the costs (Elish, 2019; Hood, 2010).

Displacement is a common outcome of algorithmic discrimination and climate injustice. In algorithmic cases, displacement often happens within a still-intact social world. Horizon victims lost businesses, savings, employment, and sometimes their homes. Welfare recipients facing automated debt recovery suffered financial collapse, lost childcare or housing, and saw severe family disruptions, including children removed from their families and cases of suicide. Platform users may not be physically expelled but can be excluded from economic spaces, reputation, and communication, amounting to civic or social death. What is displaced here is not just location but standing, credibility, and public access.

Disasters and slow changes, like sea-level rise or drought, in a nutshell, the ecological conditions for life, force relocation as a result of global warming. Communities may be separated from land, livelihood, memory, and social continuity. Yet, as in algorithmic discrimination, the spatial dimension is coupled with the institutional one: a lack of protection, recognition, and remedy for victims, while responsibility remains diffuse and ignored.

Ultimately, control institutions, such as courts or commissions, may also lose their fact-finding role if they rely on inaccessible technologies or partial records, as the chapters have shown. Displacement extends beyond people and places. It affects who can know, contest, and make reality legible (Koulu, 2019).

Algorithmic discrimination, climate change harm, and ODR-P incontestable decisions suggest that the most significant local responses to contemporary forms of institutional discrimination arise through the reconstruction of contestability. This effort is made difficult since technological systems, bureaucratic routines, and concentrated organisational power have rendered harm and discrimination difficult to perceive, name, and challenge. Academic works are helping to dissect cases and build explanations. Investigative commissions are helping to make truth emerge in its brutality. In March 2026, the Australian National Anti-Corruption Commission handed down findings of "serious corrupt conduct" by two of the six officers referred for investigation. Reporting on these findings, SBS recalled the human consequences of the scheme through the testimony of a mother whose 22-year-old son, Jarrad, received a notice stating that he owed $2,000 to Centrelink in 2019:

> Around two and a half, three hours later he walked out of the house and [took] his own life over this notice that he got. . . . You know, nothing's been public.

> It's business as usual, and the loss and the pain, and the anguish that we've all been through has fallen on deaf ears.[3]

The importance of local responses lies precisely in their capacity to break this cycle. They convert dispersed experiences of suffering and injustice into shared knowledge, collective claims, and demands for redress. The chapters on algorithmic discrimination repeatedly show that victimisation persists when those affected remain isolated, while the response becomes effective when intermediary actors help break that isolation. Civil society organisations, trade unions, journalists, activists, legal aid bodies, researchers, and community advocates emerge as crucial agents because they aggregate cases, identify patterns, sustain public scrutiny, and translate private suffering into collective actions. Local responses function as mechanisms of recognition: they make it possible to see that what appears to be individual failure, error, or misconduct is often the product of systemic and discriminatory actions by public or private institutions.

As a further step, local responses found in Part III coalesce around demands for transparency, disclosure, explanation, and auditability (Pasquale, 2015): opening the black box is a precondition for an effective independent review and for the quest for justice.

From global injustice to local responses

After having analysed the commonalities of each of the three parts in which the book is organised, it is now time to take a final step to identify the commonalities across the book.

Law's routine production of discrimination, victimisation, and displacement

A first commonality is the tight coupling between material violence and symbolic work. In Part I, colonisation is discussed not as a past episode but as an ongoing regime that joins physical coercion and power asymmetries, converting violence into something administrable, legitimate, and repeatable. Violence appears in its blunt forms—murder, conquest, extrajudicial disappearance, prison, and police violence—supported by exploitation, impunity, and dispossession.

Law normalises violence by abstracting it from the lived reality of spilt blood and profound loss into the legal categories of "evidence" and "fact". The linguistic register moves from the cry for help or the shriek of pain to the anodyne note in the file or the archive. The universal applicability of legal processes, by their institutional design, shifts attention from the individual to the general, from the victim to the system. Yet, the promise of universal application and redress can make it harder to recognise injustice when remedies fail to materialise in practice.

A key insight that emerges throughout the volume is that displaceability is shaped differently across the cases examined. In Parts I and III, it often appears as the result of classificatory moves that authorise expropriation, relocation, containment, imprisonment, and disappearance as if they were ordinary acts of governance, at times, as the successful stabilisation of conquest and discrimination into routine. Part II points to a different dynamic in which removal is renamed as "protection". In this context, displacement emerges from institutional practices and strategies that, while often intended to provide safety, may nonetheless require victims to relocate to protected locations, thereby disrupting victims' social ties and everyday lives.

In Part III, dealing with cases of climate displacement, Scutt shows how states make "undertakings" to UN Councils of the Parties or sign up to general recommendations of UN committees in the absence of any tangible action to protect the vulnerable (Chapter 10). The other chapters demonstrate how classificatory practices can be embedded into digital systems and then re-presented as neutral, incontestable outputs. Welfare recipients are transformed into fraudsters (Chapter 13); postmasters into thieves (Chapter 12); platform users into rule-breakers (Chapter 11)—through what can look like the "plain application" of rules, now mediated by technology. In this sense, part of what the volume documents is the continuity of institutional technique: the power to define who is credible, who is suspicious, and who can be displaced from rights, livelihoods, or place—sometimes deliberately, sometimes inadvertently, and sometimes through processes that appear voluntary but are shaped by structural constraints.

The myth of law and its technological recast

A second, deeper convergence concerns the "mythology of modern law" as universal, rational, factual, hence non-mythical governance tool. This account explains why legal pluralism is so often unequal even where formal recognition exists: dominant legal orders can relegate Indigenous law to "culture" or "belief", thereby disqualifying it as modern law, while denying the mythic character of their own foundational narratives (Fitzpatrick, 1992; Latour, 1996).

The struggle across Part I is repeatedly over *who can speak the law* and what counts as a valid source of normativity. Part II probes the interplay between the mythic status of formal law and the institutional grammars and operations that mediate and mask its translation into real consequences for victims and other participants. Part III suggests that this mythology is undergoing an important update. Where modern law once relied on its own aura of rationality, it can now wrap itself in a new cloak of techno-rationality: automated decisions, machine-generated records, and platform decisions are presented as objective, mechanical, and therefore equal. This makes technology-enabled law, or computable law (Casanovas et al., 2008), hard for ordinary people to challenge and hard for courts to assess: systems are complex and inaccessible, and their authority is pre-validated by institutional narratives of trustworthiness and neutrality. This can also be sealed by law, assuming algorithmic operations are reliable and correct by default (Chapter 12), or creating a reverse onus of proof, placing the victims of algorithmic discrimination in an impossible position (Chapter 13). This is why the chapters on algorithmic discrimination insist that discrimination is not the result of a technical malfunction. Algorithmic discrimination appears as a human–technological interplay in which technological features are *exploited* to reach institutional ends. As noted, the result is a familiar institutional pattern in a new register: organisations deny malfunction, assert robustness, resist accountability, and construct alternative explanations that blame victims or reframe them as perpetrators. The "myth" here is not only a story that provides context for legal or technological facts; it is also an operational resource that stabilises institutional closure.

Vulnerability and displacements: responsibility, temporality, social and spatial

Part I foregrounds conquest and oppression in space by expropriation of land and over time by denials of experience and long-standing legal systems. Part III focuses on technology-driven or mediated discrimination and victimisation, whether from techno-institutional power or environmental changes. Part II examines how modern justice systems struggle to recognise vulnerability and how entrenched characteristics of the institutions involved undermine attempts to enhance victims' protections. Although in different ways, all these paths lead to a vicious cycle of victimisation and displacement. Each chapter identifies recurring institutional patterns so pervasive that common threads emerge across all the work collected here. In criminal, civil, and family-law contexts, the chapters converge on a shared concern: institutions repeatedly struggle to recognise, govern, and respond adequately to vulnerability as it is lived by those who come into contact with justice. The dynamics examined—around the management of family conflict and children's rights (Chapter 7), intimate partner violence (Chapters 8 and 9), the removal of First Nations mothers and children, and even the ensuing deaths, in custody and from homicide (Chapter 3)—are not isolated mistakes. They emerge from institutional trajectories that recurrently misread risk, normalise power asymmetry, and prioritise procedural order, neutrality, or efficiency over safety and dignity and overall challenge the very idea of fairness. Here, four cross-cutting themes stand out.

First of all, across the chapters, legal and institutional arrangements, for a variety of reasons, are either *designed to discriminate* against groups (Part I) or result in *discriminatory outcomes* because of the difficult balancing between contrasting institutional requirements and principles (Part II). In Part III, two different paths leading to discrimination have been identified. In the context of global warming there is a clear contrast between dominant economic, military and urbanistic interests and the protection of environment and the people most affected by climate change (Chapter 10). In the case of algorithmic applications, technological features are exploited by their owners (ministries, public agencies, and companies) to punish welfare recipients (Chapter 13) or protect companies' interests (Chapters 11 and 12).

Second, *victimisation remains unintelligible due to political opportunities and systemic features.* In Part I, allegedly political necessities (Chapter 2), legal rationality (Chapters 1 and 3), and ultimately, the myth of modern law (Chapter 4) are used to mask and justify injustice and brutal violence. In Part II, victimisation unfolds over time, through earlier complaints, archived cases, weak protective measures, and unmonitored decisions. Injustice is not sudden but sedimented: it accrues through institutional delay, narrowed evidentiary frames, and routinised under-reaction to increasing risk (Chapters 7, 8, and 9). In all the chapters of Part III, as already discussed, the very features of technology make the harm it produces hard to detect and challenge.

Third, across the chapters, protection frequently operates by *shifting the locus of responsibility from institutions onto those most affected.* Institutional responses often individualise risk and fragment responsibility, requiring individuals to navigate violence, dispossession, or discrimination within frameworks that prioritise procedural order, neutrality, or efficiency. The transfer of responsibility is particularly evident in Parts I and III. Institutions formalise protection while leaving those exposed to its consequences to manage the risks it is meant to address. The pattern of transferring responsibility from the institution to the individual recurs in surprising ways. Algorithms mask institutional responsibility as individual failure or even criminality. In climate debates, the responsibility for carbon emissions was passed to individuals when the personal "carbon footprint" was promoted by the second-biggest non-state-owned oil company in the world (Solnit, 2021). In Part II, what is transferred is more the burden than the responsibility. In cases of domestic violence, for instance, victims are often required to bear the weight of their own protection by being relocated, rather than benefiting from measures designed to ensure distance from the perpetrator. Victims are also frequently required to establish their credibility and "prove" their truth well before formal investigation and fact-finding procedures begin, with serious consequences that can delay necessary interventions and contribute to escalation, potentially leading to fatal outcomes. A similar dynamic emerges in civil cases. Mothers, in particular, must work to make visible forms of inequality and harm that institutions tend to interpret as neutral, even in cases where signs of coercion are downplayed in custody decisions. Across these situations, the practical weight of protection falls on those who seek it, rather than on those responsible for ensuring it.

Fourth, *physical displacement*, as a further expression of institutional harm, then becomes an outcome of a combination of intent, legal frameworks and decisions, and practical arrangements, sometimes impelled by the consequences of technology, whether algorithms or carbon emissions. Examples range from colonisation to relocation from a home when living environments are rendered uninhabitable, unsafe, or unable to sustain life. In algorithmic discrimination, displacement often arrives as "collateral damage" of techno-institutional arrangements. It is particularly striking that, across the volume, displacement also appears as an *institutional outcome* that can be strategically useful: removing people from place, from rights, from markets, or from visibility is a recurring method through which governance avoids confronting underlying violence, inequality, or institutional responsibility. In Part I, colonial dispossession, beginning with spatial displacement, gives rise to the denial or "invisiblisation" of Indigenous culture, law or suffering. In Part II, the relocation of victims to shelters or other "safe" places points to a related dynamic: protection is secured through the displacement of victims themselves, often without fully disrupting the relations of power, coercion, and proximity from which the danger arises. In Part III, the displacement of accountability onto individuals is enabled by means of technological closure and institutional defensiveness. Displacement is justified as "protection" both of victims of IPV and of First Nations people under "Aboriginal Protection Acts" (Chapter 1).

Situated justice and local responses

If the volume were only diagnostic, its story would be bleak: institutions that routinise harm, legal ideals that mask asymmetry, and technologies that harden discrimination. However, the chapters also insistently show that people and communities do not simply endure injustice; they build practices of *survival, meaning, and resistance*. In doing so, they show that normativity does not reside only in formal law and institutions but is also carried and reproduced in communities, collective practices, memories, and struggles.

Part I is especially important here. It shows that communities carry their own laws across time: Indigenous law and collective norms persist as lived practice, even under repression, incarceration, and state sovereignty. A stroke of the pen may change formal law, but implementation must move through institutions with histories, routines, and tacit norms. Alongside this, communities continue to reproduce normativity through memory, culture, and practice. Law survives not only in statutes and courts, but also as a communal struggle—as it was put earlier, "on country and on the streets, in the courts and the colonial prisons". The proximity between the myth of La Llorona and the experiences of First Nations women in prison points to forms of repair-from-below: mourning and memory, which keep the absent present and refuse closure without justice; and community-making under pressure, which sustains life, normativity, and identity in spaces meant to break them.

Refusal of closure without justice and community-making under pressure also emerges in Part III. The testimonies collected in recent Robodebt investigative commissions continue to demand justice and to make the damages and deaths caused by the scheme public.

Such testimonies illustrate how mourning and memory continue to sustain demands for accountability even where institutional responses remain partial or delayed. Across the volume, these local responses do not remain confined to community life. The book shows how similar principles—attentiveness, memory, contestability, and collective accountability—can inform institutional design.

Specialised prosecutorial units, coordinated protection networks, attentive judicial listening, and sustained case management are presented as the means by which general norms can be translated into real protection. Likewise, contestability, independent audit, exportable logs, procedural guarantees, and mechanisms that shift the burden of reliability back onto system owners are forms of re-embedding justice in places where people can actually get justice.

Overall, across these domains, the "local responses" referred to in this book appear as practices that restore voice, rebuild meaning, and create accountability where institutions have become closed.

The book chapters, then, cut across domains by showing pathways forward to overcome the limits of contemporary justice systems when systemic issues are treated as isolated cases or purely procedural matters.

Reallocating responsibility and burden: from victims back to institutions. The shifting of responsibility and the burden of the solution onto those affected should be reversed. Institutions must bear the organisational burden of protection and the evidentiary burden of reliability. For example, the force of scientific methods for attributing specific climatic disasters should be properly considered in tort actions seeking to compensate victims of climate displacement. As a litigant in such a case put it, "People who emit less carbon must be protected, and companies with huge emissions should be held accountable by law" (Lewton, 2026).

Treating vulnerability as systemic, cumulative, and enduring. When institutions build organisational arrangements that can track escalation, recognise coercive control, and maintain engagement over time, they make an effort to see violence and vulnerability in their full complexity and intrinsic interdependency and treat them accordingly.

Contestability and access to relevant knowledge. Since power often operates through the capacity to shape and stabilise meanings (who can speak, what counts as law, and what counts as evidence), access to relevant knowledge becomes essential for framing, assessing, and challenging the facts and the truth as built by the system. In techno-institutional contexts, this becomes a matter of audit, transparency, and rights to explanation; in plural legal frameworks, it becomes a matter of recognition that does not simply "include" Indigenous law while subordinating it as culture or relegating it to history. In the context of domestic and family violence, this requires mechanisms that ensure the adequate production, interpretation, and circulation of knowledge—across evidence-gathering practices, institutional routines, and understandings of the phenomenon—while maintaining continuity over time and ensuring protection from the outset.

Institutional openness rather than closure. The recurring pattern of denial and defensiveness must be met with an effort to make institutional processes and settings accountable and open to external scrutiny, thereby making accountability enforceable. This effort should also be complemented by arrangements supporting institutional reflexivity and learning to adapt approaches and operational strategies. This also means considering external inputs and developing a better awareness of the phenomena addressed, as well as the social, economic, and practical implications of institutional action. The achievement of this improved understanding requires a mix of better application of existing regulations and machinery, taking the opinions of official advisory bodies, civil society, and professionals seriously, and, in some cases, better regulations that force the opening of enduring institutional closure. In a nutshell, structures and procedures that make learning possible, make errors visible, and make accountability enforceable.

Strengthening community capacity as justice capacity. The book's most consistent empirical lesson is that communities do not simply "cope"; they generate normativity, memory, solidarity, and practical protection. The role of communities across the book makes clear that justice systems cannot deliver protection without the social infrastructures—networks, shelters, collectives of search and mourning, Indigenous institutions of law—through which people sustain life and meaning under pressure. This is a spatial practice that can be maintained in places meant to exclude or incarcerate them: on traditional lands, on settlers' streets, and in colonial prisons.

The chapters in this volume suggest that displacement, discrimination and victimisation persist because institutions routinise harm, legal and technological devices make violence administrable, and because responsibility is repeatedly displaced—from state to individual, from perpetrator to victim, from institution to "system", from decision to algorithm, from accountability to opacity.

To break cycles, then, is not only to punish wrongdoing after the fact. It is to interrupt the institutional production of displaceability, discrimination, and victimisation; to refuse classifications that make certain lives disposable; to dismantle the myths that present law or technology as objective, rational, and neutral while reproducing power and causing widespread harm and injustice. Breaking cycles means rebuilding the conditions under which people can contest, narrate, mourn, and organise.

Even if minimal at times, the book has identified positive directions for breaking cycles. In that sense, the volume's argument is ultimately constructive. Global injustice materialises through everyday legal routines; meaningful responses begin where those routines can be reworked—locally, relationally, and with sustained attention over time.

Notes

1 "Sovereignty" in Anthony's usage refers to the unceded sovereignty of the First Nations.
2 This analogy to First Nations law recalls Marx's characterisation of revolution as an "old mole" burrowing its way through purgatory, until the time is right to emerge. (Marx, 1926, p. 130)
3 SBS News 2026. https://www.sbs.com.au/news/podcast-episode/anti-corruption-commission-says-two-people-involved-in-robodebt-engaged-in-corrupt-conduct/j7yfxs41z Accessed on the 30 March 2026.

References

Alaimo, C., & Kallinikos, J. (2022). Organizations decentered: Data objects, technology and knowledge. *Organization Science*, *33*(1), 19–37. https://doi.org/10.1287/orsc.2021.1552

Bartlett, R. P., Morse, A., Wallace, N. E., & Stanton, R. H. (2021). Algorithmic discrimination and input accountability under the civil rights acts. *Berkeley Technology Law Journal, 36*(2), 675–736. https://doi.org/10.15779/z381n7xn5b

Cappelletti, M., & Garth, B. (1978). Access to justice: The worldwide movement to make rights effective. *Buffalo Law Review, 27*(2), 181–292. Retrieved from https://www.repository.law.indiana.edu/facpub/1142

Casanovas, P., Sartor, G., Casellas, N., & Rubino, R. (2008). *Computable Models of the Law: Languages, Dialogues, Games, Ontologies*, LNCS 4884, Springer, https://doi.org/10.1007/978-3-540-85569-9

Elish, M. C. (2019). Moral crumple zones: Cautionary tales in human-robot interaction. *Engaging Science, Technology, and Society, 5*, 40–60. https://doi.org/10.17351/ests2019.260

Eubanks, V. (2018). *Automating Inequality: How High-Tech Tools Profile, Police, and Punish the Poor*. New York: St. Martin's Press.

Fineman, M. A. (2008). The vulnerable subject: Anchoring equality in the human condition. *Yale Journal of Law & Feminism, 20*(1), 1–23.

Fitzpatrick, P. (1992). *The Mythology of Modern Law*. London: Routledge.

Hood, C. (2010). *The Blame Game: Spin, Bureaucracy, and Self-Preservation in Government*. Princeton, NJ: Princeton University Press.

Koulu, R. (2019). *Law, Technology and Dispute Resolution: The Privatisation of Coercion*. Abingdon: Routledge.

Kroll, J. A., Huey, J., Barocas, S., Felten, E. W., Reidenberg, J. R., Robinson, D. G., & Yu, H. (2017). Accountable algorithms. *University of Pennsylvania Law Review, 165*(3), 633–705. Retrieved from https://scholarship.law.upenn.edu/penn_law_review/vol165/iss3/3/

Lamb, W. F., Mattioli, G., Levi, S., Roberts, J. T., Capstick, S., Creutzig, F., . . . Steinberger, J. K. (2020). Discourses of climate delay. *Global Sustainability, 3*, e17. https://doi.org/10.1017/sus.2020.13

Lanzara, G. F. (2009). Building digital institutions: ICT and the rise of assemblages in government. In G. F. Lanzara (Ed.), *ICT and Innovation in the Public Sector: European Studies in the Making of e-Government* (pp. 9–48): Palgrave Macmillan.

Latour, B. (1996). *Petite réflexion sur le culte moderne des dieux faitiches*. Paris: Synthélabo.

Lewton, T. (2026, January 7). The secret weapon that could finally force climate action. *New Scientist*. Retrieved from https://www.newscientist.com/article/2508956-the-secret-weapon-that-could-finally-force-climate-action/

Lipsky, M. (1980). *Street-Level Bureaucracy: Dilemmas of the Individual in Public Services*. Russell Sage Foundation.

Marx, K. (1926 [1852]). *The Eighteenth Brumaire of Louis Bonaparte* (E. and C. Paul, Trans.). George Allen & Unwin.

Pasquale, F. (2015). *The Black Box Society: The Secret Algorithms That Control Money and Information*. Cambridge, MA: Harvard University Press.

Pelizzon, A. (2025). *Ecological Jurisprudence: The Law of Nature and the Nature of Law*. Singapore: Springer Nature Singapore.

Pound, R. (1910). Law in books and law in action. *American Law Review, 44*, 12–36.

Solnit, R. (2021, August 23). Big oil coined 'carbon footprints' to blame us for their greed. Keep them on the hook. *The Guardian*. Retrieved from https://www.theguardian.com/commentisfree/2021/aug/23/big-oil-coined-carbon-footprints-to-blame-us-for-their-greed-keep-them-on-the-hook

Tamanaha, B. Z. (2001). *A General Jurisprudence of Law and Society*. Oxford University Press.

Veitch, S. (2007). *Law and Irresponsibility: On the Legitimation of Human Suffering*. Abingdon, Oxon: Routledge-Cavendish.

Wong, W., & Welch, E. (2004). Does e-government promote accountability? A comparative analysis of website openness and government accountability. *Governance, 17*(2), 275–297. https://doi.org/10.1111/j.1468-0491.2004.00246.x

INDEX

For Product Safety Concerns and Information please contact our EU representative GPSR@taylorandfrancis.com Taylor & Francis Verlag GmbH, Kaufingerstraße 24, 80331 München, Germany